D0897827

❧ BROTHERLY LOVE

BROTHERLY LOVE

FREEMASONRY AND MALE FRIENDSHIP IN ENLIGHTENMENT FRANCE

KENNETH LOISELLE

CORNELL UNIVERSITY PRESS
Ithaca and London

First published 2014 by Cornell University Press
Printed in the United States of America

Library of Congress Cataloging-in-Publication Data

Loiselle, Kenneth, 1975– author.
    Brotherly love : freemasonry and male friendship in Enlightenment France / Kenneth Loiselle.
        pages cm
    Includes bibliographical references and index.
    ISBN 978-0-8014-5243-7 (cloth : alk. paper)
    1. Freemasonry—France—History—18th century.
2. Male friendship—France—History—18th century.
3. Enlightenment—France.   4. France—Social life and customs—18th century.   I. Title.

    HS603.L65 2014
    366'.1094409033—dc23

                                                    2014005279

Cloth printing   10 9 8 7 6 5 4 3 2 1

To Gisela, Sarah, and Nathaniel, with much love

❧ CONTENTS

❧ ACKNOWLEDGMENTS

Many institutions and individuals helped me complete this book. The Yale Center for International and Area Studies and the Georges Lurcy Trust supported my initial research. A circle of scholars made my graduate work both a social and an intellectual experience, notably Jennifer Boittin, Rachel Chrastil, Ulrike Decoene, Brooke Donaldson, Catherine Dunlop, Katherine Foshko, Jens-Uwe Guettel, Eva Guggenomos, Sylvaine Guyot, Charles Keith, Charles Lansing, Jake Lundberg, Karen Marrero, John Monroe, Bob Morrissey, George Trumbull, and Helen Veit, as well as the members of the Eliezer Society, notably Rabbi Shmully Hecht. The idea of friendship as an object of historical inquiry first occurred to me in a seminar with Keith Wrightson, whose ability to foster creative pathways into early modern European social life still inspires. Thomas Kavanagh and Jay Winter also offered helpful feedback at various stages. The untimely passing of Frank Turner robbed the scholarly community of a great mentor for graduate students; his patience and thoughtfulness will be terribly missed. Outside Yale, a number of historians helped me immeasurably, notably David Bell, who encouraged me to reshape this project at a critical juncture. Others who offered valuable suggestions and criticisms include Ronald Asch, Steven Auerbach, Yves-Marie Bercé, Peter Burke, Peter R. Campbell, Roger Chartier, Malcolm Crook, Robert Darnton, Maurice Daumas, Natalie Zemon Davis, Jonathan Dewald, Michel Figeac, Alan Forrest, Katsumi Fukasawa, John Garrigus, David Garrioch, Matthieu Glaumaud-Carbonnier, Dena Goodman, Daniel Gordon, Bernard Hann, Julie Hardwick, Olivia Harman, Colin Jones, Steven Kaplan, the late Sharon Kettering, Wim Klooster, Christian Kühner, Marisa Linton, Darrin McMahon, Jean-Marie Mercier, Jeffrey Merrick, Paul Monod, Nathan Perl-Rosenthal, Jeremy Popkin, the late Charles Porset, Christophe Portalez, Céline Sala, Eric Saunier, James Smith-Allen, Naomi Tadmor, Dale Van Kley, Charlotta Wolff, Kent Wright, and Thierry Zarcone. Sylvie Bourrel, Pierre Mollier, and the many other archivists in Paris and the provinces, too numerous to be mentioned here, are warmly thanked for their patient guidance. In France, I had the pleasure of the hospitality and friendship of the Azimov, Guyot, Lomax, Merriman, and Vannini families.

I am grateful to the faculty and staff within the history departments at the University of Oklahoma and Trinity University for having created a congenial atmosphere in which to research and write. I would like to thank especially my successive chairs for having fully supported this project at every stage: Rob Griswold, Carey Latimore, and David Lesch. I would also like to thank the Faculty Development Fund at Trinity for having enabled summer stints of research and writing. I completed this book as an External Fellow at Rice University's Humanities Research Center, whose staff I commend for their amiability and professionalism: Carolyn Adams, Melissa Bailar, and Lauren Kleinschmidt. I also learned much from conversations with Bernard Aresu, Daniel Cohen, Julie Fette, Alida Metcalf, Scott McGill, and Jack Zammito.

The chapters that follow are heavily indebted to the groundbreaking scholarship of Margaret Jacob, who has kindly shared archival information and methodological insight on numerous occasions. In recent years, the numerous books of Pierre-Yves Beaurepaire have reshaped completely the history of Freemasonry and sociability in Enlightenment Europe. Since our first meeting on a foggy train platform in Orléans one winter morning several years ago, I have benefited immensely from his friendship and assistance in all matters, both masonic and profane. His willingness to allow me to present my work in different venues at the Université de Nice Sophia-Antipolis from 2005 to 2010 has also strengthened this book. Put simply, this book could not have been written without him.

As this manuscript became a book, Darrin McMahon and John Monroe offered helpful advice on how to proceed. Jeremy Caradonna and Charles Walton are singled out for special praise, as they both read through the entire manuscript and made a number of astute and insightful comments that helped me introduce key revisions. I would like to thank warmly copyeditor Susan Campbell; of Westchester Publishing Services; and Susan Barnett Michael Bohrer-Clancy and Karen Hwa of Cornell University Press and Westchester Publishing Services for their assistance. John Ackerman's insightful editorial comments have much improved this book. This manuscript also benefited greatly from the exhaustive and constructive reader reports. Portions of chapters 2 and 6 have been previously published in article form, respectively, in "Nouveaux mais vrais amis: La Franc-maçonnerie et les rites de l'amitié au dix-huitième siècle," *Dix-huitième siècle* 39 (2007): 303–18; and "Living the Enlightenment in an Age of Revolution: Freemasonry in Bordeaux (1788–1794)," *French History* 24 (Oxford University Press, 2010): 60–81.

Parts of chapters 3 and 4 were published, respectively, in *Diffusions et circulations des pratiques maçonniques, XVIIIᵉ–XXᵉ siècle* (Classiques Garnier, 2012); and *Colloque archive épistolaire et histoire* (Connaissances et savoirs, 2007). I thank these publications for permission to include this material. Unless otherwise noted, all translations from the French in this book are my own.

Throughout this entire process, I am most indebted to my two wonderful mentors, John Merriman and Timothy Tackett. At every turn, they have provided me with unflagging support and sound advice, and have led me down rewarding paths I did not anticipate. The bewildered expressions of my parents and siblings when I spoke about Freemasonry constituted a critical and welcome lifeline to the world of the profane. Finally, I would like to thank my lovely wife, Gisela, and my children, Nathaniel and Sarah. In their constant support of this book over the years, they remind me that, *pace* most Old Regime moralists, love and friendship are not always mutually exclusive.

❧ ABBREVIATIONS

ADG	Archives départementales de la Gironde
ADM	Archives départementales de la Marne
ADPA	Archives départementales des Pyrénées-Atlantiques
AHRF	*Annales Historiques de la Révolution Française*
AMB	Archives municipales de Bordeaux
AP	Archives parlementaires
BMB	Bibliothèque municipale de Besançon
BMC	Bibliothèque municipale de Châlons-en-Champagne
BME	Bibliothèque municipale d'Épernay
BML	Bibliothèque municipale de Lyon
BMO	Bibliothèque municipale d'Orléans
BMR	Bibliothèque municipale de Rouen
BN AB	Bibliothèque nationale, archives de la Bastille (Arsenal)
BN FM	Bibliothèque nationale, fonds maçonnique
BN NAF	Bibliothèque nationale, nouvelles acquisitions françaises
BSG	Bibliothèque Sainte-Geneviève
GLDF	Bibliothèque de la Grande Loge de France
GODF	Bibliothèque du Grand Orient de France

Introduction

Friendship created the first two Masons in the world.
It was friendship that brought these two men together
and united their hearts and feelings. This is the origin
of Freemasonry.

—Anonymous orator of Amitié et Hospitalité lodge
in Sète

Late in the evening on 12 July 1786, silk mer-
chant Jean-Baptiste Willermoz made his way through the winding streets of
Lyon to visit a dying friend. For nearly a year, retired military officer Gaspard
de Savaron had complained about an unspecified illness and, likely sensing
that his days were numbered, urged Willermoz to visit often. For months,
Savaron's worsening condition had prevented him from attending their masonic lodge, to which they had devoted considerable energies for decades.
When word went out that Savaron was on his deathbed, Willermoz hurried
to be at his side. Remaining with his companion until the end, a tearful
Willermoz held Savaron in his arms as he passed away shortly after mid-
night. In a moving account of loss penned shortly afterward, Willermoz
praised his fellow Mason as "the intimate friend of my heart for whom I cry
and pray."[1]

The friendly feeling that Willermoz expressed toward Savaron was part
of a larger story that sociologist Allan Silver has called the "transformation of
friendship" in eighteenth-century Europe.[2] In his pioneering examination

---

1. Personal account of Jean-Baptiste Willermoz, 1786, BML MS 5869.

2. Allan Silver, "Friendship in Commercial Society: Eighteenth-Century Social Theory and Modern Sociology," *American Journal of Sociology* 95 (1990): 1474–1504.

of Scottish Enlightenment views on friendship, Silver has shown how social theorists such as David Hume and Adam Smith contrasted friendship ties with the cool and impersonal relations taking form in the burgeoning commercial-industrial society of their day. He argues that the advent of a public space that ordered itself according to an impersonal exchange of goods and services became the exclusive site of instrumentality. At the same time, these philosophers recognized that private relations did not follow any economic model of exchange and divested friendship of its utilitarian component, conceiving it as a tie grounded in a "natural sympathy" that was unconstrained by practical necessity. Such a friendship marked a distinct departure from an earlier "necessitous" understanding that considered friends as political or economic allies rather than as companions with whom one shared an emotional tie and common virtues. Silver thus sees in the Scottish Enlightenment "the liberation of friendship from instrumental concerns"; friendship as we know it today was beginning to take form.

This profound rethinking of friendship as a bond anchored in emotional investment and shared values was also underway in France. As historians of early modern France have shown, the terms *ami* and *amitié* were quite protean before the eighteenth century. They could, of course, refer to what we mean today by "friend," but they also were used for advisors, business associates, kin, parents, spouses, lovers, neighbors, and patrons.[3] The entries for "friendship" in both Antoine Furetière's *Dictionnaire universel* (1690) and the Académie française's 1694 dictionary offered muddled definitions: the term referred to people of equal or unequal status whose sentiments varied from general well-wishing to intense love that may or may not be reciprocated. By the middle of the next century, the Académie had done away with much of the previous ambiguity surrounding friendship and succinctly defined it as a relationship between equals grounded in reciprocal affection, offering the reader this maxim as a point of illustration: "There is hardly ever true friendship except between equals." In 1732, the popular *Dictionnaire de Trévoux* also upheld the importance of reciprocity in friendship when it stated in order "to use or bestow upon another the title of friend, it is necessary that friendship be reciprocal." A few decades later,

---

3. Jean-Marie Constant, *Nobles et paysans en Beauce aux XVIᵉ et XVIIᵉ siècles* (Lille: Service de reproduction des thèses, 1981), 239–64; Arlette Jouanna, *Le devoir de la révolte: La noblesse française et la gestation de l'état moderne, 1559–1661* (Paris: Fayard, 1989), 65–90; Christian Kühner, *Politische Freundschaft bei Hofe: Repräsentation und Praxis einer sozialen Beziehung im französischen Adel des 17. Jahrhunderts* (Göttingen: V&R Unipress, 2013); Sharon Kettering, "Friendship and Clientage in Early Modern France," *French History* 6 (1992): 139–58. Jacques Savary's popular merchant manual, *Le parfait négociant* (1675), also refers on a number of occasions to merchants as bound in "friendship."

abbé Claude Yvon clarified in his entry on *amitié* for the first volume of the *Encyclopédie* that there existed a much deeper bond with a friend than with an "acquaintance." He praised friendship as a freely contracted relationship between equals that appealed to both the heart and mind, and celebrated it for its "great freedom of feeling and language." The following decade, another moralist clearly demarcated kinship from friendship, arguing that a friend was someone with whom "you spoke about everything as freely as you would with yourself."[4] Although the language of friendship could still be used in reference to family ties and political patronage well into the nineteenth century, by the closing decades of the Old Regime a highly significant shift was underway in which the language of friendship increasingly referred to a benevolent, voluntary bond of solidarity, distinct from love and prized for its emotional and moral qualities. Sarah Horowitz has demonstrated that even when the terms *ami* and *amitié* were used in the utilitarian political realm in modern France, they usually referred to a relationship that was anchored in equality, trust, and affection.[5]

As the intellectual historian Robert Mauzi has shown, the normative principles of this new form of affectionate friendship were laid down in meticulous detail in the considerable body of prescriptive and descriptive literature published during the period: the literary sphere of the French Enlightenment was awash with titles such as "L'Amitié," "De l'amitié," "Traité sur l'amitié," "Caractères de l'amitié," "Réflexions sur l'amitié," "Conseils de l'amitié," and so on.[6] These writings celebrated friendship as the key to temporal happiness—one of the primary concerns of Enlightenment authors—and advised the reader on how to choose one's friends wisely, how to maintain and nurture friendships, how to pen letters to friends, and how to effectively divide one's time between friendships, work, and family. Sustained treatment of friendship also found its way into the more popular novels of the century, from Prevost's *Histoire du Chevalier des Grieux et de Manon Lescaut* (1731) to Diderot's *Jacques le fataliste et son maître* (1796). Taken

4. *Dictionnaire universel François et Latin . . .* (Paris, 1732), 1:345–46. Fortunato Bartolomeo de Felice, *Code de l'humanité, ou la législation universelle, naturelle, civile et politique* (Yverdon (CH), 1778), 1:279; Antoine Furetière, *Dictionnaire universel, contenant généralement tous les mots françois tant vieux que modernes et les termes de toutes les sciences et des arts* (The Hague, 1690), 1:95. Entries from 1694 and 1762 Académie française dictionaries and *Encyclopédie* accessed via ARTFL website, http://artfl-project.uchicago.edu/.

5. Sarah Horowitz, *Friendship and Politics in Post-Revolutionary France* (University Park: Pennsylvania State University Press, 2013).

6. For a list of the relevant philosophical and literary works, see Robert Mauzi, *L'idée du bonheur dans la littérature et la pensée françaises au XVIIIe siècle* (Paris: Slatkine, 1960), 664–83.

together with Michel Foucault's observation that the eighteenth century witnessed a remarkable surge in writing about sexuality, this sustained pre-occupation with friendship shows that the private sphere was not immune to the Enlightenment penchant to describe and classify.[7]

Although Mauzi's book is now over fifty years old, the study of friend-ship in Enlightenment France is still confined primarily to works of phi-losophy or literary studies. Historians of literature have examined in great detail the place of friendship in the moral thought and literary careers of the century's canonical writers, such as Condorcet, Diderot, Rousseau, and Voltaire.[8] Scholars more inclined toward philosophy have adopted Mauzi's decontextualized history-of-ideas approach, charting the evolution of the discussion of friendship in the formal writings of the Enlightenment from the late seventeenth century down to the Revolution.[9] Although this intel-lectual history has successfully revealed the complexity of the moral writ-ings of some of the French Enlightenment's most celebrated thinkers, it has not told us very much about how friendship was lived among ordinary people who did not necessarily devote philosophical treatises or literary works to the topic.[10] This is a notable lacuna compared with the Anglo-American historiography of the period, which has more richly explored the rhetoric and practices of male friendship on a much broader scale.[11] This reluctance to explore friendship in the wider social world is also surprising given that Philippe Ariès and William Reddy have identified this relation-

---

7. Michel Foucault, *The History of Sexuality: An Introduction*, trans. Robert Hurley (New York: Pan-theon, 1976).

8. William Acher, *Jean-Jacques Rousseau, écrivain de l'amitié* (Paris: A.-G. Nizet, 1971); Rosena Davi-son, *Diderot et Galiani: Etude d'une amitié philosophique* (Oxford: Voltaire Foundation, 1985); Anne Vincent-Buffault, *L'exercice de l'amitié: Pour une histoire des pratiques amicales aux XVIIIe et XIXe siècles* (Paris: Seuil, 1995).

9. Frédérick Gerson, *L'amitié au XVIIIe siècle* (Paris: La Pensée Universelle, 1974); Edward Johnson, *Once There Were Two True Friends: Idealized Male Friendship in French Narrative from the Middle Ages through the Enlightenment* (Birmingham, AL: Summa Publications, 2003).

10. For "ordinary," we follow the definition of Robert Forster, who used the term to refer to those individuals "rich or poor, who have not left a special mark on history," in "Family Biography," *Bi-ographie und Geschichtswissenschaft: Aufsätze zur Theorie und Praxis biographischer Arbeit*, ed. Wolfdieter Bihl and Gernot Heiss (Vienna: Verlage für Theorie und Politik, 1979), 111. The only attempt to study male friendship beyond its intellectual history in eighteenth-century France is made by Jeffrey Merrick, "Male Friendship in Prerevolutionary France," *GLQ: A Journal of Lesbian and Gay Studies*, 10 (2004), 407–32.

11. Richard Godbeer, *The Overflowing of Friendship: Love between Men and the Creation of the American Republic* (Baltimore, MD: Johns Hopkins University Press, 2009); Naomi Tadmor, *Family and Friends in Eighteenth-Century England: Household, Kinship, and Patronage* (New York: Cambridge Uni-versity Press, 2001).

ship as an essential part of a new culture of privacy in eighteenth-century France that was emerging in the many voluntary organizations of the period.[12] Outside the sphere of the family and the state, individuals (mostly, but not exclusively, men) during the reigns of Louis XV and Louis XVI voluntarily came together to enjoy a variety of pastimes: reading, dining, gambling, giving charity, and so on. As Peter Clark has shown in the case of Britain, these new social practices gave rise to an "associational revolution" during which thousands of voluntary organizations appeared, from theatrical troupes to mutual aid associations. Although many groups in Enlightenment France have yet to attract their historian, extant inventories suggest that a similar phenomenon was underway across the Channel, with several hundred clubs having emerged.[13]

In eighteenth-century France, Freemasonry was the most widespread voluntary organization; it has attracted sustained attention from historians since the nineteenth century.[14] Despite this interest, the importance of friendship for the fraternity has managed to escape most investigations. And yet the most cursory examination of Freemasonry reveals that friendship was a significant part of the masonic project of creating a unique space of leisure within eighteenth-century civil society. When the leaders of the brotherhood sat down to draft their founding charter in 1735, they proclaimed in the very first article that "Masonry becomes the center and the union of a solid and desirable friendship between individuals who otherwise would have always been separated from one another."[15] From the fraternity's inception, members throughout metropolitan and colonial France adorned their lodges with names such as "Amis Choisis," "Amis Constants," "Amitié Parfaite," "Amitié Eternelle," and so on. Friendship was not only an essential criterion of masonic identity but also played a key role in distinguishing the lodge from the hundreds of other voluntary organizations, from theatrical groups to agricultural societies, vying for men's time and membership fees.

---

12. Philippe Ariès, "Introduction," in *A History of Private Life*, ed. Roger Chartier and trans. Arthur Goldhammer, vol.3, *Passions of the Renaissance* (Cambridge, MA: Belknap Press of Harvard University Press, 1989), 1–11; William Reddy, *The Navigation of Feeling: A Framework for the History of Emotions* (New York: Cambridge University Press, 2001), 149–54.

13. Peter Clark, *British Clubs and Societies, 1580–1800: The Origins of an Associational World* (New York: Oxford University Press, 2000). On French clubs, see the inventory of Arthur Dinaux, *Les sociétés badines, bachiques, littéraires et chantantes: Leur histoire et leurs travaux*, 2 vols. (Paris, 1867).

14. For an overview of masonic historiography, see Charles Porset, *Hiram sans culotte? Franc-maçonnerie, lumières et Révolution: Trente ans d'études et de recherches* (Paris: Honoré Champion, 1998).

15. This document was based on James Anderson's *Constitutions*, drafted in London the previous decade. However, the French version differs in important ways, to be discussed in chapter 2.

Freemasons lashed out against these competing social arenas as morally bank-rupt, part of what they called the "profane" world, and declared that *amitié* among non-Masons was a "meaningless word," for true friendship as they understood it was highly problematic, if not impossible to achieve in French society. If friendly association did exist, it was described as "deformed," be-ing typically of an ethereal and unstable quality, anchored in the unbridled pleasures of drink or the pursuit of sexual gratification.[16]

Some of Freemasonry's more acute contemporaries also remarked on the importance of conviviality and friendship for the organization. From the moment Masonry emerged in the 1720s, anti-masonic pamphleteers lam-pooned the fraternity as a tremendous waste of time and money, neverthe-less acknowledging that it was, above all, friendly feeling that brought men together in lodges. In 1745, Gabriel-Louis Pérau published his popular *L'ordre des Francs-maçons trahi*, in which he exposed the inner workings and symbolism of the fraternity. "They kiss one another as brothers," he wrote, "and converse with one another with all of the openness of heart that the most tender friendship can inspire."[17] Political authorities also did not fail to notice the importance of friendship to Masons. In a 1757 letter composed to his counterpart in Angers, the *procureur général* of the Parlement of Paris, Guillaume-François Joly de Fleury, attempted to allay fears that Freema-sonry was politically dangerous on account of its secrecy. He considered lodges a benign act of sociability that simply comprised "friends who gather together to drink and eat."[18] Others, however, anxiously saw in these same ties of masonic friendship a rival set of allegiances that conjured up images of the powerful aristocratic networks that had plunged France into civil war during the previous century. One anti-masonic pamphleteer toward the end of the Old Regime went as far as to label Masonry a sort of "state within the state" and urged the government to curb all masonic activity.[19]

In conjunction with the sharing of drink, ritual, and song, the idealistic visions of friendship men elaborated in their speeches and published writings provided the platform for a robust solidarity network among brethren out-side of the lodge. Like other varieties of friendship in early modern Europe, masonic friendship in practice constituted a delicate blend of affection and

---

16. Dossier of Trinité (Paris), BN FM²119bis, fol. 21v.

17. Abbé Gabriel-Louis Pérau, *L'ordre des Francs-maçons trahi et le secret des Mopses révélé*, ed. Daniel Ligou (Geneva: Slatkine Reprints, 1980), 13, 136.

18. Letter published in Charles Gérin, "Les Francs-maçons et la magistrature française au XVIIIe siècle," *Revue des questions historiques* 18 (1875): 556.

19. *Apologie de l'ordre des Francs-maçons par le frère* **** (Philadelphia (?), 1779), 39.

instrumentality (providing services).[20] The range of instrumentality could vary considerably, and included furnishing advice on particular topics of expertise, lending money or books, and helping brethren from abroad transition into French life; Benjamin Franklin was but the most renowned of the thousand or so foreigners who used lodges as a gateway to the world of the French Enlightenment.[21] Masons often helped one another at great personal risk, putting their friendships ahead of professional obligations and the law.

But friendship within Freemasonry was, above all, grounded in great mutual affection and emotional investment. Men—through the conviviality of lodge activities, letter writing, or personal visits—created a set of private spaces where an egalitarian and affective ethos reigned. There they professed a deep love for another in a language that many men today would find uncomfortably romantic. Consider, for example, a letter exchange between two Freemasons during the fraternity's early years. It was 24 December 1748, and Jean-Philippe de Béla, a military officer then stationed in Bayonne, composed a letter to his fellow Mason, Philippe-Valentin Bertin du Rocheret, at Épernay in the Champagne region. Although hundreds of miles separated them, and they had not laid eyes on one another for some time, Béla hoped to come to Épernay in the near future "to see and embrace you, to swear to you that I love you, that I adore you, to swear to you an eternal steadfastness. . . . What I feel for you is what a passionate lover feels for his mistress in her absence."[22] Such a celebration of Freemasonry as a bastion of male friendship persisted down to the final years of the century. Standing in front of his fellows at the newly established Centre des Amis lodge in Paris, one officer exercised a degree of literary imagination in directly addressing a personified friendship in 1797: "Friendship, celestial gift of the Supreme Being; the pleasure and need of sensitive souls, enter into this august Assembly. May your tender influence vivify with your sacred flame the heart of everyone here. Yes, I feel it, o divine Friendship, that you are granting my prayer! . . . Stay, stay with us forever, and make all Masons . . . a people of friends."[23]

---

20. See, for example, the comments in Katharine W. Swett, "'The Account between Us': Honor, Reciprocity and Companionship in Male Friendship in the Later Seventeenth Century," *Albion: A Quarterly Journal Concerned with British Studies* 31 (1999): 3–4.

21. Pierre-Yves Beaurepaire, *L'autre et le frère: L'étranger et la Franc-maçonnerie en France au XVIIIᵉ siècle* (Paris: Honoré Champion, 1998), 767–832.

22. BN NAF MS 15175, fol. 310r.

23. Pierre-Louis-Paul de Lucenay de Randon, *Installation de la loge du Centre des Amis* (Paris, 1797), 18–19.

Because Freemasons inside and outside the lodge prized friendship as the underlying rationale for their association, my primary aim in this book is to use the movement as a prism to understand more clearly how ordinary men conceived of and lived friendship in eighteenth-century France. Because of its size and diverse membership, Freemasonry is an ideal case study. Although there were hundreds of voluntary associations emerging during the reigns of Louis XV and Louis XVI that undoubtedly offered convivial spaces to nurture and develop friendship, none were as widespread as masonic lodges. Lodges welcomed at least fifty thousand men who came from all walks of life, from artisans to the highest echelons of the nobility.[24] The very fact that Freemasonry was the most prevalent voluntary organization in the French Enlightenment also meant that it served as a prototype for club life: the Chevalerie de la Coignée, Frères des Quatre Vents, and Ordre des Fendeurs were but a handful of the many *sociétés de plaisir* that explicitly adopted the vocabulary, rituals, and meeting format of lodges.[25] Because these societies were quite similar to lodges, understanding the story of masonic friendship not only helps us better make sense of the masonic experience but it also sheds light on a key element of the wider French associational world.

In addition, Freemasonry's rich documentary record makes the masonic setting a fitting one in which to explore friendly feeling between men. Since the pioneering work of Pierre Chevallier in the 1960s, French historians have excavated vast amounts of quantitative data on membership trends and lodge proliferation.[26] Although I do not ignore statistical data when relevant, I attempt to follow the work of Margaret Jacob and Pierre-Yves Beaurepaire in placing emphasis on a close reading and contextualization of a variety of documentation.[27] My analysis makes use of three different types of sources, each offering the historian a distinct way into reconstructing the multi-stranded world of masonic friendship.[28] First, anti-masonic exposures and apologias intended for a wider public conveyed what life in the lodge *ap-*

24. Daniel Roche, *France in the Enlightenment*, trans. Arthur Goldhammer (Cambridge, MA: Harvard University Press, 1998), 436.

25. Dinaux, *Les sociétés badines*.

26. The best example of this work is Ran Halévi, *Les loges maçonniques dans la France d'Ancien Régime: Aux origines de la sociabilité démocratique* (Paris: Armand Colin, 1984).

27. Pierre-Yves Beaurepaire, *L'espace des Francs-maçons: Une sociabilité européenne au XVIIIᵉ siècle* (Rennes: Presses Universitaires de Rennes, 2003); Margaret Jacob, *Living the Enlightenment: Freemasonry and Politics in Eighteenth-Century Europe* (New York: Oxford University Press, 1991).

28. This typology follows the helpful model put forth in Malcolm Gaskill, *Crime and Mentalities in Early Modern England* (New York: Cambridge University Press, 2000), 21.

peared to be like to outsiders; second, normative documents such as lodge speeches, ritual procedures, and statutes intended solely for internal use reflected what was *supposed* to be going on within masonic meetings; and finally, other sources, such as brethren's private and administrative correspondence and lodge meeting registers, tell us how things *likely* were inside and outside the lodge. Taken together, these disparate materials help us understand not only the normative ideals and actual behavior that undergirded masonic friendship but also the dynamic interplay and tensions between them. So, although analyzing what the terms *ami* and *amitié* meant for the men who frequented lodges constitutes an essential part of our investigation—especially in chapter 1 and a long section of chapter 5—our concern for the practices of masonic friendship in other parts of the book requires us to move beyond a mere history of ideas writ large.

A second objective of this study is to show how Freemasonry played an important role in the transformation of friendship in eighteenth-century France by offering men an institutional platform where they could work out and perhaps achieve the ideals of sentimentalized male friendship that were put forth in the literary and philosophical works of the period. By looking at how brethren inside and outside lodges appropriated—and sometimes actively reshaped—Enlightenment thought, my analysis seeks to contribute to a social history of ideas pioneered in the work of Robert Darnton.[29] I share Darnton's view that one of the most fruitful ways to assess the relevance of the century's ideas is by "grubbing in archives" to piece together how people selectively culled from and appropriated various strands of *philosophie* to provide their lives with meaning. It will come to light that the ideal depictions of friendship brethren articulated in their speeches, apologias, and letters drew from many strands of eighteenth-century thought, including physiognomy, sensationalist psychology, and especially Rousseauean ideas about friendship as a transparent union of hearts. But men also looked to Greco-Roman antiquity for inspiration. Within the masonic mental world, Cicero figured prominently, and brethren hoped to model themselves after celebrated pairs like Damon and Pythias or Pylades and Orestes. Freemasonry's indebtedness to classical models demonstrates that the Enlightenment's "appeal to antiquity," so brilliantly portrayed by Peter Gay, had relevance not just for the Enlightenment's ideas, but also in shaping its social world.[30]

---

29. Robert Darnton, "In Search of the Enlightenment: Recent Attempts to Create a Social History of Ideas," *Journal of Modern History* 43 (1971): 113–32.

30. Peter Gay, *The Enlightenment: The Rise of Modern Paganism* (New York: Norton & Company, [1969] 1995).

To explain the visions and practices of friendship within French Freemasonry, this book comprises six thematic chapters that span from the appearance of the fraternity early in the reign of Louis XV to the Reign of Terror
seventy years later. In chapter 1 I describe how the organization grew during the 1730s and 1740s and situate this development within France's larger
associational world. Then I examine the prominence of male friendship in
the masonic foundational texts of this period and undertake a close examination of the thought of Andrew-Michael Ramsay, one of the founding
fathers of the movement in France. From this analysis, a paradox within
masonic sociability will become clear: brethren like Ramsay optimistically
anchored masonic life in male friendship, but they also recognized that
friendship was a problematic bond because of the assumed nature of the
self. Specifically, the concern over the presence of self-love (*amour-propre*)
and the power of the passions over reason brought into question the extent to
which friendship could function as a durable link that cemented individuals
together. In chapter 2 we pursue how Masons dealt with this problem of
friendship and explore the relationship between friendship and the transfor-
mational aspects of the initiation ritual (*rite d'apprenti*). Here, I argue that
the initiation symbolically recast the neophyte into a new form, emptying
him of specific undesirable psychological elements which otherwise would
have made friendship a problematic, unstable relationship. The masonic initiation generated a form of ritualized friendship between men that was imbued with a Christian ethics and characterized by a measured closeness.

In chapter 3 we turn our attention to the presence of women in masonic
life by examining what were known as "adoption lodges," periodical gatherings in which brethren invited their spouses or female kin to participate in
the ritual life of the fraternity. Adoption lodges appeared at some point in
the 1730s or 1740s and were widespread by the eve of the Revolution. I argue
in this chapter that the fundamental reason why women were introduced
into Masonry via the adoption format was because their presence defended
Freemasons against the frequent accusations of sodomy that the wider French
public leveled against them. The introduction of female relatives into the lodge
explicitly defined brethren as heterosexual, thus defusing any potentially erotic
component associated with male friendship.

In chapter 4, the narrative leaves behind the world of the lodge to explore how masonic friendship was lived in daily life. Here I focus on Masons
who comprised one of the first lodges in the Paris of Louis XV, paying
particular attention to the correspondence network of a wine merchant and
civil servant based in Champagne, Philippe-Valentin Bertin du Rocheret.
Despite the fact that police pressure closed down Rocheret's lodge in the

mid-1730s, he and his masonic friends actively wrote and visited each other over the next two decades. Similar to the brand of ritualized friendship highlighted in chapter 2, the bond between these men was anchored in a Christian system of ethics. However, in borrowing from the typology of anthropologist Julian Pitt-Rivers, I have defined these personal friendships as "unritualized friendships" to distinguish them from the collective bond of solidarity contracted through the initiation.[31] Unlike the more formal ritualized friendship, the ties between Rocheret and his friends were more casual and emotionally effusive. Just as historians of women have shown that the public sphere was not as masculinist as earlier scholarship has suggested, I show in this chapter how men inhabited a private sphere that closely mirrored female experiences of the period.[32] Rocheret and his fellows put quill pen to paper to connect with dear friends, traveled great distances to rekindle old friendships, and turned to friends in times of difficulty or crisis.

From the 1760s to the outbreak of the Revolution in 1789, Freemasonry attracted greater interest than ever before. Although the nobility tended to control masonic life during the first half of the century, the fraternity became more diverse in its membership profile during the final decades of the Old Regime. This period saw the establishment of hundreds of lodges across the kingdom for men from many backgrounds, such as *parlementaires*, merchants, military officers, and skilled artisans. By examining hundreds of lodge speeches that were delivered on festive occasions, I make clear in chapter 5 that the prerevolutionary decades also underwent a qualitative shift in masonic thinking about friendship. Although their words in private could be intense, brethren tended to exhibit what I have called a "restrained sentimentalism" inside the lodge during Freemasonry's early decades, when ideal friendship was defined as striking a balance between feeling and rational engagement in which the role of the passions was minimized. By the prerevolutionary decades, however, lodges embraced feeling much more effusively, and had come to define friendship as a bond grounded in passionate expression and emotional sensitivity. This new culture of sentimentalized

---

31. Julian Pitt-Rivers, "The Kith and the Kin," in *The Character of Kinship*, ed. Jack Goody (New York: Cambridge University Press, 1975), 89–105.

32. Friendships between women have been examined in Dena Goodman, *Becoming a Woman in the Age of Letters* (Ithaca, NY: Cornell University Press, 2009), chaps. 1 and 2. The argument for the increasing exclusion of women from the public sphere during the prerevolutionary and revolutionary eras has been made most forcefully in Joan Landes, *Women and the Public Sphere in the Age of the French Revolution* (Ithaca, NY: Cornell University Press, 1988). For challenges to this thesis, see the helpful overview of Suzanne Desan, "What's after Political Culture? Recent French Revolutionary Historiography," *French Historical Studies* 23 (2000): 190–92.

friendship within Freemasonry cannot be ascribed to any specific social or legal group, for it weaved its way into speeches pronounced by craftsmen and noblemen alike. Masons now did not hesitate to couch their friendships in the rhetoric of the heart and display powerful signs of devotion to one another, notably the shedding of tears. This change occurred in part because of the major influence Rousseau had on the topic of friendship in France, but it also reflected the wider cultural current known as "sensibility" that traversed the entire Western world during the second half of the eighteenth century.[33]

It was unfortunate for Freemasons that life in the lodge did not always line up neatly with the lofty idealizations of friendship pronounced in their speeches. The impressive expansion of Freemasonry during the second half of the century was also accompanied by growing pains characterized by disputes between members that could lead to the ejection of men from lodges. In the final section of chapter 5 I explore why brethren were expelled in Parisian Masonry from the early 1760s to the end of the 1780s. I argue that membership expulsion during these years occurred primarily when two or more individuals were accused of forming self-oriented particular friendship groups at the expense of the lodge's affective collective solidarity. In this way, we demonstrate that the ritualized friendship forged between all lodge members through initiation did not always coexist harmoniously with more intimate friendships between men.

In chapter 6, we enter the revolutionary era and offer a fresh perspective on the question of the relationship between Freemasonry and the French Revolution. This question has been a polemical one since the early nineteenth century, with historians falling into one of two camps. One camp has argued that Freemasonry triumphantly ushered in political modernity, pointing to the role lodges played in fostering a political culture that prefigured some aspect of revolutionary political culture. François Furet and Ran Halévi have seen lodges as representing new egalitarian, proto-democratic arenas, where commoner and noble could intermingle and leave behind the rigid hierarchy of the society of orders.[34] In a more nuanced approach, Margaret Jacob has drawn attention to the masonic emphasis on constitu-

33. Robert Darnton, "Readers Respond to Rousseau: The Fabrication of Romantic Sensitivity," in *The Great Cat Massacre and Other Episodes in French Cultural History* (New York: Basic Books, 1984), 215–56.

34. François Furet, *Interpreting the French Revolution*, trans. Elborg Forster (New York: Cambridge University Press, 1981), 38; Halévi, *Aux origines de la sociabilité démocratique*.

tions, laws and elections, and revolutionary politics, arguing that Freemasonry played an important part in the development of constitutionalism that connected the English and French Revolutions.[35] In arguing that the masonic legacy was significant for the Revolution, these historians have taken what I call a "maximalist" view of Masonry's role in the revolutionary upheaval. The opposing camp, however, has challenged this interpretation by suggesting that Freemasonry's consequences for the Revolution were negligible. In their respective work on Maine, Normandy, and Toulouse, André Bouton, Eric Saunier, and Michel Taillefer have followed the political trajectory of Freemasons through the tumultuous revolutionary dynamic. They have observed that most lodges quickly closed once the political chaos began and that the masonic view and reaction to events was no different from that of the wider public; brethren were not transparent personifications of some type of coherent masonic vision toward political authority.[36] These historians have argued that responses to political events among Masons were more likely to be embedded in contingency, a reflection of how the evolving revolutionary dynamic affected their non-masonic lives. For these "minimalist" historians, masonic affiliation emerges as a rather unpredictable variable for determining revolutionary political orientation, as individuals and their lodges made choices based on other factors, notably their profession, social status, regional setting, and personal relationship to the local government.

These two historiographical camps diverge largely because they have chosen to focus on different aspects of Freemasonry: the "minimalists" have examined individual Masons and lodges and the "maximalists" have analyzed the ideas and electoral practices within lodges. But to do justice to the richness of the masonic experience in the Revolution, historians must account for all of these elements, and I attempt to offer such a synthesis in the final chapter. In following the approach of the "minimalists," I consider how the revolutionary tumult affected both individual masonic friendships and the collective life of lodges. My analysis revises the prevailing interpretation of the "minimalists" in two ways. First, it will be made clear that not all

35. Jacob, *Living the Enlightenment*, esp. 9, 17, 51, and 219.

36. André Bouton, "Dispersion politique des francs-maçons du Maine au printemps 1792," *AHRF* 41 (1969): 487–99; Eric Saunier, *Révolution et sociabilité en Normandie au tournant des XVIIIe et XIXe siècles: 6000 francs-maçons de 1740 à 1830* (Rouen: Publications de l'Université de Rouen, 1998), 433; Michel Taillefer, *La Franc-maçonnerie toulousaine sous l'Ancien Régime et la Révolution, 1741–1799* (Paris: E.N.S.B.-C.T.H.S., 1984), 234–35.

brethren abandoned Freemasonry once the political tumult began, but that some men remained deeply connected during the Revolution, and that their friendships helped them navigate the political process. Second, although many lodges closed their doors shortly after 1789, a handful remained remarkably active down into the final weeks of the Terror. But even these stubborn lodges were eventually closed down because the Committee of Public Safety deemed masonic friendship dangerous to the new regime. The Jacobins saw in masonic friendship a rival set of secretive allegiances that did not sit well with a political order that was nominally anchored in transparency between all citizens.

In my analysis of how masonic friendship possibly laid the groundwork for revolutionary political culture, I argue that the "maximalists" have overlooked a crucial link between Freemasonry and the Revolution: classical republicanism. The work of J. G. A. Pocock has most strongly associated this variant of political thought with early modern England and its colonies, but French historians have also identified classical republicanism in the writings of some of the major figures of the period—such as the abbé de Mably, Montesquieu and Rousseau—and in the writings of revolutionaries from members of the Cordelier Club to Robespierre and Saint-Just.[37] Antiquity was central to the classical republican tradition because it provided a record of the rise and fall of states, and there was sustained interest in the fate of Athens, Rome, and Sparta.[38] Because this history clearly demonstrated that the body politic was remarkably fragile, classical republicans were primarily interested in understanding what their contemporaneous European states should emulate or avoid from the Greco-Roman past in order to stave off political decay. These thinkers argued that the most effective way for a political community to retain its vitality was by nurturing a robust public spirit among its citizenry. Mably and Rousseau

---

37. J. G. A. Pocock, *The Machiavellian Moment: Florentine Political Thought and the Atlantic Republican Tradition* (Princeton, NJ: Princeton University Press, [1975] 2003). On classical republicanism in the French Enlightenment, see Dan Edelstein, *The Terror of Natural Right: Republicanism, the Cult of Nature, & the French Revolution* (Chicago: University of Chicago Press, 2009), 68–82; see also Johnson Kent Wright, *A Classical Republican in Eighteenth-Century France: The Political Thought of Mably* (Stanford, CA: Stanford University Press, 1997). On the Cordelier Club as a channel for classical republicanism, see Rachel Hammersley, "English Republicanism in Revolutionary France: The Case of the Cordelier Club," *Journal of British Studies* 43 (2004): 464–81. On the mutation of classical republicanism in the political thought of Marat, Robespierre, and Saint-Just, see Keith Michael Baker, "Transformations of Classical Republicanism in Eighteenth-Century France," *The Journal of Modern History* 73 (2001): 43–53.

38. Edelstein, *Terror of Natural Right*, 45–51.

duly praised Lycurgian Sparta because its laws, education and collective rites mitigated individuals' inherent selfishness and enabled them to acquire a sense of shared morals and purpose. Conversely, classical republicans critiqued luxury and the pursuit of excessive wealth as undermining civic virtue and all sense of community; commitment to one's public duties was deemed incongruous with the pursuit of individual material gain. To the classical republican mind, the moral corruption brought on by avarice and egotism was a sign of impending political doom. This is why Mably warned his readers at the end of the Old Regime that self-regarding passions were the "secret poison" that could erode Europe from within and that *moeurs* "should be the principle object of politics . . . good or ill, they decide the fate of states."[39]

Mably and other classical republicans, like theorist Jean Bodin, concurred with those authors from whom they drew so much—notably Aristotle, Cicero and Plato—that friendship between virtuous men was the backbone of the ideal political community. There was a general praise of friendship for both promoting solidarity beyond kinship and because it was grounded in a shared moral vision of the world that served as the bedrock of a collective identity.[40] As I suggest in the final chapter of this book, Freemasons were tightly bound to a similar classical notion of friendship that straddled the public and private spheres, as they hoped that their friendships could instill civic virtue and morally regenerate French society to fend off political decay. Since a significant group of the deputies of the National Assembly were Freemasons, Old Regime lodges undoubtedly provided these future revolutionaries with a concrete social space in which to experiment with some of the key themes of classical republicanism that would later shape their revolutionary experiences. The classical legacy within Freemasonry necessarily complicates Allan Silver's picture of the Enlightenment as a watershed moment when friendship began to assume its modern form, and it reminds us that what makes the eighteenth century such a fascinating period of

---

39. Wright, *A Classical Republican in Eighteenth-Century France*, 106, 194.

40. On friendship in antiquity, see David Konstan, *Friendship in the Classical World* (New York: Cambridge University Press, 1997); Paul Rahe, *Republics Ancient and Modern: Classical Republicanism and the American Revolution* (Chapel Hill: University of North Carolina Press, 1992), 24–25, 30–31, 56–57, 106, 122; Judith Shklar, "Politics and Friendship," *Proceedings of the American Philosophical Society* 137 (1993): 207–8. On the classical republican celebration of friendship as a political bond, see Sara Miglietti, "Amitié, harmonie et paix politique chez Aristote et Jean Bodin," *Astérion* 7 (2010): http://asterion.revues.org/1660; Peter Miller, "Friendship and Conversation in Seventeenth-Century Venice," *Journal of Modern History* 73 (2001): 1–31.

study is that it was a transitory moment in which the old and the new jostled one another in novel ways.

✒ A Note on Methodology

Whereas most work on Enlightenment Freemasonry has confined itself typically to a particular city or region, the following chapters span widely throughout Paris and the provinces. I have also integrated material from manuscript collections that have only recently, during the past decade or so, been made available to scholars. A new, centralized archival source has emerged that is particularly rich for the Enlightenment and revolutionary periods: twenty-seven thousand dossiers now housed at the Grand Orient and Grand Lodge libraries. It is within these "Russian archives"—which migrated during the postwar period to the Soviet Union via East Germany and returned to France only in 2000—that one finds a rich record of eighteenth-century masonic life.[41]

Such an examination of hundreds of lodges across France necessarily means including a number of ritual systems and masonic styles into our analysis. Besides the tension between the Grand Lodge and the Grand Orient over administrative control of the kingdom's lodges in the prerevolutionary era, there were also mystical variants operating in Bordeaux, Lyon, and Strasbourg, as well as the Illuminé movement in Avignon, and more philosophically inclined lodges, such as the famous Nine Sisters lodge in Paris. Despite these differences, I share the view of other scholars that French Freemasonry remained relatively uniform in how it structured masonic sociability.[42] Whether a lodge was a standard "blue" lodge, offering only the first three degrees of Freemasonry—apprentice, journeyman, and master—or a follower of one of the more elaborate ritual systems enumerated above, these lodges remained similar in their underlying structure: all Freemasons sought out lodge members whose socioeconomic status reflected their own, and all lodges had similar officer ranks, meeting formats, written guidelines, and con-

---

41. Charles Porset, "Un nouveau massif de sources: Les archives du KGB," in *Franc-maçonnerie et histoire: Bilan et perspectives*, ed. Christine Gaudin and Eric Saunier (Rouen: Publications des universités de Rouen et du Havre, 2003), 37–43. Margaret Jacob has devoted some attention to this new archive in *Strangers Nowhere in the World: Cosmopolitanism in Early Modern Europe* (Philadelphia: University of Pennsylvania Press, 2006), 107–14.

42. Our argument for a structural uniformity is limited to French lodges, but Margaret Jacob has suggested this to be valid for Freemasonry within the broader eighteenth-century Atlantic world. Jacob, *Living the Enlightenment*, 18.

ducted comparable initiation rituals. Such an institutional uniformity within French Freemasonry makes it possible to study the structural influences on friendship within Freemasonry across multiple lodges, because the opportunities and limitations for sociability within them were patterned in a similar way.

The study of male friendship within Old Regime Freemasonry provides an account of how tens of thousands of Frenchmen embraced different ways of relating to other men. By showing how men in the Enlightenment were much more than aloof statesmen, shrewd businessmen, and stern philosophers, I seek to offer a new way of thinking about masculinity and gender in this period. By listening closely to the words Freemasons used, following the ceremonies they performed, and retracing the activities they shared, inside and outside the lodge, that gave shape and meaning to the masonic experience, I hope to demonstrate that the French Enlightenment was just as much an Age of Sentiment as it was an Age of Reason.[43]

---

43. From the vantage point of intellectual history, a similar argument has been made in Jessica Riskin, *Science in the Age of Sensibility: The Sentimental Empiricists of the French Enlightenment* (Chicago: University of Chicago Press, 2002).

✦ CHAPTER 1

The Masonic Utopia of Friendship

In France, Freemasonry first attracted widespread attention in the mid-1730s, a little over a decade after its appearance in Paris and elsewhere. Reactions to the brotherhood varied from mild curiosity to outright hostility, and despite the fact that Ludovician France already had its share of academies and intellectual coteries, most observers identified the brotherhood as something different in the French associational landscape. In early 1737, a gazetteer announced to his readers that a new import from across the Channel recently had established itself in Paris: "A new order has been recently established in Paris that one calls *Fritz-massons*, [*sic*] which means in French *Francs-Maçons*."[1] And in March of that same year, the ever-attentive chronicler of Paris, *parlementaire* Edmond-Jean-François Barbier, mentioned Masonry disapprovingly as the latest episode in aristocratic frivolity: "Our lords . . . have recently invented an order called *Frimassons* [*sic*] following the example of England, where there are as many different associations as there are individuals. We do not waste time in imitating foreign impertinences."[2] Others, such as the duc de Luynes,

---

1. Georges Luquet, *La Franc-maçonnerie et l'état en France au XVIIIᵉ siècle* (Paris: Éditions Vitiano, 1963), 192.

2. Edmond-Jean-François Barbier, *Chronique de la régence et du règne de Louis XV, 1718–1763, ou Journal de Barbier* (Paris, 1858), 3:80–81.

reacted to this new form of association by simply gathering, describing, and interpreting as much masonic activity as possible.[3]

Although we know a considerable amount about how observers reacted to Freemasonry when it first burst upon the scene in Paris, little is known about how Masons themselves envisioned and ordered lodge life in the first half of the eighteenth century. How did Freemasonry's participants outline the principles of order and collective identity of their organization? How did they understand their relationship to other modes of sociability and to French society at large? By what values and ideals did Masons distinguish their association, how did Masons understand their social bonds with fellow brethren, and what were their expectations of these relationships?

Answering these questions is important for a number of reasons. First, this line of inquiry can help historians gain a clearer understanding of why individuals would have been attracted to Freemasonry in the first place and what subsequent social aspirations they hoped to realize through the brotherhood. Second, these questions necessarily address the topic of organizational self-definition, a topic particularly relevant to an early Masonry that was forced to differentiate itself from the other voluntary associations emerging during this period; as I demonstrate in this chapter, France, like Great Britain, had a rich "associational world" in the eighteenth century, of which Freemasonry was a part.[4] Too often scholars have disagreed about whether a given private society was a lodge or something else—such as an eating or drinking club—simply because there is still not enough known about the beliefs and values that shaped the fraternity during its early years.[5] And finally, recovering the salient themes at the heart of masonic communal identity is essential if one bears in mind that Freemasonry functioned as a micropolitical entity of sorts—a "state within the state," as one outsider disapprovingly noted—operating according to a set of constitutions and statutes to which members theoretically adhered.[6]

---

3. Charles-Philippe d'Albert, duc de Luynes, *Mémoires du duc de Luynes sur la cour de Louis XV (1735–1758)*, ed. Louis Dussieux and Eudoxe Soulié (Paris, 1860), 1:204.

4. The term "associational world" is taken from Peter Clark, *British Clubs and Societies, 1580–1800: The Origins of an Associational World* (New York: Oxford University Press, 2000).

5. See, for example, the disagreement between Christiane Berkvens-Stevelinck and Margaret Jacob over the masonic status of the Dutch Knights of Jubilation in Berkvens-Stevelinck, "Les Chevaliers de la Jubilation: Maçonnerie ou libertinage? A propos de quelques publications de Margaret C. Jacob," *Quaerendo* 13 (1983): 50–73, 124–48. Jacob's reply may be found in "The Knights of Jubilation—Masonic and Libertine. A Reply," *Quaerendo* 14 (1984): 63–75.

6. *Apologie de l'ordre des Francs-maçons par le frère ****** (Philadelphie (?), 1779), 39. A similar moniker— "a . . . little republic at the center of the state"—was applied to the Parisian Order of Barristers in

The early decades of Freemasonry have attracted far less attention than the prerevolutionary era, a scholarly trend that reflects the coverage of the archival holdings at the Bibliothèque Nationale.[7] But if the historian is willing to move beyond this easily consultable yet chronologically limited archive, a great wealth of normative texts, including lodge speeches and songbooks, private correspondence, apologias, and anti-masonic exposures abounds for earlier decades in the century; published works alone numbered approximately seventy before 1750.[8] We focus on these sources, and particularly on the writings of one of the founding fathers of the movement in France, Andrew-Michael Ramsay, because a close reading of these documents can help us recover how brethren intended to shape and infuse meaning into lodge life during this under-studied period in masonic French history.

Actively participating in masonic meetings or banquets was by no means a mundane act of sociability in early eighteenth-century France. Indeed, it could prove dangerous. In contrast with the organization's ambiguous but semi-legal status during the reign of Louis XVI, when authorities tolerated but stopped short of officially endorsing masonic activity, lodges were routinely hounded by the state and the Catholic Church during the earlier part of the century. Reflecting the Old Regime's prohibition against any assembly not approved by the state, police in Paris and elsewhere arrested Masons and fined shopkeepers who rented out meeting spaces.[9] The Church went after brethren with even more determination: bishops publicly condemned them, the Vatican issued a series of papal decrees against the order (in 1738 and again in 1751), and one French Mason even ended up in front of the Inquisition in Lisbon.[10] Such sustained surveillance and persecution clearly

---

the 1730s. David Bell, *Lawyers and Citizens: The Making of a Political Elite in Old Regime France* (New York: Oxford University Press, 1993), 6.

7. The *fonds maçonnique* at the Bibliothèque Nationale mostly contains the archives of the Grand Orient, established in 1773 as the central administrative organ of French Freemasonry and successor to the Grand Lodge.

8. Johel Coutura, ed., *Le parfait maçon: Les débuts de la Maçonnerie française (1736–1748)* (Saint-Etienne: Université de Saint-Etienne, 1994), 7–25.

9. Assemblies not authorized by the state had been banned since at least the fourteenth century, and the Parlement of Paris reiterated this prohibition in a 1660 *arrêt* that forbade all "public and private assemblies or congregations of all types without the express permission and consent of His Majesty." Cited in Pierre Chevallier, *Le sceptre, la crosse et l'équerre sous Louis XV et XVI, 1725–1789* (Paris: Honoré Champion, 1996), 286.

10. John Coustos, master of a Parisian lodge in the 1730s, published an account of his persecution at the hands of the Inquisition in *Procédures curieuses de l'Inquisition de Portugal contre les Francs-maçons . . . par un frère maçon sorti de l'Inquisition* (The Hague, 1747).

would have made it difficult for individuals to regularly meet face to face. Like the early modern Republic of Letters, the early masonic community thus was to some degree an imagined one, where Frenchmen placed themselves in Freemasonry either through personal letter exchange—a topic examined in chapter 4—or by the writing and reading of many of the texts encountered below.[11]

✒ The Origins of Freemasonry in France

The first masonic lodges emerged at some point in seventeenth-century Scotland.[12] As early as 1600, non-stonemasons had begun seeking membership in stonemason lodges. These so-called non-operatives emerged from a wide swath of Scottish society, but many were of the gentry. Although the paucity of records does not permit any firm conclusions, it appears that they were attracted to the stonemason lodge for a number of reasons, including the heavily ritualized associative life and secrecy, and the conviviality and "cult of friendship" among men.[13] Stonemasons, for their part, saw in these outsiders a reliable source of dues and a conferral of prestige onto their organization among the general public. Although the entry of non-operatives proceeded at varying paces in different places and moments over the course of the 1600s, the end result is clear. By the opening decade of the eighteenth century, at least twenty-five "modern" lodges, comprising both stonemasons and non-stonemasons, had been established throughout Scotland.

These early Scottish lodges governed themselves autonomously and shared few standard operating procedures. This contrasted sharply with Dutch, English, and French lodges that appeared at later dates, all of which were to nominally follow regulations emanating from The Hague, London, and Paris respectively. The first efforts at standardizing masonic practice under a central authority took place in England.[14] English lodges began to appear in the second half of the seventeenth century, and in 1716, a group of Masons

---

11. Robert Mayhew, "British Geography's Republic of Letters: Mapping an Imaginary Community, 1600–1800," *Journal of the History of Ideas* 65 (2004): 251–76.

12. The following section draws from David Stevenson, *The Origins of Freemasonry: Scotland's Century, 1590–1710* (New York: Cambridge University Press, 1988), 190–233.

13. The expression is Stevenson's (*Origins of Freemasonry*, 179).

14. A synopsis of the early English lodges may be found in Steven Bullock, *Revolutionary Brotherhood: Freemasonry and the Transformation of the American Social Order* (Chapel Hill: University of North Carolina Press, 1996), 9–41.

in London undertook the first efforts to establish common practices. To encourage socializing between lodges, they agreed to hold an annual meeting and banquet on Saint John's Day (late June). In 1717, masters of the same Londonian lodges constituted the first Grand Lodge. By the early 1720s, the number of lodges affiliated to the Grand Lodge had grown from just a handful to twenty-four in the capital. Over the following two decades, this central administrative hub began to assume regulatory powers—such as transmitting basic guidelines for lodge format and candidate admission—over lodges throughout the entire kingdom, on the continent, and in colonial America.

In France, lodges began to appear during the mid-1720s, mainly in Paris but also in provincial cities with either an established military presence or commercial links with the wider Atlantic or Mediterranean worlds.[15] Unlike Masonry across the channel in the previous century, Freemasonry in France had no direct ties to any professional guilds. Many of its early adherents instead originated as members of the sizeable and mostly noble Jacobite diaspora arriving in and around Paris. The first three Grand Masters of the fraternity in France in fact were English or Scottish supporters of the Stuart cause: Philip Wharton, James-Hector Maclean, and Charles Radcliffe. The first French Grand Master would not appear until the duc d'Antin assumed leadership of the brotherhood in 1738. As Voltaire's *Lettres philosophiques* and Montesquieu's *Esprit des lois* testify, early eighteenth-century France was gripped by a definite *anglomanie*, a fascination with English politics and culture. The *philosophes* were particularly attracted to Hanoverian England's freedoms of religion, opinion, and association, and Freemasonry of course embodied the latter.[16] As Barbier's journal entry cited in the beginning of this chapter suggests, Freemasonry's appeal had much to do with its foreign quality; by the early 1730s the French elite had begun to swell the ranks of lodges. The absence of any strong central administrative body makes estimation difficult at this time, but one may safely discard one Mason's extraordinarily inflated estimate that by the mid-1730s there were already "more than two thousand" members in France.[17] There were likely only five functioning lodges in Paris at the time, with less than one hundred members.

---

15. On the early stages of the organization in France, see Pierre Chevallier, *Les Ducs sous l'acacia ou les premiers pas de la Franc-maçonnerie française, 1725–43* (Paris: Vrin, 1964); and Chevallier, *La première profanation du temple maçonnique ou Louis XV et la fraternité 1737–1755* (Paris: Vrin, 1968).

16. Josephine Grieder, *Anglomania in France, 1740–1789: Fact, Fiction, and Political Discourse* (Geneva: Droz, 1985).

17. The estimate is of Philippe-Valentin Bertin du Rocheret, member of the Bussi-Aumont lodge. BMC MS 125, fol. 249r.

Outside Paris, Freemasons began meeting in a small number of provincial cities, beginning with Bordeaux in 1732 and then in the important fortress town of Valenciennes on the Escaut River in 1733. Frenchmen during this period also founded lodges on or near the Atlantic and Mediterranean coasts in places such as Beaucaire, Caen, Le Havre, and Niort. Many urban centers had no visible trace of Freemasonry until after midcentury; Masons did not open a lodge in Lyon until 1756.[18]

Because French Freemasonry was not yet the centralized organization it would become in the prerevolutionary decades, it is quite difficult to reconstruct with precision masonic membership for the earlier decades. However, the police raids on lodges in Paris during this period did leave behind some sporadic documentary traces of participation. Although historians like Margaret Jacob have emphasized the social heterogeneity of French Freemasonry from its very beginnings, these sources depict an organization in which the Second Estate typically led lodge meetings held in fashionable districts like the western faubourgs of Saint-Germain and Saint-Honoré and in which the nobility also made up the majority of members. A similar trend can be found in early provincial lodges as well.[19] From the three masonic groups in Paris for which we have reliable membership data in the 1730s—Bussi-Aumont, Coustos-Villeroy, and Louis d'Argent—the nobility comprised between nearly 60 percent to over 80 percent of identifiable members.[20] Note that when a member of the Third Estate was initiated, his admission was, in the majority of cases, on wholly utilitarian grounds and not intended to enhance the social standing of the lodge. It is significant

18. See the lodge lists in Alain Le Bihan, *Loges et chapitres de la Grande Loge et du Grand Orient de France . . .* (Paris: Bibliothèque nationale, 1967); and Françoise Weil, "La Franc-maçonnerie en France jusqu'en 1755," *Studies on Voltaire and the Eighteenth Century* 27 (1963), 1787–1815.

19. On the supposed social mixing going on in early lodges, see Margaret Jacob, *Living the Enlightenment: Freemasonry and Politics in Eighteenth-Century Europe* (New York: Oxford University Press, 1991), 3–4. Cities whose early lodges (founding dates are in parentheses) had a strong noble presence include Avignon (1736), Caen (1741), Toulouse (1741), Le Mans (1744), Perpignan (1744), Tarascon (1748), and Hesdin (1749). See André Bouton and Marius Lepage, *Histoire de la Franc-maçonnerie dans la Mayenne (1756–1951)* (Le Mans: Imprimerie Monnoyer, 1951), 23; Émile Lesueur, *La Franc-maçonnerie artésienne au XVIIIe siècle* (Paris: Ernest Leroux, 1914), 53–55; Jean-Marie Mercier, *Les Francs-maçons du pape: L'Art Royal à Avignon au XVIIIe siècle* (Paris: Classiques Garnier, 2010), 23; Jean-Marie Mercier and Thierry Zarcone, *Les Francs-maçons du pays de Daudet: Beaucaire et Tarascon. Destins croisés du XVIIIe au XXe siècles* (Aix-en-Provence: Edisud, 2004), 24; Céline Sala, *Les Francs-maçons en terres catalanes entre Lumières et Restauration: L'Art Royal de Perpignan à Barcelone (1740–1830)* (Paris: Honoré Champion, 2009), 78; Eric Saunier, *Révolution et sociabilité en Normandie au tournant des XVIIIe et XIXe siècles: 6000 francs-maçons de 1740 à 1830* (Rouen: Publications de l'Université de Rouen, 1998), 47; Michel Taillefer, *La Franc-maçonnerie toulousaine sous l'Ancien Régime et la Révolution, 1741–1799* (Paris: E.N.S.B.-C.T.H.S., 1984), 14–16.

20. Figures have been tabulated from Chevallier, *Ducs sous l'acacia*, chaps. 2 and 3.

that at least two-thirds of commoners with a known profession were musicians, jewelers, poets, or artists. This trend indicates that their admission
depended on whether or not the lodge thought they possessed a talent or
trade that would enhance masonic festivities. The remaining minority of
non-nobles, like the Protestant banker Bauer, were able to access early
lodges largely because of their extraordinary wealth, but this did not mean
they were considered social equals with the Second Estate. In early April
1737, for example, the duc d'Aumont held a masonic banquet to which he
invited only noble Freemasons.[21] The membership of early lodges indeed
reflected the reality of a converging or "regrouping" of the nobility of the
high robe and of the sword from the death of the Sun King to midcentury.[22] Whereas the military nobility had a tendency to differentiate itself culturally from the robe during the sixteenth and seventeenth centuries,
both groups could be found congregating in masonic lodges in the 1730s.
Such was the case, for example, of the Louis d'Argent lodge, whose dozen
identifiable members were drawn almost exclusively from the high robe associated with the Parlement of Paris or from the sword. Other lodges in the
capital, such as Coustos-Villeroy and Bussi-Aumont also followed this trend.
Even though non-nobles would begin to start their own lodges possibly as
early as the mid-1740s and later go on to become the majority of recruits
in the final decades of the Old Regime, masonic social events—banquets,
poetry readings, and so forth—would continue to pattern themselves after
aristocratic models of sociability. Antoine Lilti has explored, for example,
the intriguing links between lodges and salons in the prerevolutionary era,
and in later chapters I will explore in greater detail parallels between lodge
events and elite socializing.[23]

✦ Freemasonry and the Associational World of Eighteenth-Century France

Congregating in the secluded space of the masonic lodge reflected the continuing effort of early modern French elites to differentiate themselves from

---

21. Chevallier, *Ducs sous l'acacia*, 68.

22. Franklin Ford, *Robe and Sword: The Regrouping of the French Aristocracy after Louis XIV* (Cambridge, MA: Harvard University Press, [1953] 1962), 201.

23. Antoine Lilti, *Le monde des salons: Sociabilité et mondanité à Paris au XVIIIᵉ siècle* (Paris: Fayard,
2005), 70–72. Police reports suggest possible activity of commoner lodges in Paris in the mid-
1740s, although no official lodge documentation or correspondence between brethren has confirmed these findings. Pierre Chevallier, *Histoire de la Franc-maçonnerie française. La Maçonnerie: École
de l'égalité, 1725–1799* (Paris: Fayard, 1974), 65–71.

the wider public. Although this gradual process of withdrawal from what Peter Burke has perhaps too simplistically defined as "popular culture" had arguably been underway since the reign of Louis XIII, the eighteenth century witnessed a rapid acceleration of the creation of sites of exclusive sociability for privileged urban dwellers.[24] By the end of the Old Regime, it is indeed possible to identify at least two general cultural realms existing alongside one another, one anchored in new private institutions like Freemasonry and the other based on older patterns of collective, public sociability that played out in the city street, such as municipal processions and religious festivals.[25]

This burgeoning elite culture of privacy found its home in the clubs and societies emerging during the Enlightenment. As John Roberts has indicated, Freemasonry was one of the most widespread institutional responses to a growing human need to develop bonds of solidarity beyond the increasingly rigid expectations of family and work.[26] Although the associational world of Great Britain was undoubtedly more robust than in other parts of Europe, one still finds a remarkable diversity of voluntary organizations on the continent. Historians have yet to carry out substantive research on many French clubs and societies, but it is nevertheless possible to offer a general picture of associational life by looking at a number of extant, albeit incomplete, inventories.[27] These sources indicate that nearly one hundred fifty private organizations were founded in France from the late seventeenth century to 1750, and approximately four hundred over the course of the eighteenth century. These groups varied considerably in both how they organized themselves and what activities they pursued. Some voluntary associations

---

24. Peter Burke, *Popular Culture in Early Modern Europe* (Burlington, VT: Ashgate, [1978] 2009), chap. 9.

25. See the remarks of Robert Schneider, *Public Life in Toulouse, 1463–1789: From Municipal Republic to Cosmopolitan City* (Ithaca, NY: Cornell University Press, 1989), 357.

26. John Roberts, *The Mythology of the Secret Societies* (New York: Charles Scribner's Sons, 1972), 17.

27. This figure is based on a tabulation drawn from a number of disparate sources: F.-T. Bègue Clavel, *Histoire pittoresque de la Franc-maçonnerie et des sociétés secrètes anciennes et modernes* (Paris, 1843), 389–90; Arthur Dinaux, *Les sociétés badines, bachiques, littéraires et chantantes: Leur histoire et leurs travaux*, 2 vols. (Paris, 1867); Nicolas-Jules-Henri Gourdon de Genouillac, *Dictionnaire historique des ordres de chevalerie créés chez les différents peuples, depuis les premiers siècles jusqu'à nos jours* (Paris, 1860); and David Trott's online database of private theatrical groups at http://www.chass.utoronto.ca/~trott/societe/societe.htm. In our understanding of civil society, we have followed the Hegelian notion that refers to the distinct social space between the family and the state, in which autonomous individuals can form new bonds of solidarity. In order to focus on only those arenas of sociability that emerged spontaneously within this space, we have not included in the analysis those organizations formally bound to either the Catholic Church or the state: confraternities and chivalric orders founded by the monarchy and academies, for example, have all been excluded. On Hegel's definition of civil society, see Z. A. Pelczynski, ed., *The State and Civil Society: Studies in Hegel's Political Philosophy* (New York: Cambridge University Press, 1984).

closely resembled Freemasonry in their formality, as they also patterned their meetings after an elaborate set of written rules.[28] Others, meanwhile, were more fluid in format, mirroring a salon or dinner gathering rather than a masonic lodge. These societies' interests ranged widely, but they can be broken down into three broad categories. First, a remarkable preponderance of small, private theatrical troupes flourished under the patronage of a particular individual or family. The Société Dramatique du Château de Morville in Normandy, for example (founded in 1737), operated under the auspices of the marquise de Morville, and its half a dozen or so members both wrote and acted out a variety of plays.[29] Second, intellectual circles devoted to literature or philosophy such as the well-known Entresol Club (founded in 1724) that included luminaries such as Helvétius and Montesquieu could be found. These groups would become increasingly focused on political topics, as the *musées* of the prerevolutionary period illustrated. And third, on the other end of the spectrum, one finds clubs whose primary objective was simply dining and heavy drinking. To be sure, nearly all voluntary associations in the early eighteenth century infused their social arenas with meals and drink, but few likely went as far as the Ordre de la Boisson (founded in 1703), where officers held colorful titles such as *Bois-sans-cesse*, *l'Altéré*, *Flaconville*, *la Buvette*, and so on.[30] Particularly striking is that this pursuit of bodily pleasure knew few bounds: one finds organizations devoted to flatulence as well as, possibly, to heterosexual and homosexual relations.[31] Masons were aware of these other societies and often drew stark differences between lodges and more bacchanalian venues. Writing later in the century, an author who employed the moniker "brother Enoch" urged his readers to distinguish lodges from those "so-called societies" where the "biggest drinkers are the most zealous brethren" and in which members congregated simply to "sacrifice themselves to their stomach."[32]

---

28. See for example the statutes of the Ordre de la Malice (founded in 1734 in Paris) in Dinaux, *Sociétés badines*, 2:3–4.

29. Ibid., 2:75.

30. Ibid., 1:106.

31. Societies possibly engaged in sexual activities include the Ordre des Chevaliers de la Joie (1696), the Ordre des Pédérastes (possibly 1733) and the Ordre et Société de la Culotte (1724). On flatulence, see the Société des Francs-Péteurs (1743). Whereas Dinaux affirms the reality of the Francs-Péteurs, Eric Saunier has argued that this was likely a satirical anti-masonic invention. Saunier, *Révolution et sociabilité*, 46, n1.

32. Frère Enoch, *Le vrai Franc-maçon, qui donne l'origine et le but de la Franc-maçonnerie* (Liège, 1773), 98.

This brief survey of associational life provides the necessary backdrop to the emergence of Freemasonry during the second quarter of the eighteenth century, and it also compels us to reject the widely held assumption that Masonry was the first voluntary organization whose members congregated for nonprofessional purposes during the Old Regime.[33] Just as French political writers began to envision France as a consciously constructed nation in the eighteenth century, so too did these voluntary societies envision themselves as voluntary, self-willed communities.[34] But Freemasons faced a particular challenge in this task of self-fashioning because their rationale for congregating in lodges was far less apparent than for most of the organizations outlined above, whose activities could be inferred by simply looking at their names. Because of this challenge, and since Freemasonry was not inherently patterned after professional or family ties, brethren had to state explicitly why they were assembling and how they envisioned their relationship to each other. Unlike a trade guild or a theatrical troupe, the collective identity and objectives of a lodge could not be assumed. Instead, the salient themes, symbols, and values shaping masonic associational life were carefully spelled out in a wide variety of texts during the early decades of the movement, from lodge speeches to apologias and anti-masonic exposures.

✦ The Masonic Utopia of Friendship

One of the earliest such documents in France was a speech proclaimed at a general masonic assembly held at the lodge of Jacobite Lord Charles Radcliffe on 26 December 1736. The author of this speech was one of the more colorful and distinguished characters of early Freemasonry: the chevalier Andrew-Michael de Ramsay (1686–1743). Besides his masonic activity in France, Ramsay is perhaps best known today as the author of the 1727 best seller, *Les voyages de Cyrus.* A Scotsman by birth, Ramsay was the archetypical eighteenth-century cosmopolitan *homme de lettres,* having made his literary reputation in France, a country he rarely left after his arrival in 1710.[35]

---

33. Chevallier, *Le sceptre, la crosse et l'équerre,* 12; Ran Halévi, *Les loges maçonniques dans la France d'Ancien Régime: Aux origines de la sociabilité démocratique* (Paris: Armand Colin, 1984), 16.

34. David Bell, *The Cult of the Nation in France: Inventing Nationalism, 1680–1800* (Cambridge, MA: Harvard University Press, 2001).

35. The following account of Ramsay's life is based on George Henderson, *Chevalier Ramsay* (New York: Thomas Nelson and Sons, 1952).

Ramsay entered Freemasonry in the late 1720s, though it is not clear in what lodge or country, and he enthusiastically embraced the movement until the end of his life. We do know that during his 1729–1730 stay in England, Ramsay was readily received into the Horn lodge in London as well as the Gentleman's Society of Spalding, a club frequented by a number of prominent Masons, notably the reverends Jean-Théophile Desaguliers and James Anderson.[36] Records of Ramsay's masonic activities in France during the first half of the 1730s are sketchy at best, but it is clear that he was becoming well known in the movement by this time, having himself claimed to be Grand Orator of the order in France.

An expanded version of Ramsay's speech was to be delivered at a general meeting in Paris in March 1737, but a police crackdown on masonic assemblies the same month likely forced him to renounce his plans; a definitive version of the text survived and was published, under the title "Discours prononcé à la Réception des Frée-Maçons [*sic*]" the following year.[37] The "Discours" represented the first clear articulation in France of the order's requirements for membership and moral aspirations, and for this reason our study begins here. This text was not merely a by-product of masonic socializing, for there were but a handful of lodges in Paris and elsewhere when Ramsay first put quill pen to paper. Similar to Anderson's *Constitutions* in the British context a decade earlier, Ramsay's speech was an innovative document that served as an urtext for French Masons. It is apparent that his vision was widely shared and that it held broad appeal: brethren sent one another copies of his discourse, and lodges in provincial cities like Alençon, Lyon, Toulouse, and Troyes possessed Ramsay's text.[38] It was also reprinted at least a dozen times before the Revolution, perhaps most visibly in the masonic guide of Louis-François de la Tierce, which went through four editions during the middle of the century.[39] La Tierce inserted Ramsay's speech as a prologue to Anderson's *Constitutions* and declared the former to be the best "introduction to the responsibilities, statutes, and rules of our venerable confraternity."[40] Until 1789, lodge officers in Paris and the prov-

---

36. In 1723, Anderson wrote the founding document of British Freemasonry, *The Constitutions of the Freemasons*.

37. Ramsay's text was published in *Lettre philosophique par M. de V***. Avec plusieurs pièces galantes et nouvelles de différens auteurs* (London, [1738] 1775), 42–61.

38. BME MS 124, unfoliated, and Jacques Léglise, *Catalogue des manuscrits maçonniques des bibliothèques publiques de France* (Paris: Éditions Sepp, 1984), 1:19, 29, 76; 2:5, 71.

39. Alain Bernheim, *Ramsay et ses deux discours* (Paris: Éditions Télètes, 2011), 42–44.

40. Louis-François de la Tierce, *Histoire, obligations et statuts de la très vénérable confraternité des Francsmaçons* (Frankfurt, 1742), 127. La Tierce intended his work solely for Freemasons, informing his

inces weaved the "Discours" into their own speeches, and apologists and detractors alike identified Ramsay's oration as a touchstone of masonic ideals.[41] By examining the "Discours" and comparing it with other documents of the period, a clearer picture of the organizational culture of early Freemasonry begins to emerge. This analysis is informed by a basic yet fundamental question that historians have yet to adequately address: How did Ramsay and early Masons, in their speeches, songs, and letters, characterize the internal dynamics of lodge life, and specifically, how did they understand the bonds forged between men through Masonry?

The most prevalent idiom used to describe the interpersonal relationships of Masons in the "Discours" was male or fraternal friendship. It was the masonic preoccupation with friendship that in fact distinguished the order from other modes of association. Ramsay claimed that, whereas military orders were erected only to cultivate love of glory, Freemasonry was instituted to form "friendly men" who were "loyal worshipers of the God of Friendship."[42] Ramsay reiterated this quasi-mystical vision of masonic friendship when he quoted a Latin phrase—likely from Horace—indicating that, as Masons, "we have promised to be loyal, to venerate the saint divinity of friendship, to love virtue and not rewards."[43] His ideal Mason was a self-policing gentleman who avoided "indecent excesses" and "discordant passions" when interacting in the lodge in order to ensure "tranquility of mind, gentle morals and the sentiments of friendship."[44] Ramsay not only made recourse to friendship when describing relationships between men in the "Discours," but he also employed it as a principle of exclusion. When explaining, for example, why women were not admitted into the order, he argued it was because their presence introduced the element of sexuality (a topic addressed in chapter 3) and that this posed a serious threat to the masculine friendship cultivated in the lodge: "We fear that love

---

publisher to sell the book only to "authorized persons." Jacques Lemaire, *Les origines françaises de l'antimaçonnisme (1744–1797)* (Brussels: Éditions de l'Université de Bruxelles, 1985), 38.

41. On the invocation of the "Discours" in French lodges, see Dossier of Constance Éprouvée (Paris), BN FM²65, fol. 24r; Museum of our National Heritage, *Sharp Documents*, vol.1, *The Story of Les Élus Parfaits, the Mother Ecossais Lodge of Bordeaux* (Lexington, MA: Museum of our National Heritage, 1993), ii–vi; Pierre-Yves Beaurepaire, *L'autre et le frère: L'étranger et la Franc-maçonnerie en France au XVIIIᵉ siècle* (Paris: Honoré Champion, 1998), 648–50. For examples of Ramsay in apologias and anti-masonic exposures, see Nicolas de Bonneville, *Les Jésuites chassés de la Maçonnerie et leur poignard brisé par les Maçons* (London, 1788), 1:80; Théodore-Henry baron de Tschoudy, *L'étoile flamboyante, ou la société des Francs-maçons considérée sous tous les aspects* (Paris, 1766), 1:209.

42. *Lettre philosophique par M. de V****, 45.

43. Ibid., 47–48.

44. Ibid., 48.

entering with its charms may make us forget our fraternity. The names of brother and of friend would be weak arms to safeguard our hearts from rivalry."[45]

Widening our lens beyond Ramsay and his "Discours," we see that other brethren in the 1730s and 1740s also invoked male or fraternal friendship as the tie that bound them. An early collection of lodge songs composed by Jacques-Christophe Naudot, member of the Coustos-Villeroy lodge in Paris during the 1730s, made frequent use of the terms "friend" and "friendship" when describing masonic interaction. When asked what the purpose of Freemasonry was, a lodge master was to reply, "To pay the tribute of a tender and dear friendship: this is the lone statute of our charming institution." Another couplet exclaimed that the "first secret" of all perfect Masons was to be a subject full of zeal as well as a "tender and loyal friend" to his fellows.[46] In lodges the following decade, orators reiterated the centrality of friendship to the brotherhood, exclaiming that "Masonry is a sanctuary devoted to friendship" and that "every Mason must necessarily be a good friend."[47] This message was also emphasized at the conclusion of a candidate's initiation into Freemasonry, when the lodge master informed him that Masonry seeks "calm men, susceptible to friendship and worthy to inspire it."[48] Following a candidate's formal entry into Masonry, he was normally read a document titled, "Instructions on what a Mason must think about Masonry in general." Here, he was to be told by the lodge master that "friendship is the chain that unites us all" and, because "the affinity of characters and the conformity of principles are the sources of friendship," it was absolutely essential for a Mason to always "observe everything which can cement his union with his brothers."[49]

Outsiders and detractors also understood that Freemasonry's primary objective was to cultivate and develop male friendships between members. When the inquisitive wife of a Freemason published her supposed clandestine visit to an all-male meeting in 1744, she informed her reader that "she was

---

45. Ibid., 52.

46. Naudot's songs are published in his *Chansons notées de la très vénérable confrérie des Francs-maçons. Précédées de quelques pièces de poésie, convenable au sujet, et d'une marche* (Paris, 1737).

47. "Discours de réception dans un temps critique" and "Discours de rentrée sur l'amitié," originally published in *L'École des francs-maçons* (1748) and reprinted in Coutura, *Parfait maçon*, 184–89.

48. "Lettre à Madame D★★★," in Coutura, *Parfait maçon*, 222. Like today, the three basic masonic ranks in the eighteenth century were apprentice (*apprenti* [often spelled *apprentif*]), fellowcraft (*compagnon*) and master (*maître*).

49. "Instructions sur ce qu'un maçon doit penser de la maçonnerie en général," BN FM⁴149, fol. 5r.

agreeably surprised . . . the Masons are so charming!"[50] Behind a curtain, she claimed to witness her husband and fellows dining, drinking, and enjoying one another's conversation. She also reported on the topic of speeches, and here again friendship emerges as the idiom of choice to describe relations between brethren. Each Mason, the lodge orator explained, was a "living stone" of the masonic temple, linked to every other member by the "precious cement of friendship." All lodges, he continued, "must be cemented by the friendship of all brethren" in order to ensure their longevity.[51] In 1745, Gabriel-Louis Pérau published his *L'ordre des Francs-maçons trahi*, in which he exposed the inner workings and symbolism of a typical lodge of the period. Friendship also appeared in Pérau's text as the bond forged between Masons. When describing the physical layout of the masonic lodge, Pérau indicated that most of the space was "filled with symbols of friendship that one can modify according to one's tastes."[52]

Why did Ramsay and others choose male friendship as the binding tie of this organization? An answer to this question may be gleaned by reading the "Discours" alongside Ramsay's earlier political writings. Nearly twenty years before the publishing of the "Discours" and a decade before his active involvement in Freemasonry in France, Ramsay composed a political tract that has remained relatively obscure, the *Essai philosophique sur le gouvernment civil* (1719). His objective, by no means groundbreaking in the early eighteenth century, was to "remedy the ills of the great political body" and to "establish the maxims which will incline to make all men good citizens and subjects."[53] This document represented a minor contribution to a long-running conversation in early modern political thought that began with Jean Bodin and was devoted to rethinking political authority in the wake of the religious strife of the Reformations. Ramsay was a part of a constellation of thinkers who sought to move beyond erecting political communities on confessional uniformity and to devise new ways of defining sovereignty and communal bonds, an objective that entailed fundamentally recasting the

---

50. This anonymous account, impossible to verify as either a lived experience or a purely romantic fabrication, was published as *La Franc-maçonne ou révélation des mystères des Francs-maçons. Par Madame ★★★* (Brussels, 1744).

51. Ibid., 51, 70.

52. Abbé Gabriel-Louis Pérau, *L'ordre des Francs-maçons trahi et le secret des Mopses révélé*, ed. Daniel Ligou (Geneva: Slatkine Reprints, 1980), 136.

53. Andrew-Michael Ramsay, *Essai philosophique sur le gouvernment civil où l'on traite de la nécessité, de l'origine, des droits, des bornes, & des différentes formes de la Souveraineté . . .* (London, [1719] 1721), a3.

relationship between state and society and reinventing the codes of individual and collective social behavior.

Like all early Enlightenment writings on politics, Ramsay's *Essai* was composed in the shadow of Thomas Hobbes and John Locke. Hobbes's celebrated 1651 *Leviathan* was a frontal assault on the Aristotelian notion that there was in men some type of natural attraction toward the good and toward living in society; his writings represented, in the words of one critic, a profound "paradigm transformation" away from Aristotle's optimistic view of humanity.[54] Hobbes instead found, or rather conjured up, a man who, in his natural state, was an apolitical, asocial entity, and whose sole desire was that of self-preservation. Individuals came together, forged political societies, and accepted the laws of an absolute sovereign not because of some innate desire to frequent one another, but rather to ensure their own physical and mental well-being. Outside of and preceding the political structure, the aggressive competition for both material resources and collective esteem led men to live anxiety-ridden lives, which Hobbes famously described as "solitary, poore, nasty, brutish, and short." Although Locke disagreed with Hobbes's pessimistic view that the natural state of man was one of constant war, he nevertheless held that egoism lay at the center of bringing people together under a social contract. In his *Two Treatises of Government*, likely published in 1689 but written earlier, Locke argued that individuals' fundamental end in forging civil societies was the preservation of their already acquired material possessions and personal freedoms—what Locke broadly termed "property."

In the opening pages of the *Essai*, Ramsay took aim at both the Hobbesian and Lockean explanations for communal living. He considers "monstrous" the Hobbesian argument that an irrational fear of destruction could possibly serve as an effective means to forge a political community: "Far from here are all the monstrous ideas that teach us that man is naturally and originally engaged to be sociable solely by the fear of being oppressed. In other words, if he were assured to suffer nothing himself, he could live freely and inde-

---

54. Thomas A. Spragens, *The Politics of Motion: The World of Thomas Hobbes* (Lexington: University Press of Kentucky, 1973), 41. Hobbes openly attacks Aristotle at a number of points in *Leviathan*, most clearly in the following passage: "And I beleeve that scarce any thing can be more absurdly said in naturall Philosophy, than that which now is called *Aristotles Metaphysiques*; nor more repugnant to Government, than much of that hee hath said in his *Politiques*; nor more ignorantly, than a great part of his *Ethiques*." Thomas Hobbes, *Leviathan*, ed. Richard Tuck (New York: Cambridge University Press, 1996), 461–62. On Aristotle's conception of humankind as naturally sociable, see Michael Pakaluk, *Aristotle's Nicomachean Ethics: An Introduction* (New York: Cambridge University Press, 2005), chap. 9.

pendently from of all others." Ramsay, prefiguring David Hume's position three decades later, then proceeds to dismiss Lockean rational self-interest as well.[55] Societies formed by either tacit or overt contract agreement between individuals are nothing more than "trading companies which associate together to do business, and then break apart when they no longer find any profit!"[56] Ramsay's critique of Locke and Hobbes stemmed from the fact that he saw in both his predecessors the tendency to overemphasize self-love (*amour-propre*) as the driving force that brought individuals into society. "Those who have examined politics," Ramsay informs his readers, "have wanted to establish two types of principles which are entirely contradictory to one another. They relate moral and political virtues, as well as what we call natural law, to self-love and particular interests."[57]

Parting ways with both Hobbes and Locke, Ramsay believed that politics was not simply a matter of self-interest, although he did not deny that the individual must look after his immediate material needs. But he stressed emphatically that "self-love is the last of all loves," and that men must always strive to put collective interests ahead of their own concerns.[58] Ramsay rejects self-love as the force animating the building of communal ties between men, and instead reclaims the Aristotelian notion that "to be sociable is a character of humanity," titling the third chapter of the *Essai*, "Man is born sociable." In this section, he explains quite clearly what he meant by the term "sociable": "By sociable, I do not mean to live together and to see one another in certain places and at certain moments. The most ferocious beasts are sociable in this manner. Men can see each other every day without interacting in a sociable way. By sociable, I understand a *mutual exchange of friendship*."[59] This idea, continues Ramsay, "is beautiful and luminous and shows us what is the first principal of union and of society among men." Ramsay's premise that humans are naturally sociable and peaceable beings was already quite apparent a century earlier in the thought of Hugo Grotius, who grounded his politics in the axiom that all individuals possessed an *appetitus societatis*, as well as in the work of legal scholar Samuel Pufendorf. Later, a whole host of continental and English thinkers—the Earl of Shaftes-

---

55. Like Ramsay, Hume criticized Hobbes and Locke for having "maintained the selfish system of Morals." David Hume, *An Enquiry concerning the Principles of Morals* (London, 1751), 13.

56. Ramsay, *Essai philosophique*, 26.

57. Ibid., 1.

58. Ibid., 10.

59. Ibid., 19–20. Ramsay's emphasis.

bury and later Jean-Jacques Rousseau being the most notable—held that humans possess an inherent capacity for sociability.[60] The presence of moralists with such beliefs thus reminds us that, although the religious wars of the sixteenth and seventeenth centuries dealt a severe blow to the Aristotelian notion of individuals as naturally sociable, not all philosophers reverted to varied degrees of egoism, as did Hobbes and Locke when conceiving of sustainable political communities.

When Ramsay conceived of friendship as the bedrock of political life, he was drawing from classical sources—Cicero, for example, is cited at numerous points in the *Essai*.[61] Peter Gay has drawn attention to the Roman's elevated status during the Enlightenment, and Chantal Grell has quantitatively confirmed this by showing that Cicero was by far the most published classical author in the Enlightenment.[62] On friendship, eighteenth-century authors readily acknowledged Cicero as the formative authority on the topic, and his celebrated treatise, *De amicitia*, enjoyed over a dozen editions from the turn of the century to the Revolution.[63] It is worth recalling that Cicero's discussion on friendship in *De amicitia* was not unprecedented, as similar themes are found in Aristotle's *Nichomachean Ethics* (Books 7 and 8). Cicero celebrated friendship because it was a private bond with public benefits that could serve to buttress the Roman republic.[64] This was because, unlike modern understandings in the West, friendship for Cicero was less about intimately engaging with a unique self than it was about identifying in another person a set of shared objective criteria he variably termed "the good," "virtue," or a "community of views on all matters human and divine."[65] This idea pervaded the classical world; Aristotle described "perfect friendship" as the relationship between "men who are virtuous and who resemble

60. John Andrew Bernstein, "Shaftesbury's Optimism and Eighteenth-Century Social Thought," in *Anticipations of the Enlightenment in England, France, and Germany*, ed. Alan Charles Kors and Paul J. Korshin (Philadelphia: University Press of Pennsylvania, 1987), 86–101; Daniel Gordon, *Citizens without Sovereignty: Equality and Sociability in French Thought, 1670–1789* (Princeton, NJ: Princeton University Press, 1994), 54–73.

61. On Ramsay's familiarity with classical authors, see Henderson, *Chevalier Ramsay*, 1–12, 109–226.

62. Peter Gay, *The Enlightenment: The Rise of Modern Paganism* (New York: Norton & Company, [1969] 1995), 31–71, 105–06; Chantal Grell, *Le dix-huitième siècle et l'antiquité en France, 1680–1789* (Oxford: Voltaire Foundation, 1995), 1:297–301.

63. Jesuit Claude Buffier refers to Cicero as the "master" on friendship in *Traité de la societé civile et du moyen de se rendre heureux* . . . (Paris, 1726), 150.

64. This concern over the vitality of the state was particularly acute when Cicero sat down to compose his treatise on friendship in 44 BCE, shortly after Caesar's assassination in the Roman Senate.

65. Philippe Dubois-Goibaud, *Les livres de Cicéron de la vieillesse et de l'amitié, avec les paradoxes du même autheur* (Paris, 1708), 150.

each other by their virtue."[66] Similarly, the Stoics—whose influence on Cicero was significant—argued that friendship was based on shared values rather than inexplicable emotional attraction.[67] If the bedrock of Ciceronian friendship was virtue, then at the core of the virtuous Roman lay his love for the Republic. So important was patriotism to Cicero that he advocated abandoning any friend who sought to inflict harm upon "the public interest."[68] Because friendship could serve as an effective means to bring Roman male elites—such as the two central figures of *De amicitia*, statesmen Scipio Aemilianus and Gaius Laelius—outside the traditional orbit of family and kin and into the realm of Roman civic life, the body politic would be strengthened: "Indeed, friendship is so valuable that, if one were to remove it from our lives, no family and no Republic could survive. . . . What house is so well established, what state is so strong that it may not be entirely torn to pieces by hatred and division? From this it may be judged how great is the good in friendship."[69]

In light of this discussion, Ramsay's emphasis on friendship in his "Discours" becomes clear. He chose to ground the masonic community in friendship because, mirroring the civic friendship of Aristotle and Cicero, he saw this bond of solidarity as lying at the heart of his conception of the ideal *vita communis* as outlined in the *Essai* he had composed the previous decade. In this way, Ramsay envisioned Freemasonry as a utopian community in which the political ideals put forth in his earlier theoretical work could be worked out and perhaps achieved. Other brethren shared Ramsay's views, and understood the masonic brand of friendship as mirroring classical models. Just as Aristotle and Cicero grounded friendship in men exhibiting mutual respect for the "good" or the "virtuous," so too did brethren consider their relations as grounded in a shared moral framework and out-

66. Jules Barthélemy Saint-Hilaire, ed., *Morale d'Aristote* (Paris, 1856), 2:320. On the importance of moral character in constituting friendship in the classical world more generally, see David Konstan, *Friendship in the Classical World* (New York: Cambridge University Press, 1997), 72–78, 130–31, 152, 159; and Frédérick Gerson, *L'amitié au XVIIIᵉ siècle* (Paris: La Pensée Universelle, 1974) 13–14, 25, 29.

67. A recent treatment of Stoic friendship has described its basis as "not warm feelings of affection, but like-mindedness or *homonoia*—commitment to the cause." Dirk Baltzly and Nick Eliopoulos, "The Classical Ideals of Friendship," in *Friendship: A History*, ed. Barbara Caine (Oakville, CT: Equinox, 2009), 35.

68. Recounting the fate of recalcitrant politician Tiberius Gracchus (died 133 BCE), Cicero explains that Gracchus died without friends "for, since the belief in each other's good character was what brought friends together in the first place, it is difficult for friendship to remain if one leaves the path of goodness." Dubois-Goibaud, *Livres de Cicéron*, 178–79.

69. Ibid., 157.

look on the world. All men entering into the order, remarked a midcentury apologist, exhibited a similar "love of the good," which he defined as "a magnet which has the benefit of attracting the friendship of hearts"; shared morals thus served as the initial catalyst to bring individuals together who then derived emotional satisfaction from their fellowship. The author's indebtedness to the classics becomes explicit when he elaborates on the ethical basis of friendship in the lodge by following the Greco-Roman Stoic Epictetus. "When one wants to know if two men are truly friends," he remarks, "one should not find out if they are related or if they were raised or brought up together. These are poor indications. . . . One needs only to instruct oneself on their views and morals. If you recognize that they are both truly good people [*honnêtes gens*], . . . they are definitely friends." "It is by morals," he concludes, "that a man finds true friends."[70]

The masonic utopia of friendship Ramsay and others put forth was not, in the words of scholar Lewis Mumford, a "utopia of escape" that sought a complete and permanent separation from the outside world in order to establish a new and perfect order. This "utopia of escape" was, however, the model of many religious institutions. Since the medieval period, male friendship anchored monastic communities, and minority groups like the Jansenists at Port-Royal des Champs in the Chevreuse Valley outside of Paris also saw themselves as a tightly bound, egalitarian friendship community. However, whereas Masonry hoped to improve society at large, these institutions clearly embodied Mumfordian escapist utopias that functioned as totalizing institutions whose participants sought to seal themselves off from the outside world.[71] Freemasonry, on the other hand, should be conceived as a fine example of Mumford's "utopia of reconstruction," in which the masonic lodge promoted "a new set of habits," "a fresh scale of values," and a "new net of relationships" intended to improve the outside world.[72] It was indeed engagement and not withdrawal from French society that motivated Ramsay to state in the "Discours" his hope that Masonry would not only "resurrect and spread" the spirit of friendship between brethren but also cultivate the virtue of philanthropy (notably through charitable

---

70. *Moeurs des Francs-maçons* (Poliastrée [likely Paris], 1745), 62. In this passage, the author specifically references an abridged collection of Epicetus's teachings, likely the *Manuel d'Epictète* (Paris, 1715).

71. Maurice Daumas, *Des trésors d'amitié: De la Renaissance aux Lumières* (Paris: Armand Colin, 2011), 113–17; Brian McGuire, *Friendship and Community: The Monastic Experience, 350–1250* (Ithaca, NY: Cornell University Press, 2010).

72. Lewis Mumford, *The Story of Utopias* (New York: Boni and Liveright, 1922), 19–22.

work and alms giving) toward all of humanity. He saw such a program as having practical relevance beyond Freemasonry, as he hoped it could contribute to the moral instruction of the French nobility entering into the brotherhood, who in turn, he reasoned, would ensure the overall political health of the kingdom. Looking again to the ancients for guidance, Ramsay warned in the "Discours" that the fall of past republics was the direct result of the lack of virtue and lust for military conquest among their inhabitants: "Lycurge, Solon, Numa, and all the other political legislators were not able to make their establishments lasting. . . . Excessive love of the *patrie* often destroyed in these warring republics love of humanity in general."[73] In his emphasis on the order's usefulness, Ramsay was perhaps marked by his close association with the archbishop Fénelon, whose 1699 masterpiece, *Aventures de Télémaque*, described Boetica, a utopia of reconstruction celebrated for its civic virtue, patriotism, and social harmony. As Dan Edelstein notes, Boetica differed from utopias of escape like Francis Bacon's New Atlantis because it was not sealed off from its neighbors; Fénelon instead believed that Boetica's positive traits could be transposed to other states.[74]

☙ A Private Bond with Public Benefits

In late March 1737, Ramsay, so convinced of the public utility of Freemasonry, contacted Louis XV's chief advisor, the Cardinal de Fleury, requesting that the crown officially endorse the organization. In his letters to the minister, Ramsay envisioned Freemasonry as an institutional support of the monarchy, similar to the Académie française. "These assemblies," he remarked to the cardinal in one letter, "could become very useful to religion, the state and letters." Ramsay even sent Fleury a copy of a speech—presumably the "Discours"—he was to read to "the young nobility of France" at a general meeting of Parisian lodges, and he hoped the minister would recognize in the text the masonic "love of virtue" and look favorably upon it and perhaps bestow the order with a royal charter. Why would Ramsay have invested such high hopes in Fleury? Although the correspondence between them offers no clear answers, it is quite possible that Fleury's tacit support during the previous decade for the politically inclined and largely noble

---

73. Ramsay, "Discours," 39–40.

74. Dan Edelstein, *The Terror of Natural Right: Republicanism, the Cult of Nature, & the French Revolution* (Chicago: University of Chicago Press, 2009), 58.

Entresol Club—of which Ramsay was an active participant—signaled to Ramsay a willingness on behalf of the minister to support new institutions that claimed to rejuvenate the monarchy.[75]

Ramsay's hope that Freemasonry would serve as a privileged vehicle through which noble men would cultivate friendship and moral virtues like philanthropy thus represented one of the many solutions emerging during the early eighteenth century that sought, as Jay Smith has observed, to "reimagine" the French political system and the role of the nobility within this power structure. Toward the end of Louis XIV's reign, the French nobility was growing increasingly frustrated with a monarchy many viewed as operating in a despotic fashion. Critics pointed to the crown's tightening fiscal and administrative grip on the entire kingdom, its revocation of religious toleration in 1685, the continual involvement in warfare abroad (1689–1697 and 1701–1714) and especially the egoistic, self-referential political culture of Versailles, hermetically sealed off from the rest of France and erected solely around the king himself.[76] Dissatisfied with this arbitrary style of rule they saw as inevitably weakening the kingdom, aristocratic observers looked to antiquity in their rethinking of how the Second Estate could help improve the political health of the monarchy. They were particularly attracted to the classical emphasis on civic virtue and moral perfection and hoped their readers would strive to put these values into practice. Following Louis XIV's death in 1715, the political role the nobility could play became even more apparent. The provisional government of the Polysynodie (1715–1718), run by an aristocratic council, offered the French nobility a concrete, albeit brief, example of its possible function in the future reign of Louis XV.[77] Although Freemasons in the Old Regime remained firmly supportive of Bourbon monarchy well into the Revolution, it is significant that we detect in the writings of some early brethren traces of this dissatisfaction with the Versailles status quo. The author of an apologia in the mid-1730s praised his fellow "illustrious citizens" who chose Masonry over the "tumult" and pride of the court. In their letters to one another during the same time period, military officers stationed in Versailles complained constantly of their servile status and the general tediousness at court, and looked forward to the future moment when they would gather with other Masons in Paris. Although brethren never uttered any explicit criticism of monar-

---

75. These letters have been reprinted in Luquet, *La Franc-maçonnerie et l'état*, 157–59.

76. Jay M. Smith, *Nobility Reimagined: The Patriotic Nation in Eighteenth-Century France* (Ithaca, NY: Cornell University Press, 2005), 29.

77. Ibid., 27.

chy as a form of government or toward the king himself, such a negative view toward the social dynamics at the court remained a recurrent theme in masonic speeches well into the prerevolutionary period.[78]

There was not a mere ideological affinity between Ramsay's vision of a nobility morally purified through Freemasonry and the cultural current Smith describes, but in fact a concrete link in the person of the archbishop Fénelon. The nobility's burrowing into classical texts to reformulate its manners originated in the political and Romanesque writings of Fénelon, notably in his immensely popular *Aventures de Télémaque* (first published in 1699).[79] After traveling from Scotland to the Dutch Republic, Ramsay eventually ended up in France, where he resided with Fénelon from 1710 to 1715. During this five-year period, Ramsay studied under the bishop, and his later writings openly acknowledged this intellectual debt. The preface to his *Essai* indicated that he had been "nourished for several years by the knowledge and sentiments" of Fénelon and had "benefited from the instructions of this illustrative prelate in order to write this *Essai*."[80]

Once in France, Ramsay was also in frequent contact with other Enlightenment thinkers who hoped to reinvigorate the French nobility and who also grounded ideal political communities in friendship. Montesquieu and Ramsay, for instance, both frequented the Entresol Club during the 1720s. The former—coincidentally also a Freemason—lauded Fénelon's work as "divine" and critiqued the obsequious and morally corrupt posture of the nobility under absolutism.[81] Specifically, Montesquieu frowned upon a French aristocracy he saw as more preoccupied with personal ambition and the pursuit of luxury and pleasure than with devoting itself to the public good. He hoped, however, that the nobility's energies could be channeled into the *parlements* of the kingdom—he himself served as *président à mortier* of the *parlement* of Bordeaux—which would check the power of the monarch, ensuring that French absolutism would not begin the perilous slide into despotism.[82] Friendship also was of great political import to Montesquieu, and this can be clearly seen in the utopian fable of the Troglodytes in the

---

78. Chevallier, *Ducs sous l'acacia*, 178–79; BN NAF MS 15175; Dossier of Saint Nicholas de la Parfaite Egalité (Paris), BN FM²108, fol. 14v.

79. Smith, *Nobility Reimagined*, 42–44.

80. Ramsay, *Essai philosophique*, a4.

81. Nick Childs, *A Political Academy in Paris, 1724–1731: The Entresol and its Members* (Oxford: Voltaire Foundation, 2000), 148.

82. Mark Hulliung, *Montesquieu and the Old Regime* (Berkeley: University of California Press, 1976), chap. 2.

opening pages of his celebrated *Lettres persanes* (1721). Like Ramsay in the *Essai*, Montesquieu uses the story of this mythical people to reject both the Hobbesian and Lockean arguments for political legitimacy: successive generations of Troglodytes bear witness to the assassination of a tyrannical monarch—an example of Hobbes's all-powerful, severe ruler—and the later dissolution of Locke's society of self-interested individuals.[83] From these ashes, two families emerge, and they embody the classical ideals of civic virtue and ties of friendship: "From so many families, only two remained. . . . They worked with a common solicitude for the public interest and they had no disagreements except those sometimes born of a tender and kind friendship."[84] In contrast, the absence of friendship strongly marks Montesquieu's dystopian community in this story—the harem—which immediately follows the story of the Trogolytes so as to invite the reader to compare and contrast the two societies. In it, the First Eunuch of the harem informs his colleague that "I have never known the tie that men call friendship" and am "entirely wrapped up in myself." A similar declaration can be found later in the work when Montesquieu writes that Turks and other non-Europeans "do not see each other unless they are forced to by ceremonial. Friendship, this tender engagement of the heart, which in France is the pleasure of life, is essentially unknown to them. They remain in their homes. . . . Every family is thus isolated."[85] The emphasis on friendship as the elemental bond of solidarity in political thought thus likely represented a key value shared among some members of the Entresol, and it also offers us a possible ideological connection between the masonic experience and this earlier political club about which so little is known due to lack of documentation.

⟿ The Fragility of Friendship in Society: The Problem of Self-Love and the Passions

An examination of early eighteenth-century masonic visions of friendship would be incomplete without also considering brethren's distinctly pessimistic view of social life outside their organization. Reflecting Umberto Eco's observation that "a cultural unit . . . is defined inasmuch as it is *placed*

---

83. Charles-Louis Secondat de Montesquieu, *Lettres Persanes*, ed. Jean Starobinski (Paris: Gallimard, 1973), 66–70.

84. Ibid., 71.

85. Ibid., 77, 109.

in a system of other cultural units which are opposed to it," Freemasonry's very identity required a continual manufacturing of distinction between its members and the wider public.[86] This topic will receive extended treatment in a later chapter, but it was already apparent early in the century that friendship lay at the heart of this meaningful exercise. Reflecting a distinctly Shaftesburian viewpoint, an orator in the 1740s spoke of Masons as naturally sociable: "Their character is that of men predisposed to social interaction [la société], of friends a thousand times more attached to one another than kin." However, once outside the walls of Freemasonry, friendship remained elusive in all segments of society. At the top of the social pyramid in the Old Regime, genuine friendship remained elusive to the powerful and wealthy because their high status made asymmetrical relationships nearly inevitable. "The Great," the orator continued, "confuse friendship with the respect that is due to their rank; they are more interested in attracting homage than hearts." On the opposite end of the spectrum, the impoverished masses, "burdened with a thousand distressing worries proportionate to their sad situation," could not hope to cultivate friendly relations either because friendship required leisure time outside work and family. For this reason, this Mason believed that friendship among le peuple was "mercenary" in nature, a highly instrumental relationship heavily predicated on rendering services to others rather than comprising a blend of emotional and material investment.[87]

For Masons, a major problem with social exchange outside the fraternity was that self-love and the passions made social harmony impossible, reducing relationships to relentless competition and inevitable conflict for prestige and material resources.[88] An orator in mid-1740s Paris defined French society as a "sad spectacle" due to the "disorders" unleashed by "unbridled and unregulated human passions," and a similar view could be found in the widely circulated writings of Joseph Uriot, an apologist for the fraternity.[89]

---

86. Umberto Eco, *A Theory of Semiotics* (Bloomington: Indiana University Press, 1976), 73.

87. *Lettre et discours d'un Maçon libre servant de réponse à la lettre et la consultation anonymes sur la société des Francs-maçons* (The Hague, 1749), 15–17.

88. Although Masons conceived of self-love and the passions as interrelated, they were imprecise in distinguishing between the two. At times, they considered them to be synonymous; at other times they saw one as the product of the other. When they spoke of the "passions," they usually referred to one of the eleven passions (anger, hope, fear, joy, etc.) identified in Christian writings, such as in Aquinas's *Summa Theologiae*.

89. Joseph Uriot, "Éloge de la Franc-maçonnerie et des Maçons: Prononcé par un frère dans une loge qui se tint à Paris le 25 novembre 1744," in *Lettre écrite par un Maçon à un de ses amis de province* (Paris, 1744), 14.

Uriot derided the individual outside Masonry as nothing more than a "mediocre man" whose thought and actions were determined by a self-love that "perverted his heart." He designated the profane as an entity "in obscurity," a state in which "every passion, one after the other, makes us imagine and seek out happiness precisely where it does not exist." These passions were nothing more than "unworthy guides" that dragged men from one error to the next.[90]

Brethren realized that friendship would remain a problematic relationship if passion and self-love remained unchecked. Thémiseul de Saint-Hyacinthe (1684–1746), who was in close contact with English Grand Master Jean Desaguliers and Montesquieu in England, and later with Ramsay in France, discussed friendship in a treatise published in 1736.[91] In it he defined friendship as a form of pure love, unadulterated by the passions; it was "happy and constant." This form of attraction required one to shun exaggerated sentimentalism, what Saint-Hyacinthe defined as "cupidity." "Attachment to cupidity," he wrote, "is nothing more than a boiling of blood which attacks the heart and the brain; it excites thousands of tumultuous passions." A member of the Louis d'Argent lodge in Paris during the 1730s, the abbé Pernetti, also declared in his *Conseils de l'amitié* that "it is not so easy to succeed in tranquilizing one's passions" and that "people subject to strong passions are not very susceptible to friendship."[92] Vanity, jealousy, and self-interest often too easily destroyed friendship, and for these reasons he concluded that individuals have "an infinity of acquaintances" but few true friends in life.[93]

Uncovering Masonry's gloomy view of the self and friendship outside the organization, we are reminded of Peter Gay's caution against simplistically associating the Enlightenment with an unfettered confidence about sociability and human nature.[94] On one hand, Robert Mauzi and William Reddy have found, in the sentimental novels, conduct books, and private correspondence of eighteenth-century France, friendship praised as an

---

90. Joseph Uriot, "Le secret des Francs-maçons mis en évidence: Seconde lettre," reprinted in Coutura, *Parfait maçon*, 83.

91. Themiseul de Saint-Hyacinthe, *Recueil de divers écrits sur l'amour et l'amitié* (Paris, 1736). On Saint-Hyacinthe's masonic activity, see Margaret Jacob, *The Radical Enlightenment: Pantheists, Freemasons, and Republicans* (Burlington, NC: Temple Publishers, [1981] 2003), 197–234.

92. Abbé Jacques Pernetti, *Conseils de l'amitié* (Lyon, 1747), 103, 126.

93. Ibid., 103.

94. Peter Gay, *The Enlightenment: An Interpretation* (New York: Norton, [1966–69] 1995), 1: chap. 1; 2: chap. 2.

"emotional refuge" that offered a key to achieving one of the century's most elusive goals: temporal happiness.[95] This increased optimism in friendship as a calm and durable bond was the result of a host of factors affecting France and Western Europe generally after 1700, including rising literacy, falling mortality rates, expanding consumer economies, and progress in agrarian science.[96] On the other, we also detect in the same Enlightenment texts a lingering pessimism, originating from the intellectual and religious developments of the seventeenth century, regarding friendship. Whether it was the mechanistic philosophy of Thomas Hobbes, who believed human behavior was dictated by the physical needs of the body—defined most often as "the passions"—or the religious wars plaguing the Continent that made Europeans acutely aware of senseless violence, man was cast during the reign of Louis XIV as irrational and involuntarily led astray by his passions. In France, the passions and self-love were accorded an especially prominent place within the Jansenist movement, and this group would exercise a notable influence on moral and social theory during the second half of the seventeenth century.[97] Contrary to the Renaissance celebration of man as capable of shaping his own destiny through reason, Jansenists contended that humankind's actions were involuntarily dictated by the pangs of jealousy and self-love. Although Jansenism was by no means a monolithic movement, its luminaries tended to express great skepticism on the matter of friendship. Pierre Nicole and Blaise Pascal categorically rejected it because they considered the self as too corrupt and imperfect to merit the special attraction friendship normally bestowed. Nicole starkly made this point in the first volume of his popular *Essais de morale* (1671): "To seek the love of men is unjust because it is required that we judge ourselves likeable and this is false. This stems from a voluntary ignorance of our faults."[98] Even thinkers from outside the movement such as La Rochefoucauld reiterated the notion that self-love had deformed friendship into a relationship into which one entered solely for personal gain: "What men name friendship is nothing more than

95. Robert Mauzi, *L'idée du bonheur dans la littérature et la pensée françaises au XVIIIᵉ siècle* (Paris: Slatkine, 1960), 359–62; William Reddy, *The Navigation of Feeling: A Framework for the History of Emotions* (New York: Cambridge University Press, 2002), 153–54. For a similar assessment, see Anne Vincent-Buffault, *L'exercice de l'amitié: Pour une histoire des pratiques amicales aux XVIIIᵉ et XIXᵉ siècles* (Paris: Seuil, 1995), chap 1.

96. Daniel Roche, *France in the Enlightenment*, trans. Arthur Goldhammer (Cambridge, MA: Harvard University Press, 1998), chap. 15.

97. Nannerl O. Keohane, *Philosophy and the State in France: The Renaissance to the Enlightenment* (Princeton, NJ: Princeton University Press, 1980), 183–88, 262–311.

98. Pierre Nicole, *Essais de morale* . . . (The Hague, 1700), 1:322.

an acquaintance, a reciprocal arrangement of interests. . . . It is nothing more than a commerce where self-love always has something to gain."[99]

Perhaps because Jansenist moralizing continued to resonate widely in France—Nicole's *Essais* alone enjoyed more than thirty editions during the eighteenth century—a weariness regarding sociability persisted.[100] Although clearly less despairing about human nature than their Jansenist counterparts, a number of eighteenth-century authors shared the concern that *amour-propre* and the passions constantly threatened to tear apart friendly ties. At the turn of the century, Louis-Silvestre de Sacy repeatedly warned the readers of his *Traité de l'amitié* (1703) that self-love was a potentially destructive force. "No matter what man says, no matter what he does," he lamented, self-love "disguises itself in a thousand different ways." "It is against this self-love," he continued, "that one must constantly make war, if one desires a durable and constant friendship."[101] In his popular *Traité de la société civile* (1723), Claude Buffier cautioned that friendship with another person could naturally provoke an outpouring of "sentiments and desires," "involuntary movements," or "movements of passion" toward the friend that could, if left unchecked, drive one to material ruin or even the laying down of one's life.[102] In the 1760 preface to his *Caractères de l'amitié*, the marquis de Caraccioli describes friendship as so essential to life that one "does not know truly how to be a person" without it. He then immediately remarked, however, that because "society is degenerating day after day, and only listens to self-love and personal interest," perhaps durable and virtuous friendship would remain forever elusive.[103]

The ideas of these moralists, praising friendship as a rewarding bond while also acknowledging its fragility due to the potentially deleterious effects of the passions and self-love, thus resonated closely with Freemasonry. Uncovering this equivocal position toward friendly feeling also leaves the

---

99. François, duc de La Rochefoucauld, *Oeuvres complètes*, ed. Robert Kanters, Louis Martin-Chauffier, and Jean Marchand (Paris: Gallimard, 1964), 414.

100. Dale van Kley, "The Jansenist Constitutional Legacy in the French Prerevolution," in *The French Revolution and the Creation of Modern Political Culture*, vol. 1, *The Political Culture of the Old Regime*, ed. Keith Michael Baker (New York: Pergamon Press, 1987), 198n15.

101. Louis-Silvestre de Sacy, *Traité de l'amitié* (Paris, 1703), 90, 284.

102. Buffier, *Traité de la société civile*, 152–56. Buffier's views on friendship had a lasting influence, as the abbé Claude Yvon lifted entire passage's from Buffier's text when he composed his article on friendship for the first volume of the *Encyclopédie* nearly three decades later.

103. Louis-Antoine de Caraccioli, *Les caractères de l'amitié* (Liège, 1760), iii–iv.

historian with an important question: How was it possible for the fraternity to realize its utopia of male friendship, explored earlier in this chapter, if, at the same time, brethren remained so skeptical of human sociability because of *amour-propre* and the passions? In most cases, eighteenth-century moralists addressed this problem by simply warning readers of the great power of these harmful desires and cautioning them to form friendships that were, in the words of Buffier, "always circumspect and regulated" by a critical reflection on the relationship into which they were entering.[104] Others, however, devised a more ambitious program that sought to overcome the egoism that marred social exchange. Rousseau, for example, whose best-selling *Nouvelle Héloïse* offered the French public one of the most powerful images of male friendship in the couple of Saint-Preux and Lord Edouard, remained nevertheless wary of the destructive power of selfishness. In his landmark, *Émile* (1762), he declared friendship to be "the most sacred" and elemental of all relationships that stood above love, but he also recognized that *amour-propre* often disfigured even the closest of friendships by provoking jealousy and dissent. He did not believe, however, that enmity was the inevitable result of human association, but that harmonious relations were in fact possible. One of the key goals of his educational treatise was to show how philosophy, embodied in the tutor (presumably Rousseau himself), could help a typical individual (Émile) develop compassion toward others while keeping his self-love and passions in check.[105]

To transform into a reality the lofty ideal of friendship they articulated in the speeches and normative texts explored over the course of this chapter, Freemasons had to adopt a more robust Rousseauean solution to the fragility of friendship. Even though Masons, like Rousseau, held a bleak vision of friendship in society at large, they elaborated an institutional process that, in their view, served as both an effective ethical filter and an ontological passageway between the outside "profane" world and the sacred space of the lodge: the initiation ritual. In chapter 2, I examine how this *rite de passage* functioned in a manner similar to the educational program of Émile's tutor, since it was through the initiation that Freemasonry proceeded to redefine the masonic self as free of the undesirable psychological elements that otherwise would have made friendship so problematic. By imparting

---

104. Buffier, *Traité de la societé civile*, 162–63.

105. Jean-Jacques Rousseau, *Émile, or On Education*, introd. and trans. Allan Bloom (New York: Basic Books, 1979), 17–20, 220–23, 233.

Freemasonry's collective belief system onto new members, this cultural performance also provided an effective means to ensure that the fraternity adhered to the classical style of friendship, in which every Mason nominally possessed a shared moral vision of the world, or as Cicero put it, "a community of views on all matters human and divine."[106]

---

106. Dubois-Goibaud, *Livres de Cicéron*, 150.

☛ CHAPTER 2

Friendship in Ritual

> Every ceremonial in all societies always appears
> ridiculous when one does not seek out its spirit.
>
> —Abbé Robin, *Recherches sur les initiations anciennes
> et modernes* (1779)

In this chapter I reconstruct in detail Enlight-
enment Freemasonry's initiation, known as the "apprentice ritual" (*rite
d'apprenti*). As we saw in chapter 1, Freemasonry's anxiety over *amour-propre*
and the passions frustrated the organization's optimistic praise of male friendship as a collective bond of solidarity. In the following pages we examine
how brethren overcame these psychological defects they saw in human nature and answered a question an orator asked his lodge in the late 1780s:
"By what mysterious charms," he wondered, were Masons "able to draw
close together, to renounce amongst them all those pretentious and mundane frivolities, and all those distinctions of convenience that are so flatter-
ing to self-love?"[1] By arguing that it was the initiation that performed this
task of ontological transformation, we are echoing the consensus of anthropologists and cultural historians that the ritual act mattered for institutions
like Freemasonry because it forged deep, lasting bonds between individuals
who did not necessarily have a previous record of social relations.

Rituals like the *rite d'apprenti* pervaded all aspects of early modern European life, from elaborate royal funerals to village youth groups taunting

---

1. Dossier of Réunion des Étrangers (Paris), BN FM²177, *Planche à tracer de la cérémonie de
l'inauguration de la R. L. de St. Jean . . . sous le titre distinctif de la Réunion des Étrangers*, fol. 62r.

unwed or childless couples.[2] Rituals have by no means disappeared from the modern world, but they were particularly relevant for a largely semi-literate continent because performing the series of gestures and actions intended to convey a message (such as civic processions) or transform a being (such as baptism) often did not require reading or writing. Ritual acts demanded a great deal of preparation as well as faith in their efficacy; the French king's coronation ceremony at the Reims cathedral, for instance, was a complex, drawn out affair where observers and participants collectively affirmed the semi-divine status of the newly crowned monarch.[3]

Because so much of early modern French ritual life was tied to Roman Catholicism, the anticlerical sentiments that pervaded the Enlightenment have often been seen as incompatible with rituals and ceremonies. In his classic treatment on wills and inventories in Provence, Michel Vovelle found a marked decline in the more external manifestations of a baroque Catholic faith, from the decline of legacies for requiem masses to a drop in the weight of candles burned before religious images and statues.[4] Even within the clerical establishment, some priests complained that seminaries placed far too much emphasis on memorizing the minutiae of ritual gestures, such as genuflection, instead of learning the catechism and studying the Bible.[5] In part it was Enlightenment thinkers who, mostly rejecting the idea of communication with the divine or, at the very least, questioning the ability of Christian rituals to enable it, incited these changes. David Hume considered religion a social-psychological phenomenon rather than a spiritual one, and ridiculed practices such as fasting and self-flagellation as "frivolous observances" with no soteriological benefit for the individual or practical relevance for society.[6] In France, Voltaire's midcentury campaign to boldly "crush the infamous thing" (*écraser l'infâme*) of traditional religion

---

2. Natalie Davis, "The Reasons of Misrule: Youth Groups and Charivaris in Sixteenth-Century France," *Past & Present* 50 (1971): 41–75; Ralph E. Giesey, *Royal Funeral Ceremony in Renaissance France* (Geneva: Droz, 1960).

3. A detailed account of this ceremony can be found in John McManners, *Church and Society in Eighteenth-Century France,* vol. 1: *The Clerical Establishment and its Social Ramifications* (New York: Oxford University Press, 1998), 7–11.

4. Michel Vovelle, *Piété baroque et déchristianisation en Provence au XVIIIᵉ siècle* (Paris: Éditions du C.T.H.S., [1973] 1997), esp. chap. 2.

5. McManners, *The Clerical Establishment,* 204.

6. David Hume, *Four Dissertations* (London, 1757), 103.

already had echoes in earlier writings of the Radical Enlightenment.[7] So sustained was the eighteenth-century attack on rituals and external piety that Edward Muir claims that "by the eighteenth century, 'ritual' had become a dirty word . . . ritual came to imply insincerity and empty formality, the very antithesis of the Enlightenment values that prized individual spontaneity and authenticity."[8] Although Muir's argument does not work for Freemasonry, it is clear that the Enlightenment represented a watershed moment where the ritual underwent a slow process of objectification, transformed from an inward expression of faith to an external object of scholarly inquiry.[9]

Once Freemasonry in France had begun to attract detractors in the 1730s, authors almost always took aim at Masonry's elaborate ritual system. One libertine midcentury author mockingly derided the fraternity as "a society of crazies" and "the height of human madness," whose hierarchy was based on passing through a number of "ridiculous" rituals.[10] Despite the best efforts of zealous brethren to counter these accusations in print, the public continued to look upon the lodge as an irrational environment with strange practices. In Nîmes, a young noblewoman wrote to her future spouse, the marquis de Valfons, about his recent entry into the order. "I have heard that you have just become a Freemason and I compliment you." However, respect quickly turned to ridicule when she recounted a supposed dream about his initiation ceremony: "In my dream . . . you had surrounding you all these people making a thousand monkey tricks [*singeries*]."[11] Members were well aware of this mockery and strove to ensure that men were entering into lodges for sincere reasons. "Do not think that this is a joke," a Mason sternly warned a potential new recruit before then bluntly asking if he had ever "ridiculed the ceremonies that the profane think we

7. Jonathan Israel, *The Radical Enlightenment: Philosophy and the Making of Modernity, 1650–1750* (New York: Oxford University Press, 2001), esp. chaps. 30–32.

8. Edward Muir, *Ritual in Early Modern Europe* (New York: Cambridge University Press, 2005), 294.

9. The best-known work on comparative religious rituals during this period is the multivolume work of Jean-Frédéric Bernard and Bernard Picart, *Cérémonies et coutumes religieuses de tous les peuples du monde*, published from 1723 to 1737. On this work, see Lynn Hunt, Margaret Jacob, and Wijnand Mijnhardt, *The Book That Changed Europe: Picart and Bernard's Religious Ceremonies of the World* (Cambridge, MA: Belknap Press of Harvard University Press, 2010).

10. Henri-Joseph Dulaurens, *Le compère Matthieu ou les bigarrures de l'esprit humain* (London, 1732), 1:274–76.

11. Jean-Marie Mercier, *Les Francs-maçons du pape: L'Art Royal à Avignon au XVIIIe siècle* (Paris: Classiques Garnier, 2010), 97.

practice?"[12] Even during the Revolution, when anti-masonic literature was largely preoccupied with the supposed deleterious political effects of Free-masonry, authors still drew readers' attention to its unfathomably esoteric set of rituals; Girondist Jacques-Pierre Brissot was initiated into the order only to quickly dismiss it as utter "silliness."[13]

Historians have often followed the lead of such critics and dismissed ma-sonic ritual as an incoherent, puzzling mass of arcana. John Roberts wrote some time ago that Freemasonry was a neglected topic because professional historians tended to shy away from an organization that was so fraught with conspiracy theories. "Because the historian passed by," Roberts lamented, "the charlatan, the axe-grinder and the paranoiac long had the field to themselves."[14] Although this fortunately is no longer the case when speak-ing of the organization as a whole, the close study of masonic male ritual among professional historians still remains largely neglected.[15] This lack of attention is due in part to the conventional focus on Freemasonry's political significance for the Revolution, in which historians such as François Furet, Ran Halévi, and Margaret Jacob have interpreted lodges alternatively as proto-democratic, harbingers of Jacobinism, or proponents of constitutional-ism. Such a teleological approach distorts the picture we have of lodges by drawing attention to modern aspects of the order while leaving aside other elements that were not corrosive to the Old Regime and yet were still quite meaningful for eighteenth-century Masons.

The following discussion draws from over twenty different manuals brethren used to perform the apprentice ritual, dating from the 1740s to the Revolution; these documents are analyzed as a group because the basic perfor-mative and structural elements of the ritual varied little during the century.[16] Some masonic antiquarians may feel uneasy that this chapter introduces a

---

12. "Réception d'apprentif," cited in *The Rituals of the Count de la Barre*, ed. Library of the Count de Lichtervelde (Latomia Foundation for Masonic Excavations, 2000), unfoliated.

13. Claude Perroud, ed., *J.-P. Brissot, Mémoires* (Paris: A. Picard et fils, 1911), 1:134.

14. John Roberts, *The Mythology of the Secret Societies* (New York: Charles Scribner's Sons, 1972), 10.

15. One notable exception to this is Pierre-Yves Beaurepaire, *Les Francs-maçons à l'orient de Clermont-Ferrand au XVIIIe siècle* (Clermont-Ferrand: Université Blaise-Pascal, 1991), 182–91. Women's rituals within the mixed gender "adoption" meetings, on the other hand, have received far more atten-tion. Janet Burke and Margaret Jacob, "French Freemasonry, Women, and Feminist Scholarship," *The Journal of Modern History* 68 (1996): 513–49; and Jan Snoek, *Initiating Women in Freemasonry: The Adoption Rite* (Leiden: Brill, 2011). Adoption Freemasonry will be examined in chapter 3.

16. The initiation rites range from 1740 to the end of the century; dates are based on the *fonds ma-çonnique* card catalog. A similar approach to initiation in *compagnonnage* may be found in Cynthia

variety of strands of Freemasonry into this analysis, from the standard "blue" Masonry to the more elaborate Scottish rite. We nevertheless contend that this is possible because these ritual systems had initiations that were remarkably similar in form and content, despite the important differences between them in higher ranks. The apprentice ritual arises as a privileged site of analysis because it represented the lowest common denominator of the eighteenth-century masonic experience. No matter how ambivalent a man could become regarding his involvement in lodge life—and many members quickly did lose interest—every man was required to pass through this critical *rite de passage*.

We unfortunately have just a handful of personal accounts of the initiation. In addition, the close study of lodge procedures that I propose to undertake only enables the historian to reconstruct what an apprentice candidate *likely* experienced once he stepped into a French lodge some two hundred and fifty years ago. Such scant documentation limits our scope of inquiry in two important ways. First, it is impossible to know how this ceremony differed between noble and non-noble lodges, or how cultural differences across regions might have affected how the initiation proceeded. Furthermore, this approach is inevitably logocentric, as there is simply no way to recapture the extralinguistic components that would have been so important in shaping the meaning of this performance: bodily gestures, facial expressions, and prolonged moments of tense silence between initiand and lodge members are all irretrievably lost.

Despite this incomplete picture, we contend that these manuals were not just normative texts, but undoubtedly reflected what men actually experienced during Old Regime initiations for three reasons. First, the majority of these guides were handwritten, and thus solely intended for internal lodge use. Even the published ritual procedures from which we draw in this chapter likely illustrated what went on in lodges. This is confirmed in the numerous complaints the Grand Lodge and Grand Orient fielded about them, such as the following from the small Breton town of Dinan in late July 1760: "I am aware of some books that are widespread amongst the public, entitled *Le secret des Francs-maçons révélé* [of Gabriel-Louis Pérau, first published in 1742] and *Les Francs-maçons écrasés* [of an author using the pseudonym "Larudan," first published in 1747]. These books treat us very

---

Truant, *The Rites of Labor: Brotherhoods of Compagnonnage in Old and New Regime France* (Ithaca, NY: Cornell University Press, 1994), esp. chap. 3.

badly, and reveal our passwords, signs and gestures."[17] Second, lodges prided themselves on closely following such official procedural guidelines. Throughout the century, societies that consciously mimicked Freemasonry to attract members, as well as unauthorized lodges, appeared in towns alongside those assemblies the Grand Lodge and later Grand Orient formally endorsed. The masters of official lodges knew that their status as legitimate—as a *loge regulière*—in the eyes of the masonic bureaucracy depended on the possession of official documents and careful adhesion to their instructions. It was not uncommon, for example, for lodge members to complain if standard ritual procedures were not followed. A group of Parisian brethren in the mid-1760s informed the Grand Lodge of their master's rather odd improvisations to the initiation ritual. "Since it is true that the order of Freemasonry is respectable," they reported, "it is surprising that the master dresses up in a Franciscan robe, a beard and a moustache which causes candidates to deride and despise our order."[18] And third, lodge officers were so committed to following the ritual manuals that they could spend hours reviewing in painstaking detail a grade's catechisms, passwords, hand gestures, and overall symbolic import. Having spent nearly twelve hours preparing his lodge and membership for an upcoming ceremony, one master of a Toulousian lodge at midcentury reflected afterward in a letter to Paris that "I believe that it has been the hardest day I have ever lived in my life."[19] The physical layout of the lodge and theatrical aspects of the ritual were so important that the Grand Orient also deemed the blind to be ineligible to become Freemasons.[20]

It is also likely that most candidates for admission had little knowledge of what lay ahead. There were some reports of men hurriedly fleeing from lodges in "panicked terror" in the middle of the initiation, and other reports that claimed that a number of masonic hopefuls were routinely "gripped by a complete fright, losing the use of their legs and voice."[21] It therefore

---

17. BN FM^{1}111, vol. v, fol. 358r.

18. Dossier of La Bonne Foi (Paris), GODF MS AR.113.1.75, fol. 18r (early 1766).

19. Gerry Prinsen, ed., *The Story of the Ecossais Lodge in the Town of Toulouse* (Lexington, MA: Museum of our National Heritage, 1993), 28–30. Meetings could be quite drawn out when initiations occurred. In early 1782 in Rouen, for example, elderly professor Jacques Formage regretfully informed his brethren that he would no longer be able to participate in Freemasonry because his declining health did not allow him to remain "enclosed with you for six hours." BMR MS G.165/division 247, pièce 7.

20. *Consultation sur cette question maçonnique: Un aveugle peut-il être reçu maçon?* (Paris, 1783).

21. *Le Franc-maçon tel qu'il doit être ou avis fraternels à tous les maçons qui éclairent les quatre points cardinaux, de l'Occident à l'Orient et du Nord au Midi* (Jerusalem [certainly false], 1775), 29; Larudan, *Les*

would be quite wrong to see the initiation ritual as a mere empty formality, as lodge records indicated that if a candidate did not present himself appropriately—if he were intoxicated, for example—or did not perform satisfactorily during his ceremony, he would be escorted promptly from the lodge.[22]

In sum, in this chapter we follow Robert Darnton's sound counsel that "when we cannot get a proverb, or a joke, or a ritual, or a poem, we know we are on to something."[23] Following the candidate on his laborious journey from the non-masonic world of the "profane" to the inner sanctum of the lodge, we will witness the initiate's multiple encounters with lodge members and spatial zones in our effort to understand how these interactions fit into the wider pedagogical project of symbolically breaking down the candidate's egoistic self. We will show how the initiation generated a form of "ritualized friendship" that was anchored in the moral foundation of an ecumenical Christianity. Although this meant that lodges nominally welcomed both Protestants and Catholics, it also translated into the systematic exclusion of freethinkers, Jews, and Muslims. We also situate Freemasonry's ritualized friendship in the *longue durée*, arguing that lodges served as privileged enclaves through which persisted an older, more formalized form of friendship whose origins stretched back to at least the medieval period.

◄ Leaving Behind the World of the Profane

The first stage of the eighteenth-century apprentice ritual was the physical separation and isolation of the candidate. For as few as fifteen minutes and as long as two hours, the initiate was placed in a dark room designated as the "reflection chamber," sometimes alternatively called an obscure chamber. As its name implied, this stage afforded the candidate the opportunity to reflect on the decision to enter the brotherhood; it also signified his separation from the socioeconomic structure and distinctions of eighteenth-century society. The marquis d'Evry, an officer of the Grand Orient during the 1780s, indicated in a speech to a Parisian lodge that at this moment the ini-

---

Francs-maçons écrasés: Suite du livre intitulé l'ordre des Francs-maçons trahi (Amsterdam, 1747), 333.

22. BN FM⁴514, fols. 26r–27r; Dossier of St. Julien de la Tranquilité (Paris), GODF MS AR.113.1.94, fol. 2v.

23. Robert Darnton, *The Great Cat Massacre and Other Episodes in French Cultural History* (New York: Basic Books, 1984), 5.

tiate was "left to all his reflections."[24] In his work on African tribal rites, anthropologist Victor Turner observes that this first stage of physical isolation of the neophyte marked the individual's departure from the position previously inhabited in society. It is during this moment that the ritual subject begins his symbolic "death" from his previous existence, leaving behind his earlier status and acquired socioeconomic distinctions.[25] The death of the candidate's former status in society was emphasized in the reflection chamber by the presence of an image of a skull, and he was required in certain rites to write out his last will and testament.[26]

It was through the initiation that the fraternity redefined the masonic self as free of the undesirable psychological elements that otherwise would have made friendship so problematic in society. As we saw in the chapter 1, Freemasons acknowledged that the mental defects of the passions and self-love made men unlikely to become friends in society. Masons also believed that they could logically take concrete steps to purge these undesirable psychological elements from neophytes or, at the very least, mitigate their effects on social behavior. This was the purpose of every stage of the initiation beginning with the time spent in the reflection chamber.

Just as Descartes's new system of metaphysics in the previous century began with the philosopher closing himself up in a room to rid himself of distracting passions—"happily disturbed by no passions," he claimed in his *Meditations*—so too did the lodge hope that the candidate's isolation would free him from the power of harmful desires. Speaking to the initiate later in the ceremony, the lodge master explained the significance of the reflection chamber: "We wanted to teach you through this that it is in silence, retreat and the calm of the senses that the lodge purges passions." Another ritual manual explained in similar terms that it was only this "solitary and isolated space" that could furnish the "necessary tranquility" to facilitate "reflection that is free from the passions, sensual objects and

---

24. Dossier of Réunion des Arts (Paris), BN FM²97, fol. 13r.

25. Unless otherwise noted, Turner's views on ritual are taken from his *Ritual Process: Structure and Anti-structure*, with a foreword by Roger D. Abrahams (New York: Aldine de Gruyter, 1995), chap. 3. Although Turner's perspective on rituals has not been applied to the masonic context, it has had a tremendous influence on the study of early modern France, notably Natalie Davis, *Society and Culture in Early Modern France: Eight Essays* (Stanford, CA: Stanford University Press, 1975); and Emmanuel Le Roy Ladurie, *Carnival in Romans*, trans. Mary Feeney (New York: G. Braziller, 1979).

26. BN FM⁴514, fol. 5r; *Un aveugle peut-il être reçu Maçon?*, 14. If writing was expected of the candidate at this time, a candle could be lit.

prejudices."[27] By identifying the power of external "sensual objects" and "the senses" to involuntarily shape human behavior, brethren echoed the Lockean map of the mind prevalent in France since Condillac's *Essai sur les connaissances humaines* (1746). Lodges defined the reflection chamber as a "moral time" because it played the pedagogical role of instructing the candidate that harmful passions such as self-love, anger, and hate were very real and could wreak havoc, but they could at the same time be minimized and controlled by carefully orchestrating the social environment around the individual.[28] This masonic effort to exclude external stimuli deemed to jeopardize male friendship was already apparent in the order's very beginnings; as we saw in the last chapter, Ramsay's "Discours" explained that women were kept out of lodges because they were feared to incite jealousy between Masons.

Once the separation period in the reflection chamber had ended, a lodge member escorted the ritual subject into a second room, usually known as the preparation chamber.[29] At this point began the most significant stage of the ritual process, what Turner describes as "liminality," the physical and mental "grinding down" or "leveling" of the initiate, an action that symbolically transforms the individual into a *tabula rasa* onto which the group's values and relationships then may be inscribed. Three elements constitute this liminal state: the physical anonymity of the neophyte, his posture of humility before the entire group achieved through physical and verbal abuse, and the imparting of a community's values and norms onto the initiate. Turner describes liminality as the moment during which the ritual subject "may be represented as possessing nothing." What he means by this qualification is that "as liminal beings they have no status, property, insignia, secular clothing indicating rank or role, position in a kinship system—in short, nothing that may distinguish them from their fellow neophytes or initiands."[30] For this reason, initiates are either stripped naked, scantily clad, or dressed identically to all those individuals that are undergoing or have

---

27. BN FM⁴513, fol. 2v; BN FM⁴180ᵇⁱˢ, fol. 23r.

28. On the reflection chamber defined as a "moral time," see the deliberations of the Anglaise lodge in Bordeaux, GODF MS AR 113.2.102, fol. 171v.

29. Later in the century, the reflection and preparation chambers could be combined into one room. See, for example, BN FM⁴514, fol. 5r. In order to maintain the formality of the ritual, lodges stressed that all members involved in a candidate's initiation should not be personal friends. BN FM⁴180ᵇⁱˢ, fol. 7r.

30. Turner, *Ritual Process*, 95.

previously undergone the initiation process. In this way, the ritual subject is no longer portrayed as a distinct entity alongside others, but instead takes on the character of anonymity within the ritual community.

Escorted—sometimes shoved—into the preparation chamber, the candidate encountered a second member of the lodge, known as the "Dreadful Brother" (*frère terrible*): "Armed with a sword like the angel of death in order to test the steadfastness of the recipient," as one early masonic exposure described this officer.[31] The extant rituals describe his role in a similar fashion (though armed with a dagger rather than a sword), as his task was to verbally and physically attack the neophyte. Dressed in a long black robe and wearing a large worn hat, the *frère terrible* was typically seated at a small, dimly lit table in the middle of the room, on which was placed a large book and a dagger stained in what was to appear to be blood. Beside the table was a coffin. He presented himself as completely absorbed in his reflections, reading intently with his elbows on the table and his hands pressed against the sides of his head.

Another lodge member, known as the "Master of Ceremonies," accompanied the initiate and presented him to the *frère terrible*.[32] "Pardon if I interrupt for an instant your profound reflections," he said, "but here is a profane—." Upon hearing this last word, the *frère terrible* threw a glance of horror at the neophyte, rose quickly from his seat, grabbed the dagger, and toppled the table in anger. He insulted the candidate as an unworthy "indiscrete profane" and a "parasite" who merited nothing less than death for his intrusion into the lodge.[33] Pointing to the coffin, he remarked in a cold and discourteous tone that this was the fate awaiting the initiate.[34] It is significant that the *tu* form was here to be used during this dialogue, whereas brethren typically addressed each other with the more respectful *vous*. When *tutoiement* did appear between among Freemasons, it almost always signaled

---

31. *Le sceau rompu ou la loge ouverte aux profanes par un Franc-maçon* (Rouvray: Les Éditions du Prieuré, [1745] 1994), 26. The most detailed account of the preparation chamber can be found in Baylot BN FM⁴124, fols. 6r–8r, and Baylot BN FM⁴125, fols. 2v–9v. The following discussion is based on these documents. In some rituals, it is the *frère expert* who replaced the *frère terrible* in the preparation chamber.

32. In some later versions, the neophyte is left alone with the *frère terrible* at this point.

33. The following quatrain published late in the century reflected the typical dialogue between the candidate and the *frère terrible*: "Frère terrible en fonction, / Lui dit que veux-tu parasite? / Hélas! Je suis un néophyte, / Modèle de discrétion." G.-P. Legret, *Le troubadour Franc-maçon, ou recueil de cantiques maçonniques* (1793), 27.

34. Baylot BN FM⁴125, fol. 3v.

hostility rather than harmony. It can be found, for example, in the verbatim reports of fighting between members.[35]

A chase through the room ensued, ending when the *frère terrible* violently seized the candidate and raised his arm in the feigned attempt to deal a mortal blow. The Master of Ceremonies then intervened, pleading that the neophyte solicited membership not for any malicious reasons, but simply to obtain "the happiness to be admitted." In some cases, the initiate could still receive a minor cut.[36] The *frère terrible* again turned to the candidate, addressing him in a "brusque and lugubrious tone," and pressed the candidate on his reasons for desiring to enter into the fraternity. He was, in the words of one ritual guide, to "become acquainted with the dominant passions of the candidate."[37] It is also clear that some form of extended dialogue occurred between the two men in order that the *frère terrible* could acquire a "clear picture of the religious beliefs and manner of thinking [of the candidate] in order to keep out of lodges any pretext of dispute . . . tending to destroy the union which must always reign."[38] Such an inquiry into the individual's views on secular and spiritual matters was necessary because masonic friendship, as pointed out in chapter 1, was grounded in a shared moral vision between all brethren. Although the candidate's sponsor had already been required to vouch for his integrity, this questioning represented an additional precautionary screening before the aspiring Mason would be fully exposed to the lodge's values and norms later in the initiation.

After this interview, the *frère terrible* stressed that commitment to Masonry would demand nothing short of total obedience of the individual to the community, "the sacrifice of your passions and of your will, a blind submission to all decrees . . . such is the essence of our duties as Masons."[39] Once the candidate had agreed to the submissive nature of his engagement, he assumed a state of physical anonymity where, according to Turner,

---

35. In the early 1780s, for example, a brawl between factions within the Aménité lodge that spilled out onto the streets of Paris began with the following insult: "Te voilà donc Frère Drôle, Frère Polisson, Frère Gascon, c'est toi. . . . Je t'apprendrai à vivre, je te corrigerai." Dossier of Aménité (Paris), BN FM²31bis. On the *tu* as an indicator of conflict in eighteenth-century Paris, see David Garrioch, "Verbal Insults in Eighteenth-Century Paris," in *The Social History of Language*, ed. Peter Burke and Roy Porter (New York: Cambridge University Press, 1987), 114.

36. Baylot BN FM⁴123, fol. 8r.

37. BN FM⁴180bis, fol. 7r.

38. BN FM⁴514, fols. 21r–22r.

39. Baylot BN FM⁴124, fol. 7v.

"symbolically, all attributes that distinguish categories and groups in the structured social order are . . . in abeyance."[40] "Brother Master of Ceremonies," the *frère terrible* said at this moment, "take this gentleman away, and put him in the appropriate state so that we may accord him entry into our august temple. And so that he starts to give us a proof of his submission, have him abandon himself entirely to you."[41] The submissive posture of the candidate was emphasized in the renouncing of the physical elements of his distinctive individuality. A lodge member removed any distinguishing accouterments or clothing, known masonically as his "metals." "One undressed you and took away all metals," a lodge master explained, because "this state is the symbol of the purity of the first age of man. One removed all that signified distinction in society in order to return you to this happy time."[42] To accentuate this symbolic status as a clean slate onto which Freemasonry would inscribe its collective values, the candidate could also have his eyes, ears, and mouth thoroughly washed at this point.[43] Before entering the lodge, the initiate was made to resemble all those who had passed through the apprentice ritual before him: his right knee was exposed, his left boot was partially unlaced, his left arm was removed from his shirt, and finally he was blindfolded.

The initiate was next introduced into the lodge in this awkward and passive position. This space represented the final stage of liminality for the neophyte. It was within this space that Masonry completed the "grinding down" and tempering of the ritual subject through physical and psychological intimidation, and it was also within the lodge that the candidate was fully exposed to the group's values and norms. Pushed roughly through the main entryway, the initiate was immediately seized by a high-ranking officer of the lodge—usually the second Warden—who then rested the tip of his sword on the chest of the candidate. "The tip of this sword placed against your heart," the Warden warned, "is only a small indication of the surrounding dangers threatening you if you do not follow me exactly and without hesitation."[44] The candidate was then ushered through a precipitous series of tours around the lodge. This was designed to be a "long and

---

40. Turner, *Ritual Process*, 103.

41. Baylot BN FM⁴125, fol. 4r.

42. BN FM⁴149, fol. 14r.

43. "Secrets des Francs-maçons: Réception des apprentifs," in Johel Coutura, ed., *Le parfait maçon: Les débuts de la Maçonnerie française (1736–1748)* (Saint-Etienne: Université de Saint-Etienne, 1994), 40.

44. BN FM⁴622, fol. 8r. See also BN FM⁴566, fol. 92v.

fatiguing walk" during which the candidate was led and jerked about; stones or other objects were sometimes placed in his path and doors were opened and shut to disorient him. A masonic exposure tract described the tour in the following terms: "Once it is finished, one is as tired as if a long journey has just been completed."[45] While this was occurring, lodge members made noises such as the clashing of swords or the sharpening of tools, and threw combustible material into a flame; all of this was carried out "in the view to intimidate the recipient."[46] Some lodges later in the century added a truly theatrical touch to this episode by employing a "machine to imitate the noise of thunder."[47] No doubt this ceremony strikes us as it did outsiders of the time as highly amusing, but it must be emphasized that, for Masons, it was no laughing matter: a manuscript sternly warned that there was to be absolutely "no sort of clowning" at this point, for "Masonry is not a joke for the instructed Mason."[48]

What followed for the candidate was a continuation of the psychological abuse first experienced in the preparation chamber. Still blindfolded, he was brought in front of the lodge master, who addressed him in a firm and impolite tone (the *tu* form again appeared): "What are you, a profane, looking for here? What do you want? What is your motive? Answer! Why do you come and trouble us in our saintly mysteries?" Another lodge officer, usually the orator, accompanied the master in this harangue: "What motive propels your steps? What audacity! What boldness! What can possibly justify your actions?" Both the master and the orator, whose responsibility was the preservation of lodge order, continued the inquiry into the neophyte's moral fitness initially undertaken by the *frère terrible*. The orator hoped that the candidate did not think of masonic assemblies as privileged spaces of "intemperance and depravation" where "we give into unbridled pleasures and passions." The master also advised the neophyte that if he did not possess an "honest heart" and "irreproachable morals," then he should quickly leave the lodge.[49] During most of this exchange, the candidate was instructed to remain silent. His few answers were expected to be short, and sometimes

---

45. Abbé Gabriel-Louis Pérau, *L'ordre des Francs-maçons trahi et le secret des Mopses révélé*, ed. Daniel Ligou (Geneva: Slatkine Reprints, 1980), 35.

46. "Secrets des francs-maçons: Réception des apprentifs," in Coutura, *Parfait maçon*, 40. The Saint-Théodore de la Sincérité lodge in Paris referred to this moment in its statutes as the "great trial of charcoal fire." GODF MS AR 113.1.100 fol. 6r, Article XI.

47. BN FM⁴514, fol. 5r.

48. BN FM⁴149, fol. 5r.

49. BN FM⁴628, fol. 14v.

another lodge officer would answer on his behalf. The threat of severe physical harm also reappeared at this point. Following the interrogation of the
candidate, the lodge master asked aloud, "Is the iron hot? Is it red? Have someone bring it to me." He then placed a hot iron close to the initiate's skin,
misleading him into believing that he was to be deeply burnt. Fearfully an-
ticipating a painful wound, the candidate would be relieved to feel only the
application of a cold substance.[50] Other forms of physical intimidation to
which the candidate was subjected while blindfolded included pretending
to cut his skin or forcing him to drink a beverage that was supposed to be
poison or blood. Looking back on his masonic experience in France and
the Austrian Netherlands during the Old Regime, military officer Charles-
Joseph de Ligne recounted in his memoirs how during one apprentice ritual
he "made the recipient drink some hot water in making him believe that it
was his own blood."[51]

❧ The Making of the Masonic Man

The "grinding down" process of liminality was thus complete at this point
and the ritual subject was now in the condition to be infused with Masonry's values and norms. To emphasize the candidate's complete departure or
death from his previous state, he could at this stage be lowered into a casket
and have a veil placed over his face.[52] He was indeed a *tabula rasa*, for when
the master asked him, "What is your speech?" the neophyte was to answer,
"I know neither how to read nor how to write."[53]

What were the masonic models of conduct now inscribed onto the candidate? Evidence indicates that Freemasonry drew its legitimacy above all
from an ecumenical Christianity. Historians of Enlightenment Freemasonry
in France have largely overlooked just how much lodge life was infused
with Christian elements, instead preferring to see an organization that was,
in Maurice Agulhon's words, "free of all religious character"; Daniel Ligou
has similarly argued that French lodges gradually became more deistic as the
Enlightenment progressed, abandoning the Bible at some point after mid-

---

50. BN FM⁴182, fol. 6r; BN FM⁴628, fol. 15r.

51. Prince Charles-Joseph de Ligne, *Fragments de l'histoire de ma vie*, ed. Jeroom Vercruysse (Paris:
Honoré Champion, 2000), 1:228.

52. Pérau, *L'ordre des Francs-maçons trahi*, 76.

53. Baylot BN FM⁴123, fol. 13v.

century.[54] Envisioning Freemasonry as a secular voluntary organization devoid of religious sentiment is objectionable not only because it is factually incorrect, but also because this interpretation smacks of teleology, understanding Old Regime Freemasonry as the necessary origin of the fraternity in the nineteenth century. Although it is true that the anti-masonic literature of the Revolution and the highly visible conflicts between the Catholic Church and an anti-clerical faction of Masons in the Third Republic have depicted modern Freemasonry as fundamentally at odds with Christianity, we should resist projecting this image back onto Enlightenment Masonry.[55]

Similar to most initiations of *compagnonnage* in the Old Regime, the entire apprentice ritual may be understood as a time of mutual affirmation during which both the lodge and the candidate confirmed their Christian beliefs.[56] This process advanced incrementally—presumably to allow for either party to withdraw at any time—with the lodge first stressing the importance of providential theism and then later Christianity. The first basic element apparent is a firm belief in one God who could actively intervene in human affairs and with whom one could personally communicate. The apprentice lodge opened with a prayer to the "Grand Architect of the Universe." At first glance, the use of this term would seemingly place Freemasonry squarely within a deistic rather than Christian cosmogony. We immediately conjure images of the divine watchmaker, a Creator that represented little more than an abstract, architectonic principle that constructed the world according to an ordered plan and did not involve itself in human affairs. This was the God of the High Enlightenment described in works such as Voltaire's *Candide* (1759) and Diderot's *Jacques le fataliste et son maître* (1796). The affinity between deism and Freemasonry is apparently reinforced

---

54. Maurice Agulhon, *Pénitents et francs-maçons dans l'ancienne Provence: Essai sur la sociabilité mériodionale* (Paris: Fayard, [1968] 1984), 19; Daniel Ligou, "Recherche sur le rite français," in *Franc-maçonnerie et Lumières au seuil de la Révolution française* (Paris: Grand Orient de France, 1985), 80–81. See similar comments in Ran Halévi, *Les Loges maçonniques dans la France d'Ancien Régime: Aux origines de la sociabilité démocratique* (Paris: Librairie Armand Colin, 1984), 71–72, 99–100.

55. Pierre-Yves Beaurepaire, "Lumières maçonniques et christianisme," *Dix-huitième siècle* 34 (2002): 27. This historiographical problem appears to be unique to France, as masonic scholarship in other national contexts has acknowledged the importance of Christianity in eighteenth-century lodges. On German lodges, for example, see the comments of Margaret Jacob in "Franc-maçonnerie," in *Le Monde des Lumières,* ed. Vincenzo Ferrone and Daniel Roche (Paris: Fayard, 1999), 271.

56. Truant, *Rites of Labor,* 88–92, 104–8. Truant indicates (279n15) that despite their structural affinities, it is not clear if *compagnonnage* and Masonry directly borrowed from one another before the Revolution.

by the fact that well-known deists such as Franklin, Montesquieu, and Voltaire were all Masons in France.

But it becomes clear, on further inspection of the opening prayer during the apprentice ritual, that these figures represented a fringe within the organization and that French Freemasonry generally did not subscribe to deism.[57] The masonic Grand Architect represented more than a vague First Cause but was instead conceived of as actively intervening in lodge life. He inhabited a "celestial abode" where "angelical company" accompanied and worked alongside Him, and the orator expressed hope that He could descend upon the lodge and shower it with His "lights."[58] It is also clear that, unlike the deistic position, Masons believed that God could shape lodge affairs. Before beginning the initiation, the orator asked Him to "cast a favorable glance on this lodge and on all the brothers who compose it" and to cover them in "your celestial light so that your spirit of wisdom and of equity accompanies us incessantly . . . let our actions please you to the extent that our motives are saintly, and let the burning desire to serve you gather us together, so that none of us be neglected by your adorable view." He also hoped that a "divine breath" would inspire the lodge in their choice of members, so that Freemasonry would continue to be a "saintly refuge" of happiness and virtue.[59] Toward the conclusion of the apprentice ritual, the lodge master again turned to Him for guidance when he uttered aloud: "Preserve us, enlighten me so that I know if what I do is pleasing to you and if the candidate who is presenting himself is worthy to enter." Freemasonry thus did not conceive of any unbridgeable wedge between God and the world. The "Grand Architect" in this opening prayer was a personal and intimate God whom the orator addressed with the *tu* form, to whom one prayed and sought advice, and whose laws one strove to follow

---

57. We understand "deism" to be the philosophical position of the late-seventeenth and early-eighteenth centuries that critiqued ecclesiastical institutions and questioned certain basic tenets of Christian faith such as the divinity of Jesus Christ, the validity of the prophecies, and of the Bible generally. Composed in the early 1750s, Voltaire's *Sermon of the Fifty* qualified the Old and New Testaments as "absurd fables" and accused early Christians of mythologizing Jesus into a God. Peter Gay, *Deism: An Anthology* (Princeton, NJ: D. van Nostrand Company, 1968), 145, 153–56.

58. See, for example, the prayer in Baylot BN FM⁴124, fol. 10v.

59. In the employment of the term "divine breath" (*le souffle divin*), Freemasonry was perhaps alluding to the numerous Biblical passages where this expression symbolized God's intervening in human affairs. In his exhaustive study on the occurrence of the Hebrew word *ruach* (breath) in the Hebrew Bible, scholar Daniel Lys writes that the phrase "breath of God" signifies "God turned towards creation, acting on it, in relationship with his creation." Daniel Lys, *Rûach: Le souffle dans l'Ancien Testament. Enquête anthropologique à travers l'histoire théologique d'Israël* (Paris: PUF, 1962), 56.

in order to attain eternal salvation where all lodge members, the orator hoped, would be reunited after death "in the celestial, adorable and eternal lodge."[60]

Masons themselves in fact did not think that the term "Grand Architect" inevitably invoked the specter of deism. After all, the expression had been in use since at least the sixteenth century, well before deism first emerged as a serious intellectual position in the late seventeenth century.[61] It appeared in the first volume of *L'Architecture* of Tuileries palace architect Philibert de l'Orme in 1567, and Kepler employed the term in his 1609 *Astronomia nova*. In the masonic context, the terms "Grand Architect" and "God" could in fact be used interchangeably. During the apprentice ritual, the candidate was to take an oath of loyalty to the order "in the presence of the Grand Architect of the Universe, who is God."[62] Similar to the Hebrew Bible, in which we find God called by more than one name to refer to different divine attributes—Adonai, Elohim, Shaddai, and so forth—lodges used expressions like "Grand Architect" in order to respectfully invoke Him. "His saintly name will never be uttered by accident, nor will it be profaned in any manner," explained a set of statutes of a Parisian lodge active in the 1770s, "It will be pronounced when necessary, with fear, respect and trembling, naming him by the Eternal, the All Powerful, or the Grand Architect of the Universe."[63]

Within the reflection chamber, some lodges gave candidates a Bible as well as a piece of paper with the following message: "In this apparent solitude, do not think that you are alone. Completely separated from other men . . . see that there is a Being that is closest to you and to which you owe your existence and life." Reading on, the candidate learned that becoming a Freemason not only meant expunging self-love and other harmful passions but also required complete submission to divine laws. "To succeed," the document concluded somberly, "you will have to perform a difficult labor, seek and suffer! Are you sure to continue?"[64] Once inside the preparation chamber, the *frère terrible* asked the initiate: "In whom do you place your

60. Baylot BN FM⁴125, fols. 2r–5r.

61. Charles Porset, "Grand Architecte de l'Univers," in *Encyclopédie de la Franc-maçonnerie*, ed. Eric Saunier (Paris: Librairie Générale Francaise, 2000), 345–47.

62. BN FM⁴149, fol. 8r; Baylot BN FM⁴123, fol. 10v.

63. Alain Le Bihan, *Francs-maçons et ateliers parisiens de la Grande Loge de France au XVIIIᵉ siècle (1760–1795)* (Paris: Bibliothèque Nationale, 1973), 435.

64. BN FM⁴514, fol. 31r.

trust?" When the latter answered "in God," the former replied, "In this case, follow your guide and fear no danger."[65]

The candidate, upon entering the lodge, was posed a series of questions by the master. This interrogation illustrates the important point that Masonry conceived religion as one of the basic elements of a person's identity: "What is this profane's name? What age is he? What religion does he profess? What is his social condition [*état*]? What is his place of birth?"[66] From this point forward, the lodge left behind providential theism to explicitly embed the masonic engagement within a Christian framework. Nearing the conclusion of his journey from profane to brother, the candidate was brought in front of the master. In between the two men lay a Bible, typically open to the Gospel of Saint John, the patron saint of Freemasonry (figure 2.1).[67] With his right hand on the scriptures, he was to take a solemn oath never to reveal the secrets of the fraternity and always to be ready to emotionally or materially assist a fellow Mason. The lodge master made clear that the Gospels represented the moral and spiritual basis of the lodge and masonic solidarity. "You have your hand on the holy writings," he explained, "Do you now want to swear your allegiance?"[68] In August 1785, a lodge master warned a candidate that, "I remind you once again, because you are about to adopt or refuse them [the responsibilities of Masonry] if you are uneasy. A Mason must be religious, an observer of the Laws of God. Sir, do you want to become a Mason?"[69] Other ritual manuals stressed in similar terms that the candidate was to promise to "be loyal to the saintly Christian religion, to my sovereign, and to the civil laws" and that "the Gospels are the law of the Mason which he must incessantly think about and follow." Rituals referred to the Gospels as "the book of truth" and the lodge master explained that the Bible's presence was required in order to "regulate our faith." It was also within Holy Scripture that the Masons claimed to derive all of their organizational principles. "It is from the book of God," observed a lodge master to the newly initiated apprentice, "that we have drawn our decrees. We revere His supreme law, [for] it contains all our secrets." And in a century where the concept of divine monarchy

65. BN FM⁴180ᵇⁱˢ, fol. 10r.

66. BN FM⁴149, fol. 4r.

67. Masons venerated the two saints John, the Baptist and the Evangelist, and celebrated their feast days on 24 June and 27 December, respectively.

68. BN FM⁴149, fol. 7r.

69. Dossier of Union et Fraternité (Caen), BN FM²190, fol. 129r.

FIGURE 2.1.   Facing the lodge master with the orator to his right, a candidate solemnly swears on the Gospels to never reveal the secrets of Freemasonry. Detail from an engraving modeled after Johann Martin Bernigeroth's *Assemblée de* [sic] *Francs-Maçons, pour la réception des Apprentifs*, 1745. Courtesy of the Grand Orient de France.

gradually but surely was giving way to a secular concept of the "nation," we still find Freemasons during the reign of Louis XVI explaining that members must obey civil laws because "the ruling power emanates from God." In order to discourage candidates from thinking that the apprentice ritual's opening emphasis on a general theism meant that Freemasonry did not differentiate between Christianity and other monotheistic religions, lodges took care to stress the New rather than the Old Testament as their foundational text. One ritual manual specified that the "promises of a Freemason" were to be sworn "on the Holy Gospels and not on the Old Testament." During the actual oath, the candidate was explicitly made aware that the Grand Architect and the Christian God were one and the same when he declared, "I swear and promise on the Holy Gospels, in the face of Almighty God, Grand Architect of the Universe."[70] Seeking to inscribe Freemasonry within the history of the secularization of French society in the Enlightenment, historians like Daniel Ligou have argued that the Gospels gradually disappeared from masonic ritual over the course of the century. Such an assertion cannot stand up against the overwhelming evidence that the New Testament was continually used in French lodges down to the Revolution and perhaps beyond.[71]

A series of questions and answers marked the end of the ritual. These "catechisms" or "instructions" made recourse to Jesus's teachings when explaining the moral significance of certain actions the apprentice had performed during the ritual. Three knocks had been required to enter the lodge. "What do these three distinct knocks signify?" The apprentice was taught to quote Matthew (7:7–8) in answering, "the three words of Scripture: knock, and the door will be opened, ask, and you will receive, seek and you will find."[72] Much of the apprentice ritual was in fact symbolically infused with the number three, sacred in Christianity because its represents the Trinity. Messin parliamentarian and lodge master Baron de Tschoudy explained that "everything is done by the number three in Freemasonry," because it is "the most august object of our faith, the greatest vehicle of our hopes."[73] After the three knocks at the door, the apprentice normally made three blindfolded trips around the lodge, after which he took three steps forward to be presented to the lodge master. There, he was instructed that there were three pieces of furniture in the lodge (the Bible, the compass, and the gavel), three windows in the lodge, three "mobile jewels" (the square, the level, and the plumb line), and three "immobile jewels" (the rough stone, the finished stone, and the writing board [*planche à tracer*]).[74] The

---

70. Description of the function of the Gospels and the Bible has been drawn from, in order of appearance, BN FM⁴566, fol. 96r; BN FM⁴513, fol. 5r; Baylot BN FM⁴123, fol. 10v; BN FM-⁴180ᵇⁱˢ, fol. 37r; BN FM⁴151, fols. 15r–15v; BN FM⁴180ᵇⁱˢ, fol. 16r; BN FM⁴112, fol. 16r; BN FM⁴513, fol. 5v.

71. On the supposed secularization of rituals, see Ligou, "Recherche sur le rite français," 80–81. For examples of lodges that used the Gospels into the 1790s, see the meeting minutes of Anglaise (Bordeaux) and Parfaite Sincerité (Marseille) in GODF MS AR 113.2.101 and 113.2.102, and BN FM³387, respectively.

72. BN FM⁴628, fol. 16r.

73. Théodore-Henry baron de Tschoudy, *L'étoile flamboyante, ou la société des Francs-maçons considérée sous tous les aspects* (Paris, 1766), 1:74, 77.

74. In the initiation context, the term "jewel" (*bijou*) referred to specific items on which the candidate was to meditate. In the higher grades, the Mason was later explained the moral and spiritual

apprentice also learned at the end of his induction that three was the minimum number of members required to hold a meeting. There were also three signs of the apprentice: of the throat (which could be cut if the apprentice revealed any secrets to non-Masons), of the hand (it was through manual gestures that the apprentice identified himself), and of the foot (the apprentice was always to walk in the path of virtue). The apprentice gesture itself comprised three movements of the thumb and index finger.

Despite the fact that the Paris Grand Lodge's general statutes in the middle of the century could only be followed by Catholics—requiring Roman baptism of all Masons, for instance—and that the overwhelming majority of French Masons were Catholic, lodges and apologists were careful to speak of their relationship to "Christianity" rather than "Catholicism."[75] Just as the deists of the High Enlightenment represented one minority group within lodges, Lyonnais Jean-Baptiste Willermoz and his associates, with their explicitly Catholic brand of Masonry, occupied another. Mainstream Freemasonry in France, on the other hand, was neither fashionably deist nor resolutely Catholic. As Pierre-Yves Beaurepaire has argued, the masonic project in the eighteenth century was fundamentally ecumenical.[76] There were, of course, cases of exclusively Catholic or Protestant lodges to be found—such as in Sedan—but in general Freemasonry sought to reunite Protestants and Catholics in the wake of France's religious wars and continuing discrimination of Huguenots following the 1685 Edict of Fontainebleau.[77] Although such an ecumenical position opened the brotherhood to criticism from the Vatican and other stalwarts of orthodoxy, Masons were not breaking any new ground but were merely acting out what Christian rationalists had already advocated in the previous century. In Ramsay's thinking, for example, there is the clear presence of Latitudinarianism, embodied in the hope that Christians could move beyond the sectarian divisions—the "fatal discords" he called them in his "Discours"—that had proven so

---

significance of some of these objects, such as the compass: "Through the compass, you should understand that God makes everything perfectly, just as the compass forms a circle in which all the points of the circumference are equally distant from the center. God is the central point of all things . . . which are equally close and distant from a central point, which is God." BN FM⁴149, fols. 137r–137v.

75. Pierre Chevallier, *Histoire de la Franc-maçonnerie française. La Maçonnerie: École de l'égalité, 1725–1799* (Paris: Fayard, 1974), 121–22.

76. Beaurepaire, "Lumières maçonniques," 30.

77. On Catholic and Protestant lodges in Sedan, see Gérard Gayot, "Le problème de la double appartenance: Protestants et Francs-maçons à Sedan au XVIIIᵉ siècle," *Revue d'histoire moderne et contemporaine* 18 (1971): 415–29.

destructive throughout much of recent European history. In the "Discours," he placed Freemasonry squarely in the history of Christian brotherhood, for like "our ancestors, the Crusaders," he hoped that the order would bind Christians together into a "spiritual nation" that would transcend national, linguistic, and denominational differences. Ramsay was also a great admirer of Ralph Cudworth, a member of the Cambridge Platonists, a group close to the Anglican Latitudinarians.[78]

Over the course of the eighteenth century, this ecumenism evolved from the level of ideas to practice to the extent that one often found a general "doctrinal indifference" where Catholics and Protestants coexisted relatively peacefully; even lower clergy had become increasingly reluctant to persecute illicit Huguenot assemblies in many areas of the kingdom.[79] Freemasonry, then, must be seen as one of the leading indicators of this trend, for its ecumenism was routinely affirmed in lodge speeches and in practice. One orator summed up this position when he stated that "all those who believe in Jesus Christ, regardless of their denomination, can be admitted into the order."[80] And although some Catholic brethren may have privately wished that the followers of Calvin and Luther recognize their supposed errors, apologists urged members to keep the space of the lodge free from proselytizing efforts. Catholics within Freemasonry were not expected to consider Protestants heretical or even schismatic, but rather part of the wider Christian community. Although Huguenots were "unfortunately separated from our Communion," wrote one Catholic Mason, "they nevertheless have been touched and edified by morality."[81] In a similar vein, a document from an unknown lodge in Bordeaux indicated that Protestants could be admitted into lodges as long as their "Christian disposition" and "goodwill" could be affirmed.[82] Protestant Masons could be found in the

---

78. George Henderson, *Chevalier Ramsay* (New York: Thomas Nelson and Sons, 1952), 114, 128, 174, 218, 220, 224, 227, 234. Ramsay's ecumenical convictions also found expression in his posthumous *Philosophical Principles of Natural and Revealed Religion* (1748).

79. The expression has been coined in David Bien, *The Calas Affair: Persecution, Toleration, and Heresy in Eighteenth-Century Toulouse* (Westport, CT: Greenwood Press, [1960] 1979), chap. 2. On clerical toleration of Huguenots, see John McManners, *Church and Society in Eighteenth-Century France,* vol. 2: *The Religion of the People and the Politics of Religion* (New York: Oxford University Press, 1998), 623–25.

80. Frère Jarrhetti, *L'orateur Franc-maçon* (Berlin, 1766), 67.

81. Tschoudy, *Etoile flamboyante,* 1:132; Frère Enoch, *Le vrai Franc-maçon, qui donne l'origine et le but de la Franc-maçonnerie* (Liège, 1773), 91–92.

82. ADG, 6^E9, unfoliated. It is probable that this document pertained to the Anglaise lodge, as other material from Anglaise is included in the same dossier.

major cities of the kingdom—Paris, Lyon, Marseille, and Bordeaux—as well as in traditional bastions of the reformed faith such as Nîmes and Montauban.[83] Lodges indeed facilitated Protestant integration into their fold by often making optional those ceremonies feared to make them uncomfortable. For example, in the Atlantic port town of Rochefort, where many Huguenot families had remained after the 1685 Revocation, the Aimable Concorde lodge in the 1770s excused its non-Catholic members from attending the mass in celebration of the feast of Saint John the Baptist.[84]

It is important to note that Freemasonry expressed deep concern that outsiders understood their organization as something other than Christian. One of the earliest apologias to directly confront this issue was the *Apologie pour l'ordre des Francs-Maçons* (1742), and brethren would reiterate its arguments throughout the century in the effort to allay public fear in France that the order was a hotbed of freethinking. The author recognized that Freemasonry's novelty compelled some to see in the order "a thousand chimerical dangers." In particular, it was necessary to "respond very seriously to the suspicions of atheism, of deism, of indifference in religious matters . . . subjects [which] by their very atrocity refute themselves, but it nevertheless seemed necessary that the core of our order offer some explanation to the public."[85] The author readily acknowledged that "all Christian communions have rights in the order, and are admitted indifferently: this is a constant truth." And because Freemasonry theoretically treated all Christians equally, he saw no logical reason why one particular denomination would be favored. The objective of the order was to reunite men who, despite "a difference of explication in dogma and in religious services," nevertheless hoped and trusted in Jesus, "the eternal sacrifice of a God who really wanted to die for them."[86]

But this spirit of Christian inclusiveness was accompanied by—and arguably required—the unequivocal exclusion of two types of religious outsiders. First, it was clarified that men of unorthodox or questionable religious conviction were unwelcome: "We carefully avoid admitting in our order atheists and deists, at least as much as it is possible to recognize in an initiate such opinions that could lead to deism or atheism." It was not simply

---

83. Gayot, "Le problème de la double appartenance," 415.

84. Francis Masgnaud, *Franc-maçonnerie et Francs-maçons en Aunis et Saintonge sous l'Ancien Régime et la Révolution* (La Rochelle: Rumeur des Ages, 1989), 84.

85. "Apologie pour l'ordre des Francs-maçons par Mr. N★★★, membre de l'ordre. Avec deux chansons composées par le frère américain," in Coutura, *Parfait maçon,* 94.

86. Ibid., 124.

enough for a candidate to possess a personal Christian faith, but he must also express it publicly. The *Apologie pour l'ordre des Francs-Maçons* clarified that he who "neglected to publicly serve God according to the denomination in which he had been baptized" did not merit masonic affiliation, "regardless of his qualities in civil society." Non-Christians were a second group categorically excluded from membership. Whereas John Toland and other late-seventeenth and early-eighteenth-century deists believed that the principles of an ideal Christianity could correspond with a number of other religious traditions, Freemasonry did not embrace all faiths under the general rubric of "natural religion." "The order admits only Christians," the author firmly stated. "Outside of the Christian church, it is not possible, and it must not occur, that anyone be received as a Free Mason. This is why Jews, Muslims and pagans are excluded as infidels." The *Apologie* reassured its readers that "it was from the profession of Christianity that flowed the fundamental principles of the Order."[87]

This message that Freemasonry accepted all Christians but rejected other faiths held true in eighteenth-century lodge life. Contrary to Jacob Katz's assertion that Jews in France experienced little difficulty in entering lodges, Pierre-Yves Beaurepaire has marshaled much evidence to demonstrate how Jews were kept out of Masonry.[88] In 1767, the Parfaite Sincerité lodge of Marseille indicated in its regulations that any individual "who has the unhappiness of being a Jew, Negro or Muslim must not be proposed [for initiation]." Other provincial cities where Sephardic Jews could be found—such as Toulouse and Bordeaux—disqualified Jews from initiation and even refused entry to foreign Jewish Masons. Consider, for example, the regrettable experience of a Jew by the name of Cappadoce who was traveling in Bordeaux in late November 1747. Having been initiated into Freemasonry in Amsterdam, he sought to visit one of the city's lodges, Anglaise. Visibly taken aback by Cappadoce's request, not only did the lodge's doors remain closed to this unfortunate individual, but his very status as a Mason was denied. Undeterred, Cappadoce made a second attempt to enter the lodge in February 1749. This time, however, he also presented Anglaise with a recommendation from his lodge master back in Amsterdam. The lodge

---

87. Ibid., 98.

88. Pierre-Yves Beaurepaire, *L'autre et le frère: L'étranger et la Franc-maçonnerie en France au XVIIIe siècle* (Paris: Honoré Champion, 1998), 553–76. Beaurepaire takes issue with the remarks of Katz in *Jews and Freemasons in Europe, 1723–1939*, trans. Leonard Oschry (Cambridge, MA: Harvard University Press, 1970), 19–20.

again refused to allow him inside and adamantly declared that "Jews will never be admitted among us."[89]

The decidedly Christian brand of Freemasonry appears to have been the norm for much of continental Europe and stands in contrast with Anglo-American Masonry of the eighteenth century. The wider circle of tolerance within British—and presumably American—lodges becomes apparent when comparing side by side the first set of general guidelines for French Freemasonry, the *Devoirs Enjoints aux Maçons Libres* (1735), with the British equivalent, the *Constitutions* (1723) of Anderson and Desaguliers. Whereas the latter document required all Masons to profess the "Religion in which all Men agree," the French version sharpened the language to read "the Religion in which all *Christians* agree."[90]

✒ Masonic Friendship: A "Proper Economy of the Passions"

The time has now come to review our findings on the initiation ritual and understand how this institutional process permitted Freemasonry to posit friendship as a stable human relationship. In chapter 1 we probed masonic understandings of friendship and uncovered the problematic nature of this bond. Masonry recognized that the dangerous vicissitudes of the passions and harmful desires of self-love made friendship an unstable, fleeting relationship that could dissolve as quickly as it could take form. The problem of friendship for Freemasonry in Enlightenment France therefore was fundamentally a problem of the self, and to reconfigure friendship thus meant first reconstructing the individual. The principal argument made in this chapter is that brethren undertook this task of constructing an individual into a reliable friend through the apprentice ritual. As we have examined in detail, this effort first required the symbolic tearing down of a candidate's previous sense of individuality; this is the "leveling" or "grinding down" process to which Turner has referred. The candidate was stripped of his distinguishing characteristics as a distinctive self, forced to humbly submit to physical and psychological abuse, and repeatedly warned that a Mason must

---

89. 30 November 1747 and 11 February 1749 entries in "Extrait de tout ce qui s'est passé de plus intéressant pendant les séances à la respectable loge Anglaise n° 204, orient de Bordeaux depuis sa fondation qui date du 27 avril 1732 jusqu'au 29 juin 1817." GODF MS AR 113.2.96, pièce 1.

90. BN FM⁴146. My emphasis.

learn to control his self-regarding impulses. Masonic friendship thus required that the passions be tempered and that self-love be expunged.

The initiation ceremony then recast the candidate into a new form, actively constructing a new self. During a visit to a Parisian lodge in late 1778, an officer of the Grand Orient who had just participated in an initiation claimed that "everything that he [the candidate] has just experienced has purified his soul and his heart; he has acquired a new existence."[91] Lodge masters celebrated the newly received Freemason as a "new being" and the apprentice ritual as an opportunity to "leave behind the previous man, the man of our century, and become a new man, the masonic man."[92] The apprentice ritual infused this new self with an ecumenical Christianity.

By affirming that the candidate would behave as a virtuous Christian, and symbolically cleansing him of the moral imperfections that made friendship so problematic, the apprentice ritual logically represented the gateway to the masonic friendship community. Only at its conclusion, therefore, did the lodge master invite the new member to formally accept the lodge's friendship. "What did you receive in entering into apprenticeship?" asked the lodge master. "The friendship of those who received me," the apprentice replied. This pledging of friendship was understood to be reciprocal: "Question: How did you recognize this advantage? Answer: In according to them in turn the most sincere friendship."[93] The newly formed apprentice was also warned: "You have taken a solemn but voluntary oath, and never forget its importance. Its exact observation will procure you true friends just as its infraction will certainly expose you to disdain and shame."[94]

Brethren throughout the century reiterated this view that Masonry bound together men who possessed a shared moral vision of the world. In a midcentury letter to the Grand Lodge in which the master of the Amitié lodge in Bordeaux reflected back on his quarter-century engagement with the order, he praised the term *frère*, for those who held this title not only were bound in a "particular bond" but also adhered to a "uniform way of thinking."[95] By grounding masonic friendship in a common set of moral guidelines, Freemasonry closely followed the classical models of friendship outlined in the previous chapter that saw friendship as only possible be-

---

91. Dossier of Réunion des Arts (Paris), BN FM²97, fol. 15v.

92. Dossier of Saint-Julien (Brioude), BN FM²188 (1), fol. 43r; Tschoudy, *Etoile Flamboyante*, 2:96.

93. "Catéchisme des apprentis," in Coutura, *Parfait maçon*, 155–56.

94. BN FM⁴180bis, fol. 26r.

95. GODF MS AR 113.2.14, fol. 20r (28 May 1765).

tween the virtuous, who held, in the words of Cicero, a "community of views on all matters human and divine."[96] This classical vision was emphasized at the conclusion of the apprentice ritual when the lodge master urged the newly received Mason to always remember that "the conformity of morals is the source of friendship just as their differences are the source of hate."[97] Masons believed that this absolute uniformity in morals meant that the lodge functioned as a ready-made friendship network for brethren who traveled far from home. In the spring of 1777, for example, military officer Jean-François de Bar tearfully bid farewell to his Parisian lodge, but took solace in the fact that "since there are Masons everywhere in the world, I must find friends everywhere. . . . The Freemason is everywhere the same (I must believe this). Virtue is his foundation, . . . friendship his torch."[98]

Freemasonry intended these ritually grounded friendships to display both affective and practical components.[99] The lodge master made clear to the newly received apprentice that the safeguarding of this material aspect of friendship was the primary motive for the creation of a masonic language of signs: "As all brothers owe each other friendship and assistance, even beyond our lodges, we have signs, gestures and words to recognize ourselves."[100] Speeches, apologias, and anti-masonic exposures throughout the century all referred to the concrete assistance members could expect from one another, even in times of acute crisis. "Who is not aware," one orator asked, "that where we find Masons, we also find friends?" He envisioned masonic friendship as a vast network of solidarity on which a man could always depend if he were to fall upon hard times for any reason, from an unsuccessful business venture to a shipwreck.[101]

And yet Freemasonry above all stressed that their brand of friendship was not merely encapsulated by instrumentality. They surely would render

---

96. Philippe Dubois-Goibaud, *Les livres de Cicéron de la vieillesse et de l'amitié, avec les paradoxes du même autheur* (Paris, 1708), 150.

97. BN FM⁴149, fol. 5r.

98. Dossier of Celeste Amitié (Paris), BN FM²59, fols. 23v–24r.

99. Anthropologist Julian Pitt-Rivers emphasizes that "by definition all friendship must be both sentimental in inspiration and instrumental in effects, since there is no other way to demonstrate one's sentiments than through those actions which speak plainer than words. The instrumental aspect validates the affect." Julian Pitt-Rivers, "The Kith and the Kin," in *The Character of Kinship*, ed. Jack Goody (New York: Cambridge University Press, 1973), 97.

100. BN FM⁴149, fols. 11r–12r; BN FM⁴180ᵇⁱˢ, fol. 21r.

101. Jarrhetti, *L'orateur Franc-maçon*, 25–26.

services to one another when required, but this was not the underlying principle of the relationship: masonic friendship was "a commerce where one never counts" one orator stressed, and the new apprentice promised at the end of his reception to unconditionally love his fellow brethren.[102] Masons complained that individuals too often called "friendships" relationships that were motivated solely by calculating self-interest and characterized by "conditional flattery," "frivolous deference," and a "false cordiality." Freemasonry was in fact likely reacting to and defining itself against a specific form of utilitarian friendship Sharon Kettering and others have identified in Old Regime France. Although she observes that some early modern friendships were grounded in affection, a far more frequent type of friendship was "public, utilitarian, and calculating—the support sought from a patron or offered to a client. Clientage did not derive its impetus or justification from friendship, but its use of the same language forced the connection between them in all its ambiguity."[103]

But even despite the symbolic recasting of the individual in the apprentice ritual, Masons remained cautious about the emotional quality of male bonding. Before the prerevolutionary current of *sensibilité* ushered in an unprecedented optimism about sentimental friendship (a topic explored in chapter 5), brethren did not posit friendship as a relationship grounded in deep promptings of feelings or tender affection, but rather presented it as a form of restrained closeness between the virtuous. In this way, masonic friendship embodied the Stoic ideal that man can, with effort, regulate his passions. In an open letter to a female acquaintance curious about the inner workings of the fraternity, Breton Mason Elie-Catherine Fréron recounted some details about lodge life, specifically the speech following his own initiation in the early 1740s. His lodge master defined the masonic bond as occupying a middle ground of carefully demarcated sentimentalism, situated somewhere in between "the constant coldness of vulgar friendships and the passing ardor of love."[104] Other speeches of the same period defined masonic friendship as an "enjoyable sentiment," a "simple cordiality," as well as a "*proper economy of the passions that does not exclude virtue*."[105]

---

102. Baylot BN FM⁴123, fol. 11r.

103. Sharon Kettering, "Friendship and Clientage in Early Modern France," *French History* 6 (1992): 142.

104. "Lettre à Madame de ★★★," in Coutura, *Parfait maçon*, 222.

105. "Discours de réception dans un temps critique" and "Discours de rentrée sur l'amitié" in ibid., 186–89. My emphasis.

This emphasis on emotional restraint can be found not only in the speeches and rituals of the order but also in its material artifacts. Perhaps intended to commemorate the inauguration of a lodge or to be offered as a memento to a departing member, an unknown lodge during the eighteenth century commissioned the manufacture of a porcelain gourd on which two Freemasons are clasping hands while separated by the masonic compass and square (figure 2.2). This depiction resembled a cultural practice common in early modern male friendship: the friendship portrait. Originating at some point in the mid-fifteenth century, the friendship portrait was especially

FIGURE 2.2. *Gourde aux deux frères* (faïence de Nevers, eighteenth century). Photo courtesy of the Grand Orient de France.

prevalent among humanist circles, but endured at least until the eighteenth century.[106] The image on the vase bears striking resemblance to these paintings in that these Masons are portrayed as equals in many respects, as they are dressed and posing in a similar fashion. The emotional component of their relationship is stressed with the clasping of hands, but a number of formal elements in the work suggest that these men were bound by a Ciceronian brand of friendship that was grounded in a shared moral system rather than inexplicable personal attraction. First, the artist confers a decidedly Stoic character to their friendship in that their gaze is deliberately cast outward, towards the viewer rather than one another. Second, their physical proximity is restricted to the hands as the compass and square keep the men from physically touching. The artist not only uses these two visual motifs to limit emotional closeness, but also to convey the message that a shared moral character lies at the heart of their relationship; their grasping of hands is patterned exactly after the geometric shape of the compass, perhaps the best-known synecdoche of masonic ethics.

✐ Ritualized Friendship

It is important to note the specific quality of the friendship we are observing in the apprentice ritual. In his system of "amiable relations," Julian Pitt-Rivers classifies friendship into two categories: ritualized and unritualized friendship (figure 2.3).[107] Both forms of friendship bind together non-kin in a voluntary relationship that possesses both instrumental and affective components, but the latter is an essentially private, casual relationship generated and sustained through an extended process of interaction during the life cycle. The former, on the other hand, is ritually contracted between individuals who did not necessarily have any previous trace of personal relations.[108] It was this second form of sworn friendship the apprentice

---

106. On the friendship portrait in the Renaissance, see Peter Burke, "Humanism and Friendship in Sixteenth-Century Europe," in *Friendship in Medieval Europe*, ed. Julian Haseldine (Stroud, UK: Sutton, 1999), 268. On Enlightenment varieties, see Jessica Fripp, "Portraits of Artists and the Social Commerce of Friendship in Eighteenth-Century France" (PhD diss., University of Michigan, 2012), chap. 3.

107. Pitt-Rivers, "Kith and Kin," 96.

108. I am indebted to Gabriel Herman's discussion of Pitt-Rivers' typology in his *Ritualised Friendship and the Greek City* (New York: Cambridge University Press, 1987), 32–33.

"Amiable Relations"

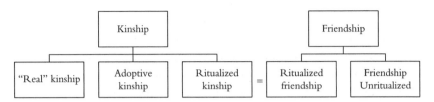

FIGURE 2.3. "Amiable relations." Adapted from Julian Pitt-Rivers, "The Kith and the Kin," in *The Character of Kinship*, ed. Jack Goody (New York: Cambridge University Press, 1973), 96.

forged during his initiation ceremony, the precise moment that the candidate theoretically established a bond of solidarity with every member of the lodge. In other words, a connection of friendship between the apprentice and his brethren took form not through any prior sustained personal exchange, but in quite an abrupt manner, through the ritual act and the formal pledging of friendship.

Because ritualized friendship was a formal and objective bond that could be shared by strangers, Freemasonry could define itself as a mode of sociability that created friendships between individuals who did not know one another previously. One of the founding documents of French Freemasonry, the *Devoirs Enjoints aux Maçons Libres*, opened with six articles that outlined in broad strokes the expected behavior of the ideal member. The first article enunciated in clear terms the order's aspirations, and the vision of Freemasonry as a privileged space of male friendship again appears. It was hoped that the order would become the "center and union of a solid and desirable friendship between those, whom, without the order, would be forever separated from each other."[109] In their letters to one another, brethren also evoked the idea that their ritualized friendships were not necessarily embedded in the context of personal relations. In May 1750, a certain brother named Boulard from Paris wrote the Élus Parfaits lodge in Bordeaux, offering his modifications of a specific ritual. He closed this technical letter on a warm note: "Goodbye, dear brethren. Love a little a brother who loves you even though he does not know you." He could consider himself friends with individuals whom he had never seen because the ritual bond of Freemasonry necessarily entailed that of friendship. He in fact immediately eschewed the distinction between a "brother" and a "friend" and went on to declare that "are we not friends as soon as we become brothers?"[110]

Membership in the masonic friendship community therefore preceded and transcended personal relationships. It was possible for Masons to consider strangers reliable friends because the ritual functioned as both a filter and an ontological passageway through which all candidates were theoretically reshaped. The ritualized, formal bond of sworn friendship generated in the apprentice ritual undoubtedly strikes the modern reader as something decidedly different from what we would today consider friendship. Friendship today conceptually distinguishes itself from other relationships such as marriage or kinship in that it is essentially a private, informal matter (ordinarily) between non-kin. The modern understanding of friendship assumes that, unlike a relationship with a spouse or kinsman, there exist no factors external to the friendship group that may identify an individual as a part of this particular group—as a "friend."[111]

In his work on early modern English friendship, Alan Bray has contrasted this modern understanding of friendship to early modern practices. His examination of joint burial monuments erected by friends from the sixteenth to the late seventeenth centuries leads him to observe that such a ritual "gave friendship a formal and objective character markedly different from friendship in modern society."[112] Similar to marriage, early modern friendships, contends Bray, were formal relationships bound by rituals that could act as a cohesive social gel that not only bound together the friends in question, but also allied each man's respective kinship network. Bray's account of aristocratic friendships also holds true for the French case of the same period. The work of Sharon Kettering, Arlette Jouanna, and Jean-Marie Constant all indicate that early modern noblemen—including the king himself—actively mobilized their friendships in the public realm for a variety of purposes: to raise armies, to collect taxes, to advance professionally and to supplement material resources.[113]

---

110. Gerry Prinsen, ed., *The Story of Les Élus Parfaits, the Mother Ecossais Lodge of Bordeaux* (Lexington, MA: Museum of our National Heritage, 1993), 4.

111. Graham Allan, *Friendship: Developing a Sociological Perspective* (New York: Harvester Wheatsheaf, 1989), 3.

112. Alan Bray, *The Friend* (Chicago: University of Chicago Press, 2003), 25. See also 40, 174.

113. Kettering, "Friendship and Clientage"; Arlette Jouanna, *Le devoir de la révolte: La noblesse française et la gestation de l'état moderne, 1559–1661* (Paris: Fayard, 1989), 65–90; Jean-Marie Constant, *Nobles et paysans en Beauce aux XVIᵉ et XVIIᵉ siècles* (Lille: Service de reproduction des thèses, 1981), 239–64.

Bray and others contend that such formal, ritualized friendships that held political and social significance gradually began to lose currency as publicly useful relationships during the eighteenth century.[114] Beginning with Locke's criticism of friendship in his *Two Treatises of Government*, wherein he argued that friendly feeling in the public sphere inevitably led to bitter partisanship and poor judgment, the Enlightenment no longer considered friendship as an essential social link on which society could be constructed, but instead increasingly derided it—along with gift-giving—as a corrupting agent in public life that could easily lead to favoritism, the rise of political factions, and subsequent civil anarchy, such as the English Civil War and Frondes in France.[115] Such skepticism of ritualized forms of friendship can in fact be found in some anti-masonic literature that compared masonic lodges with the political machinations of Oliver Cromwell, where the latter were considered to be veritable lodges *avant la lettre*.[116] Because of such increasing suspicion over ritualized friendship, Bray argues that it gradually receded from public view. However, he also points out that friendships bound by pact or ritual did not disappear altogether but instead continued to find expression in limited private venues well into the nineteenth century.[117] In this perspective, it would appear that Freemasonry served as a privileged enclave through which persisted an older, more formalized form of friendship.

Although masonic historiography has largely ignored male rituals, this chapter suggests that doing so is a perilous enterprise, for it is through these elaborate ceremonial performances that Freemasons infused meaning into their organization and distinguished their brand of sociability from the outside world. In the case of the initiation, we have examined just how central it was to the associational culture of lodges, because it was through this initiation process that brethren resolved the Gordian knot over friendship that preoccupied Masons and moralists alike in the Old Regime: How could friendship be posited as a stable bond of solidarity if the self was plagued by self-love and the passions? Through the pedagogical and purificatory

---

114. Mark Vernon, *The Philosophy of Friendship* (New York: Palgrave Macmillan, 2005), 113.

115. Bray, *The Friend*, 205–19; Scott Yenor, "Locke and the Problem of Friendship in Modern Liberalism," in *Love and Friendship: Rethinking Politics and Affection in Modern Times*, ed. Eduardo A. Velásquez (Lanham, MD: Rowman & Littlefield, 2003), 146. On eighteenth-century criticism of the gift in public life, see Harry Liebersohn, *The Return of the Gift: European History of a Global Idea* (New York: Cambridge University Press, 2011), chap. 2.

116. Larudan, *Les Francs-maçons écrasés*, 63–100. Larudan argued that both groups utilized their friendships to defend themselves from outside attacks and to mask their grand projects of establishing a new political order on the ruins of monarchy.

117. Bray, *The Friend*, 239–46, 283–88.

qualities of the initiation, the brotherhood was able to invent a masonic man who was cleansed of undesirable psychological elements and infused with an ecumenical Christianity. The ritual journey from the reflection chamber to the lodge master represented an ontological passageway that reshaped men into perfect friends. The *rite d'apprenti* thus was not only a ceremony that communicated collective values but was also one of profound symbolic transformation.

✒ CHAPTER 3

Confronting the Specter of Sodomy

At some point in the late 1730s or early 1740s, men in French lodges began organizing what were known as lodges of adoption.[1] Unlike all-male meetings, these assemblies included both men and women. These mixed-gender assemblies typically met less frequently than regular Freemasonry and were often held in spaces distinct from all-male lodges. In addition, the Grand Orient not only required adoption meetings to be attached to a male lodge but also stipulated that men must be in attendance during adoption in order to supervise rituals. These restrictions aside, adoption Masonry afforded women the opportunity to participate fully in the ritual and social life of Masonry by undergoing initiations, delivering and listening to speeches on a variety of topics, performing plays, raising funds for charity, and so forth. Although male Masons elsewhere in Europe also organized adoption lodges, most were located in France.[2]

Why did men invite women into their fold? For the history of male friendship in Freemasonry, this question is not of passing antiquarian curiosity but of vital importance because the masonic friendship community

---

1. Jan Snoek, *Initiating Women in Freemasonry: The Adoption Rite* (Boston: Brill, 2011), 120–23.

2. On women in Freemasonry outside France, see Pierre-Yves Beaurepaire, "Théâtre de société et Franc-maçonnerie aristocratique dans l'Europe des Lumières: Une rencontre réussie," *Revue d'histoire de théâtre* 57 (2005): 53–59.

supposedly was predicated on the absence of women from the lodge. As we have seen in an earlier chapter, Andrew-Michael Ramsay in his famous address was one of the first to explain that women were not granted access to the fraternity because they inevitably introduced the element of sexuality, thus transforming masonic friends into bitter rivals for female affection. The following decade, an individual of an unnamed French lodge furthered the point, apologizing to women, metonymically addressing them as *amour*. Employing a language of combat, he exclaimed, "Pardon us, love, if in our celebrations we shelter ourselves from your blows. We respect your rights but fear your conquests. We seek friends and you make men jealous."[3] In explaining why women were not allowed, a newly elected orator fifteen years later laid the blame on men's inherent inability to resist female allure: "The [study of the] most distant centuries have made known what power a woman wields over the weakness of man and it is only in order to avoid the disastrous effects of this weakness that we do not admit women into lodges." If women were to be introduced, he warned, then the male desire to be loved would jeopardize friendly relations between brethren: "We seek to please women, we want to do so and nothing more. We view those brothers who have the same objective as we as problematic . . . dissimulation replaces trust, friendship cedes to indifference and hate."[4] The view that women and masonic friendship were somehow incompatible endured well into the prerevolutionary era. In one masonic apologia of the 1770s, a fictional dialogue between a Freemason and a self-styled *philosophe* unfolded in which the latter inquired into the purpose of the organization. At one point, the Mason explained that women were kept in the realm of the non-masonic "profane" world in order to maintain order and harmony within the lodge. This answer satisfied the *philosophe*, who echoed the masonic consensus that "love and friendship are difficult to bring together . . . whenever rivalry begins, good relations (*la bonne intelligence*) come to an end."[5] Even within adoption Masonry itself, men and women recognized the great, and sometimes destructive, power

---

3. Andrew-Michael Ramsay, "DISCOURS prononcé à la réception des Frée-maçons. Par Mr. de Ramsay, Grand-Orateur de L'Ordre," in *Lettre philosophique, par Mr. de V★★★, avec plusieurs pièces galantes et nouvelles de différens auteurs* . . . (London, [1738] 1775), 45; *Discours prononcé à la loge de★★★, et autres pièces en prose et en vers concernant l'ordre des Francs-maçons par le frère . . . orateur de la Loge* (1740), 22.

4. *Discours prononcé en loge, par un Franc-maçon, nouvellement élevé à la dignité d'orateur* (1755), 10–11.

5. S. Arbas, *Considérations filosophiques sur la Franc-maçonnerie dédiées à tous les oriens en France, par un député de Jérusalem* (Hambourg-Rome, 1776), 375–76.

of love. Following a lodge meeting in early February 1778 in Paris, the men and women of Candeur lodge acted out Marmontel's operetta, *L'Ami de la maison*, where the central female protagonist, Agatha, reduces her suitors to whimpering, trembling supplicants.[6]

This evidence appears to conflict with the fact that Freemasonry had established well over fifty mixed-gender adoption lodges by the prerevolutionary era.[7] Exploring this apparent paradox in masonic sociability, we first chart the history and contours of mixed-gender Freemasonry, describing the proliferation of adoption lodges throughout the kingdom, the socioeconomic profile of membership, and typical lodge activities. We then examine the range of possible motivations for why men would choose to integrate women into Masonry. Such an investigation is intended to shed further light on gender relations within Enlightenment Freemasonry and reveal in greater detail the underpinnings of male friendship within this particular institutional milieu. This analysis thus operates under the guiding principle that eighteenth-century norms for masculinity and, by extension, male friendship were not static but were in fact the product of social interaction between men and women.[8]

✑ Adoption Lodges in Enlightenment France

Adoption Freemasonry came into existence in France soon after the inception of its exclusively male counterpart. Although public awareness and discussion of a feminine presence in Masonry remained rather muted until the second half of the century, tangible evidence indicates that women were initiated into adoption Masonry possibly as early as the 1730s. Parisian Mason and musician Jacques-Christophe Naudot composed a banquet songbook in the mid-1730s and furnished the reader with a number of hymns intended specifically for gatherings where women—defined as "sisters"—were likely present. Stanzas such as "Brothers and sisters, let us drink together

---

6. Dossier of Candeur (Paris), BN FM²58bis, dossier 2, fol. 47r.

7. For French adoption lodge figures, see the lists in Janet Burke and Margaret Jacob, "French Freemasonry, Women, and Feminist Scholarship," *Journal of Modern History* 68 (1996), 546–49; as well as Gisèle and Yves Hivert-Messeca, *Comment la Franc-maçonnerie vint aux femmes: Deux siècles de Franc-maçonnerie d'adoption féminine et mixte en France, 1740–1940* (Paris, 1997), 63–82.

8. Michael Kimmel develops such an "interactionist" perspective in "The Contemporary 'Crisis' of Masculinity in Historical Perspective," in *The Making of Masculinities: The New Men's Studies*, ed. Harry Brod (Boston: Allen and Unwin, 1987), 121–54.

often" and "Here [in the lodge] the sister and brother / have the same wish / to enjoy oneself without effort" and "My dear sisters until tomorrow let us remain at this [banquet] table" indicate that women participated in, at the very least, the more jovial aspects of masonic sociability.[9] During Naudot's time, *lieutenant de police* René Hérault also conducted crackdown operations on early Parisian lodges, arresting both men and women.[10] Lodges in the provinces also welcomed women in the first half of the century. During the 1740s, we find scattered references to adoption lodges from Marseille to Lunéville.[11]

From the middle of the 1740s onward, adoption Freemasonry was sufficiently prevalent in the kingdom to become a topic of discussion in the growing body of printed apologias and masonic exposures. For the first time, rules and regulations were generated, and songbooks specifically designated for adoption lodges appeared.[12] In essays and works of fiction, the presence of adoption assemblies fueled the curiosity of women—a common theme to which we will return—to access masonic knowledge. Adoption Freemasonry's growth followed that of male lodges during the second half of the century. From 1760 down to the Revolution, French Masons, in both military and civil lodges, erected at least sixty adoption lodges, thirteen of which could be found in the capital. These assemblies involved perhaps three thousand women over the course of the century. These figures are likely conservative since Old Regime Freemasonry was generally less dutiful in recording adoption activity.[13]

---

9. Jacques-Christophe Naudot, *Chansons notées de la très vénérable confrérie des Francs-maçons* (Paris, 1737), 73, 78.

10. Margaret Jacob, *Living the Enlightenment: Freemasonry and Politics in Eighteenth-Century Europe* (New York: Oxford University Press), 4.

11. Hivert-Messeca and Hivert-Messeca, *Deux siècles de Franc-maçonnerie d'adoption*, 56–57. References to women at a *loge de cour* at Lunéville can also be found at BN NAF MS 15176 fol. 73v (16 April 1738).

12. See, for example, Jean-Pierre Moët, *L'antropophile* (Paris, 1746); Abbé Gabriel-Louis Pérau, *L'ordre de Francs-maçons trahi et le secret des Mopses révélé* (Amsterdam, 1745); "Le secret des Francs-maçons entièrement découvert à une jeune dame de dix-sept ans par un faux frère de quatre-vingt ans . . ." (1748) in *Le parfait maçon: Les débuts de la Maçonnerie française (1736–1748)*, ed. Johel Coutura (Saint-Etienne: Université de Saint-Etienne, 1994), 129–38; *Chansons de l'ordre de l'adoption ou la Maçonnerie des femmes* (The Hague, 1751).

13. Burke and Jacob, "French Freemasonry," 546–49; and Hivert-Messeca and Hivert-Messeca, *Deux siècles de Franc-maçonnerie d'adoption*, 63–82. A typical example of masonic negligence in transcribing adoption proceedings was the sloppy recording of the secretary of the Candeur lodge in Paris during the late 1770s and early 1780s. See Dossier of Candeur (Paris), BN FM²58bis, dossier 2.

Unlike their exclusively masculine counterparts, adoption lodges could not be found everywhere in Enlightenment France. Major masonic centers like Paris and Bordeaux had numerous adoption assemblies, whereas others such as Lyon had only a single mixed lodge during the eighteenth century.[14] No evidence survives suggesting the involvement of women in Freemasonry in other towns and cities with a strong masonic presence, such as Montpellier (twenty-two lodges), Marseille (nineteen lodges), Toulouse (eighteen lodges), Toulon (sixteen lodges), Rouen (thirteen lodges), or Strasbourg (twelve lodges). Adoption Freemasonry was indeed entirely absent in a number of regions throughout the kingdom: Alsace, Auvergne, Béarn, Bourbonnais, Corsica, Dauphiné, Flanders, Gascogny, Limousin, Maine, Massif Central, Provence, and Roussillon et Foix had no lodges integrating women.[15]

Adoption Freemasonry also differed from mainstream lodges in that it was a predominately aristocratic phenomenon throughout the century. As I will explain in chapter 5, many male lodges gradually began to admit artisans and clerks into their fold from 1760 onward. Adoption membership, however, never descended below the highest echelons of Old Regime society. Eighty-two percent of women participating in adoption Freemasonry had noble lineage, and the remaining were spouses of the financial or military non-noble elite. The adoption assemblies of the Candeur lodge in Paris offer an illustrative example of this socioeconomic composition. Out of thirty-two initiated women, we find one princess, three duchesses, nineteen countesses, and eight marquises. Only one member, the spouse of a royal finance officer, did not possess a hereditary title. In the provinces, more diversity existed among membership, but still only the most privileged women could be found in lodges. In Lorient, for example, the Heureuse Alliance was made up solely of wives of high-ranking military or civil posts, and all but two of the eight members possessed noble status.[16]

Despite their low numbers and restricted membership, adoption lodges nevertheless attracted significant attention and comment from individual brethren, lodges, and the Grand Lodge and, later, Grand Orient. Although scattered documents indicate that adoption lodges were established in other countries, French observers nevertheless saw it as a distinctively national

---

14. Albert Ladret, *Le grand siècle de la Franc-maçonnerie: La Franc-maçonnerie lyonnaise au XVIIIᵉ siècle* (Paris: Dervy-Livres, 1976), 125–42.

15. Hivert-Messeca and Hivert-Messeca, *Deux siècles de Franc-maçonnerie d'adoption*, 57.

16. Ibid., 115–21.

invention. In his fictive correspondence between two English gentlemen, "Mylord All'Eye" and "Mylord All'Ear," the hack author and *libelliste* Pidansat de Mairobert regretted the ever-growing presence of adoption Freemasonry in the kingdom. Mylord All'Eye, an English Freemason, felt that although introducing women into the fraternity in France undoubtedly had attracted more male members, it nevertheless corrupted the organization. He dismissed adoption lodges as a continental "frivolous superficiality" and claimed that women did nothing to "contribute to the progress of assemblies. . . . This nation [France] seeks only to amuse itself rather than to establish the profound principles of one of the most beautiful human establishments."[17] Masonic pamphlets in England, the Dutch Republic, and Switzerland all echoed this concern that adoption lodges had become a "disastrous abuse" within the organization in France. And because much of this material was in French, it is quite likely that French Masons displeased with the admission of women comprised a notable portion of the intended readership.[18]

Despite protests both inside and outside France, adoption Freemasonry made gradual progress as the Old Regime drew to a close. A decade before the Revolution, Louis-Guillemain de Saint-Victor offered French brethren a standardized, comprehensive set of adoption rituals that included the three basic ranks as well as the more elaborate higher degrees. His popular collection ran into fifteen editions during the 1780s and largely superseded earlier women's rituals devised by the Comte de Clermont.[19] Saint-Victor opened his ritual conduct book by regretting Freemasonry's past reticence to acknowledge publicly and endorse women's involvement in the organization. Addressing himself to "the ladies," he hoped that his work would be sufficient proof "of our error and of your glory. [We have been] rather unfair to have believed for a long time that pleasures founded on virtue were beyond the faculties of your soul. . . . We have dared to exclude you from our assemblies. . . . Let us do away with the ridiculous sentiments that a false selfishness has given us."[20]

---

17. Pidansat de Mairobert, *L'espion anglois, ou correspondance secrète entre milord All'eye et milord All'ear* (London, 1784), 10:84.

18. See, for example, abbé Robin, *Recherches sur les initiations anciennes et modernes* (Amsterdam, 1779), 153–54; *L'anti-radoteur; Ou le petit philosophe moderne* (London, 1785), 162; *Les Francs-maçons, plaideurs* (Geneva, 1786), viii; *Lettres historiques, politiques et critiques sur les événements qui se sont passés depuis 1778 jusqu'à présent* (London, 1788), 2:82–84; *L'adepte moderne; Ou le vrai secret des Francs-maçons* (London, n.d.), 115.

19. The Comte de Clermont's adoption rituals may be found in *Livre contenant tous les grades de la véritable maçonnerie . . . de l'année maçonnique 5763* [1763], BN FM⁴79, fols. 122v–140r.

20. Louis-Guillemain de Saint-Victor, *La vraie maçonnerie d'adoption* (London, 1779), v–vi.

Female Masons took a particularly active role in charity efforts in lodges. In 1778, the Candeur adoption lodge in Paris raised funds for poor relief and sponsored an essay contest on how to reform foundling hospitals, a dangerous and underfunded institution in eighteenth-century France.[21] Adoption lodge meetings also functioned as spaces where men and women partook in more mundane acts of sociability that enhanced the purely social and convivial character of Freemasonry; eyewitness accounts indicated that dancing, along with theater, drinking, and dining all highlighted the adoption experience.[22] Although we will draw attention to the differences between women's and men's rituals shortly, adoption rituals too served to connect adoption lodge members through a ritual friendship similar to that experienced in male practice. Janet Burke has shown that, similar to the men's initiation process examined in the previous chapter, the adoption rituals unquestionably were "designed to heighten dramatically the sense of friendship" between the female initiate and lodge members.[23]

As in the male lodges, symbolism from the Old and New Testament permeated all grades, and both men and women's Masonry shared the underlying Christian message that through charity and fellowship Masons could create a terrestrial Garden of Eden free of self-love and the passions. This idea was reinforced in rituals where the candidate played the role of Eve and promised to avoid vice and licentiousness in both her masonic and profane life. Such imagery had special resonance for women in the French Enlightenment, as their education—whether through a convent, at home, or in the secular *pensions* that were emerging in cities—was often imbued with traditional Christian morality.[24] Like the men examined in this study, not only did women take pleasure and find meaning in the formal rituals of Freemasonry, but they also continued their friendships beyond the lodge either through correspondence, masonic banquets, or meals at private homes.[25]

---

21. *Esquisse des travaux d'adoption, dirigés par les officiers de la loge de la Candeur . . .* (Paris, 1778), 41. Cited in Burke and Jacob, "French Freemasonry," 543.

22. In a late January 1775 entry in his private diary, Marie-Daniel Bourrée de Corberon described the adoption lodge he had attended that day: "We held an adoption lodge and we danced. There were quite a number of pretty ladies. . . . I danced with the little Josuel. . . . In bringing her home, she tenderly squeezed my hand several times." Cited in Pierre-Yves Beaurepaire, *L'espace des Francs-maçons: Une sociabilité européenne au XVIIIe siècle* (Rennes: Presses Universitaires de Rennes, 2003), 72.

23. Janet Burke, "Freemasonry, Friendship and Noblewomen: The Role of the Secret Society in Bringing Enlightenment Thought to Pre-revolutionary Women Elites," *History of European Ideas* 10 (1989): 285.

24. Martine Sonnet, *L'Education des filles au temps des Lumières* (Paris: Cerf, 1987).

25. Burke, "Freemasonry, Friendship and Noblewomen," 287–88.

By the end of the century, then, adoption lodges were a critical element of Enlightenment Freemasonry and were much more than "a supplemental and passing ornament of men's Masonry," as Pierre Chevallier has suggested.[26] Although surviving documents indicate the existence of fifty to sixty adoption lodges, the actual number was likely much higher since brethren were negligent in recording adoption activity. In any case, by the 1770s, adoption lodges were widespread enough that the Grand Orient officially sanctioned women's involvement in the organization, and guidebooks providing examples of adoption rituals and sample lodge speeches had begun to appear. By the prerevolutionary era, outsiders no longer spoke of Freemasonry as an exclusively male organization, but as one in which women played a major role.[27]

☙ Friendship and the Specter of Sodomy

Why did male Masons in France decide to integrate women into their organization? As we noted at the beginning of this chapter, such a question has particular salience for the brotherhood because its brand of male friendship was predicated on the absence of women, who were thought to introduce sexual rivalry. Even Masons whose lodges held frequent adoption assemblies warned that women could be detrimental to male friendship. The Neuf Soeurs lodge, for example, was well known for its adoption activities and yet its founder, astronomer Jérôme de Lalande, advised against integrating women into Masonry in his *Abrégé de l'histoire de la Franche-maçonnerie* (1779). His text included poems that reiterated the message that mixed-gender settings would put strain on friendly relations between Masons who unquestionably would be more interested in appealing to women than to their brethren.[28]

Perhaps this fear of women had some justification in reality, as lodges sometimes ran into trouble when they introduced adoption meetings. Tension

---

26. Pierre Chevallier, *Histoire de la Franc-maçonnerie française. La Maçonnerie: École de l'égalité, 1725–1799* (Paris: Fayard, 1974), 208.

27. Reports in the *Correspondance secrète*, for example, made frequent reference to women involved in Freemasonry. *Correspondance secrète, politique & littéraire, ou mémoires pour servir à l'histoire des cours, des sociétés & de la littérature en France, depuis la mort de Louis XV . . .* (London, 1787–90), 8:66, 342; 10:391; 13:151, 413; 17:401. See also *Lettres historiques, politiques et critiques, sur les événements, qui se sont passés depuis 1778 jusqu'à présent . . .* (London, 1788), 2:82–84.

28. Jérôme de Lalande, *Abrégé de l'histoire de la Franche-maçonnerie . . .* (Lausanne, 1779), 98.

could also arise, for instance, when brethren abused the adoption setting as an opportunity for seduction that was nearly always unwelcome. Following a typical adoption lodge in November 1786, male and female members of Amis Intimes in Paris sat down to a banquet to welcome new initiates. Like any masonic meal, it was an occasion for sociability, food, and of course plentiful consumption of wine. Over the course of the evening one member, parlementaire Louis Duverger, became so drunk that he completely "forgot himself," according to the lodge secretary's report. At some point, Duverger leaned over to a young woman seated beside him and made some type of obscene remark that "scandalized" other men nearby and so embarrassed the woman in question that the lodge secretary informed the Grand Orient that she "did not dare raise her eyes for the rest of the banquet." This episode brought Duverger into conflict with the lodge master, which eventually led to his expulsion.[29] In a subsequent chapter, we will examine other ways that adoption could split apart lodges, either because a contingent of members did not approve of this practice or because some men held private male-female gatherings to which not all brethren were invited.

Because Masons understood that integrating women into Enlightenment Freemasonry was not an unproblematic process, it is therefore important to try to identify the motivations behind this development. French Masons themselves put forth three straightforward reasons why they chose to include women. First, some proponents cited boredom (*ennui*) as the impetus behind adoption lodges, as one indicated: "We have dared to exclude you from our assemblies but . . . the isolation and boredom that your absence has made us experience . . . has convinced us that . . . we cannot separate ourselves from you."[30] Second, ill-defined French "gallantry" towards the opposite sex was a second reason why men thought adoption lodges were particularly visible in France. With some regret, one observer of the order noted that "the practice to admit women into some of its assemblies will perhaps one day lead to the decadence of Masonry in France. Little by little, French gallantry accustoms Masons to deviate from the rigorous laws of their order. Too preoccupied by entertaining this sex with brilliant ceremonies, they will lose sight of their true purpose."[31]

But the insatiable curiosity of spouses or female acquaintances was the third and most common reason Masons offered as to why they welcomed

---

29. Dossier of Amis Intimes (Paris), BN FM²43, fol. 58v.

30. Saint-Victor, *Vraie maçonnerie d'adoption*, v–vi.

31. Robin, *Recherches sur les initiations anciennes et modernes*, 151.

women into adoption. Nearly every apologia or masonic exposure that made mention of adoption lodges incorporated the figure of the curious spouse or lover.[32] Masons unflatteringly compared these women to the biblical figure of Delilah and themselves as modern-day Samsons who were coaxed into revealing the secrets of the Craft. The major plotline in narratives like *La Franc-Maçonne* (1744) involved brethren valiantly resisting the demands of their wives or lovers to know more about Freemasonry, only eventually to cede to their demands. In the opening lines of one text, the narrator regrettably conceded defeat to *les belles*: "The perseverance of beautiful women has finally defeated the formidable masonic oath. Up until this point I have been powerful Samson; but today . . . I have been vanquished by the young Delilah."[33] An orator of the Réunion des Étrangers lodge in Paris defined adoption Freemasonry as the feminine "enjoyment of satisfied curiosity."[34] Even in the course of adoption rituals, the lodge master warned that although curiosity had allowed them access into the fraternity, they must seek to suppress this natural penchant in the future: "Curiosity is a vice that can cause us the greatest unhappiness."[35] This perceived female inquisitiveness undoubtedly stemmed from the fact that all-male Masonry constituted a clear departure from aristocratic sociability in early modern France. Since at least the seventeenth century, the social world of *le monde* was defined as a space of feminine participation in which women, especially as a salon *maîtresse de maison*, organized social gatherings of the elite. Women also were involved in mixed-membership voluntary organizations like the *Ordre de la Félicité*, founded in the early 1740s. As a riposte to the masonic deviation from these conventional patterns of leisure, some women in Paris even threatened in the 1730s to form their own private "lodge" from which men would be categorically excluded.[36]

Historians have generally accepted at face value these interpretations and simply reiterated or expanded on them in their own work. Although writing two hundred years later, Pierre Chevallier echoed the Enlighten-

---

32. Over half the documents in Coutura's *Le parfait maçon* anthology mention this theme, as does Pierre Clément's 1744 play, *Les Fri-maçons*.

33. "Le secret des francs-maçons, entièrement découvert à une jeune dame," in Coutura, *Parfait maçon*, 131.

34. *Planche à tracer de la cérémonie de l'inauguration de la r.l. de St. Jean . . . sous le titre distinctif de la Réunion des Étrangers* (Philadelphia [likely Paris], 5785 [1785]), Baylot BN FM²177, fol. 34r.

35. BN FM⁴149, fol. 188r. See also BN FM⁴151, fol. 57v.

36. The 1737 gazette report on this supposed all-female lodge is cited in Georges Luquet, *La Franc-maçonnerie et l'état en France au XVIIIe siècle* (Paris: Jean Vitiano, 1963), 194. On the *Ordre de la Félicité* and similar organizations in the Old Regime, see Snoek, *Initiating Women*, 14–17.

ment trope of the woman as a creature of passion when he described the eighteenth-century feminine public as "burning with envy to access the pleasures and joys of the fraternity" and forcing brethren to "find a means to satisfy the fair sex."[37] Alec Mellor has identified the French propensity toward "gallantry" as a way of understanding why adoption assemblies occurred most prominently in France.[38] A major methodological problem with these historians is that their views are solely framed by perspectives from the past. Historical explanation undoubtedly must accommodate contemporary views, but it should not limit itself to them since these views do not preclude looking at the past in other ways as well. A comprehensive understanding of the adoption lodge phenomenon therefore must accommodate masonic visions of reality but surely must also examine other causal factors that eighteenth-century brethren may not have emphasized as strongly.

One useful way to understand why women were integrated into the fraternity in France is to remove them temporarily from the equation. How was Freemasonry viewed in the early eighteenth century when it was considered an exclusively male organization? Unlike the revolutionary criticism of abbé Barruel and others that centered on the idea of the Craft as a politically dangerous organization, attacks before 1750 tended to focus on the moral depravity of Masons.[39] The accusation of sodomy in particular appeared frequently in early masonic exposures. Randolph Trumbach has argued that the eighteenth century underwent a veritable "gender revolution" that profoundly transformed the relations between men and women and the normative sexual practices of each gender. One salient feature of this transformation was the emergence of the male sodomite as a third gender distinct from men and women. Trumbach argues that pre-1700 norms of masculinity were more tolerant toward physical intimacy with men. Most European adult men of the early modern period, he contends, could have sexual relations with

---

37. Pierre Chevallier, *Histoire de Saint-Jean d'Ecosse du Contrat Social, mère loge écossaise de France à l'orient de Paris, 1776–1791* (Montmorency: Ivoire-Clair, 2002), 243. On the Enlightenment view of women, see Paul Hoffmann, *La Femme dans la pensée des Lumières* (Paris: Éditions Ophrys, 1977).

38. Alec Mellor, *La vie quotidienne de la Franc-maçonnerie française du XVIIIᵉ siècle à nos jours* (Paris: Hachette Littérature, 1973), 175; and Mellor, *Les grands problèmes de la Franc-maçonnerie aujourd'hui* (Paris: Belfond, 1976), 109. Dena Goodman has also drawn from eighteenth-century interpretations in explaining the adoption lodge, seeing it as a result of the moment when "men seemed to become bored with their company." Dena Goodman, *The Republic of Letters: A Cultural History of the French Enlightenment* (Ithaca, NY: Cornell University Press, 1994), 253–54.

39. John Roberts, *The Mythology of the Secret Societies* (New York: Charles Scribner's Sons, 1972), 60; Jacques Lemaire, *Les origines françaises de l'antimaçonnisme (1744–1797)* (Brussels: Éditions de l'université de Bruxelles, 1985), 37–56.

other men, beginning in adolescence and continuing well into adulthood and even into married life without violating the norms of manhood. By the opening decades of the eighteenth century, however, sexual acts between men increasingly were viewed as incompatible with the prevalent cultural model of masculinity. By 1750, a man was expected to engage exclusively in sex with women, and sodomy was relegated to the marginal figure of the exclusively homosexual sodomite. Although some isolated figures did publically defend same-sex relations between men, the eighteenth century overwhelmingly saw the establishment of the paradigm of what Gregory Herek calls "heterosexual masculinity" that in many ways still endures today.[40]

Trumbach focuses exclusively on London and does not convincingly explain what factors may have facilitated this important shift in definitions of early modern manhood, but his interpretation has merit in that it identifies the increased public concern, policing, and imprisonment of sodomites in the eighteenth century. Police in Paris hired young male agents known as *mouches* (flies) to roam the public gardens and stroll along the banks of the Seine in the effort to identify sodomites for arrest.[41] The anxiety over sodomy colored behavioral expectations between men, notably in the domain of male friendship. Enlightenment authors found it at times difficult to dissociate friendship from homoerotic relations. Notable literary works such as Prévost's *Manon Lescaut* (1731) as well as morality tales such as Marmontel's "L'Amitié à l'épreuve" (1765) and Saint-Lambert's "Les Deux Amis, conte Iroquois" (1770) contained male friendships that blurred the distinction between asexual sentimental attachment and erotic desire. In his article on friendship in the *Dictionnaire philosophique*, Voltaire also stressed that friendship too frequently has been confused with erotic relations, and that even in past societies like ancient Greece where sodomy had been an accepted practice, it was not central to amicable relations.[42]

---

40. Randolph Trumbach, *Sex and the Gender Revolution*, vol. 1: *Heterosexuality and the Third Gender in Enlightenment London* (Chicago: University of Chicago Press, 1998), 3–22; Gregory Herek, "On Heterosexual Masculinity: Some Psychical Consequences of The Social Construction of Gender and Sexuality," in *Changing Men: New Directions in Research on Men and Masculinity*, ed. Michael Kimmel (Newbury Park, CA: Sage Publications, 1987), 68–82. On the few defenders of male homosexuality in the eighteenth century, see Faramerz Dabhoiwala, *The Origins of Sex: A History of the First Sexual Revolution* (New York: Oxford University Press, 2012), 128–40.

41. It has been estimated that somewhere between 20,000 and 40,000 sodomites lived in eighteenth-century Paris in Maurice Lever, *Les bûchers de Sodome: Histoire des "infâmes"* (Paris: Fayard, 1985), 249–50.

42. François-Marie Arouet de Voltaire, *Dictionnaire philosophique, portatif* (Geneva, 1764), 15. On the overlapping of male homosocial and homosexual relations in the Enlightenment more generally, see Edward Joe Johnson, *Once There Were Two True Friends: Idealized Male Friendship in French Narrative from the Middle Ages through the Enlightenment* (Birmingham, AL: Summa Publications, 2003), 183–

It was this backdrop of anxiety over male homosocial bonds that made it difficult for early Freemasonry to distinguish its asexual friendship from homoerotic relations. In early October 1737, a Parisian gazette assumed that since the comte de Clermont had enthusiastically embraced Freemasonry, he would soon abandon all of his mistresses.[43] In April of that same year, the *commissaire au Châtelet*, Simon-Henri Dubuisson, outlined the average Parisian's public reaction to the Freemasons with his correspondent in Avignon, the marquis de Caumont. "There is no longer any gossip about anything except this coterie. Everyone wants to become a Mason," Dubuisson wrote. Once again, suspicions of sodomy abounded when he continued that "its members possess a secret forbidden to reveal; even those who had intended to reveal it chose not to do so as soon as they were initiated. This secret, true or false, is the source of scandal with women. All of them believe that the order of Freemasons comes from Sodom." Dubuisson continued to relate how some wives feared that their husbands would soon neglect their "conjugal duties" because of the "different taste that they have acquired" in lodges.[44] In an exposure tract a few years later, a woman similarly wondered why her husband had become a member of the brotherhood since she noted "the effeminate behavior of so many Freemasons."[45] Such suspicions were not limited to the capital. In late September 1737, a newspaper report shockingly reported that men stripped completely naked during the initiation ceremony in a Lunéville lodge. The founding of the Prudence lodge in 1753 in Angers immediately attracted concern on behalf of the public, especially the clergy. The following year, the chapter of Saint-Maurice forbade any masonic meetings to be held on properties owned by the diocese. They feared that lodges, comprising men only, easily could give rise to the gratification of what they euphemistically called the "unnatural passions."[46]

245; Eve Kosofsky Sedgwick, *Between Men: English Literature and Male Homosocial Desire* (New York: Columbia University Press, 1985), 67–82; Robert Tobin, *Warm Brothers: Queer Theory and the Age of Goethe* (Philadelphia: University of Pennsylvania Press, 2000), 35–39.

43. Cited in Luquet, *La Franc-maçonnerie et l'état*, 197.

44. Albert Rouxel, ed., *Mémoires secrets du XVIIIᵉ siècle: Lettres du commissaire Dubuisson au marquis de Caumont, 1735–1741* (Paris, 1882), 352–53.

45. "La Franc-maçonne ou révélation des mystères des francs-maçons," (1744) in Coutura, *Parfait maçon*, 143.

46. The Lunéville report is cited in Pierre Chevallier, *Les ducs sous l'acacia ou les premiers pas de la Franc-maçonnerie française, 1725–43* (Paris: Vrin, 1964), 163. On Freemasonry in Angers, see John McManners, *French Ecclesiastical Society under the Ancien Régime: A Study of Angers in the Eighteenth Century* (Manchester, UK: Manchester University Press, 1960), 40.

The ambiguity inherent in male friendship was undoubtedly compounded by the fact that known sodomites were also prominent members and apologists of the order during its early years. Minor writer and journalist abbé Pierre Desfontaines published a defense of Freemasonry in 1744, *Lettre de l'abbé DF*** à Madame la marquise de ***, in response to blanket accusations against the Craft for questionable morals. In this short pamphlet, Desfontaines tried to convince readers that Masons did not admit into their fold those who were "impious" or "foolish children of libertinage." He sought to assure the public that brethren conducted themselves in a morally upright manner and simply enjoyed one another's company: "We are all friends," he declared innocently.[47] However, the abbé would have likely found a good number of skeptics among his readership as his name and moral character already had been well established in the eyes of the public by this time. During 1724 and 1725, Desfontaines had been arrested on more than one occasion for having attracted young boys to his Parisian residence for coerced sex. In early 1725, he was imprisoned and was to be burnt at the stake. The young Voltaire, prefiguring his role in the Calas affair some forty years later, embarked on a vocal campaign in print and in person to defend Desfontaines, who he considered a fellow *homme de lettres* in danger. These efforts were successful, securing the abbé's release a few months later. However, Desfontaines's later literary adversaries—including Voltaire himself—would remind him of these accusations, which plagued him for the remainder of his life.[48]

Police reports as well as the public at large pointed a damning finger at French Masons for harboring or encouraging sodomites like Desfontaines. Besides *sodomie*, Enlightenment France possessed a rich, albeit pejorative, vocabulary to describe male-male sexual encounters, all of which could be found in discussions on Freemasonry: *amour socratique*, *crime infâme*, *vice odieux*, *crime abominable*, *crime contre les bonnes moeurs*, and so forth.[49] One satire described how Masons, in preferring young men to women, were keepers of the "Socratic faith" much to the dismay of their spouses, and another lamented that surely brethren were condemned to eternal hellfire

---

47. Pierre-François Guyot Desfontaines, *Lettre de M. l'abbé DF*** à Madame la marquise de *** contenant le véritable secret des Francs-maçons* (Anvers, 1744), 17–18.

48. Lever, *Les bûchers de Sodome*, 288–90.

49. Ibid., 239–40; and Luquet, *La Franc-maçonnerie et l'état*, 196. It is worth noting that authorities rarely used the term *sodomie* when arresting sodomites. Officials instead referred to suspects in police reports as having the *goût de l'infamie*, having committed a *crime d'infamie*, or having perpetrated *infâmes*. See, for example, BN AB MS 10259 (1741–1748).

for their deviancy.[50] Yet other accusations from this early period were more graphic in their descriptions of masonic physical intimacy. One particularly scurrilous attack against the order suggested that lodges forced candidates to remove their trousers for initiation in order to receive a hot iron brand on their buttocks. It was reported that meetings were punctuated by group flagellation, and each crack of the whip, it was claimed, further transformed men into sodomites. On every shelf of the lodge could be found the "play of Sodom," and meetings concluded in the "tickling joy" of anal sex. In another fictitious revelation, a female vendor at Les Halles accused brethren of being "crazies" whose "little secret" was to "show the ass" in lodge. And when Masons were rounded up in Paris, similar themes arose in official correspondence between agents and the *lieutenant-général de police*.[51]

Why did the forces of order in Paris so closely associate the Freemason with the sodomite? Besides the public's penchant to blur, as we have seen, the lines between homosocial and homoerotic relations, there were a number of striking parallels between masonic social spaces and the associational life of sodomites that would have been apparent to police raiding early lodges. First, Freemasons and sodomites shared a basic temporal and spatial proximity: their meetings often occurred after dark in order to conceal their activities; they frequently took place in cabarets where wine was easily procured; and the urban core of Paris was a locale of choice for both groups. During a police interrogation in early 1744, one Mason admitted to having attended a lodge somewhere within the Hôtel de Soissons; a sodomite was apprehended in precisely the same location just a few years later.[52] Second, when police informants observed the movements of both Masons and sodomites, they remarked that both groups possessed a rich language of signs—notably hand gestures—to identify each other.[53] This comes as little surprise since many participants in the so-called *assemblées de la manchette* and lodge meetings would not have known one another beforehand, and they also had to exercise a great deal of discretion as the authorities forbade their

---

50. Anne-Gabriel Meusnier de Querlon, *Les soupers de Daphné et les dortoirs de Lacédémone* (Paris, 1740), 41–42; *Chanson sur les Francs-maçons*, in Émile Raunié, *Recueil Clairambault-Maurepas: Chansonnier historique du XVIIIᵉ siècle* (Paris, 1879–1884), 5:175. This song was composed circa 1740.

51. *Free Masons: An Hudibrastick Poem* (London, 1723), 11–20; *Lettre de Marie Bon-bec harangère de la halle à l'auteur des 'Réflexions occasionnées par la conférence d'un Franc-maçon et d'un profane,'* 10; Jacob, *Living the Enlightenment*, 5.

52. BN AB MS 11556 (dossier Potel), fol. 298r; BN AB MS 10259, reports of 16 April 1747 and 3 October 1748.

53. BN AB MS 10259, reports of 26 April and 6 September 1748.

activities.[54] Additionally, sodomites made recourse to kinship terminology similar to that of the Masons, such as "frère" and "soeur," when describing their community.[55] This association between Freemasonry and sodomy was also likely strengthened by the fact that lodges resembled in their regulations and general structure fictitious societies devoted to male-male sex, such as the Ordre des Pédérastes, which appeared in the anonymous satirical work, *La France devenue italienne*.[56]

But what is most striking about the association between Masonry and male-male sexuality in early-eighteenth-century Paris is that we find actual sodomites deploying masonic language and motifs in their own gatherings. Master sculptor Charles Feuillon of rue Saint Claude accused two merchants of having coerced him into sexual intercourse in early 1748. He recounted to the authorities how two men—named Fauconnier and Dupuis in the police report—invited him to dine at Dupuis's residence at rue Tiquetonne in central Paris. Feuillon then recounted that, at the end of the meal, "Fauconnier closed the door of the room where they were, and then asked Feuillon if he wanted to become a Freemason." At that moment, Faucounnier and Dupuis removed their trousers, presented themselves naked to Feuillon, and said to him, "Enter into our society and let's see if you have a big one (*si vous l'avez bien gros*)." When Feuillon refused to participate, Dupuis and Fauconnier proceeded to sodomize him by force.[57]

Masons clearly recognized that outsiders suspected them of homosexuality. A 1730s apologist set out to dispel the calumny that lodge meetings were "rendezvous that horrify nature." Lodge master and known apologist Joseph Uriot decried that the order had been unjustly accused of committing "those villainous mysteries (*mystères infâmes*) whose name would dirty our lodges if it were merely pronounced." Another work of the period regretted that, despite the order's efforts to portray itself as morally upright, the exclusively masculine nature of masonic sociability made the public suspect Masonry of "all that is of the most outrageous in terms of depravation." In 1737, a doctor likewise recognized in a speech to his lodge that the public accused Freemasonry of "the blackest of calumnies," and therefore much effort was required to convince the uninitiated that brethren indeed adored

---

54. Sodomitical gatherings were never allowed, and the government issued a formal judgment banning masonic lodges from the kingdom in September 1737. BME MS 124, fols. 17r–18r.

55. Authorities remarked that the terms *frère* and *soeur* were "terms of infamy" in use amongst Parisian sodomites. BN AB MS 10259, reports of 25 June and 15 October 1748.

56. Roger de Rabutin de Bussy, *Histoire amoureuse des Gaules* (London, 1777), 5:12–19.

57. BN AB MS 10260, report of February 1749.

the "fair sex." Jean Coustos, a Parisian lodge master of the 1730s, was more forthcoming when he lamented that the Church condemned Freemasonry as "a monstrous and horrible combination of sacrileges, of sodomy and of several other abominable crimes." This situation compelled one orator to lament that French society was simply incapable of conceiving that men could be "affectionate towards one another without sin."[58]

In its early years, French Freemasonry therefore faced the formidable challenge of affirming the asexual nature of the male friendship cultivated within and beyond its lodges. How did the brotherhood address this issue and empty male socializing of its homoerotic potential? The most straight-forward way brethren went about desexualizing their relationships was by making great efforts to affirm to outsiders their heterosexuality and affection for women. Shortly after his initiation in September 1737, the Épernay wine merchant and *lieutenant-criminel* Philippe-Valentin Bertin du Rocheret composed a lengthy letter to two female correspondents in which he assured them that "the dreadful idea that one has put forth about Freemasonry concerning . . . the fair sex" is nothing more than a "miserable calumny." He further urged them to chase from their minds the "abominable thought" that Masons preferred the intimate company of men to women.[59] The earliest statutes of the order also made a visible effort to show that brethren rejected sodomy. In one set of widely circulated regulations in the 1730s, a Mason's sexual orientation was deemed so important that it immediately followed the fundamental principles of believing in God and respecting the French monarchy. Even those simply suspected of sodomy could not be considered for membership until all accusatory clouds had dissipated: "No man," indicated the third statute, "suspected of infamous and perverted vices (*vices infâmes et dénaturés*) will be admitted unless after three years, he has given resounding proof of his love for the fair sex."[60] Masonic initiation also made explicit that heterosexuality was the normative

---

58. *Relation apologique et historique de la société des Francs-maçons* (Nîmes, 1738), 44; Joseph Uriot, "Le secret des Francs-maçons mis en évidence: Seconde lettre," in Coutura, *Parfait maçon*, 84; "Apologie pour l'ordre des Francs-maçons," in Coutura, *Parfait maçon*, 113; Antoine La Barre de Beaumarchais, *Amusemens littéraires, ou correspondance politique, historique, philosophique, critique, & galante* (The Hague, 1741), 1:7–9; Jean Coustos, *Procédures curieuses de l'Inquisition de Portugal contre les Francs-maçons, pour découvrir leur secret* (The Hague, 1747), 50; "Discours abrégé sur l'origine de la maçonnerie," in Coutura, *Parfait maçon*, 177.

59. Rocheret to Mesdames de la Vieuville and d'Allée (22 September 1737). BMC MS 125, fols. 244r and 250r.

60. These statutes were published in 1738 and inserted after Ramsay's "Discours" in *Lettre philosophique par M. de V****, 62.

behavior of Masons. At the end of his induction, the new member typically received two pairs of white gloves, one of which he was to offer to the woman that he "most appreciated." This exchange formed a part of the conscious effort to shore up Masonry's heterosexual identity. "These gloves," the lodge master explained, "will make further known that we are quite removed from those sentiments that the vulgar believe we possess, and that we loyally preserve the respect and care . . . for their (the female) sex."[61]

Viewed in this context of confronting the inherent issue of sodomy in male friendship, the purpose of adoption lodges now becomes unmistakably clear. The slow yet constant integration of women into Freemasonry via adoption assemblies from the late 1730s onward was the most concerted effort on behalf of French brethren to affirm their identity as heterosexual. By inviting spouses, female love interests, or women from their extended kinship network (such as nieces) into their fold, Masons were able to display in a straightforward and visible manner their conventional social and moral character. The inversely proportional relationship between accusations of sodomy and the number of adoption lodges attests to the success of this strategy. During the second half of the century, attacks against Freemasonry were no longer preoccupied with sodomy and moral depravity, but rather shifted ground to focus on the political dangers that the Craft's growing membership posed to the strict hierarchy of Old Regime society. In the wake of the Revolution, this political variant of anti-Masonry would become the most dominant form of attack against the fraternity as conservatives— most notably the abbé Barruel—lashed out against the *philosophes* and modes of sociability like Freemasonry for having either influenced or inspired the revolutionary tumult.[62]

Brethren recognized that the adoption lodge was important in shoring up male friendship against the shadow of sodomy. In 1762, the Trinité lodge in Paris wrote to the Grand Lodge, explaining that they had decided to implement adoption in order to placate public "murmuring" about what men in the lodge were up to behind closed doors.[63] So important was the adoption lodge for the purpose of publically demonstrating heteronormativity that Masons were willing to tolerate a great deal of disorder engendered by these mixed assemblies. In 1777, the Saint Sophie lodge of Paris initiated an inter-

---

61. BN FM⁴182, fols. 6r–7r.

62. Lemaire, *Les origines françaises de l'antimaçonnisme*, 81–97.

63. Dossier of Trinité (Paris), GODF MS AR 113.1.104, fol. 1v.

nal debate on the place, utility, and future of adoption ceremonies in their establishment. The manuscript record of this discussion indicates that the lodge leadership and perhaps members of the Grand Orient administration as well were shocked to discover that some brethren in the city—it is not indicated if Saint Sophie members were among them—were using the adoption format as a venue to invite prostitutes to the lodge. "It is only too true," lamented lawyer Louis Trincano, "that under the pretext of an adoption lodge, some Masons unworthy of this name have assembled women of corrupted morals and they have committed very condemnable excesses under the auspices of our respectable mysteries." He argued, however, that although the presence of these *filles publiques* was a scandalous abuse to be eradicated swiftly, it was nevertheless essential to maintain the adoption lodge format. "Otherwise," he warned in citing well-known examples of homosexuality from classical literature, "what would become of Masonry? Could it avoid the odious reputation that the Sacred Band of Thebes had long ago in Greece; [and the] reputation that has obscured the glory of Socrates?"[64] Agreeing with Trincano, the rest of the lodge decided to leave intact the adoption format despite recent problems.

By using the figure of the woman to empty male friendship of its potential eroticism, Freemasonry reflected wider cultural trends at work during the Enlightenment. In his work on male friendship in French literature in the eighteenth century, Edward Johnson has demonstrated how authors defused the moral and sexual ambiguity of friendship between men by explicitly showing them to be within the heterosexual norm. Such a paradigm was achieved, argues Johnson, by making women a prominent object of sexual desire, demonstrated through marriage, courtship, or even episodes of rivalry between friends.[65] Likewise, Freemasons affirmed the nonsexual nature of their male bonding by using the woman—and by extension the adoption lodge—as a powerful instrument in mediating the sexual ambiguity inherent in male friendship. In this way, the presence of women in Freemasonry did not jeopardize friendship as some brethren feared but, on the contrary, reinforced its distinctiveness as a nonerotic, sentimental relationship.

---

64. Louis-Charles-Victor Trincano, "Réflexions sur les loges d'adoption," in Dossier of Sainte-Sophie (Paris), BN FM²112, fols. 17r–18v. On reports of prostitutes in adoption lodges, see Dossier of Saint Louis de la Martinique des Frères Réunis (Paris), GODF MS AR 113.1.96, fols. 24v–25r.

65. Johnson, *Once There Were Two True Friends*, 183–245. Johnson's perspective draws from Sedgwick, *Between Men*, 21–29.

↜ The Spatial Foundations of Masonic Friendship

The adoption lodge thus served a critical role in cementing male friendship by deflecting suspicions of sodomy away from Freemasonry. However, a lingering problem had yet to be addressed and resolved. Throughout the eighteenth century, Masons conceived their social space as free of women. How was it possible for brethren to continue to posit their mode of sociability as anchored in an exclusively masculine brand of friendship if adoption lodges had existed possibly as early as the 1730s? Why did Masons throughout the century speak of women as not included in the masonic lodge if they were already active participants through adoption?

Evidence suggests that Enlightenment Freemasonry held fast to a vision of exclusively masculine friendship because Masons clearly distinguished between adoption assemblies and meetings intended for men only, viewing the former primarily as an enjoyable social gathering auxiliary to what they considered "normal" lodge activity. This conscious act of spatial segregation can be perceived in all stages of planning the adoption lodge. First, adoption meetings often took place in physical settings outside the usual lodge meeting space, notably the private or public gardens dotting the capital and its environs.[66] In 1777, the Contrat Social lodge of Paris debated whether to allow another group of Masons to hold an adoption ceremony on its premises. It clearly stated that "the lodge will never lend its facilities for this type of assembly." And when it decided to organize an adoption lodge of its own two years later, it was careful to hold this event not in the lodge, but in the Vauxhall of the Saint-Germain district.[67] The pattern of holding adoption lodges in spaces physically distinct from the normal lodge location persisted into the postrevolutionary era. In March 1800, Parisian lodges Amitié and Amis Intimes held a communal adoption lodge in an unnamed public garden where banquet tables were laid out and musicians performed.[68]

When logistical or financial concerns precluded holding the adoption lodge in a different setting, great care was taken to empty the lodge space of

---

66. Gardens were associated with adoption in Dossier of Candeur (Paris), Baylot BN FM²53, fol. 17r. See also the remarks of Beaurepaire, *L'espace des Francs-maçons*, 140–41; and David Hays, "Carmontelle's Design for The Jardin de Monceau: A Freemasonic Garden in Late-eighteenth-century France," *Eighteenth-Century Studies* 32 (1999): 447–62.

67. Chevallier, *Saint-Jean d'Ecosse du Contrat Social*, 243–45.

68. BN FM²35 (5), *Echelle tracée aux travaux de l'assemblée d'adoption . . .* (Paris, 1800).

paraphernalia that conveyed symbolic import. In August 1765, the Amitié lodge of Toulouse decided to hold an adoption ceremony but only after having "removed all attributes which could divulge our mysteries."[69] A ritual instruction booklet likewise indicated that "after having removed from the masonic lodge all of its attributes, such as the square, the compass, etc., one can hold an adoption here. On the table in front of the master, there is only an angel, a spade and candles. Furthermore, the lodge must be decorated like a ballroom."[70] Writing during the Directory, counterrevolutionary Jacques-Louis de Bougrenet de la Tocnaye recalled nostalgically that adoption lodges under the Old Regime were splendid moments where "one thought only of pleasure and where the assemblies were charming balls."[71]

This masonic effort to carefully demarcate between social spaces of male socializing and those providing the opportunity for interaction between men and women is an example of what architectural historian Daphne Spain has defined as the spatial foundations of male friendship.[72] Drawing largely from nonindustrial societies of the nineteenth and twentieth centuries, she demonstrates that male friendships are solidified and confirmed when social units or voluntary organizations erect highly segregated spaces to which women do not have access. Spain offers the ceremonial hut or house as emblematic of this gender segregation. Within its walls, only men congregate and communicate specific bodies of knowledge intended solely for their gender, such as hunting and warfare techniques. It is also within the ceremonial hut that men perform group rituals that mark a boy's passage into manhood.

At the conclusion of her study, Spain speculates on the implications of her argument for Western societies and alludes to possible manifestations of spatial segregation of social space to enhance male friendship, specifically mentioning Freemasonry. Further probing the masonic response to adoption lodges indeed reveals striking parallels between Spain's ceremonial hut of nonindustrial societies and the eighteenth-century lodge. Like the tribal societies that Spain investigates, Masons reinforced spatial segregation between men and women by ensuring that the knowledge transmitted in the

---

69. Michel Taillefer, *La Franc-maçonnerie toulousaine sous l'Ancien Régime et la Révolution, 1741–1799* (Paris: E.N.S.B.-C.T.H.S., 1984), 45.

70. "Maçonnerie des femmes," BN FM⁴149, fol. 168r.

71. Jacques-Louis de Bougrenet de la Tocnaye, *Les causes de la Révolution de France et les efforts de la noblesse pour en arrêter le progrès* (Edimbourg, 1797), 36.

72. Daphne Spain, "The Spatial Foundations of Men's Friendships and Men's Power," in *Men's Friendships*, ed. Peter M. Nardi (London: Sage Publications, 1992), 59–73.

all-male lodge was not communicated to women. Historians are quite correct to note the objective structural affinities between adoption and male Masonry—for example, both ritual sets drew heavily from biblical motifs in their rituals—but it is essential not to overlook how Masons themselves understood the relationship between adoption rituals and those performed exclusively by men.[73]

Discourses, apologias, and rituals all indicate that men believed that the knowledge revealed to women in adoption rituals had little or nothing in common with what they understood to be "true" (i.e., exclusively masculine) Masonry. In the 1740s, one member dismissed adoption rituals as "pure nonsense" invented by some brethren of questionable morals.[74] The topic of adoption also arose in a widely circulated published exchange between an inquisitive outsider and a Mason later in the century. Explaining the difference between Freemasonry and the Order of Mopses (a club prevalent among the nobility in Central and Western Europe), the Mason explained that this latter organization had abandoned "one of the fundamental articles" of the brotherhood, namely the exclusion of women. But the outsider quickly retorted, "I know that there are women who are Freemasons . . . this Masonry is it not, without a doubt, the same as the men's?" To this, the Mason simply replied, "There is not even a relationship between the two."[75]

In early 1784, future governor of the Danish West Indies Ernst Frederik von Walterstorff delivered an address to his Parisian lodge, the Réunion des Étrangers. Here he clarified that although women were welcome in the adoption context, men must never reveal to them the symbolic content of male rituals. In his words, the adoption lodge was a means to "unite them closer to us without revealing the great secrets of Masonry." And if ever a woman were to inquire into male rituals, he offered the following advice: "Let us say to our lovely companions: our hearts are yours, we offer you the most tender of praises. But the secret of Masonry is not ours. It is of our fathers and of our children. Do not ask a secret that we cannot reveal to you." By stressing that masonic knowledge could be transmitted only through the circuit of male lineage, Walterstorff affirmed that women were inherently excluded from these secrets. Walterstorff remained convinced that no Mason would reveal the inner workings of the all-male lodge. "Who

---

73. James Smith-Allen, "Sisters of Another Sort: Freemason Women in Modern France, 1725–1940," *Journal of Modern History* 75 (2003): 805–11.

74. "La Franc-maçonne ou révélation des mystères," in Coutura, *Parfait maçon*, 144.

75. Arbas, *Considérations filosophiques*, 374, 390. In a similar vein, adoption was dismissed as "not Masonry" in *Les Francs-maçons, plaideurs*, ix.

among us, my brothers," he asked his brethren, "could be so weak-willed as to violate this seal of tenderness, this seal of friendship?"[76]

The distinction between the adoption lodge and all-male meetings was not merely an imaginary one, however. It existed not only in the minds of men like Walterstorff but was also apparent at the level of actual practice in six ways. First, men were demoted in office or excluded from Freemasonry if they were found guilty of having revealed the content of male rituals or meetings to women, be they adopted or part of the wider female public. Such was the case, for example, of one former master of a lodge in Paris in the mid-1760s who was thrown out of the Freemasonry on account of the "capital offense" of performing ceremonies intended for men in front of a group of women.[77] During the same decade, a man from Mâcon in Burgundy who was a First Warden—the second-highest office in a lodge—was also expelled after the membership discovered that he had instructed two young women in the initiation, decorations, and handshakes of the Craft.[78] On a related note, brethren could also deem a lodge insufficiently discreet and abandon it if they felt that women had witnessed ceremonies solely intended for men.[79] Second, whereas masonic lodges could meet several times per month or even more than once a week, even the most active adoption groups sometimes met only a few times per year; this was the case, for instance, of the adoption assembly of the Candeur lodge in 1778.[80] Third, unlike the male initiation ceremony, the adoption ritual did not necessarily represent the establishment of a permanent ritual bond between the candidate and a specific group of individuals. A woman could in fact be "initiated" into more than one lodge in the same city within a very short time period. At some point in 1779, the daughter of an unnamed *fermier général* in Paris was received into the adoption lodges of Neuf Soeurs and then of Fidelité in short succession.[81] Fourth, Masons were not very strict in their use

---

76. "Planche à tracer de la cérémonie de l'inauguration de . . . la Réunion des Étrangers," Baylot BN FM²177, fol. 34r.

77. Dossier of Saint-François des Parfaits Amis (Paris), GODF MS AR 113.1.101, fols. 6r–8r. A similar event occurred in Paris earlier in the decade: BN FM¹111bis, fol. 2r.

78. GODF MS AR 113.1.52, fols. 10r–10v.

79. See, for example, the mass exodus reported in Dossier of Bonne Foi (Paris), GODF MS AR 113.1.75, fol. 18v.

80. Dossier of Candeur (Paris), BN FM²58bis, dossier 2.

81. Following the young woman's initiation into Neuf Soeurs, the Grand Orient received a complaint from the family from this young "Mademoiselle de Gen . . ." who, they claimed, had been inducted into the adoption lodge without her consent. The lodge questioned how troubling this

of the terms *maçonne* or *soeur*, as they often could simply apply to spouses who had never attended actual adoption ceremonies.[82]

Fifth, the relative paucity of archives, despite the fact that there were at least sixty adoption lodges in the eighteenth century, must also give reason for pause. Eighteenth-century Freemasonry drew its legitimacy from its possession of a wide variety of documents, such as constitutions, statutes and regulations, membership lists, ritual handbooks, catechisms, and so forth. Without these items, a lodge would quite simply cease to be perceived as authentically masonic. Every lodge had a secretary who minutely recorded discourses, meeting minutes, reasons for exclusion of members, and also drafted requests for rituals and masonic certificates. The lodge preserved most of this material in their own archives, and—fortunately for historians— a great deal of it also found its way to the Grand Orient's central holdings. The regrettable absence of any equivalent for adoption gatherings leads us to believe that Masons simply did not view these social gatherings as "worthy" of recording or circulating. Even within the dossiers that pertain to adoption lodge proceedings, historians are confronted with frustrating lapses of silence where discourses by women were announced but never recorded.[83]

The sixth and final important structural distinction between the adoption lodge and the regular male lodge was that the former was inextricably bound to the latter. Adoption lodges possessed no autonomy of their own and ceased to exist if the male lodge sponsoring their activities dissolved or decided to terminate adoption assemblies. Although it is true that male lodges themselves depended upon the Grand Lodge and later Grand Orient for their own legitimacy, they could and did exist outside of these constitutional frameworks. Lodges were established, for example, during the tumultuous transitory moment during the late 1760s and early 1770s when there was no clear central administrative head in Paris. The Grand Orient did not later deem these institutions as invalid, but rather recognized their existence as fact and subsequently invited them to renew their constitutions.

---

had been either for her or her family since she was again initiated into the Fidelité adoption assembly eleven days later. "Mémoire pour la loge des Neuf Soeurs," Baylot BN FM²148, fol. 39r.

82. In the 1730s and 1740s, members of Bussi-Aumont in Paris, for example, referred to each other's wives as *soeurs* although they were never involved in adoption Masonry. See BN NAF MS 15175–15176.

83. See, for example, the January 1778 meeting of Candeur. Dossier of Candeur (Paris), BN FM²58ᵇⁱˢ, dossier 2, fol. 40v.

So strong was the need to spatially segregate male lodges from adoption assemblies that even among brethren who were well known for their adoption activity, great care was taken not to confuse regular meetings with mixed-gender gatherings. One-time master of the Neuf Soeurs lodge, Jérôme de Lalande, affirmed in his writings that the adoption format bore no resemblance to male Masonry. "One has . . . for some time initiated through adoption women into the mysteries of Freemasonry. These mysteries, however, are not the same as the men's."[84] It was not uncommon for lodges like Neuf Soeurs to hold activities where women were invited following the normal lodge meeting. Brethren clarified, however, in which social spaces women would be admitted and which were reserved for men. In August 1779, Neuf Soeurs sent out invitations announcing a poetry reading and banquet that would be held following the regular lodge meeting. Although these events were open to both men and women, the lodge secretary was careful to point out that only the male members of Neuf Soeurs would be admitted to the lodge.[85] It is quite possible that this particular lodge was acutely aware of the importance of differentiating between all-male Masonry and adoption because of the difficulty it experienced in having its lodge title accepted back in 1776. The Grand Orient initially rejected the title of Neuf Soeurs on the grounds that outsiders would assume that it referred to a meeting of both men and women. Only after a lengthy back and forth, replete with an etymological history of the title, was the lodge successful in gaining its title.[86]

This did not mean, however, that women and men did not at times seek to merge adoption and all-male Masonry into one meeting. During a Saint John's Day banquet in the summer of 1776 in Paris, an unknown party proposed to "incorporate Masonry of the ladies to that of the men." The Grand Orient does not appear to have seriously considered this request, for one of its dignitaries—possibly the marquis de Belabre—composed a mocking poem entitled, "The Triumph of Friendship over Love" in which he imagined himself in a dialogue with a frustrated *soeur* who presumably was at the point of abandoning an adoption lodge. "What, are you leaving?" he began. He justified the strict separation between mixed and all-male assemblies by pointing out to her that he has discovered "true friendship" among his brethren, which has afforded him a "durable happiness" found nowhere else. If

84. Lalande, *Abrégé de l'histoire de la Franche-maçonnerie*, 47n2.

85. Barbara Oberg, ed., *The Papers of Benjamin Franklin* (New Haven: Yale University Press, 1993), 30: 237–39.

86. Dossier of Neuf Soeurs (Paris), GODF MS AR 113.1.81, fol. 14v; Charles Porset, "Pourquoi les Neuf Soeurs?" *Renaissance Traditionnelle* 131–32 (2002): 282–88.

women were allowed into all-male meetings, he feared that "the terrible arrows" of love would destroy male conviviality. In sum, he predicted for Masonry a "terrible collapse if we were to risk such a perilous undertaking."[87]

The intriguing episode of the chevalier d'Éon (figure 3.1) illustrates the importance the Grand Orient placed in keeping the all-male lodge entirely free of the feminine presence.[88] Éon served France in a variety of diplomatic posts in London during and after the Seven Years' War, and in 1768 joined the francophone lodge Immortalité de l'Ordre in London, where he proceeded quickly through the three basic degrees in Masonry and served as a Second Warden. Although historians do not know its precise origins, a rumor concerning Éon's gender had become a matter of public debate in Paris and London by 1771. Bets were placed on whether he was a man or a woman that apparently reached up to 120,000 British pounds, and he was the center of discussion in cafés and taverns as well as the subject of numerous libels and cartoons. Although this matter receded from the public eye for the next few years—likely due in part to his reception into Freemasonry, an all-male fraternity—it again became a matter of discussion in 1777 when parties who had bet that Éon was a woman began clamoring for payment. A London surgeon, William Hayes, brought the matter to trial, and was eventually successful in convincing a jury that the chevalier d'Éon was indeed a woman. By the end of the summer, Éon himself conceded that he was indeed of the female sex, began dressing as a woman, and henceforth signed all correspondence as *La Chevalière d'Éon*.

Although Éon's identity was now female from 1777 onward, this did not prevent her from trying to enter masonic lodges. Less than two years later, she tried to gain admittance into the Amis Réunis lodge in her Burgundy hometown of Tonnerre. What is striking is that the membership did admit *cette personne*—as they ambiguously called her—into their meetings despite the fact that they were fully aware of Éon's previous gender switch. Writing to the Grand Orient, the master justified this action because Éon was already fully aware of Masonry's male rituals and ceremonial due to his extended masonic career in England. The master feared that if refused admission, Éon would have otherwise proceeded to reveal the brotherhood's secrets to the public. Faced with a unique and challenging set of circumstances,

---

87. BSG, MS 1973, fols. 4r–5r.

88. Gary Kates, *Monsieur d'Éon is a Woman: A Tale of Political Intrigue and Sexual Masquerade* (New York: Basic Books, 1995). For his involvement in Freemasonry, we have relied on W. J. Chetwode Crawley, "The Chevalier d'Éon: J. W. of Lodge No. 376 Grand Lodge of England," *Ars Quatuor Coronatorum* 16 (1908): 231–51.

MADEMOISELLE de BEAUMONT, or the
CHEVALIER D'EON.
Female Minister Plenipo. Capt. of Dragoons &c.&c.

FIGURE 3.1. After her highly anticipated gender switch, d'Éon is depicted as half-man and half-woman. *Mademoiselle de Beaumont, or the Chevalier d'Éon* (1777). Engraving courtesy of the Lewis Walpole Library, Yale University.

this lodge thus demonstrated a remarkable degree of tolerance and flexibility, which the Grand Orient regrettably did not share. Earlier that year, Paris had clarified that if a woman were to be received as a Mason, either clandestinely or because she had hidden her gender by wearing men's clothing, she would be stripped of her masonic status the moment that she was recognized as a woman "because this character [of a Mason] can only be given to a man." Following this logic, the masonic leadership insisted that the Tonnerre brethren expel Éon immediately, and her name subsequently disappeared from the lodge record.[89]

As the Éon case indicates, brethren strove to include women into Freemasonry, but only when it was done through the carefully demarcated space of the adoption lodge. Men clearly understood adoption as something other than their brand of Masonry and took great care to demarcate between mixed-gender and all-male social spaces. *Maçonnes* indeed were aware that their rituals were different from the male versions, but, as Janet Burke and Margaret Jacob have shown, this did not preclude them from deriving great meaning and satisfaction from their lodge experience. This did not mean, however, that adoption served as a chance to play out a "fantasy of gender equality" as Jacob has argued, since it was rather gender difference and not equality that was the core principle guiding male Masons who took such great pains to spatially and temporally separate their lodge from adoption assemblies. James Smith-Allen is therefore quite accurate when he argues that the adoption lodge was a privileged site of "relational feminism" in which women could experience greater freedom and autonomy, but within well-defined and closely regulated gender roles.[90]

Studying the adoption lodge also makes clear that Freemasonry did not divide the world in a straightforward, Manichaean way between brethren and the non-masonic "profane" world. Clearly men did not consider adoption lodges on the same footing as all-male meetings, but initiated *maçonnes* could not be counted among the general public either, as they partook in secretive rituals to which others did not have access. Women in adoption Masonry thus inhabited an intermediate middle ground between public and private where their primary role—at least from the vantage point of men— was to publically represent the private bonds of male friendship as unambiguously nonsexual. The adoption lodge also straddled the public and private spheres in that it served as the setting of choice for brethren when they held activities that engaged French society at large, such as charity

---

89. Deliberations of the Chambre des Provinces, FM¹87bis, fol. 326r; Dossier of Amis Réunis (Tonnerre), BN FM²433, fols. 19r–20r. I am greatly indebted to James Smith-Allen for alerting me to this second source.

90. Smith-Allen, "Sisters of Another Sort," 785. He borrows the notion of relational feminism from Karen Offen, "Defining Feminism: A Comparative Historical Approach," *Signs* 14 (1988), 134–50. Dena Goodman advances a similar, though less optimistic argument in *The Republic of Letters*, 253–59. Jacob's comments on adoption offering parity between men and women can be found in *Living the Enlightenment*, 130.

efforts or general cultural events like poetry readings. Adoption Freemasonry thus illustrates effectively the ambiguous and paradoxical status of women in Enlightenment France. Experiencing "mixity without parity," as one scholar has described it, they enjoyed increased access to venues like masonic lodges that typically had been the preserve of men while nevertheless remaining the second sex.[91]

91. Dominique Godineau, "The Woman," in *Enlightenment Portraits*, ed. Michel Vovelle and trans. Lydia G. Cochrane (Chicago: University of Chicago Press, 1997), 394.

✒ CHAPTER 4

"New but True Friends"

The Friendship Network of Philippe-Valentin Bertin du Rocheret

In September 1737, Freemasonry suffered a major setback when police authorities in Paris raided a banquet on the rue de la Rapée in the Faubourg Saint-Antoine. Reinforcing the Old Regime ban on private assemblies held without the specific authorization of the monarchy, the *lieutenant-général de police* imposed a hefty one thousand *livre* fine on a wine merchant who had rented space to the Masons, and closed down his shop for six months. The brotherhood had experienced similar incidents before, but this time chief minister cardinal de Fleury issued a formal judgment against them, which forbade "any person, regardless of their order (*état*), quality or condition, to assemble or to form any type of association . . . notably that of the Freemasons."[1]

The very evening before this raid, Philippe-Valentin Bertin du Rocheret stood looking at the door of an apartment in the cloister of Saint-Nicolas-du-Louvre on the rue d'Orléans, just north of the Hôtel de Soubise. At the end of his annual summer stay in Paris, Rocheret awaited induction into one of the first masonic establishments in France, the Bussi-Aumont lodge. Less than a week later, he returned to his native Épernay in Champagne to

---

1. "Sentence de Police qui deffend toutes sortes d'Associations, & notamment celle des FREYS-MAÇONS. . . ." BME MS 124, fols. 17r–18r. This edict was dated 16 September 1737.

oversee the *vendanges* and resume his responsibilities as the town's *lieutenant-criminel*. Although he possessed little prior knowledge of Freemasonry before his initiation and had not participated in any lodge activity in Paris besides his reception, Rocheret was clearly pleased with his new affiliation. In mid-September, he told a longtime correspondent that "I have become a Freemason" and concluded a letter to another that he remained, "with the faith of a Freemason," his most humble and obedient servant.[2]

Judging from their correspondence, the Bussi-Aumont lodge clearly saw the police raid and Fleury's pronouncement as the end of their organization. In early October, one member, the chevalier de Raucourt, lamented in a letter to Épernay that "I am quite upset, my dear brother, that the first mark of my attention is limited to sending you a judgment which orders the dissolution, the discontinuity . . . [and] the separation of all the members of a group distinguished as much by its union as by its purity of morals." For Raucourt, it was clear that Bussi-Aumont would respect the official ruling. "We are now forever separated from one another," he continued, "unless we would want to directly displease the government, something no reasonable person must do." Others in the lodge apparently agreed with his reasoning: Bussi-Aumont met only three more times, definitively breaking apart by the end of 1737.[3]

The fact that this lodge had a very short institutional life span means that Rocheret's masonic community cannot be considered typical of most in the Old Regime that met in person on a weekly basis. But it is precisely this difference that makes this set of correspondence so revealing for the historian, because written documentation replaced face-to-face gatherings that would have mostly occurred without leaving a trace. Despite the demise of their lodge, these men would continue to communicate and visit with one another over the next two decades. Although separated geographically— members resided in Avignon, Épernay, Lunéville, and Paris, as well as abroad— and constrained by professional and familial obligations, these Masons maintained and developed their relationships through an active correspondence, of which hundreds of letters survive. By closely reading these

2. Bertin du Rocheret recorded the details of his initiation in his correspondence notebook, BME MS 156, fol. 21r.

3. BN NAF MS 15176, fols. 11r–11v. Letters indicate that the lodge held only three more meetings in late 1737 during which members were under constant pressure to conceal their activities. One member informed Rocheret in early December that "the persecutions which continue to overwhelm us do not allow us to have a fixed point for our assemblies and we are constantly and often obliged to change the meeting place." Ibid., fol. 29r.

documents, it is possible to gain a clearer understanding of the social dynamics at work within Freemasonry and to identify the values these men held and employed that made their relationships meaningful. Such a study thus can help us better make sense of Freemasonry because it illuminates the nature of the experiences and exchanges to which the organization gave rise. Clearly, further research into other correspondence networks—such as that of Lyonnais silk merchant Jean-Baptiste Willermoz, or of lawyer Pierre-Jacques Astruc in Montpellier—is needed to confirm whether this chapter's findings on the Rocheret community can be applied to Freemasonry in Enlightenment France more generally.

Of course, these letters do not grant the historian unfettered access to the minds of these Freemasons who lived over two hundred and fifty years ago. We cannot reconstruct the emotional life of these men as they actually lived it, since their writings were not neutral, mimetic windows onto their inner worlds. Like nearly all Old Regime epistolarians, they followed the general guidelines found in the hundreds of letter-writing manuals that inundated the literary marketplace. Understanding that these letters were cultural constructs does not mean, however, that we should understand them as empty epistolary performances devoid of emotional import. Unlike more formal bureaucratic correspondence or letters exchanged between patron and clients in the Old Regime, the familiar letters in this chapter inhabited and indeed helped construct a realm of leisure where pleasure rather than attaining favors or moving up in the social world was the ultimate rationale behind writing.[4]

It is also essential to ask the important preliminary question of whether the relationships under investigation can be considered truly "masonic" since these men devoted little space to the discussion of rituals and esoteric matters; Rocheret, for instance, had very little formal knowledge about the fraternity since his lodge institutionally dissolved shortly after his induction. We nevertheless contend that these relationships were very much masonic because it was through the initiation and lodges in Paris and Lunéville that these men first became acquainted. In addition, the very fact that these men continually referred to each other as "brother" indicates clearly that masonic identity mediated their social relations. This network thus reflected wider trends within Freemasonry in the French Enlightenment, in that esoteric doctrine *stricto sensu* did not always play a major role in bringing

---

4. A similar contrast between "formal" and "familiar" letters for women in Enlightenment France is discussed in Dena Goodman, *Becoming a Woman in the Age of Letters* (Ithaca, NY: Cornell University Press, 2009), 133–39.

together members. Banquets, balls, charity functions, drinking, letter exchange, personal visits, hypnosis *séances*, poetry readings, operetta performances, and speeches on a variety of non-esoteric topics were all commonplace in French Masonry down to the Revolution. Looking back on his time in Freemasonry in the 1780s, for instance, playwright Antoine-Vincent Arnault recounted that the lodge functioned as a "philanthropic society during its ordinary moments and became from time to time an academic society. . . . During banquets, its members, between the pear and cheese, would read plays in verse or in prose."[5] If we were to pass by all of this non-esoteric activity on the grounds that it was "not masonic," we would regrettably eliminate much of the history of Enlightenment Freemasonry, obfuscating the rich and hybrid sociability that made the fraternity so attractive for so many.

We begin with a brief biographical sketch of these men, examining in turn their frequency of writing and visits. The content and purpose of these masonic letters will then be scrutinized in greater detail, with particular emphasis on identifying the terminology and categories of thought these men used when describing themselves as "friends." We will lastly consider the extent to which these friendships were instrumental ties, examining how these men provided one another both emotional and practical support. The range of instrumentality could vary considerably, from furnishing advice on particular topics of expertise to helping another sell his wine to a wider drinking public. We even encounter one extraordinary circumstance where members placed their friendships above professional responsibilities and the law of the Old Regime.

✎ The Lodge of Bussi-Aumont

The lodge of Bussi-Aumont took form under the auspices of the duc d'Aumont in December 1735. The fifteen other members were primarily noblemen, employed either in the government or the military. From this initial group, eight continued to correspond actively with Bertin du Rocheret after the lodge's formal disappearance.[6]

---

5. Antoine-Vincent Arnault, *Souvenirs d'un sexagénaire* (Paris, 1833), 1:153–54.

6. Member biographies rely on Pierre Chevallier, *Les ducs sous l'acacia ou les premiers pas de la Franc-maçonnerie française, 1725–43* (Paris: Vrin, 1964), 64–70; Chevallier, *La première profanation du temple maçonnique ou Louis XV et la fraternité, 1737–1755* (Paris: Vrin, 1968), 34–40; Jean de Jaurgain, "Notice sur le Chevalier de Béla" in *Mémoires militaires du chevalier de Béla*, ed. E. Ducéré (Bayonne,

Philippe-Valentin Bertin du Rocheret, the recipient or composer of the majority of the letters under investigation, was born in 1693 in Épernay, a town he described in one of his manuscripts as "situated on the Marne [river] 5 *lieues* from Reims, to the west of Châlons, between two forests."[7] After having studied with the Jesuits in Reims, he set off for the capital where he completed his law training and later argued cases at the Châtelet de Paris. He then returned to his native Épernay in 1716, succeeding his father as *lieutenant-criminel*. He supplemented his income with wine production in the neighboring hillside village of Aÿ. Although his administrative responsibilities kept him in Épernay most of the year, he spent numerous summers in Paris, renting a furnished room from his cousin on the rue des Arcis, just west of the Place de Grève. In the capital, he frequently paid visit to the marquis de Souvré, whose primary residence was near Louvois, a hamlet northeast of Épernay. Rocheret and Souvré were connected not only geographically but also in their mutual participation in the local chivalric organization, the Chevaliers du Jeu de l'Arc.[8] Just as Maurice Agulhon demonstrated long ago that membership in Catholic confraternities and masonic lodges overlapped considerably in the eighteenth century, so too has Pierre-Yves Beaurepaire shown that these archery clubs bore many structural similarities to lodges and had many members in common. Additionally, Souvré was a Freemason, and although there is no solid evidence to confirm that he was in Bussi-Aumont with Bertin du Rocheret, it was through the marquis that Rocheret was first introduced to a member of this lodge, chevalier Charles-Joseph-Pierre Tanchon de Castagnet, in August 1737. A member of the prestigious military Order of Saint Louis, Castagnet was a quartermaster in the Villeroy company, and three other Bussi-Aumont members—a brother Gonor, the abbé Le Camus and the marquis de Calvières—also served under Villeroy in some capacity.[9] Calvières showed

---

1896), 7–25; Jean-Marie Mercier, *Les Francs-maçons du pape: L'Art Royal à Avignon au XVIIIe siècle* (Paris: Éditions Classiques Garnier, 2010), chap. 1; Léonce Pingaud, *Les Saulx-Tavannes: Études sur l'ancienne société française. Lettres et documents inédits* (Paris, 1876), chap. 8.

7. BME MS 191, fol. 1v.

8. A 1732 membership list of Épernay's compagnie de l'Arc lists both men. Reprinted in Léon Frémont, "Mélanges," *Revue de Champagne et de Brie* 18 (January 1885): 92.

9. Pierre-Yves Beaurepaire, *Nobles jeux de l'arc et loges maçonniques dans la France des Lumières: Enquête sur une sociabilité en mutation* (Groslay: Éditions Ivoire-Clair, 2002). In letters to others, Rocheret referred to the marquis as "frère Souvré," although they do not address one another in this manner in their own correspondence. After having learned about Freemasonry at some point in July or early August 1737, Bertin du Rocheret wrote Souvré on 20 August in Paris, requesting a meeting with Castagnet. BME MS 209, fol. 58v.

great enthusiasm for Freemasonry; he remained involved in the fraternity throughout his life and was instrumental in helping found the first lodge in Avignon in 1737. Marquis Henri de Mirebel-Tavannes (1705–1747) originated from Burgundy and also pursued a military career, first as a cavalry lieutenant in the Luynes regiment and later as captain of the duc de Bourbon guards. Little information can be found about two other Bussi-Aumont members who remained in some written contact with Rocheret, the chevalier de Raucourt and a brother de Roblastre.

Of all masonic correspondents, the most frequent correspondent was a brother formally outside of the Bussi-Aumont cadre, the chevalier de Béla. Béla first wrote to Épernay in early February 1738 through the marquis de Tavannes. Both Tavannes and Béla were residing at the Lunéville court of Stanisław Leszczyński, deposed king of Poland and duke of Lorraine. Born in 1709 in the Basque-speaking town of Mauléon in the southwest, Jean-Philippe de Béla served in the royal artillery regiment from 1727 before entering into the service of Leszczyński in Poland and later in a special guard unit at Lunéville. Béla belonged to a masonic lodge in Lunéville that took form in late 1737 whose members later wrote and visited Rocheret.[10]

This overview of the Bertin du Rocheret masonic correspondence circle reflected the predominately aristocratic profile of early-eighteenth-century French Freemasonry.[11] The majority of the group belonged to the *noblesse d'épée*: Béla, Calvières, Castagnet, Gonor, Raucourt, Roblastre, and Tavannes. Besides Roblastre and Raucourt, about which we know virtually nothing, the rest had all actively served in the king's armies. This preponderance of the military in Bussi-Aumont has led one historian to mistakenly label Bertin du Rocheret as a "French general," although his status as a legal official clearly placed him in the *noblesse de robe*.[12] The abbé Le Camus was the sole cleric in the group. These Masons also shared a similar age profile, ranging from their late twenties to early forties and nearly all of them—with the exception of Rocheret and Calvières—were unmarried at the time of their initiation. These men thus embraced Freemasonry and one another's friendships

10. A 23 September 1737 gazette noted that "the order has become very active in Lorraine." It is not clear whether the duke of Lorraine was himself a Mason. Anne Muratori-Philip, *Le roi Stanislas* (Paris: Fayard, 2000), 299–300.

11. Chevallier, *Ducs sous l'acacia*, 52, 72–76. On the *noblesse d'épée* in Freemasonry, see Pierre-Yves Beaurepaire, "Officiers 'moyens,' sociabilité et Franc-maçonnerie: Un chantier prometteur," *Histoire, Economie et Société* 23 (2004): 541–50.

12. William Weisberger, *Speculative Freemasonry and the Enlightenment: A Study of the Craft in London, Paris, Prague, and Vienna* (New York: Columbia University Press, 1993), 68.

at a similar point in their lives: they were professionally established, although most had not yet contracted conjugal responsibilities.

❧ Correspondence and Visits

Rocheret's meticulous writing habits offer a fairly comprehensive picture of his masonic letter writing, which spanned more than two decades. Although it is impossible to determine how many letters were discarded or later lost, we have available those he either carefully bound in thick leather tomes or recopied. And to the historian's delight, he also consistently maintained a detailed correspondence journal from 1724 until his death in 1761. Each entry contained Rocheret's location, the date, and correspondent, followed by a sentence or two detailing each letter's content.[13]

From this documentation, we are able to reconstruct the frequency of letter writing of Bertin du Rocheret's correspondence circle. From his initiation in September 1737 until he drafted his final masonic epistle in December 1759 (just three years before his death), at least 487 letters were exchanged between Bertin du Rocheret and his brethren. As table 4.1 indicates, the vast majority of this correspondence (96 percent) occurred between 1737 and 1751. A flurry of activity marked the beginning of this period, with 35 percent of all letters written between 1737 and 1741. In-consistency characterized the epistolary output between 1742 and 1748, when annual totals varied from thirteen to forty-five. The variability during this period was the result of the increased mobility of Béla, Calvières, Cast-agnet, Gonor, and Le Camus because of their military service in the War of the Austrian Succession (1740–1748). The final years, 1749 to 1751, repre-sented a brief resurgence of activity when Rocheret actively corresponded with a handful of Masons, especially the chevalier de Béla.

It was Béla and Rocheret who exchanged the largest group of letters— nearly 40 percent of the total. Their epistolary commerce stood out not merely for its bulk, but also for its longevity, spanning over two decades (1738–1759). These two men's writing habits mirrored the irregularity of the wider network and were inversely proportionate to Béla's professional

---

13. These journals can be found at BME MS 156 and 209. Because of his multiple administrative responsibilities and wine production in Épernay, he sent the vast majority of these letters to either colleagues or customers. Rocheret's entire letter production over these four decades is currently under analysis and will be appearing in a forthcoming study. Regarding his masonic correspon-dence, the full text remains for 170 letters, slightly over 20 percent of the estimated total.

Table 4.1   Letter Production of the Bertin du Rocheret
Masonic Correspondence Circle, 1737–1759[1]

1737–1740	146
1741–1745	132
1746–1750	161
1751–1755	41
1756–1759	7
Total	**487**

[1] Figures include letters sent directly to the correspondent and indirectly via family members.

obligations. Although they would interrupt their writing for over a year during Béla's military campaigns or travels—such as in 1742, 1753–1754 and 1758—they spent some years, especially between 1749 and 1751, writing to one another several times each month.

Bertin du Rocheret's other correspondents generally followed a slow yet steady pattern of decline in their letter writing. Although a few individuals— like Paris de la Montagne in 1737 and de Raucourt in 1739—lost enthusiasm shortly after the formal dissolution of the lodge, most Bussi-Aumont Masons broke off contact with Rocheret at some point in the mid-1740s. Consider the case of Tanchon de Castagnet, with whom Rocheret exchanged nearly 20 percent of all letters. The two had met one another before the Champenois's formal entry into Bussi-Aumont, and remained in regular communication during the first five years after the police crackdown on their lodge. By 1742, however, Castagnet's active service in the Villeroy company prevented him from continually writing, and the two slowly neglected their writing for the remainder of the decade.

Although physical separation forced these men to depend on these letters as the primary vehicle through which their amicable feelings continued to find expression, personal visits were even more valued. In his work on lodgings in eighteenth-century Paris, Daniel Roche has underscored the close association between acts of hospitality and friendship bonds in the eighteenth century. Even in a century with an increasing number of lodging houses and inns, welcoming personal friends or friends of family members into one's home continued to hold as expected practice for all segments of the population, including the urban poor.[14] For these Masons, these face-to-face

---

14. Daniel Roche, *Humeurs vagabondes: De la circulation des hommes et de l'utilité des voyages* (Paris: Fayard, 2003), chap. 8.

meetings represented a welcome temporary break in their epistolary friendships, a brief moment during which they could once again share food and
drink and enjoy each other's company. Some of these visits were entirely
spontaneous and brief, such as when the marquis de Tavannes arrived in
Épernay on 5 December 1741, traveling from Lunéville to Versailles. In a
letter to his cousin a few days later, Bertin du Rocheret recounted how the
marquis entered his house in the early morning hours and "agreeably surprised me in my bed. I calmly woke up and kept him company." Tavannes
had bid him farewell before breakfast.[15]

Other meetings were planned well in advance. These men sought to reciprocate visits, generally extending invitations in response to a previous act of
hospitality. Shortly after his first visit to Épernay in March 1738, for example,
the chevalier de Béla thanked his host for the "good food" and in turn promised Rocheret that "if you leave Épernay and come to Lunéville . . . we will
make every effort to convince you, myself in particular, of our sincere zeal.
This lodge will be entirely attentive to your happy stay in this region." Writing
to Rocheret from Versailles in mid-January 1744, Béla framed a visit to
Lunéville in more explicit bacchanalian terms: "I think I'll remain here for
five or six more days after which I'll make arrangements for the trip back to
the court of Lorraine. If your health allows you to make this voyage with
me . . . I will provide you with a good bed, a good table . . . a warm fire, young
ladies; in a word, nothing will be forgotten."[16]

Between 1737 and 1751, these Masons met with each other at least fifty-
seven times. The actual number was undoubtedly far higher since these men
did not record all their meetings in a systematic manner. This would have
been especially true during the May to August period when two or more of
them were residing in Paris for the summer. They saw each other most often
during March (nine visits), as this month marked the end of the long winter
in Champagne and Lorraine where frozen rivers and damaged roads made
travel difficult.[17] Frequent visitations continued in the months of April and
May (both seven visits), again peaking in July with nine meetings. Over half
of their meetings (thirty-four) took place in Paris. The capital occupied an
important place in the years immediately following the dissolution of the

---

15. BME MS 129, fol. 8r.

16. BN NAF MS 15176, fol. 64r (28 March 1738); BN NAF MS 15175, fol. 49r (15 January 1744).

17. This was particularly the case in 1740 and 1747, when freezing temperatures and inclement
weather completely sealed off major roads and damaged bridges. BME MS 209, fols. 74r and 108r.

Bussi-Aumont lodge: from 1737 to 1743 only seven out of thirty-six visits occurred in the provinces. These Parisian get-togethers did not tend to be lengthy, but were usually informal evening meals (*soupers*) at someone's apartment. Consumption of wine punctuated these gatherings, as the abbé Le Camus made clear in a late December 1737 letter to Épernay: "We drank more than once, brothers Gonor and Castagnet and I, to your health." The following summer, Rocheret was residing in Paris when Castagnet invited him to his residence to drink with Le Camus and Gonor. And when he received a shipment of wine from Épernay in early 1740, Castagnet thanked Rocheret from Paris and hoped to "conserve a few bottles in order to have the pleasure of drinking them with you." To ensure that wine from Épernay would always be flowing when these men gathered around a table, Castagnet even offered to transform two rooms in his building into a wine cellar.[18]

By the mid-1740s, Paris had declined as the preferred meeting place of the Bussi-Aumont Masons. Between 1744 and 1755, only 20 percent of their visits occurred there. The tendency now favored more extended stays at an individual's residence, usually in Lunéville or Épernay. Castagnet and Gonor spent two days in Épernay with Bertin du Rocheret in November 1743, and Béla remained there for nearly a fortnight in early 1749. Rocheret stayed with Castagnet at his countryside home in Senlis northeast of Paris for ten days in 1747 and remained in Lunéville for three weeks in 1745. This change in visiting patterns occurred primarily because the Bussi-Aumont Masons found less and less time to come to Paris over the course of the 1740s. In a letter to Voltaire in 1732, for example, Rocheret informed the *philosophe* that he came to Paris often and looked forward to meeting in the capital to discuss Arouet's recent history of Charles XII.[19] He spent at least every summer (May–August) in Paris during the late 1730s and early 1740s, but voyages to the capital became less frequent by the mid-1740s. According to his journal, he never again set foot in Paris after September 1747. Rocheret's age—like Béla, he suffered frequently from rheumatism and lower back pain—and professional responsibilities likely played an important role in this decreasing mobility. Such ailments were exacerbated by Rocheret's systematic distrust of doctors. "Our town," he wrote, "contains only 4,000 inhabitants and yet there are 3,999 doctors. If I dared to compose a list of all

18. BN NAF MS 15176, fol. 27r (23 December 1737), fol. 29r (12 December 1737), fol. 157r (undated), fol. 223v (22 February 1740).

19. BMC MS 125, fol. 44r (27 April 1732).

the remedies that they have put forth, I would end up with volumes thicker than the *Summa* of Saint Thomas." By 1755, his movements from Épernay had declined to the point that he decided to sell his carriage.[20]

Although visits were nearly ten times less frequent than letter writing, the pattern of masonic visits nevertheless mirrored that of their correspondence. The majority of meetings (60 percent) occurred during the period between 1737 and 1743, in the aftermath of the breakup of the Bussi-Aumont lodge. And despite two years of renewed contact (1747 and 1749), these men's interest in maintaining their masonic relationships slowly waned, and they never again met in person after 1751.

For the remainder of the chapter, we will direct our attention away from these structural aspects of masonic sociability and toward a closer reading of the letters themselves in order to understand the nature of the bond these men shared. A series of basic questions hitherto unaddressed will guide the following section. What role did the letter play in defining and maintaining these relationships? What made these Masons consider one another "friends"? What were the different affective, intellectual, and moral aspects of these friendships? Once we have formed a clear picture of the internal dynamics of friendship, we will then consider the variety of ways in which their friendships were instrumentally expressed during their lives.

☙ Friendship and Letter Writing

Private epistolary contact between brethren was essentially an informal activity that the institutions of Freemasonry did not regulate. Within the entire massive Grand Orient archive at the Bibliothèque Nationale, for example, there exists one lone model for individual letter exchange, entitled *Modèle pour écrire une lettre maçonnique,* which was composed in the 1780s.[21] This brief one-page manuscript document simply stated that when writing to another Mason, it was necessary to use the masonic calendar (which meant adding four thousand years to the Gregorian date and beginning the year in March), address him as "brother," and begin and conclude the letter with a reference to the number three because "Masons do everything in lodge and at table by this number." Beyond these general guidelines, it of-

---

20. Auguste Nicaise, *Oeuvres choisies: Mémoires et correspondance de Bertin du Rocheret* (Paris, 1865), 194.

21. BN FM⁴199, fol. 20r. The document is dated 5786 (1786).

fered no further advice about the epistle's structure, progression or expected tone of language, and it made no commentary on the purpose of the personal letter.

To uncover the objective of the Bertin du Rocheret epistolary commerce, we must therefore focus our attention on the content of the letters themselves rather than on the order's formal documents. Following the police crackdown on Parisian Masonry in September 1737, the abbé Le Camus regretted to inform Rocheret that Bussi-Aumont's formal activity must cease. However, he found some room for optimism when he declared that "if the laws of the State separate us, they cannot forbid us from loving one another (*de nous aimer*), from drinking together, and from demonstrating to all the Earth that nothing is above the knots that link us as brothers."[22] Le Camus thus hoped that the personal relationships first established in the formal cadre of the lodge somehow could continue in an informal fashion.

But what precisely was the nature of this "love" Le Camus evoked? They were not kin, and *pace* Freemasonry's detractors encountered in the last chapter, there is no evidence to suggest any sexual component to their relationships. For these men, the letter became an important space where their friendships with one another developed. In a January 1738 note, the chevalier de Raucourt agreed with Rocheret that, despite their recent persecution from authorities, they would continue to cultivate individual friendships: "M. de Calvières and M. de Gonor, whom I have just left, and all concerned brothers are in despair . . . but, like you have said . . . what consoles them is that each one of us personally has made an acquisition of a friend with whom we will continue to be linked." Rocheret also had in his possession a long poem dedicated to the order in which Masons were described as "new, but true friends."[23]

These men frequently designated one another as "friend" in their correspondence. During the first months of their epistolary commerce in the autumn of 1737, however, these men of Bussi-Aumont would also refer to one another formally as "Monsieur." But as these epistolary relationships continued, their tone gradually became more familiar. Friendship and kinship terminology could overlap in the eighteenth century, and these men employed both the language of friendship and that of fictive kinship to

---

22. BN NAF MS 15176, fol. 34r.

23. BN NAF MS 15175, fol. 42r; BME MS 124, fol. 16r.

describe their relationships with each other. By early 1738, common monikers included "dear brother," "very dear brother," "friend," "dear friend," "good friend," "kind friend," "dignified friend," and so forth.

In the case of the Béla-Rocheret dyad, which maintained itself into the 1750s, their terms of address became more expressively intimate. By the early 1740s, Béla had begun to qualify his relationship with Bertin du Rocheret as exceptionally close. In a mid–September 1743 letter, Béla declared that he was Rocheret's "most loyal and sincere friend" and referred to him in a later epistle as "the most friendly man in the world."[24] We detect that Béla's conception of his friendship with Rocheret relied on a degree of mutuality when he wrote in 1749 that he considered him as "the most privileged among all my friends, because I assume to occupy the first rank among yours." Bertin du Rocheret himself declared in a 1746 letter to Béla that he was a "dear brother that I love with all of my heart." The two also confirmed and deepened their emotional tie by adopting a playful register in their correspondence. They both gave Béla the Latin sobriquet *indomitus Cantaber* ("wild Cantabrian") and Béla jokingly called his friend a "very silly boy" (*un fort joly garçon*) when he neglected his writing.[25]

Because these men saw each other infrequently, they relied upon writing as the primary means through which they could continue to experience their friendships, and the audience of the letters could be either individual Masons or a select group. Throughout the period between 1737 and 1759, they viewed the letter as a "testimony" or "sign" of friendship and indeed saw writing as a form of dialogue—albeit an inferior one—for the amicable conversation they had first begun in Paris. Over the past several decades, literary scholars have examined in great detail the correspondence of the century's most celebrated writers and have noted how French Enlightenment authors conceived of the act of writing as analogous to speech, specifically as a form of dialogue.[26] Such a vision also found expression in the Bertin du Rocheret letters. For this reason, the idea of the letter as an ongoing conversation surfaced in their writings. In mid–November 1737, for example, Le Camus reassured his friend after a long letter that "I never tire of

---

24. BN NAF MS 15175, fol. 49r; BME MS 130, fol. 616r. Béla again employed the superlative when he described himself to Rocheret in early 1750 as his "best brother." BN NAF MS 15175, fol. 373r.

25. BN NAF MS 15175, fol. 306r; BMC MS 125, fol. 457r.

26. On the topic of the letter as conversation in the Old Regime, see Anne Vincent-Buffault, *L'exercice de l'amitié: Pour une histoire des pratiques amicales aux XVIIIe et XIXe siècles* (Paris: Seuil, 1995), 25.

conversing (*entretenir*) with a brother, not being able to assemble with him."[27] Their repeated employment of a vocabulary conveying orality—notably the verbs "entretenir," "s'entretenir avec," "parler," and "dire"—to describe epistolary activity reinforced the analogy of the letter and conversation. These Masons even transformed the written word into speech when they read their letters aloud collectively rather than silently. On more than one occasion, Béla transmitted Rocheret's news, poetry, and humor to the entire Lunéville lodge.[28] Conversely, correspondents also used the letter to convert speech into print when they passed along others' regards and best wishes.

Since their personal letters served as the primary medium through which their friendships continued to find expression, these Masons hoped that friendly feeling rather than mechanical habit would serve as the impulsion to write. Béla wrote Bertin du Rocheret in early January 1739 from Lunéville and wished him a pleasant stay in Paris. He recognized that the pleasures of the capital were likely to take up most of his time, and yet he still hoped that their sentimental bond would compel his friend to send personal news. "Will you be in Paris for a long time, my dear brother, and will you send me sometimes your news? You must do so, even if it is only to repay the sentiments which I will hold for you until the last breath." A few years later, we find Béla sending him a letter in the midst of an active military campaign in the Austrian Netherlands. Visibly lonely and tired—he had received a severe head wound only days before—he concluded his letter by urging his correspondent to let the emotions of friendship dictate his writing patterns: "Goodbye dear brother. I hope that your friendship will inspire you to sometimes send me your news and that it will always say that nobody loves you more tenderly than I." Like his fellow brethren, Rocheret too believed that sentiment should be the underlying motor of the masonic letter. When writing to the marquis de Tavannes in September 1746, he wondered if his letter would safely arrive: "I am writing you by chance at the last address you left me. I imagine that you are no longer there." However, he quickly regained confidence that despite the marquis's frequent change of residence, this letter would eventually reach its intended addressee because it was "animated by the sentiments that I have devoted to you."[29]

The Bertin du Rocheret network placed emphasis on consistency, expecting letters to be sent and replied to in a fairly regular pattern. As

27. BN NAF MS 15176, fol. 23r.

28. See, for example, BN NAF MS 15175, fols. 73v, 142r, and 306r.

29. BN NAF MS 15176, fols. 146v–147r; BME MS 131, fol. 816v; BMC MS 125, fol. 404r.

Table 4.2   Monthly Distribution of Letter Production,
1737–1759

MONTH	PERCENTAGE
January	14
February	6
March	9
April	5
May	10
June	7
July	5
August	7
September	7
October	9
November	9
December	12

table 4.2 shows, the correspondence between Rocheret and his friends followed a general chronological continuity throughout the year.

This table reveals that at no point did these Masons wholly neglect their writing. December and January were particularly active months for correspondence because these men traveled little during this time. Although Rocheret frequently went to Paris between 1737 and 1747, for example, his correspondence journal indicates that he never once ventured beyond the immediate Épernay region in December or January during this decade.[30] Conversely, the month of July saw a slowed rhythm of writing as travel to the capital or elsewhere picked up. It was indeed possible that they were visiting one another in person—July was the most active month for visits among this group—and hence could temporarily dispense with the letter as the means for maintaining their friendships.

These letter patterns reflected the emphasis these men placed on continual communication despite physical separation. Research on contemporary friendship suggests that friends generally place little obligation on each other to keep up the relationship.[31] This eighteenth-century group of Masons, on the other hand, invited each other to send along news whenever

---

30. Besides Épernay, he only traveled to the neighboring villages of Mancy and Aÿ during this time.

31. Rebecca G. Adams and Rosemary Blieszner, *Adult Friendship* (Newbury Park, CA: Sage Publications, 1992), 66–67.

possible. In early November 1737, Castagnet invited Rocheret to write him because "you will bring me great pleasure to send along your news. Please, whenever your affairs permit you . . . ." Having described recent court activity and his life at Lunéville, Béla ended a January 1740 letter with a gentle yet firm reminder for his friend to do likewise: "Goodbye, my dear brother. Give me your news a little more often." Bertin du Rocheret also shared this view that the letter functioned as a window through which these men kept one another updated on their daily life. "I will be here for a good portion of the summer," he wrote Béla in May 1747, "Write me, dear brother, during all of your free moments. Tell me about your successes, tell me every week what is going on; a word for each occasion."[32]

If an individual recognized his failure to fulfill the implied obligation of consistently writing and responding, he was usually quick to apologize and justify his behavior. When explaining why so much time had elapsed since writing, these men most often cited laziness, illness, or a simple lack of time due to professional responsibilities or the pursuit of other leisurely activities. Béla informed Rocheret in early 1739 that the "continual entertainment" at the Lunéville court had prevented him from writing, and he beseeched his friend to pardon this temporary lack of attention: "I ask from you a thousand pardons for my negligence. I am counting on your indulgence during a time which is so inconvenient for epistolary matters." One could also inform correspondents beforehand if the demands to reciprocate would not be able to be met for a time. Because of his wine production, Rocheret wrote Le Camus in late 1737 that he should "write me without hope of a reply." If much time had elapsed, this self-correction could take on a more uncomfortable tone. Responding to complaints from Épernay about neglecting his epistolary "duties" for well over a year, Castagnet displayed noticeable awkwardness when he rekindled correspondence with his friend in the mid-summer of 1745: "My rest affords me the occasion to return to my duties towards you. . . . I no longer know how to go about it. Please forgive my past wrongs."[33]

Letter writing thus signified the continuity of friendship, and to neglect correspondence could place this relationship at risk. In early December 1740, Castagnet opened his epistle by declaring to Bertin du Rocheret that not having written has made him an "unworthy" friend: "I have made myself unworthy of your friendship in my negligence to respond to your

---

32. BN NAF MS 15176, fols. 17r and 215r; BMC MS 125, fol. 418r.

33. BMC MS 125, fol. 146r; BME MS 209, fol. 60v; BME MS 132, fol. 156r.

letters." As their correspondence became more erratic over the course of the 1740s, Castagnet's reassurances of friendship became more frequent. "Never doubt my attachment for you, my dear brother and good friend, if I have not had the pleasure of responding to your previous letter," he wrote in late 1747, "You know that at Versailles our service gives us only the time to eat. . . . I am quite excusable." A few months later, in February 1748, we again find Castagnet trying to convince Rocheret that lack of writing in no way implied a waning in friendly feeling: "If I do not write you often . . . do not doubt my friendship and my attachment for you. Be persuaded that I do not forget you and that very often I think of you and that I consider you a good and dignified friend." Even Béla, who made a more consistent effort to maintain his correspondence, had to offer reassuring words on occasion. Following his lapse in communication for a few months in September 1743, he urged Rocheret to "suspend your judgment. . . . I did not respond to your first letter for many reasons." After describing in detail his numerous professional obligations at Lunéville that had prevented him from sending personal news, he closed by reaffirming to his friend that "you know that I am neither negligent nor lazy and I do not think that you doubt that I care for you deeply (*que je vous aime*)."[34]

If one did forget to answer a letter and offered no apology, correspondents would cry out in protest. Likely because of his relative isolation in Épernay and Aÿ, Rocheret especially looked forward to receiving news from his fellow brethren and voiced displeasure when they neglected putting quill pen to paper for an extended period. He complained to the Masons of Lunéville at one point that "their court is the court of silence," and his most emotional outburst came in a late July 1743 letter to Béla. Having received no mail from his friend for well over a month, he emotionally demanded to know the whereabouts of the chevalier: "What have you become, my dear and friendly brother?" he began. "What! Not even the smallest word since my letter of 2 June, not a sign of life since your departure from this town! My friendship has become alarmed." Rocheret recognized that his masonic correspondents did not always have sufficient time to compose lengthy notes, but he did not believe that this excused them from completely neglecting their epistolary responsibilities. Writing to the marquis de Tavannes in early September 1746, he informed his friend that only

---

34. BN NAF MS 15176, fol. 249r; BN NAF MS 15175, fols. 205r and 210v; BME MS 130, fols. 616r–616v.

a few lines would suffice to maintain the sentimental link between them: "If you have but a few minutes to give me . . . you will tell me all that pleases you. . . . I have been delayed to be assured of your happiness."[35]

Expectations for regular letter writing were also complicated by a host of external factors, from mail delivery to these men's unpredictable movements. With the publication of the *Almanach Royal* in 1699, the royal postal service claimed to be operating under the principles of consistency and predictability. By 1763, the post had become a big enough business to begin annual publication of its *Guide des Lettres*. The author of this guide explained to his reader that this publication was "a useful work for all those engaged in epistolary commerce" and that now "one can easily know, in whatever city one may be, the days and hours of the departure of letters and those of their arrival at their place of destination."[36] Bertin du Rocheret's experience with local carriers just a couple of decades earlier was quite different. His frustration with lost letters and misplaced packages prompted this outburst in 1744: "I am horribly unhappy with our messenger who is a careless drunk."[37] Besides such human negligence, Enlightenment France was still characterized by unsure roads and waterways, highway crime, and tampering with the post, all of which would have disrupted the flow of letters to and from Épernay. Additionally, because of the peripatetic nature of the military career, many of these Masons were in constant movement for several months of the year, also making correspondence difficult. We noted earlier that Castagnet, Le Camus, and Gonor interrupted writing at many points during the 1740s because of their active campaigning in northern France and the Austrian Netherlands. Béla's devotion to writing was also strained for similar reasons. In the course of December 1747, he covered several hundred kilometers when traveling from Paris to Auch in Gascogne where his regiment was stationed.[38] He and others plainly acknowledged the unpredictability of their movements; indeed one important function of the letter was to update Rocheret of their whereabouts. His letters also frequently missed their mark when addressed to the marquis de Calvières, who shuttled between Paris and his native Avignon. Before safely arriving in the

---

35. BME MS 209, fol. 66r; BMC MS 125, fols. 357r and 404r.

36. Cited in Dena Goodman, *The Republic of Letters: A Cultural History of the French Enlightenment* (Ithaca, NY: Cornell University Press, 1994), 140.

37. BN NAF MS 15175, fol. 9r.

38. BME MS 132, unfoliated.

marquis's hands, letters from Épernay could travel back and forth between these destinations. Writing him from Paris in late January 1746, Calvières confirmed reception of a month-old letter addressed to Avignon and regretted that his "friendly letter had twice made the trip."[39]

☙ The Meaning of Friendship

We have so far examined the importance these men placed in letter writing in maintaining their personal friendships. The time has now come to scrutinize in greater detail the content of these prized letters to assess the meaning that these Masons attributed to their friendships. Here we will examine, in turn, the importance of three recurrent elements underpinning this friendship community: perceived closeness, shared intellectual pursuits, and the ethic of *honnêteté*.

Although these men believed their voluntary ties to be distinct from the rigid demands of family life and professional obligations, they also imbued their friendships with features modern readers would find unfamiliar. They displayed, for instance, a degree of formality that contrasts sharply with modern understandings of friendship. We will recall from an earlier chapter that the masonic bond began as a formal, ritualized friendship contracted through initiation. And although the exchange of letters and personal visits between Rocheret and his masonic brethren gradually transformed these ritualized friendships into "unritualized" ones that took on a more casual and dynamic quality, traces of the initial formality endured. It was not uncommon, for example, for these men to formally declare their friendship in their letters, and they also frequently reaffirmed their alliance through the mutual pledging of eternal oaths.[40] Also noteworthy is that a certain emotional distance, compared to modern forms of address, was maintained by the avoidance of the *tu* form in correspondence. Unlike friendship today, friends in the Old Regime generally avoided *tutoiement* even with their closest companions, because they viewed it as too familiar for use with non-kin. In his 1709 manual, moralist Jean-Léonor de Grimarest categorically rejected

---

39. BME MS 133, unfoliated.

40. Some examples can be found in the following letters: BME MS 209, fol. 60v (Bertin du Rocheret to Raucourt, November 1737); BN NAF MS 15176, fol. 27r (Le Camus to Bertin du Rocheret, December 1737); BN NAF MS 15175, fols. 128r (Castagnet to Bertin du Rocheret, September 1746) and 150r (Béla to Bertin du Rocheret, October 1746).

the *tu* form as an "uncouth practice." A letter manual published at the turn of the eighteenth century offered readers dozens of examples of correspondence between friends, none of which employed the *tu*. Another conduct book that enjoyed numerous editions during the century admitted that, although a few celebrated French writers felt comfortable using *tutoiement* in their letters to each other, the *vous* form was the best practice for everyone else. One Enlightenment moralist even cautioned against such familiarity between kin: "*tutoiement* is exceptional; even amongst family one must be careful."[41] Besides his wife, Bertin du Rocheret only used the *tu* form with his sister, a cousin, and a nephew. As far as we know, the only case in French archives of friendly *tutoiement* between Freemasons in the Old Regime was a brief letter exchange between two Parisian brethren in the mid-1760s.[42]

Despite the fact that these men retained such formality in their emotional expression, the first important element anchoring their friendships was a degree of perceived emotional proximity. Bertin du Rocheret was quite familiar with the literature of Greco-Roman antiquity due to his education at the Jesuit *collège* in Reims, and he continued to read and refer to the work of Cicero and other classical authors throughout his life. He owned, for example, a French translation of Cicero's treatise on friendship and held it in high enough regard to request its return after having lent it out to a friend's son in 1736.[43] Just as Greco-Roman antiquity shaped the wider associational life of Freemasonry as examined in earlier chapters, so too was Rocheret's own understanding of his masonic friendships imbued with Ciceronian visions. On more than one occasion, for example, he echoed the classical notion of the friend as a second self, found in *De Amicitia* in which Cicero claims that "he who looks at a true friend, sees as an image of himself."[44] In a similar vein, when writing to the chevalier de Béla—who

---

41. Marie-Claire Grassi, *L'art de la lettre au temps de la* Nouvelle Héloïse *et du romantisme* (Geneva: Slatkine, 1994), 175; René Milleran, *Lettres familières, galantes, et autres, sur toutes sortes de sujets, avec leurs réponses* (Lyon, 1700), 50–240; Pierre Richelet, *Les plus belles lettres françoises sur toutes sortes de sujets, tirées des meilleurs auteurs, avec des notes* (Amsterdam, 1721), xxiv.

42. Dossier of Saint Louis de la Martinique des Frères Réunis (Paris), GODF MS AR.113.1.96, fol. 34v.

43. BME MS 209, fol. 60r. Although Cicero was the most frequently cited classical author, Rocheret did own or borrow other Greco-Roman works, notably those of Anacreon, Epicurus, Horace, Juvenal, Sappho, and Vitruvius.

44. Philippe Dubois-Goibaud, *Les livres de Cicéron de la vieillesse et de l'amitié, avec les paradoxes du même autheur* (Paris, 1708), 156. As noted in an earlier chapter, Cicero's ideas about friendship—including the notion of the friend as a "second self"—stretches back to Aristotle's *Nicomachean Ethics*, and

was also quite familiar with writers of ancient Rome as his personal library comprised primarily books in Latin rather than in French—Rocheret claimed that they shared all thoughts and feelings because their decade-old friendship implied that they were no longer two distinct individuals, but rather one interconnected being. "I am your friend only because I have always thought like you," he wrote in May 1747, "You would not know how to separate yourself from me, you think always as I do. . . . I know you in depth (à fond). I am your support."[45] These men also viewed their friendships with one another as fundamentally grounded in a perceived closeness where transparency ideally reigned, a theme moralists throughout the century—notably Rousseau—championed.[46] The marquis de Calvières, for example, expressed the idea of an unmediated connection between Masons in the course of a lengthy note to Bertin du Rocheret in mid-1741. In a rush to finish the letter because of family matters, he apologized for his sloppy handwriting but remained convinced that his friend would be able to decipher its meaning regardless: "When I am plagued by these inconveniences, my writing becomes unreadable, but Masons understand each other without having to say anything."[47]

These men believed that to maintain a rhetoric of intimacy, letters should be relatively free of formulaic language and compliments. Excusing himself for not immediately responding to Rocheret's letter in early 1749, Calvières clearly separated letters to friends from those shrouded in formality. "I assume that friendship is always a little more indulgent than the compliments of etiquette," he declared, "and that is why it is sometimes attended to a little later." Soon after a more informal tone took hold in their letters, Bertin du Rocheret and others happily left behind the tediously lengthy forms of closure so characteristic of epistolary commerce in the Old Regime.[48] When Castagnet informed his friend in Épernay that mutual acquaintances bid him "a thousand compliments," he refused to do likewise but instead

---

possibly earlier. Carolinne White, *Christian Friendship in the Fourth Century* (New York: Cambridge University Press, 2002), 18–20.

45. BMC MS 125, fol. 417r. Béla's personal library of nearly 350 works has been discussed in Michel Etcheverry, *Le chevalier de Béla dans sa retraite* (Bayonne: Darracq, 1952), 75.

46. Jean Starobinski, *Jean-Jacques Rousseau, la transparence et l'obstacle* (Paris: Plon, 1957).

47. BN NAF MS 15176, fol. 270r.

48. For an example of the detailed etiquette in eighteenth-century letter closings (which could number well over one hundred and varied according to the station of the addressee), see Jon Rudd, "A Perception of Hierarchy in Eighteenth-Century France: An Epistolary Etiquette Manual for the Controller General of Finances," *French Historical Studies* 17 (1992): 791–801.

closed his letter by simply assuring him that he was a "good brother" and "friend." Calvières also avoided excessively ornate language when bidding farewell for fear of boring his masonic correspondent. And Béla, true to his military profession, preferred metaphors of combat when describing how standard compliments were unflinchingly "cut" and "sliced" from his correspondence. By the middle of the 1740s, he was also prone to abandon even the minimum formality of signing his name at the end of his letters.[49]

Such an emphasis on open and natural communications resulted in letters of varying length and penmanship. Like Bertin du Rocheret, many of his correspondents undoubtedly acquired letter-writing proficiency during their primary education at a Jesuit *collège* through classical models such as Cicero's *Epistulae ad Familiares* and more recent conduct books like Pierre Richelet's successful *Les Plus belles lettres françoises sur toutes sortes de sujets*, which underwent seven editions between 1689 and 1747.[50] These texts instructed readers on how to compose epistles to friends, acquaintances, and family, and stressed self-consciousness about handwriting, margins, layout, and organization of prose. Most writers in the Bertin du Rocheret network, however, felt comfortable enough within their correspondence circle to compose epistles that could sometimes read as unbroken streams of consciousness that paid little or no attention to paragraph transitions, punctuation, or spelling. A correspondent nevertheless apologized if he caught himself in the act of writing a particularly incoherent letter. After detailed instructions about where to send his wine shipment in Avignon and a tangent about his father's drinking habits, Calvières apologized to Rocheret for his "verbiage," but remained convinced that "friendship excuses some things." And at the conclusion of a meandering letter in early 1746 about his recent movements, Béla playfully excused himself for his missive's length: "Do not complain my dear brother that my letter is too short, but I complain that you read it from beginning to end. Try to forget about this letter, as I will do by not signing it. [I am] convinced that you will recognize me by my drivel."[51]

Even when they felt compelled to write one another at ceremonial moments of the year, every effort was made to carefully inscribe their action as beyond the parameters of tradition or habit. Béla opened his 1739 New Year's greeting by eschewing the formulaic wishes of polite society, deriding

---

49. BN NAF MS 15175, fols. 92r, 158r, 170r, and 255r; BN NAF MS 15176, fol. 229r.

50. L. W. B. Brockliss, *Calvet's Web: Enlightenment and the Republic of Letters in Eighteenth-Century France* (New York: Oxford University Press, 2002), 97–98.

51. BN NAF MS 15176, fol. 266v; BME MS 135, unfoliated.

this practice as motivated by the self-regarding impulses of ambition: "If a Freemason were susceptible . . . of all of the ambition of a profane, I would desire for you on the occasion of this new year all that is wished by everyone else." He instead preferred to remind his friend of the symbolic content of Freemasonry they both first encountered in the apprentice ritual and the eternal bond of friendship this event established between them: "But, since such compliments are not admitted among us, I think that my duty and inclination are satisfied once I have exhorted you to never lose sight of the symbols of the compass, the square and the plumb rule, and to never forget all that you owe to your dear brothers, particularly to he who has sworn to you *ad eternum* friendship, zeal and truth in all circumstances." Rocheret likewise assured his masonic correspondents that his *bonne année* would be an antidote to the otherwise unoriginal mishmash so common to this occasion. "Do not fear any compliments," he declared to the marquis de Calvières in early January 1746, "I am too much your friend for such a vulgar ceremonial. On quite the contrary to such a foolish custom, I send you my best wishes in order to stave off, if I can, the boredom and blandness of this day."[52]

Their perceived intimate connection to each other through the letter not only meant to refuse what they understood to be more formal rhetorical strategies, but it also meant an attempt to connect the innermost element of one's friend—the heart. Although these men did not inhabit the prerevolutionary decades during which Rousseau urged his extensive reading public to follow the dictates of feeling rather than the rigidity of social etiquette, one nevertheless finds these Masons couching their friendships in the rhetoric of the heart. Such a choice of words suggests that the pre-Rousseauean discourse of sensibility Gustave Lanson identified long ago in Nivelle de la Chaussée's successful *comédie larmoyante* of the 1730s and 1740s extended well beyond the literary sphere.[53] For these Masons, the heart represented the depths of the friend, where his sincere thoughts and feelings were housed. Because membership selection and the ritual process theoretically assured that the masonic man was free of the convulsions of passion and selfishness, Bertin du Rocheret and his correspondents were able to posit the heart as the motor and anchor of their friendship. Shortly after the dissolution of Bussi-Aumont, Raucourt declared that in his Épernay brother he perceived a "well-formed heart" and for this reason could be assured of his continual correspondence. Throughout the 1740s, the vocabulary of the

52. BN NAF MS 15176, fols. 134r–134v; BMC MS 125, fol. 386r.

53. Gustave Lanson, *Nivelle de La Chaussée et la comédie larmoyante* (Paris: Hachette, 1887), 225.

heart continued to frame the way these men described their intimate connection. "Always care for me (*Aimez-moi toujours*)," Béla urged Rocheret in December 1749, "You owe me the most tender sentiments of your heart, because mine knows no other sentiments than those that I have pledged to you for life." The elemental expressions of friendship—congratulations, well-wishing and embraces—were always sent "with all of the heart," and the act of writing ideally was understood as a concrete manifestation of the friend's innermost feelings. Once their correspondence had been established for over a year, Béla hoped that his regular and familiar letters convinced Rocheret of "the movements that I feel in my heart towards you. . . . I tell you only what my heart inspires me, and by consequence, everything I write can only be good."[54]

This employment of the figurative metaphor of the heart coupled with the avoidance of overly formulaic language permitted the masonic letter to function as a privileged space through which feelings could be not only openly expressed but also activated. The sender hoped that the receiver would delight in good news and conversely express dismay toward the bad. Complaining to Bertin du Rocheret about his multiple responsibilities toward the duke of Lorraine and the French crown, Béla hoped that his friend fully empathized: "I belong to two kings, [and am] subject to many orders. . . . I don't know if you completely sense my situation. . . . If it touches you, it must move your fraternity. I am going to die of boredom here." After spending six months at Fort l'Évêque prison for assaulting a fellow officer in 1749— an episode to which we will turn our attention later in this chapter—Béla again implicitly understood that he and his friend from Épernay were bound by an unbroken emotional circuit in which feelings were equally experienced: "Yesterday evening, I left my sad sanctuary and I convey to you a joy that equals that which you will express upon reception of this news." These men emphasized that reading each other's epistles provoked a gamut of emotions, from pleasure to anger; words "penetrated" the reader. At times, writing could be so effective in triggering sentiment that it actually provoked its own destruction—the tearing up of the letter. "Oh! What a sad state for the chevalier de Béla!" exclaimed Bertin du Rocheret after learning that his correspondent wished to retire from the military because of slowness in rising through the ranks. In responding to Béla's request to conceal his career plans, he informed him that "I tore up your letter, out of indignation and fury."[55]

---

54. BN NAF MS 15176, fols. 11r and 81r; BN NAF MS 15175, fol. 352r.

55. BN NAF MS 15175, fols. 218r, 352r, and 382r; BMC MS 125, fol. 417r.

Besides conveying perceived emotional closeness through the letter, the less frequent personal visit served as an even more prized occasion during which these men could display the emotional content of their friendships. Their descriptions of past and future trips reveal a degree of informal physicality in which these men clasped one another's hands, laughed together, embraced, talked at length, dined, and, of course, drank copious amounts of wine. Trying to convince Rocheret to visit him in Lunéville, Béla assured his friend that there would be a "a good bed . . . a good table, good wine . . . and the very happy face of your host. I promise you all this."[56] Although the reference to a bed in this passage could have referred to a guestroom, it remains ambiguous. Unlike today, the eighteenth-century bedchamber was not exclusively private but was often a collective social space, and the sharing of beds between men was not uncommon.[57] Although there is no evidence indicating sexual intimacy between Béla and Bertin du Rocheret, this does not exclude the possibility of the bed affording an additional opportunity for some type of physical proximity.

Because letters could be intended to impact a wider audience beyond the receiver, friendly feeling was not necessarily directed to particular Masons, but could inclusively embrace a number of individuals. In early January 1747, for example, Béla acknowledged reception of Bertin du Rocheret's letter containing an unspecified humorous remark. He relayed to his friend that the entire Lunéville lodge was amused: "You are adorable by three times three [a common masonic expression] my dear brother. Your letter made me laugh uncontrollably [and] all present company laughed until tears came to their eyes. I am still laughing." Rocheret also used Béla to send regards to the marquis de Tavannes, whose frequent movements around Europe made direct correspondence difficult. Besides Masons, these men also used the letter to transmit sentimental greetings to and from common friends. Writing in Paris during a brief return from the battlefield in northern France in the springtime of 1743, Calvières informed Rocheret that his group of officers whom he "knew and cared for . . . have all entrusted me to thank you for remembering them." Their friendships could also be ex-

---

56. BN NAF MS 15175, fol. 150r.

57. On sleeping arrangements in early modern France, see Jean-Louis Flandrin, *Families in Former Times: Kinship, Household and Sexuality*, trans. Richard Southern (New York: Cambridge University Press, 1979), 98–102; Annik Pardailhé-Galabrun, *The Birth of Intimacy: Privacy and Domestic Life in Early Modern Paris*, trans. Jocelyn Phelps (Philadelphia: University of Pennsylvania Press, 1991), 42–66, 73–82.

tended to encompass family members and especially the spouses of Masons, generally referred to as "sisters." Castagnet mingled friendship with the conjugal unit when he wrote the following to Rocheret in September 1746: "Care for me always dear brother. I merit this because of the sentiments of friendship . . . that I have pledged to you for my entire life. I embrace you with all of my heart with no other compliments. Please send my respects to Madame . . . and receive the quite sincere assurances of friendship from my dear half. Drink to our health as we will drink to yours."[58]

A second essential element of these friendships was shared intellectual pursuits. Like citizens of the Republic of Letters or salon goers, their letters were littered with ongoing discussions about poetry, literature, drama, history, and collectibles (notably coins); likely because of their lodge's brief life span, these men apparently had little grasp of or interest in esoteric topics historians normally associate with "masonic" knowledge.[59] It is therefore not insignificant that these men openly identified themselves not only as Freemasons but also as *gens de lettres*.[60] They not only exchanged ideas about *les belles lettres*, but in fact produced writing of their own. The letter offered many of these men a creative space in which to exercise their literary and historical imagination. The quality and topics ranged widely, from Le Camus's obscene poetry about soldiers accosting young noblewomen in the dead of night to Béla's antiquarian digressions into Basque history. And although Calvières would later publish a set of fables and Béla a history of the Basque region, most of these men never intended to render public their labors.[61] Similar to the prerevolutionary writers of Grub Street, Bertin du Rocheret viewed the quest to publish and the patronage system of the Old Regime as humiliating, wherein "the greatest poet is nothing more than a toy of the great." For him, composing poetry, drama, and history was instead understood and lived as a leisure activity essentially to be enjoyed with and shared among like-minded friends. In the preface to his slim manuscript collection

---

58. BN NAF MS 15175, fols. 128r and 306r; BN NAF MS 15176, fol. 372v.

59. A certain M. de Banzy of neighboring Châlons declared that Rocheret regrettably had "no knowledge of the secrets of Freemasonry." Apparently familiar with the first three ranks and beyond, he offered to furnish his correspondent with the masonic alphabet and initiate him into the higher degrees. It is unclear if this invitation was accepted. BN NAF MS 15175, fol. 119r.

60. Raucourt, for example, described Rocheret's letters as an "ornament to the Republic of Letters" and referred to him as an *homme de lettres*. BN NAF MS 15176, fols. 13r–15r.

61. Calvières's *Recueil de fables diverses* was published posthumously in 1792 and Béla's *Histoire des Basques* in 1760.

of poetry compiled toward the end of his life, he explained that he had always sought out "the conversation and friendship of *savants* and *beaux esprits*" during his life and that it was these friends alone that he had hoped "to please with my works."[62]

Reactions to his letter writing and poetry indicated that Bertin du Rocheret's masonic correspondents appreciated his literary talents. Béla and Calvières both praised his elegant style, flatteringly comparing him to celebrated poets such as La Fontaine; the latter even requested duplicate copies of his poetry for preservation purposes. Calvières clearly recognized that their shared love of letters was an important aspect of his friendship with Rocheret: "Long live the presidents [a reference to one of his administrative positions in Épernay] who are good Masons, who compose lovely verses and good prose and who nevertheless find the time to drink and offer drink to their friends. . . . Such men are rare, but I do know one who I care for and revere." In the wake of the police crackdown on the brotherhood in late 1737, the lodge also asked Rocheret to draft an apologia of the order for the reading public, which was eventually circulated among Bussi-Aumont and Lunéville members.[63] To whittle away idle time during their military campaigning in the 1740s, Gonor, Le Camus, and Castagnet also received a *petite comédie* from Épernay for them to perform. Because masonic affiliation in this instance bound together these officers and also provided them with entertainment, Enlightenment Freemasonry could thus alleviate two of the most visible problems plaguing the Old Regime military: boredom and the erosion of collective solidarity.[64]

The openness expected of their relationships allowed these men to rely on each other to offer candid criticism of their work. Bertin du Rocheret clearly did not view these exchanges as engaging in one-upmanship, but instead simply looked to his brethren for constructive criticism, which was itself considered a testament of friendship: "I only want to hear in all frankness from my friend . . . so that he can rectify my judgment by better and more solid reasoning than my own. . . . I like the freedom of sentiments and the outpourings of the heart." It was Calvières who most often filled this capacity as friendly reviewer, offering Rocheret detailed corrections of his

---

62. BMC MS 124, fols. 5r–7r. Besides these poems, Rocheret also left behind a manuscript of the history of Épernay and an unfinished play, both of which can be found in Épernay's municipal library.

63. BME MS 133, unfoliated; BN NAF MS 15176, fols. 13r and 153r.

64. BN NAF MS 15176, fol. 326v. On the concern over interpersonal relations in the army, see Christy Pichichero, "Le Soldat Sensible: Military Psychology and Social Egalitarianism in the Enlightenment French Army," *French Historical Studies* 31 (2008): esp. 571–72.

poetry such as rewriting stanzas and suggesting word changes. Such feedback was possible, Calvières explained, only because "you have allowed me to express my sentiment." Whereas Calvières served Rocheret as a commentator, Béla depended upon the latter for assistance with historical research. The uncomfortable feeling that his work was amateurish and lacking scholarly rigor dampened Béla's appetite for history. He openly shared his doubts with Rocheret that soldiering was incompatible with intellectual pursuits. "But tell me on what grounds do I dare to speak about history," he asked him, "having my head full of cavaliers, bridles, saddles, halters . . . brushes, combs, sponges, etc.?" And despite his friend's continual insistence that he did indeed possess the requisite *esprit*, Béla never ceased to consider himself as an intellectual inferior. Their intimacy not only created the conditions possible for such frankness, but it also assured Béla that his friend would patiently read through and respond to his lengthy queries. The chevalier also relied on Rocheret to put him into epistolary contact with scholars—typically from provincial academies—who shared his interest in the Basque country.[65]

Accompanying the expressions of affection and the similarity of intellectual interests, their recognition of each other as gentlemen or men of honorable conduct—*honnêtes hommes*—represented a third key element undergirding these friendships. Raucourt defined the Bussi-Aumont lodge as a group of "*honnêtes gens*" and Rocheret described Freemasonry as a "confederation of *honnêtes gens*, distinguished in everything they do, who seek only to enjoy themselves philosophically through the commerce of pleasing sentiments, *belles lettres*, and fine arts of all types." Béla also qualified the Masons of Lunéville in a similar fashion. Thanking Rocheret in early January 1750 for having agreed to host a Lunéville Mason in Épernay, he wrote that "I am very happy that you will meet this *honnête homme* whom I care for very much." Conversely, undesirable behavior—such as lack of writing or declining invitations to visit—was frequently defined as *malhonnête*.[66]

What did the terms *honnête* and *honnêteté* signify in masonic culture according to these men? The most revealing explanation can be found in a letter Bertin du Rocheret addressed to two longtime female correspondents in late September 1737, both of whom possessed little knowledge of the

---

65. BMC MS 124, fol. 224r; BN NAF MS 15175, fol. 222r; BN NAF MS 15176, fols. 81r, 269v, and 380r; BME MS 135, unfoliated; BMC MS 125, fol. 360r.

66. BN NAF MS 15176, fol. 42r; BN NAF MS 15175, fols. 80r, 158r, and 361r; BMC MS 125, fol. 245r.

fraternity.[67] In the wake of governmental repression, Freemasonry had captured the attention of the Parisian public. With an intent similar to the printed apologias examined earlier in this study, Rocheret attempted in these letters to adequately explain—albeit without revealing its inner workings—the nature of masonic sociability to the wider public. He clearly believed that the ideas expressed in this document accurately reflected orthodox masonic belief, as he later sent copies to lodges in Paris, Lunéville, and Lyon.

For Bertin du Rocheret, masonic *honnêteté* primarily referred to the individual's ability to regulate his passions and exercise self-restraint during moments of enjoyment. This code of conduct was closely aligned with the philosophy of neo-stoicism elaborated in the writings of Renaissance humanists, notably that of Belgian Justus Lipsius. Peter Gay has drawn attention to Lipsius's enduring popularity into the eighteenth century, and Rocheret actively endorsed the neo-stoic ideal of restraint to such a degree that he advised his nephew to practice it in his daily life.[68] Describing the lodge banquet to his correspondents, he stressed that, although Masons enjoyed the pleasures of good food and drink, they were careful to avoid excesses of the table unsuitable to *honnêtes gens*. He described Masons as "happy with a fare that is refined and delicate and in accordance with the seasons," but they viewed an "excessive enthusiasm in this regard as an attention undignified of *honnêtes gens*." In his own personal reflections, Béla expressed a similar view regarding food consumption when he wrote that "frugality at the table keeps the mind and body healthy." Rocheret also made recourse to this ethic of self-control when explaining why women were unwelcome to participate in normal lodge activities.[69] Similar to Ramsay's "Discours" examined in the first chapter, Rocheret expressed concern that if allowed into masonic lodges, women would inevitably activate male passions of jealousy and rivalry, destroying the ethos of restrained sentimentalism so carefully constructed through the ritual process. He emphasized that adopting a dispassionate nature toward the world was capital for the Freemason who strove to be "truly an *honnête homme* according to God and according to society by annihilating all the tumultuous passions

---

67. BMC MS 125, fols. 244r–252r.

68. Ibid., fol. 40r. Peter Gay, *The Enlightenment: The Rise of Modern Paganism* (New York: W. W. Norton, [1966] 1995), 300–303.

69. There did exist, however, at least since the late 1730s or early 1740s "adoption lodge" assemblies in which spouses, sisters and other family members of male Masons were present. These lodges have been discussed in the previous chapter.

which are opposed to the happy security that we seek to enjoy. This is our entire philosophy."[70]

This last passage suggests that the brethren under investigation in this chapter believed that religion and the self-restraint of *honnêteté* were enmeshed to some degree. Bertin du Rocheret indeed believed that it was possible to reconcile the secular code of conduct of the *honnête homme* with the basic moral precepts he associated with Christianity. In a short manuscript treatise entitled *Sur l'honnête homme et sur l'education des enfants* (composed in 1735), he described how "one must reconcile" God and the world, and that religion served as the foundation on which *honnêteté* and all of society stood: "I am intimately persuaded that one cannot become an *honnête homme* in the world without fully recognizing the greatness of the Creator . . . and that one cannot be loyal to the duties of civil life if one is not loyal to the religion in which one was born." He stressed that the *honnête homme* did not merely believe in a Christian God, but that he also must express his religious convictions in daily life where "the most humble and the most austere virtues of Christianity can and must be practiced." He prized the transparent connection between social interaction and inner motives as the essential Christian virtue because he claimed that "God hates grimaces, affectations and mannerisms almost as much as crimes."[71] Organizations with which Rocheret had previously been associated also advocated for the marrying of *honnêteté* and Christian ethics. From the early 1720s until 1735, he was a member of the Ordre Social de l'Aimable Commerce, a literary society whose patron was the duchesse d'Orléans. In its report on this organization, the *Journal de Verdun* stated that "one perceives here a noble alliance of the Christian man with the *honnête homme*. . . . One sees here virtue displayed and religion dominant."[72]

Did the religious views of these Masons play any noticeable role in the cultivation or expression of their friendships? Before responding to this question, we must first note that the precise religious orientation of these men is difficult to ascertain because they were virtually silent on topics of religion and theology, as their correspondence was largely devoted to the

---

70. BMC MS 125, fols. 246r–49r, and 462r–63r. On Béla's neo-stoicism, see Christian Desplat, "Le chevalier de Béla: Seigneur de village et philanthrope," *Bulletin de la Société des Sciences, Lettres et Arts de Bayonne* 129 (1973): 229.

71. Nicaise, *Mémoires et correspondance*, 199.

72. Chevallier, *Première profanation du temple*, 39. Fragments of Rocheret's correspondence with other members of this society can be found in BME MS 155.

sharing of personal news and intellectual subjects. We also have no data regarding how often they attended mass or what other manifestations of orthodox Catholicism they embraced or disavowed. And yet their substantial
correspondence and complementary material do allow us to carefully advance some observations on their religious opinions and the extent to which
these sentiments shaped their friendships.

As the previous discussion suggests, Bertin du Rocheret's vision of Christianity did not necessarily correspond to orthodox Catholicism. He rarely employed the adjective "Catholic" in his writings but instead preferred the more
inclusive term "Christian." Like Ramsay and other brethren, he believed
that sectarian conflicts—both within and outside the Church—threatened
the spiritual unity by which all Christians should be bound.[73] He saw Freemasonry as a unique space in which this ecumenical Christianity could flour-
ish, and was quite aware that the chevalier de Béla was of Huguenot ancestry.
We must nevertheless be prudent not to distance these Masons too far from
the orthodox position of the Church. There is, for instance, no trace of any
aggressive anticlericalism in their letters, and Rocheret had in fact initially
considered a career in the clergy.[74]

In sum, then, the masonic friendships under investigation in this chapter
depended on three key elements. First, they relied on the letter to communicate an ethos of emotional proximity and reciprocating self-disclosure.
Masons established a familiar, informal tone in their epistolary exchange by
eschewing overly formulaic language and employed the rhetoric of the
heart to describe their affection for one another. Second, their friendships
were also sustained by ongoing conversations and exchanges on history and
poetry in a manner similar to the early modern Republic of Letters, and the
openness of their friendships allowed them to offer candid criticism of
works in progress. Finally, their friendships were enhanced by the mutual
recognition of a shared ethical framework that was characterized by an ecumenical Christian faith and the neo-stoic conduct of the *honnête homme*.
This perceived commonality undoubtedly contributed to the ethos of social

---

73. In a strongly worded letter to a theologian of the Sorbonne, for instance, he voiced opposition
to the 1713 *Bulle Unigenitus* for having generated unnecessary friction within the Church. BMC
MS 124, fol. 104r.

74. Ibid., fol. 23r. He succumbed to his father's pressure to pursue law. Referring to two writers in
early October 1749, a certain "Grassin" and "la Morlière," Rocheret wrote to Béla that they were
"reformed like you." BME MS 156, fol. 8v. It is important to note, however, that Béla's family had
formally converted to Roman Catholicism in 1679, and that the chevalier himself regretted that his
ancestors had been "infected" by the "demon of Calvinism." ADPA, MS 1 J 62/2, fol. 15v.

equality in their relationships, a feature these men often stressed as being essential to masonic friendship.[75]

Now that we have elucidated the internal nature of these friendships, we will next direct our attention outward and try to understand how these relationships played a concrete role in these men's lives. How did they interact with and compare with other social ties, such as kinship and conjugal relations? How did Masons express their friendships instrumentally through the rendering of favors and economic services? It is to these questions that we now turn.

✎ Counting on Friends

Within the lodge, brethren defined friendship not merely as an emotional bond of solidarity but also as an instrumental one. The brotherhood expected members to offer one another assistance when requested or expected, regardless of any previous personal ties—all Masons, as noted in chapter 2, were nominally considered to be "ritual friends." The masonic ideal of friendship also assumed that services would be provided without any expectation of immediate reciprocity, but that one rather gave voluntarily and trusted to receive the same treatment in return from brethren during times of need. Mutuality and reciprocity thus underpinned the instrumentality of masonic friendship.

Bertin du Rocheret and his correspondents frequently reaffirmed the instrumental aspect of their friendships. "Send me sometimes your news," Castagnet wrote in early 1740, "[and] employ me if I can be useful to you." Béla, too, expected material support to play an integral role in friendship. The chevalier highly valued his family's commonplace book, which he credited in 1741 with helping him "dissipate from my mind the immense pain and infinite labor I have suffered in my profession." Under the heading of *Amitié*, we find the laconic affirmation that "he who helps is a friend and he who only complains [on behalf of others] is not." Béla reiterated this position in his masonic letters, informing Rocheret on a number of occasions to "rest assured that there is nothing that I would not do for you." One of the more visible ways that these men rendered services for one another was

---

75. In a January 1746 letter, for example, the marquis de Calvières linked equality with masonic solidarity when he emphasized that amongst Masons "we are concerned only with preserving equality, and consequently, unity, the most desirable possession in life." BME MS 133, unfoliated.

through the purchasing of wine from Épernay. Shortly after his initiation into Bussi-Aumont, Rocheret began shipping crates of wine down the Marne River to his brethren in Paris and was also supplying the Lunéville lodge by mid-1738. Although not as long lasting, this exchange roughly followed the patterns of letter writing and visits. Wine shipments peaked in the early 1740s and then slowly declined over the following years until they finally ceased in mid-1748.[76]

Although the paucity of records does not allow a precise accounting of the amount of wine sent, Bertin du Rocheret's own comments about these transactions do allow us to safely assume that a significant portion of his total wine sales in the 1740s was derived from masonic contacts.[77] Noticeably frustrated with a Parisian buyer's complaining over price and shipping fees, he drafted a strongly worded letter where he warned that "I want absolutely no discussion" on the matter. He further downplayed the economic importance of this single transaction in relation to his overall wine trade, because "my brethren are able to sell for me more wine than I am able to procure." Masonic friendship thus ensured Bertin du Rocheret a consistent and reliable outlet for his wine for over a decade, a clear benefit for any merchant who operated in the commercial world of the Old Regime, which was fraught with broken arrangements and contracts. Friendship also ensured that the Masons of Bussi-Aumont and Lunéville would be purchasing quality wine at a fair price. For Rocheret to treat his brethren *en amy* was expected, and meant that prices were reduced whenever possible.[78]

But such economic benefits were only one aspect of the instrumentality of friendship. Emotional support during periods of difficulty or crisis was in fact the most significant way that these men utilized these relationships. Brothers Béla, Castagnet, Gonor, and Le Camus frequently expressed in their letters boredom regarding the life of an officer; the chevalier depressingly summed up military life as a state of resignation where "[You] lower

---

76. BN NAF MS 15176, fol. 223v and 383r; ADPA, MS 1 J 62/2, fols. 15v, 86v. According to his correspondence journal, his final wine delivery to a Freemason was a fifty-bottle shipment sent to a brother Behagle (an acquaintance of Castagnet) on 4 July 1748. BME MS 156, fol. 3v.

77. Any useful comparison between Rocheret's masonic and non-masonic wine sales is unfortunately not possible given that his correspondence journal rarely cites the precise quantities or sums of money involved in a given sale.

78. In a 1745 letter to Rocheret, Castagnet indicated that an unnamed Parisian Mason would like to make a wine purchase. He wrote that he was "well convinced, knowing you as I do, that you will treat this brother in the manner that is expected among us in reducing the price if it all possible." BN NAF MS 15175, fols. 88v and 193v.

the head and march forward with your eyes closed."[79] Béla's sense of frustration with his career reached a climax in April 1747, when he informed his friend of his decision to retire from the army: "I am taking leave from disappointment and I find it necessary to resign from the service." Like many officers in the eighteenth century, he clearly viewed his failure to rise through the ranks as the fault of the war ministry which, he claimed, "has inflicted on me every injustice for the past three years, having promised to promote me to Brigadier and then instead having promoted 200 others since this time, all of them less senior than myself." Béla intended this frank complaint to his friend to be strictly limited to the confines of their relationship, a point he made explicit when he reminded his friend to "please let this remain just between us."[80]

Bertin du Rocheret's response in early May illustrated precisely how masonic friendship could help these men manage and mitigate their dissatisfaction with work. He first openly acknowledged the reality of Béla's feelings and empathized that he too perceived an "injustice" in his friend's predicament. And yet, despite affirming the reality of Béla's emotions, he strongly opposed the chevalier's retirement: "I would not know how to approve dear brother whom I care for with all of my heart . . . the disastrous resolution that you appear to want to take in leaving the service. For God's sake, do not do anything. I forbid you." Echoing the ideal of aristocratic *honnêteté*, which emphasized putting the interests of the crown above personal concerns, Rocheret reminded the chevalier that, as a *noblesse d'épée*, his social status depended on his continued military service: "Your life is dedicated to the country (*patrie*) in which you were born, to the king to whom you are bound, [and] to the honor that you owe him. The source of your blood must be inexhaustible in this regard." He also attempted to reframe the situation in a more favorable light. "It is only an annoyance, a passing disappointment," he assured. Rocheret held fast to the conviction that Béla's superiors would soon recognize his personal merits and that in the meantime he should simply adopt the neo-stoic virtue of patience in the face of adversity. "Stand firm against injustice and against your enemies. You will achieve everything that you merit." In a follow-up letter, Béla thanked him for the encouraging words and declared that "I would truly be ungrateful if

---

79. BME MS 131, fol. 816r. See also the comments of Castagnet and Le Camus in BN NAF MS 15176, fols. 326r–28r.

80. BN NAF MS 15175, fols. 176r–77r. On obstacles to promotion in the eighteenth-century French army, see David Bien, "The Army in the French Enlightenment: Reform, Reaction and Revolution," *Past and Present* 85 (1979): 68–72.

I did not care for you as I must and as I will all of my life." Their friendship thus helped Béla effectively confront and diffuse the frustration associated with his profession because his masonic relationships were wholly unconnected to his work environment. Béla could express these emotions without fear of escalating tension, and Rocheret likewise could candidly offer him constructive suggestions that enabled his friend to move beyond his initial outburst. Rocheret's advice eventually proved to be correct: Béla remained in the officer corps and was appointed brigadier-general the following January.[81]

Bertin du Rocheret himself also showed signs of profound boredom in Épernay and looked to his masonic friendships to alleviate dissatisfaction. During his youth, he had studied and practiced law in Paris, where he longed to permanently reside once again. Confined to a small town on the Marne for most of the year, he felt bogged down with multiple administrative responsibilities, which he described in 1741 as "dog's work." Comparing himself to a "galley slave" and an "exile in Siberia" (a common eighteenth-century metaphor to describe the provinces), he made repeated efforts to find employment in the capital throughout the 1730s.[82] But this project never came to fruition, and he depended on masonic correspondents to maintain connection with the political and cultural world of Paris. Le Camus regularly sent him news of all sorts, such as political intrigue, general affairs of state, diplomatic visits, recently performed plays and operas, and even the weather. Early in their correspondence, he promised to report news as objectively as possible: "I simply assume the role of an echo, repeating what I have heard." Rocheret often made use of Le Camus's information to manually cross out or add information to his personal copies of the *Leiden Gazette*.[83]

Besides offsetting the tediousness of everyday life, these masonic friendships could also offer emotional support during times of crisis. It is again the Béla-Bertin du Rocheret dyad that most fully illustrates this instrumental aspect of friendship. At the conclusion of the War of the Austrian Succession in late 1748, Béla's command over the Royal-Cantabrian regiment ended

---

81. BMC MS 125, fols. 417r–19r; BN NAF MS 15175, fol. 180r; *Mémoires militaires du chevalier de Béla*, 18.

82. He unsuccessfully attempted to find work both in the Royal Library and in diplomatic posts. The following poem composed in 1735 reflected his desire to live and work in the metropolis: "Si j'étais à Paris, bien chauffé, bien logé, / Exerçant quelqu'emploi digne d'un honnête homme, / Cinq cents écus de rente, avec le bien que j'ai / Me rendraient plus heureux que le Pape de Rome." Nicaise, *Mémoires et correspondence*, 172, 211.

83. BME MS 124, fol. 19r.

and the war ministry dissolved the unit soon after. This abrupt decision provoked outcry from a number of officers, some of whom accused Béla of personally squandering the regiment's funds and printed these slanderous attacks in a *libelle* in early 1749. Upon hearing these rumors, Béla promptly left Lunéville for Paris to confront his detractors and clear his name of this calumny. His search came to an end on 17 May at ten o'clock in the morning on the rue des Vieilles Étuves in Versailles. Identifying one of the officers in question, the chevalier approached, drew his sword, and challenged the officer to a duel on the spot. When he refused, Béla motioned to strike him anyhow ("I raised my arm in order to cut his face" he recounted the following day) but was physically restrained by another officer nearby.[84]

Béla soon after found himself in front of the *tribunaux des maréchaux de France* for his assault—deemed unwarranted—and was subsequently incarcerated for six months at the Fort l'Evêque prison. During captivity, one of his rare links to the outside world was his correspondence with Bertin du Rocheret; the two men exchanged nearly thirty letters during this period. Their friendship's ethos of transparency allowed Béla to openly display the mental anxiety brought on by his imprisonment. He described how his condition was one of "sad solitude" and that his mind was constantly "overwhelmed by sad reflections." His friend attempted to ease his loneliness in a variety of ways. Rocheret invited Béla to visit Épernay in December 1749 and assured him a couple of months earlier that there remained "just a little more of a difficult time before you come and spend the holidays with me." He also ordered Béla to chase all "lugubrious ideas" from his mind and sent him a copy of Charles-Jean-François Hénault's *Nouvel abrégé chronologique de l'histoire de France* to occupy his time with reading. Béla also borrowed an unspecified amount of money during his imprisonment to help defray legal fees. Rocheret also attempted to make Béla's stay at Fort l'Evêque more pleasing by sending him at least one shipment of wine. It is important to note that no payment was expected for this transaction, as it was understood not as an economic exchange but rather as a gift of friendship: "*un pagnier de vin amy*" as Bertin du Rocheret put it.[85]

This episode also furnishes us with a concrete example of a fundamental concept of masonic ritualized friendship introduced in the previous chapter:

---

84. This entire incident was recounted in *Lettre d'un parent de M. le chevalier de Béla, Brigadier des Armées du Roi, Chambellan du Roi de Pologne, à un ami. De Paris le 9 août 1755*. BN NAF MS 29625, fols. 14r–17r. Béla reported his encounter at Versailles in an 18 May 1749 letter to Épernay. BN NAF MS 15175, fols. 290r–91v.

85. BN NAF MS 15175, fols. 315r and 334r; BME MS 156, fols. 7r–8v.

coming to a brother's aid regardless of any previous personal ties. Soon after Béla's arrest, Rocheret sought assistance from Gonor, Castagnet, and Calvières on behalf of his friend. In an 18 June 1749 letter, he asked Gonor to "go and see our illustrious and unhappy brother" in his confinement and also to inquire if the influential duc de Villeroy, the master of a Parisian lodge, could be convinced to intervene on Béla's behalf. With the exception of the marquis de Tavannes and Rocheret, Béla had neither previously met nor written to any member of Bussi-Aumont. Nevertheless, both Gonor and Calvières met with the chevalier, who especially appreciated Calvières's encouragement. "I adore this man," Béla wrote of Calvières in a letter to Rocheret, "[and] am sad that I was not able to have the time to make him affectionate towards me (*de m'aimer*)." Although he regretted not being able to cultivate a more intimate tie with the marquis before the latter's departure for Avignon, their bond of ritualized friendship established through Freemasonry was sufficiently meaningful for Calvières to visit and console him.[86]

Béla valued these relationships and contrasted them with the lack of help he received from family members during his isolation. He dismissed his brother for having taken the side of his slanderers and for having refused to correspond with him while in prison: "It appears that he is in league with my enemies to enrage me," he grumbled. His appreciation for Bertin du Rocheret was made clear by adopting a heightened emotional tone in his correspondence. Beginning in the summer of 1749, his declarations of friendly feeling became more explicitly romantic. Expressions such as "I love you dear brother more passionately than ever," "you know that I care for you but you will never imagine just how much," and "for your friendship, I would sacrifice father, mother, sister, brother, mistress, even illegitimate child. . . . It is with these sentiments dear brother that I am yours for life" reflected the deep gratitude Béla felt toward him. He openly acknowledged that packages and letters from Épernay enabled him to keep his mindsprings going throughout this trying moment, and he especially singled out for praise the gift of wine. "When I feel my patience leave me," he explained halfway through his prison term, "I arm myself with a corkscrew and fire in all directions until the very idea of my enemies has completely disappeared from my mind." Immediately upon his release, Béla sought to return his friend's services, asking whether "now I can be useful to you. Order and I am ready to do anything you desire. . . . I still have fresh in my memory the oil you sent me to lubricate the locks and bolts of my solitude. It is a debt that is close to

86. BME MS 156, fol. 7r; BN NAF MS 15175, fol. 306r.

my heart." Béla soon fulfilled this promise of reciprocity, shipping off to Épernay various articles of clothing purchased in Paris. In this way, the gift exchange between Béla and Rocheret was characteristic of gift-giving practices in early modern Europe, as it was reciprocal rather than asymmetrical.[87]

Besides mitigating the severity of the Old Regime justice system, these Masons could also offer one another assistance during moments of family crisis. The misfortune of the marquis de Tavannes offers us a salient example of masonic friendship in opposition to the family, functioning as an emotional refuge through which these men offered the marquis both emotional and concrete support. During his youth, the marquis de Tavannes became friendly and eventually amorous of his cousin, Ferdinande de Brun, with whom he spent extended time at the family's château at La Marche in the Burgundy countryside.[88] Both hoped to eventually marry, but this project soon fell apart in early 1732 as Mademoiselle de Brun learned that her parents had already prearranged a marriage with the comte de Salives. Although such an imposition was by no means uncommon in the Old Regime, de Brun's reaction was exceptional, as she fled Burgundy with Tavannes soon after learning of her fate. They both took up residence with an unnamed relative of de Brun in the Duchy of Lorraine, and Ferdinande's father immediately placed the case in the hands of the Auxonnais *lieutenant-criminel* and was eventually successful in acquiring from the king a *lettre de cachet*. Faced with this overwhelming opposition, the two lovers were left with few options, and Mademoiselle de Brun regretfully returned to her family after nearly two years on the run. In late 1733, her father forced Ferdinande into a convent.

Meanwhile, the marquis de Brun continued legal action against Tavannes, who spent most of the remaining decade at the court of Lunéville trying to secure his safe return to France. However, this transitory state abruptly ended on 10 February 1738 when the Parlement of Dijon found Tavannes guilty of *rapt de séduction* and condemned him to be decapitated.[89] *Huissiers* confiscated his personal possessions remaining in Burgundy, and he was soon

---

87. BN NAF MS 15175, fols. 310r, 333r, 358r, and 366r. On reciprocal gift-giving in early modern France, see Natalie Davis, *The Gift in Sixteenth-Century France* (Madison: University of Wisconsin Press, 2000).

88. This event has been reconstructed from BMC MS 125, fols. 401r–15r, as well as from two published accounts of the Tavannes-Le Brun affair: *Lettre de M*** à une personne de considération* (Metz, 1734); and Gabriel-Louis Pérau, *Lettres au sujet du différend de M. le marquis de Tavannes, Brigadier des Armées de l'Empereur, avec M. le marquis de Brun, Maréchal des Camps et Armées du Roi* (1743).

89. Old Regime law dealt harshly with *ravisseurs* like Tavannes. See Jean Ghestin, "L'action des Parlements contre les mésalliances au XVIIᵉ et XVIIIᵉ siècles," *Revue historique de droit français et étranger* 34 (1956): 74–109.

after publicly executed in effigy in front of the family château. Tavannes, now realizing not only his reputation but his very life was in danger, decided to flee to the Bavarian Electorate where family connections had assured him a safe refuge.

It was precisely at this crisis point that Tavannes's masonic friendships proved to be of great assistance. According to Bertin du Rocheret's own account of the event, Tavannes learned of his death sentence while on a brief trip to Paris, "in complete security" comforted by members of the Bussi-Aumont lodge. Lodge master duc d'Aumont strongly urged him to leave France immediately and instructed him to use Rocheret's residence as a rest stop before continuing on his journey eastward out of the kingdom. Tavannes, having never physically met his fellow Freemason from Épernay, followed Aumont's advice and spent one evening in Épernay while Rocheret himself was absent. After his escape abroad, Tavannes also sought out expatriate French Masons and was affiliated with a francophone lodge in Frankfurt in the early 1740s.[90] The marquis also depended on a complex network of Freemasons to safely correspond with his beloved Ferdinande, who was now enclosed in a Parisian convent. Épernay typically was the first stop for Tavannes's letters, where Rocheret then repackaged the marquis's correspondence—likely in order to conceal the sender's true location—and shipped it off to a second Mason, a certain "frère Vincent," who was in Paris. This second brother then physically delivered Tavannes's letters to the convent. Rocheret conversely sent Tavannes letters and general news of the kingdom, as well as a loan of 280 *livres*.

Besides such practical assistance, brethren were also emotionally invested in the fate of Tavannes. Once the marquis had secured safe passage into France to plead his case in front of Louis XV himself at Versailles in late 1745, he paid a brief visit to Épernay on 6 December. This face-to-face meeting represented the sole opportunity for these two men to infuse their friendship with a physical component. In Bertin du Rocheret's words, "this was the first time that I saw and that I tenderly embraced this dear brother." They never again laid eyes on one another, but Rocheret continued to discuss Tavannes in letters to Béla. The chevalier expressed concern that this decade-long familial dispute had not only irreparably tarnished the marquis's honor but had also left him psychologically debilitated. Even if the crown would allow Tavannes to return to France, Béla believed that "he

---

90. In October 1744, an orator of the francophone Union lodge in Frankfurt cited Tavannes as a member. Joseph Uriot, "Le secret des francs-maçons," cited in Johel Coutura, ed., *Le parfait maçon: Les débuts de la Maçonnerie française (1736–1748)* (Saint-Etienne: Université de Saint-Etienne, 1994), 70.

will not be the same Tavannes as before. . . . Tavannes will find Mademoiselle de Brun the same, but she will not find the same Tavannes."[91]

The legal pursuit of Tavannes ended with the death of the marquis de Brun in early 1746. Bertin du Rocheret's discovery in a periodical that the crown had permitted Tavannes to return to France that summer prompted him to write his exiled friend in early September. "I have just learnt . . . that you have received your pardon (*lettres de grâces*). . . . You would have sooner received my compliments if I had known by another means." Rocheret clearly was disappointed that Tavannes had not personally informed him of the fortunate turn of events, and this sentiment colored the remainder of his letter. "The *Gazette de Hollande*, so often incorrect," he continued, "always leaves me with some doubt and I would like to experience no uncertainty regarding everything that contributes to your happiness. . . . You know that no one is more vehemently interested in your felicity than myself. . . . I dare complain to not be personally assured by you." Placing emphasis on his friend's happiness—the keyword of eighteenth-century friendship according to Robert Mauzi—allowed Rocheret to reaffirm the intimate, familiar status he hoped to occupy within Tavannes' social world: "This happy moment has been the object of my concern and desires for so long. . . . You have friends more essential to satisfy. However, dear and very dear brother, you do not have any friend more sincere or devoted than I."[92]

What is particularly striking about this episode is the extent to which Bertin du Rocheret placed his friendship with Tavannes above professional obligations. He derived his high social status in Épernay because of his multiple administrative and legal responsibilities in the town. His most important post was that of *lieutenant-criminel*, whose duty was to both dispense local justice and enforce royal edicts and parliamentary judgments from throughout the kingdom.[93] And yet not only did he make no attempt to arrest Tavannes, alert other authorities, or even distance himself from his friend, but in fact he actively assisted the marquis, both in his flight and in maintaining contact with de Brun's daughter, and also took explicit steps to carefully conceal the whereabouts of his friend. This incident thus illustrates the extent to which these men could place the personal bond of masonic friendship over more abstract loyalties, such as the rule of law. And similar

---

91. BMC MS 125, fol. 402r; BN NAF MS 15175, fol. 129v.

92. BMC MS 125, fols. 403r–404r.

93. On the responsibilities of the *lieutenant-criminel*, see Roland Mousnier, *The Institutions of France under The Absolute Monarchy, 1598–1789*, trans. Arthur Goldhammer (Chicago: University of Chicago Press, 1984), 2:255–75.

to the Béla case, the Rocheret-Tavannes dynamic again reveals the importance of the personal tie of friendship in negotiating the unpredictable system of justice of the Old Regime.

↩ The End of Friendship

On 3 October 1757, Bertin du Rocheret composed his final letter to the chevalier de Béla, inquiring into his foreign travels. The two men had not physically seen one another probably since 1749, when Béla had visited Épernay for ten days. This gradual atrophy of friendship was typical of the other men in the group under investigation. In order to fully understand the nature and limits of masonic friendship in eighteenth-century France, we must end this chapter by asking why these ties came apart.

Death was the most straightforward reason these friendships ended, but only the marquis de Tavannes passed away during this period, after a violent convulsion in early 1747.[94] For the majority of these men, geography clearly became the most disruptive external factor to the maintenance of friendship. After his public scandal and prison term put a premature end to his military career, Béla definitively returned to his native region of the Béarn in the southwest where he possessed a seigneurie at Hours.[95] The marquis de Calvières likewise eventually returned to the Languedoc in the 1750s, and both Castagnet and Rocheret spent gradually more time in their respective native towns of Senlis and Épernay because of declining health and professional obligations. Following a lengthy inheritance dispute with his brother, who occupied the lofty and influential post of *président de la Cour des Aides*, the abbé Le Camus found himself exiled to the Mediterranean island of Sainte-Marguerite by way of a *lettre de cachet*.[96] By 1750, then, these Masons were dispersed throughout France and beyond, with no likely opportunity to re-kindle their friendships with the pleasure of face-to-face visits. Rocheret did maintain a purely epistolary friendship with Béla into the decade, but

---

94. Tavannes suffered an unspecified illness that provoked regular bouts of internal bleeding. This condition was exacerbated by his heavy drinking, a habit brought on by legal and financial problems and the refusal of Ferdinande de Brun to marry despite the passing of her father. Celebrated eighteenth-century *femme de lettres* Madame de Graffigny, a longtime family friend, chronicled the marquis's rapid physical decline in Nicole Boursier and English Showalter, ed., *Correspondance de Madame de Graffigny*, (Oxford: Voltaire Foundation, 1985–2004) 7:441; 8:7, 203.

95. *Mémoires militaires du chevalier de Béla*, 20. Béla's *livre de raison* places him definitively in the Béarn no later than January 1759. ADPA, MS 1.J.59/2.

96. BME MS 132, fol. 157r; Chevallier, *Ducs sous l'acacia*, 65.

their writing frequency declined dramatically. It would thus appear that, although their friendships were largely experienced through the writing and reading of letters during the 1730s and 1740s, the Bertin du Rocheret circle always viewed this epistolary exchange as an inferior proxy to the moment when they would all once again gather around a table, sharing a meal and each other's company.

Another factor that eroded these friendships was a shifting among these Masons of what sociologists have defined as "foci of activity." According to Scott Feld and William Carter, foci of activity, such as masonic lodges, are able to generate friendships because they have "the common effect of bringing a relatively limited set of individuals together in repeated interactions in and around the focused activities."[97] They also point out that when a focused activity ends—because of a closing of a club, a divorce, or a change in residence—friendships initially derived from these activities usually cease as well. The only relationships that tend to endure this change are those whose participants are willing to make a sustained and conscious effort to maintain contact despite an absence of any supporting focus of activity.

This masonic network represents a clear example of robust friendships transcending an initial focus of activity, as the Bussi-Aumont lodge formally disbanded shortly after Bertin du Rocheret's initiation in 1737. However, involvement in other foci of activity that afforded similar opportunities to cultivate friendships undoubtedly contributed to the fading away of these masonic ties. In the neighboring town of Châlons-sur-Marne, for example, Rocheret decided to establish a chapter of the Ordre de la Félicité in March 1746. Like Freemasonry, this voluntary organization possessed a set of rituals and a hierarchy of ranks, and members held periodic banquets and pronounced speeches. In 1753, he also took a leading role in establishing the Académie des sciences, arts et belles lettres de Châlons. For the remaining eight years of his life, his correspondence journal indicates that he devoted the majority of his leisure time to recruiting members, soliciting scholarly papers and assuring the overall administration of this fledgling academy.[98] The marquis de Calvières also followed a similar path upon his return to Avignon, where he became involved in masonic life in the city as well as an avid participant

---

97. Scott Feld and William C. Carter, "Foci of Activity as Changing Contexts for Friendship," in Rebecca Adams and Graham Allan, ed., *Placing Friendship in Context* (New York: Cambridge University Press, 1998), 136.

98. On his involvement in the Ordre de la Félicité, see BN NAF MS 15175, fol. 113r. On his role in the Châlons Academy, see ADM, 1 J 95.

in the intellectual coterie of the doctor and *homme de lettres* Esprit Calvet.[99] Both Rocheret and Calvières thus serve as illustrative examples of members of the eighteenth-century social elite who readily moved in and out of Enlightenment foci of activity over the course of their lives. Because of decreased mobility due to age, these men naturally preferred those activities that were geographically proximate to their residence. And as participation in these new foci of activity increased, so too did the opportunity to establish new friendships that were relatively close to home and thus based in part on face-to-face meetings. Rocheret and Calvières likely privileged such relationships over their more dispersed masonic contacts established earlier in their lives because of this physical component, and also because they did not require the same degree of effort to maintain.

These friendships were not only weakened by such external pressures, but were also undermined by interactional problems between these men. There is a general consensus among social scientists that instrumentality is an essential component of friendship. William Rawlins has pointed out, however, that friends do not effortlessly negotiate between the affective and utilitarian aspects of friendship, but that a distinct fear of being perceived by others as exploitative of aid or services constantly hovers over friends. They typically address this issue in two ways. First, friends tend to downplay the role of instrumentality in their relationship by balancing the rendering of services with non-instrumental components of friendship, such as displays of affection either in writing or in person. Rawlins defines this careful action of negotiation as the "delicate traffic in sentiment and assistance." Second, individuals also distinguish friendship from mere impersonal utilitarian bonds by striving to maintain an ethos of egalitarian reciprocity in any type of exchange, giving as much as they receive. Rawlins argues that if a long-term imbalance of instrumentality does begin to develop, the friendship normally either ends or evolves into a purely economic or patron-client relationship.[100]

We have seen this effort to preserve an equitable exchange in the case of the Bertin du Rocheret-Béla dyad when the chevalier reciprocated his friend's services rendered during his prison sentence immediately upon his release. In other instances, however, an absence of mutuality and of any

---

99. Brockliss, *Calvet's Web*, 71.

100. William Rawlins, *Friendship Matters: Communication, Dialectics, and the Life Course* (New York: Aldine de Gruyter, 1991), 17–20.

significant non-instrumental elements of friendship gradually deformed the friendly exchange of goods into little more than a cool economic transaction. Such was the case of the friendship between Rocheret and Castagnet. As noted above, Castagnet purchased wine from Épernay until the late 1740s and served as an important broker between Rocheret and other customers in the capital. With the exception of the initial period of their correspondence in which they discussed Freemasonry's problems with the government, the remainder of their letter writing was overwhelmingly devoted to wine. Unlike the correspondence with Le Camus, Tavannes, Calvières, and Béla, Rocheret and Castagnet spent little time inquiring into one another's family life or work, and they did not use the letter to share in common intellectual pursuits. Castagnet also repeatedly declined invitations to visit Épernay and rarely wrote a letter without a wine purchase request. Over the course of the decade, Rocheret grew visibly tired of this purely utilitarian correspondence and gradually neglected his writing. Toward the end of their epistolary contact, Castagnet, realizing that their friendship was now in danger, attempted to reinsert an affective component into the relationship. Explicit declarations of feeling peppered his letters between 1745 and 1747, as did more non-instrumental content such as discussion of work and court life at Versailles.[101] However, these late efforts were unsuccessful in rebalancing affectivity and instrumentality and the two only exchanged a handful of letters after 1748.

Another point of tension between these men was the development of intimate ties within the masonic community that proved to be detrimental to a wider collective solidarity. As made clear above, Bertin du Rocheret and Béla formed the strongest friendship dyad among the Masons under investigation. The chevalier wrote to and visited Épernay the most often, and his letters were meandering informal conversations, filled with erudition, humor and intense expressions of love that many men today undoubtedly would find uncomfortably close to the vocabulary of erotic relationships. When Béla faced legal trouble, Rocheret mobilized his Bussi-Aumont contacts in the hope of securing an early release. However, Béla ended up serving out the entirety of his six-month sentence, and received no help from either Castagnet or Gonor, outside of the latter's brief visit to Fort l'Evêque. When Rocheret asked Béla the extent of their contact with him, he wrote that "I received two responses to the letters that I wrote to Mssrs. Gonor and Castagnet. My first thought was to send them to you, but after

---

101. See, for example, his letters in BN NAF MS 15175, fols. 147r–211r.

thinking about it, I judged that they were not even worthy of the two *sols* of postage."[102] This unwillingness to offer substantial help to Béla clearly disappointed Rocheret and, in addition to other factors already mentioned, he subsequently ceased all correspondence with both Gonor and Castagnet.

Rocheret's close affinity for Béla thus compelled him to break off ties with other members of his masonic peer group whom he perceived as not expressing sufficient concern for the chevalier. In this way, this masonic network demonstrates that the two modes of friendship within Enlightenment Freemasonry explored thus far in this book—ritualized and unritualized—could be both complementary and in conflict with one another. On the one hand, the formal, ritualized bond that the Rocheret community contracted through the initiation ritual served as the basis for the more informal, unritualized relations explored in this chapter, since most of these men had no record of personal relations with one another before induction into the fraternity. On the other hand, these unritualized friendships varied greatly in their intensity, and therefore introduced emotional imbalance and dissonance into the masonic community where uniform harmony among all members was the ideal. As the next chapter will show, smaller and more exclusive unritualized friendship cliques inside prerevolutionary lodges could threaten Freemasonry's wider collective solidarity, just as the deep friendship between Béla and Rocheret ultimately undermined the Bussi-Aumont group.

The bond these men shared during the second quarter of the eighteenth century demonstrates that the pattern of masonic socializing through writing and visits did not necessarily correspond with the institutional life span of a lodge. Although Bussi-Aumont formally closed its doors at some point in late 1737 due to police pressure, these Freemasons remained in contact with each other well afterward. Historians have often overlooked this discrepancy between the formal institution of the lodge and the personal relationships cultivated between members. This is largely because most masonic histories have relied solely on the formal documents of the brotherhood, notably lodge records readily available at the Bibliothèque Nationale. Pierre-Yves Beaurepaire has rightly criticized this approach as "lazy mono-exploitation" because, although it tells us about the more skeletal elements of a lodge—the number of members, its location, its official correspondence with the Grand Lodge or later Grand Orient—it has nothing to say about how individuals integrated

---

102. Ibid., fol. 315r.

Freemasonry into their everyday lives.[103] Poring over administrative records and tallying up membership rolls cannot tell us how Frenchmen some two hundred and fifty years ago lived their masonic ties and depended on them for emotional and practical support. Only further investigation into sources similar to the ones examined in this chapter—personal letters, diaries, and memoirs—can hope to capture the personal dimension of the masonic experience and answer the deceptively simple question Pierre Chevallier asked over four decades ago about the tens of thousands of men who walked into a lodge in eighteenth-century France: "Why did they become Freemasons?"[104]

103. Pierre-Yves Beaurepaire, *L'espace des Francs-maçons: Une sociabilité européenne au XVIIIᵉ siécle* (Rennes: Presses Universitaires de Rennes, 2003), 9.

104. Chevallier, *Première profanation du temple*, 89.

◆ CHAPTER 5

Friendship in the Age of Sensibility

By the time Philippe-Valentin Bertin du Rocheret passed away in 1762, Freemasonry had entered into a new phase of its history. From midcentury until the Revolution, the movement steadily proliferated, attracting an ever-widening swath of French society into its ranks. Whereas participation in masonic life during the time of Andrew-Michael Ramsay and Bertin du Rocheret had been largely, though not exclusively, an experience restricted to large cities and the upper echelons of society, the second half of the century saw a much more geographically and socioeconomically diverse *corps maçonnique*: low-level functionaries, local priests, merchants, and master artisans of all trades now could be found on membership rolls in lodges from Paris to Port-au-Prince. This growth was due largely to the organization's ambiguous status during the final years of Louis XV and the reign of Louis XVI, when authorities tolerated but stopped short of officially endorsing masonic activity. Lieutenant-général of the police of Paris, Jean-Charles-Pierre Le Noir, thought that lodges were simply "innocent amusements" that posed no threat to the social order or body politic.[1] Although it would never touch in any meaningful way the

---

1. "Mémoires de Jean-Charles-Pierre Le Noir," BMO, MS 1422, fol. 103r.

bulk of the population during the eighteenth century—namely the rural peasantry and urban working classes—Freemasonry by 1789 boasted at least 50,000 members in France.[2]

In this chapter we will describe how male friendship continued to serve as a key component of masonic identity in the twilight of the Old Regime. We can measure the importance of friendship by quantifying the terms *ami* and *amitié* within the semantic field of lodge titles, known as *titres distinctifs*. Throughout the century, French lodges reflected their counterparts elsewhere in Europe and the Americas by adopting a specific title for their assembly. A major reason for this consistency is that it represented one of the basic elements of a lodge's identity and endorsement by the Grand Lodge and later Grand Orient. These organizations printed up and circulated throughout the kingdom a *tableau général* of all lodges under their administration, and such a master list played a critical role in facilitating communication between lodges. Upon examining the list of lodges recently received from the Grand Orient, one secretary from a Calaisian lodge confidently declared to his brethren in 1784 that, with this document in hand, "you will never be strangers anywhere, for everywhere you will find brothers and friends."[3] The name on which members agreed rarely was chosen carelessly but was instead a product of a lengthy debate process between members, often carried out in consultation with neighboring lodges and Paris. Brethren attributed special importance to the title because it gave an identity to the lodge and shaped the character of lodge meetings.[4]

The core of this chapter comprises an exploration of the masonic mentality toward friendship through the prism of the many lodge speeches

2. Daniel Roche, *France in the Enlightenment*, trans. Arthur Goldhammer (Cambridge, MA: Harvard University Press, 1998), 436. On the diversity of membership from the 1760s onward, see the lodge rolls in Johel Coutura, *Les Francs-maçons de Bordeaux au 18ème siècle* (Marcillac: Éditions du Glorit, 1988), 57–205; Albert Ladret, *Le grand siècle de la Franc-maçonnerie: La Franc-maçonnerie lyonnaise au XVIIIe siècle* (Paris: Dervy-Livres, 1976), 429–70; Alain Le Bihan, *Francs-maçons parisiens du Grand Orient de France (fin du XVIIIe siècle)* (Paris: Bibliothèque Nationale, 1966), 31–489.

3. Cited in Pierre-Yves Beaurepaire, *L'autre et le frère: L'étranger et la Franc-maçonnerie en France au XVIIIe siècle* (Paris: Honoré Champion, 1998), 32.

4. Previous work has recognized the rich potential of the lodge title, especially Ran Halévi, "Les représentations de la démocratie maçonnique au XVIIIe siècle," *Revue d'histoire moderne et contemporaine* 31 (1984): 571–96; and Daniel Roche, *Le siècle des Lumières en province: Académies et académiciens provinciaux, 1680–1789* (Paris: Mouton, 1978), 1:277–80; 2:109.

that men delivered during the 1770s and 1780s.[5] Typically referred to as a "discourse" (*discours*) or, more esoterically, as a "piece of architecture" (*morceau d'architecture*), speeches were commonplace and served to instruct members in Freemasonry's objectives and moral code; for this reason, initiations were always followed by a talk from the lodge master or orator. But officers and visitors from the Grand Orient also offered veteran Masons insight into the art of living masonically. Lodges routinely put time aside for speeches on topics such as "the qualities that a good Mason must have" as the goal of discourses was, in the words of the orator of the Parisian Vrais Amis Réunis lodge in 1781, to remind brethren of "the virtues that the arches of our temples uphold."[6] Speeches could also be delivered to mark significant occasions, from the biannual celebration of Saint John's Day to the birth of a member of the royal family. Along with initiations and banquets, then, the pronouncement of discourses—which varied from a few paragraphs to over a dozen pages—was one of the key ways Freemasons conferred meaning onto the masonic experience, using these speeches to anchor their organization in a shared set of values and to generate a meaningful, robust framework for relating to one another, to Freemasonry as an organization, and to French society as a whole.

Unfortunately for brethren, the lofty visions of friendship that adorned their lodges and were expounded on in speeches often did not line up neatly with the concrete reality of masonic social life in the prerevolutionary era. Although collective harmony was held up as the ideal, bitter conflict often broke out between men. Meeting records reveal that many members either voluntarily left or were ejected for a variety of infractions that ranged from vocal disagreement with officers to fighting in the streets. We will consider in the final section of this chapter what role friendship played in provoking these disputes and how lodges worked to restore order following these divisive episodes.

---

5. Speeches have been studied in Gérard Gayot, "Du pouvoir et des Lumières dans la fraternité maçonnique au XVIIIᵉ siècle," in *Peuple et pouvoir: Etudes de lexicologie politique*, ed. Michel Glatigny and Jacques Guihaumou (Lille: Presses universitaires de Lille, 1981), 87–116; Margaret Jacob, *Living the Enlightenment: Freemasonry and Politics in Eighteenth-Century Europe* (New York: Oxford University Press, 1991), esp. chaps. 2 and 6; and briefly in Eric Saunier, *Révolution et sociabilité en Normandie au tournant des XVIIIᵉ et XIXᵉ siècles: 6000 Francs-maçons de 1740 à 1830* (Rouen: Publications de l'Université de Rouen, 1998), 279–85.

6. Lodge register of Anglaise (Bordeaux), GODF MS AR 113.2.101, fol. 43r; Dossier of Vrais Amis Réunis (Paris), BN FM²127, fol. 12v.

⤚ Freemasonry Expands

Between 1750 and 1793, slightly over a thousand civil and military lodges were established in Paris and the provinces.[7] Although some lodges came and went quite quickly, in table 5.1 and figure 5.1 we demonstrate that, at the very least, many new lodges were created from the 1750s onward. Whereas only eighty-three lodges had been created before 1750, nearly one hundred new lodges were erected during the period between 1750 and 1759 alone. This strong expansion continued down to the Revolution, despite the Grand Orient's efforts to exercise a firmer hand in the screening of new lodges. At the end of the Old Regime, Gérard Gayot estimates that over six hundred of these lodges were still active. Although Paris possessed far more lodges than any other city (eighty-seven, followed by Lyon with thirty), only 30 percent of all masonic assemblies could be found in the twenty most populous cities (of 31,000 inhabitants and above). It was above all in the country towns—those from 5,000 to 10,000 residents—that Freemasonry began to expand. After 1770 the growth rate in these areas tripled, whereas in larger cities, where Masonry had arrived earlier, it slowed considerably. Lodges in such intermediate-sized localities gradually comprised a greater portion of total lodges throughout the period, eventually amounting to nearly 30 percent of all lodges in France in the 1780s. During these prerevolutionary decades, masonic life touched even the smallest and most remote of places, such as the alpine village of Briançon (population 535).[8]

France's middling sort and elites were attracted to Masonry because it offered a hybrid, amorphous sociability whose appeal lay in the diversity of its content. In many provincial cities, large semiautonomous administrative

---

7. Unlike a civilian lodge, a military lodge could be a traveling lodge and typically was made up of officers of the same regiment. Unless otherwise noted, population figures are from Bernard Lepetit, *The Pre-Industrial Urban System: France, 1740–1840*, trans. Godfrey Rogers (New York: Cambridge University Press, 1994), 449–52. Lodge figures have been principally derived from Alain Le Bihan, *Loges et chapitres de la Grande Loge et du Grand Orient de France (2ᵉ moitié du XVIIIᵉ siècle)* (Paris: Bibliothèque nationale, 1967). These figures include all lodges found in both Paris and the provinces, including military lodges. The following types of lodges have been omitted: 1) Lodges created by fusions of smaller lodges; 2) Central "mother" lodges in the provinces as well as chapters devoted to the higher degrees, as both comprised Masons already affiliated to other lodges; and 3) organizations denied recognition by either the Grand Lodge or later Grand Orient. Unlike civil chapters, most military chapters did in fact function autonomously and have therefore been included in this calculation.

8. Gérard Gayot, *La Franc-maçonnerie française: Textes et pratiques (XVIIIᵉ–XIXᵉ siècles)* (Paris: Gallimard, 1980), 34–35; Ran Halévi, *Les loges maçonniques dans la France d'Ancien Régime: Aux origines de la sociabilité démocratique* (Paris: Armand Colin, 1984), 78–85.

Table 5.1   Lodges Created from 1750 to 1793

DECADE	NUMBER OF LODGES CREATED
1750–1759	99
1760–1769	221
1770–1779	276
1780–1793	405
Total lodges created	**1001**

hubs, commonly referred to as "mother lodges," erected masonic systems with a dizzying array of hierarchy and ritual. Lyon and Strasbourg, for example, became active centers of the Strict Observance of the Templars, a form of Masonry that viewed itself as the continuation of the medieval Knights Templar. Although once closely linked to the Grand Lodge early in his career, itinerant merchant Etienne Morin propagated his own version of higher degrees throughout the French Caribbean in the mid-1760s and early 1770s. The controversial figure Giuseppe Balsamo, known as the Count Cagliostro, independently devised a complex set of higher grades, dubbed "Egyptian Masonry." Masons such as Lyonnais Jean-Baptiste Willermoz also blended the fashionable current of Mesmerism with Masonry, transforming lodges into veritable *séances*.[9]

By the end of the Old Regime, then, Freemasonry had become a thriving institution present throughout metropolitan and colonial France. The organization had moved well beyond its embryonic, marginalized status earlier in the century, and brethren could be found confidently walking the streets of Paris in full lodge regalia on their way to meetings, apparently unconcerned with reprisals, harassment, or concealing their affiliation. Furthermore, a lodge's accouterments such as tapestries and uniforms were by no means carefully veiled from the public eye, as local artisans rather than Masons themselves were the typical suppliers. The members of the celebrated Neuf Soeurs lodge—a lodge that counted Benjamin Franklin and Voltaire as members—reassured the Grand Orient in 1780 that their increasingly public presence posed no danger to Freemasonry. Explaining why they made little effort to hide its activities or membership, Neuf Soeurs declared that "our ornaments are not a secret. Women manufacture them. . . . Only masonic ceremonies remain a mystery." Another active member of

---

9. Robert Darnton, *Mesmerism and the End of the Enlightenment in France* (Cambridge, MA: Harvard University Press, 1968), 67–69.

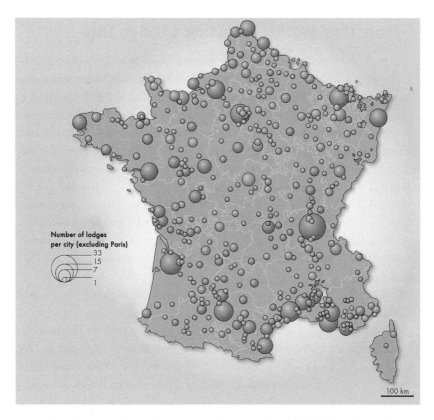

Number of lodges
per city (excluding Paris)
33
15
7
1

100 km

FIGURE 5.1. By the Revolution, Freemasonry had become widespread, with lodges in nearly every corner of the kingdom. Map adapted from *Atlas de la Révolution française*, copyright 2010 by Pierre-Yves Beaurepaire and Silvia Marzagalli.

Neuf Soeurs and celebrated chronicler of eighteenth-century Paris, Louis-Sébastien Mercier, devoted a chapter to the brotherhood in his rich panorama of prerevolutionary Parisian life. Contrasting France with less tolerable kingdoms elsewhere on the continent—such as Naples, where lodges had been closed down as recently as 1775—Mercier confidently declared that "Freemasons are not persecuted in Paris; they are allowed to hold lodge meetings as often as they wish." As in England, lodges had become so integrated into the cultural landscape that tourist guides to Paris like *Le voyageur à Paris* casually presented them alongside monuments, churches, and parks as notable sites in the capital.[10]

---

10. "Mémoire pour la loge des Neuf Soeurs," (Paris, 1780), Baylot BN FM²148, fol. 32r; Louis-Sébastien Mercier, *Tableau de Paris*, ed. Jean-Claude Bonnet (Paris: Mercure de France, 1994),

↳ More than Words: Selecting a Lodge Title

Guidebooks like *Le voyageur* typically supplied readers with only one reference point to describe lodges: their name. The Grand Orient recognized that a lodge's *titre distinctif* represented the sole initial point of contact between Freemasonry and outsiders, and therefore reviewed, and at times rejected, name proposals. During a tense exchange with one lodge, the Grand Orient explained that great care must be taken in the selection of the title because it served to "offer the public an idea of the advantages of our mysteries and lodges of which at least the names are known." If word got out that a lodge had selected its name in a manner perceived haphazard or lackadaisical, other lodges would protest to the Grand Orient. In late 1786, the Amis Intimes lodge in Paris complained that the Masons of Henri IV simply chose this name because they had "found it by accident" on the Pont Neuf.[11]

Fortunately for the Grand Orient, most lodges did not choose their names in an arbitrary manner, but rather through careful discussion. This preoccupation with naming and words in general was reflective of the Enlightenment view that semantics was of central importance. The notion that words wielded power shaped much of early modern political and social thought. Francis Bacon, Thomas Hobbes, and John Locke, for instance, had all adopted a strong nominalist position in their writings, wherein it was made explicit that truth essentially was a function of language and that, subsequently, the pursuit of knowledge entailed reasoning correctly about names.[12] As these thinkers—especially Locke—all became available in French by 1700 and as the French crown's own efforts to systematize and improve language through state institutions like the Académie Française continued to expand, the emphasis on careful word use had become a mainstay of French literate culture by the eighteenth century. Diderot, d'Holbach, and Rousseau

---

2:171; *Le voyageur à Paris, extrait du guide des amateurs et des étrangers voyageurs à Paris* (Paris, 1790), 258–59.

11. Dossier of Thalie (Paris), BN FM²117 fol. 17r. Amis Intimes was likely referring to the plaque and statue dedicated to Henri IV on the bridge. Dossier of Amis Intimes (Paris), BN FM²43, fol. 59v.

12. See, for example, the scrupulous attention paid to the definition of key words in Francis Bacon, *The Advancement of Learning*, ed. William Wright (Oxford, 1876), book 2; Thomas Hobbes, *Leviathan*, ed. Richard Tuck (New York: Cambridge University Press, 1996), 24–31; and John Locke, *An Essay Concerning Human Understanding*, ed. Peter H. Nidditch (New York: Oxford University Press, 1975), 6–14.

were just a handful of the many *philosophes* who believed that language could shape thought and action.[13]

Like these pillars of the French Enlightenment, Freemasonry invested words with transformative power. Masons went to great pains to explain why they called themselves an "order" or a "society," and what deeper significance lay at the heart of words such as "lodge" and "Royal Art."[14] They likewise recognized that the *titre distinctif* possessed not only a distinguishing but also a descriptive and prescriptive function. It displayed in emblematic form the meaning of their sociability to both the wider public and fellow brethren alike. Because of this high visibility and symbolic import, deliberation among members over lodge titles could last several weeks, even during periods of acute political and personal turmoil. Erected on the eve of the Revolution, the military lodge Guillaume Tell mainly comprised members of the king's elite Swiss Guard; many members were killed when *sans-culottes* stormed the Tuileries palace on 10 August 1792. Shortly after this incident, amid international war and unprecedented domestic tumult, surviving members decided to establish a new lodge. Seemingly unconcerned or unaffected by recent events—Austrian and Prussian armies were on French soil and Louis XVI's trial had begun—the lodge happily informed the Grand Orient that after a calm and thorough deliberation, they had all agreed on Centre des Amis as an appropriate title.[15]

A *titre distinctif* was so important to the identity of a lodge that not only did members devote considerable time to its selection, but they also would consider it as an unequivocal form of original expression to be jealously guarded. If a new lodge in the vicinity attempted to use the same name, older lodges typically would write in protest to the Grand Lodge or Grand Orient, staunchly holding firm to the notion that they alone possessed the exclusive right to a given title. Such tension occurred most frequently when an individual or group detached themselves from a lodge and attempted to establish a new assembly with the same name. Such was the case, for example, when four unnamed members of the Aménité lodge of Paris broke away and solicited the Grand Orient for constitutions under the title Élus

---

13. Sophia Rosenfeld, *A Revolution in Language: The Problem of Signs in Late Eighteenth-Century France* (Stanford, CA: Stanford University Press, 2001), chap. 1.

14. See, for instance, Théodore-Henry baron de Tschoudy, *L'étoile flamboyante, ou la société des Francs-maçons considérée sous tous les aspects* (Paris, 1766), 1:31–38, 46.

15. *Premier registre des assemblées de la respectable loge du Centre des Amis (succédant a celle de Guillaume Tell) depuis sa formation le 12 février 1793 (ère vulgaire) jusqu'au 6 août 1804 inclusivement*, BN FM³31, fol. 79r.

de la Parfaite Aménité in 1784. Aménité soon got word of their plans and angrily wrote the Grand Orient, asking on what grounds this small coterie had singled itself out as the "elect" from the lodge's other thirty-five members. The Chamber of Paris agreed and forced the new lodge to adopt the title Élus de la Parfaite Intimité.[16] Even less proximate lodges could become divided on the issue of similar titles. In 1764, the Candeur lodge of Strasbourg composed a strongly worded letter to Paris in which it complained that another lodge had unjustifiably adopted the same name. What is particularly striking is that this other group of Masons was not located in Strasbourg, but rather in Metz, which lay at least a day's coach ride away. This example illustrates that Enlightenment Freemasonry was a community constructed not only on face-to-face meetings, but also—in a more abstract manner—on the production and exchange of documents, of which lodge tables were an important part. It was indeed following this logic that these Strasbourgeois brethren feared that the two lodges likely would be confused with one another; unless some action were taken, both would be identified as Candeur on a master list the Grand Lodge had begun to compile. The lodge beseeched Paris to "quickly request it [the Metz lodge] to change its title of Candeur that one should never have granted in the first place since we have bore this name since our beginning." Otherwise, they worried, "if it persists to use this name, we will be forced to write to all lodges in the kingdom to prevent any surprises."[17]

☛ Friendship in the Semantic Field of Lodge Titles

Carefully selected and jealously guarded, titles thus represented a fundamental component of a lodge's identity. Overall, there were at least 1,130 titles created or proposed in France over the course of the eighteenth century.[18] The disparate evidence available in earlier records—principally limited to printed works lampooning or defending the order—suggests that

---

16. Dossier of Élus de la Parfaite Aménité (Paris), BN FM²73, fols. 1r–5v.

17. BN FM¹111, fol. 452r. It is not clear how the Grand Lodge responded to this request, but we are able to infer that Paris did not share the same uneasiness, as both lodges continued to bear the name *Candeur*. It is also noteworthy that lodges were quite fastidious in ensuring their names were correctly recorded on the master lists the Grand Lodge and Grand Orient circulated. In December 1765, for example, the Masons of the Parfaite Union lodge in Macon complained that the Grand Lodge had incorrectly labeled them Parfaite Réunion. GODF MS AR.113.1.52, fol. 5r.

18. This dataset is larger than Ran Halévi's (830) earlier work (see note 4 above) because it includes: 1) titles proposed by a lodge but denied by the Grand Lodge or Grand Orient; 2) new titles pro-

earlier Freemasons did not exercise any great degree of linguistic creativity in selecting their lodge names. According to one apologia of the 1740s, a lodge was commonly named simply to honor its residing master or aristo-cratic sponsor: "Today, these lodges number approximately twenty-two. One designates a lodge by those who preside over it. Thus, one says, I was received in the lodge of Monsieur N."[19] Religious references were a second recurrent point of reference during the first half of the century. The major-ity of titles before 1760 fell into this category—nearly 60 percent. This group usually included those assemblies that simply chose to leave their title as "Saint Jean," a reference to the patron saints (John the Baptist and John the Evangelist) of Freemasonry. Still others singled out for praise a specific saint such as Saint Thomas (Paris, 1729), Saint Julien (Brioude, 1744), or Saint Paul (Perpignan, 1744), and these lodges typically celebrated their chosen saint's feast day in addition to the expected festivals of Saint John the Baptist and the Evangelist (24 June and 27 December, respectively).[20] Less frequent within this category were titles referring to specific religious cere-monies, beliefs or events such as La Conversion de Saint Paul (Montpellier, 1764). Although references to individuals, geography, and especially religion could still be found during the final decades of the Old Regime, the most dominant category from 1760 onward included terms that described the nature of ideal masonic social interaction, such as Concorde, Amitié, or Sociabilité. Although a notable portion of titles fell under this "sociability" rubric even in the early decades of the brotherhood—32 percent during the period from 1720 to 1760—these titles nearly doubled to 60 percent of all names during the 1760s and remained at this level until the end of the century.

Looking in closer detail at this "sociability" category allows us to discern the prominent position friendship occupied within the semantic field of titles. Historians of Enlightenment Freemasonry have suggested that within masonic discourse, the idiom of kinship rather than friendship was singled

---

posed by an already existent lodge or following a fusion of two lodges; 3) military lodges; and most importantly, 4) lodges in Paris.

19. Gabriel-Louis Pérau, *L'ordre des Francs-maçons trahi et le secret des Mopses révélé* (Amsterdam, 1745), 32.

20. Such was the case, for example, of the Sainte Solange lodge in Bourges and the Saint Maurice lodge in Clermont-Ferrand, which stipulated in their regulations that their saint festivals (10 May and 22 September, respectively) were be celebrated with a banquet. Pierre-Yves Beaurepaire, *Les Francs-maçons à l'orient de Clermont-Ferrand au XVIIIᵉ siècle* (Clermont-Ferrand: Université Blaise-Pascal, 1991), 322; Robert Durandeau, *Histoire des Francs-maçons en Berry* (Limoges: Lucien Souny, 1990), 63.

out for praise. In reference to both all-male and mixed adoption lodges, Margaret Jacob has remarked that Masonry celebrated its distinctive brand of sociability for recreating the warm intimacy of the family unit. She observes that members called each other "brother" and "adopted" women into their lodges; in reference to Dutch lodges, Jacob identifies a penchant for brethren to select maternal figures as their iconographic symbols since lodges "were analogous to the home, intended to inculcate the virtues associated with domesticity."[21]

In general, French lodges also viewed the family in a positive light, but they usually did not consider their social space as a seamless extension of the domestic unit. They clearly understood that their brand of kinship was constructed or fictive, one that bound together non-kin in bonds that, like real kinship, possessed both affective and instrumental components. A clear differentiation between masonic relationships and other webs of obligation first appeared in one of the earliest regulatory texts, wherein Masons were instructed to "behave as wise men of good manners, and above all do not reveal to your family, friends, or neighbors what goes on in the lodge." A masonic apologist of the 1770s emphasized that the joy of the lodge was made possible because within its walls, "one forgets about all his worries and domestic concerns." In a letter to a potential recruit written during the 1780s, Lyonnais silk merchant Jean-Baptiste Willermoz stressed that Freemasonry could come into conflict with domestic life, explaining that some wives had expressed displeasure at having been excluded from the order's activities. In addition, Masons typically expressed sharp critique for those kinship relations outside the immediate family. During the inauguration ceremony of the Saint Laurent lodge in Paris on 21 August 1777, an orator announced to his brethren that the happy occasion of affiliation with the Grand Orient prompted him to "speak to you about friendship, this soft and tender passion that gave birth to Masonry." He praised this day as one in which "we are going to all swear the most solemn oaths of friendship, since I am amongst men who have formed between them a fraternity of taste and of choice, [which is] much more solid and much more pleasing than bonds of blood."[22]

---

21. Jacob, *Living the Enlightenment*, 52–72, 118.

22. "À la maison et dans le voisinage," in *Statuts généraux des Frères-maçons* which appeared in *L'École des francs-maçons* in 1748. Reprinted in Johel Coutura, ed., *Le parfait maçon: Les débuts de la Maçonnerie française (1736–1748)* (Saint-Etienne: Université de Saint-Etienne, 1994), 208; S. Arbas *Considérations filosophiques sur la Franc-maçonnerie dédiées à tous les oriens en France* . . . (Hambourg, 1776), 22; BML MS 5918, pièce 3; Dossier of Saint-Laurent (Paris), BN FM²105, fols. 5r–6r.

These statements indeed reflected a penchant among Freemasons to choose members from among their non-kin friends, typically met through the world of work. Consider, for example, the case of the Anglaise lodge in Bordeaux, one of the oldest masonic organizations in continental Europe, having been established in 1732. Unlike most Old Regime lodges, Anglaise's massive meeting register has survived from 1784 into the Revolution, numbering well over a thousand manuscript pages.[23] Such rich material enables the historian to trace in minute detail the intricacies of lodge life, including membership profiles. This record shows that at least eighty-six men were proposed for initiation from the summer of 1784 (the moment when the register begins) until the political turbulence of 1789 began to disrupt the course of routine activity. Only around six percent of these men (five proposals) were related to a member of the lodge, as brethren instead preferred to recruit Masons from their professional contacts in and around the city. In the instances that the profession of both the sponsor and the initiand can be identified (forty-three out of the eighty-one non-kin proposals), there were only seven cases where the two men did not exercise the same profession. This pattern of selecting individuals from professional peers was repeated nearly everywhere and at multiple socioeconomic levels, from the political and financial elites of the Parisian Amis Réunis lodge to the humble merchants of Eleves de Minerve in Toulon. As the master of a lodge in Amiens put it a few years before the Revolution: "When it is not feasible to frequent others in civil society it is impossible to do so as a Mason."[24]

Two forms of equal status or likeness thus were preconditions of masonic friendship in the Old Regime: not only was it necessary for brethren to endorse a similar ethical system through the initiation ritual as examined in an earlier chapter, but, because work tended to play an important role in determining the contours of the masonic community, men in lodges also were of a similar socioeconomic background. Although historians such as Margaret Jacob have interpreted the presence of humble professions on the rolls of prestigious lodges as proof of unprecedented social mixing within Enlightenment Freemasonry, many of these individuals were known as "servants," and were not considered to be full-fledged members. These

---

23. GODF MS AR 113.2.101, fols. 1r–181r and GODF MS AR 113.2.102, fols. 1r–24r.

24. Cited in Roger Chartier, *The Cultural Origins of the French Revolution,* trans. Lydia G. Cochrane (Durham, NC: Duke University Press, 1991), 165. See also Maurice Agulhon, *Pénitents et Francs-maçons dans l'ancienne Provence: Essai sur la sociabilité mériodionale* (Paris: Fayard, [1968] 1984), 176–77; Beaurepaire, *L'autre et le frère,* 454–56.

servants—who in rare cases were not even Freemasons—often lived in the same apartment building of the meeting space and oversaw the general upkeep of the lodge. To emphasize their different status, lodges either omitted servants' names from their membership tables or spatially set them clearly apart from other members on the document.[25]

Because the social world of Freemasonry was fundamentally constituted by non-kin relations, the vocabulary of friendship far outweighed that of kinship within the semantic field of titles. Within the wider category of lodges that employed a language of sociability, terms such as *fraternité, frère, famille*, and so forth never comprised more than 17 percent of civil lodge names, whereas the language of friendship was far more common, reaching over 40 percent by the Revolution. It is also significant that whereas the idiom of kinship peaked in the 1760s and then declined to near 10 percent for the remainder of the Old Regime, friendship language, on the other hand, continued to increase its proportion as the century drew to a close. From 26 percent of sociability lodges during the 1760s, it rose to 34 percent during the 1770s, and continued its gradual yet sure ascent until records trailed off in the early 1790s. Among military lodges, the prevalence of friendship was even more widespread. Kinship was found within only six military titles throughout the entire century, whereas friendship comprised over half of all sociability lodges by the Revolution.

Within the collective lexicon of titles, friendship rather than kinship thus represented the collective metaphor of choice. It is notable that, besides friendship and kinship, no other concrete models of social relations surfaced within the semantic field of titles. Other keywords in the general sociability category, such as "candor," "sincerity," and "harmony," instead operated as complementary qualifying terms that described the ideal lodge setting and expected behavior of members.

For Ran Halévi, this expansion of friendship and sociability vocabulary later in the century represented a clear trend toward "the secular model, freed from both religious and occultist connotations."[26] Although such an interpretation is suggestive—and indeed lines up neatly alongside classic hypotheses regarding the *laïcisation* in the age of Enlightenment that François Furet and others have put forth—it does not fit well with the fact that Freemasonry's rituals and lodge activities were still quite outwardly Christian as

---

25. See, for example, the membership table of the Parfaite Union in Mâcon at GODF MS AR 113.1.52, fol. 7r. On the supposed heterogeneity of French Freemasonry, see Jacob, *Living the Enlightenment*, 3–4.

26. Halévi, "Représentations de la démocratie maçonnique," 592.

examined in this book. Regarding the titles themselves, we also detect an enduring awareness of a Christian sensibility informing the Grand Orient's position vis-à-vis names submitted for approval. Some lodges, for example, had their titles rejected on these grounds. In 1787, the Grand Orient forced the Apôtres d'Heredom of Montargis to drop this name because it was considered an unacceptable muddling of Christian and non-Christian vocabulary.[27]

The rapid surge of *titres distinctifs* denoting social interaction during the closing decades of the Old Regime did not signal secularization within Freemasonry but rather reflected a growing preoccupation with the nature of the lodge experience itself; this trend may be understood, to borrow the linguistic classification espoused by John Stuart Mill, as a move from non-connotative to connotative naming. The proper names of places (such as the Loge Ancienne de Metz (1735)) that dominated the semantic field of lodge titles before 1760 did not denote any relevant information about masonic life. Mill would have considered such lodge titles as "unmeaning marks" in that they did not "convey to the hearer any information about them, except that those are their names."[28] As the century advanced, Masons left behind such non-connotative appellations and increasingly incorporated into their titles words or expressions that denoted the ideal social environment and relationships forged within the lodge. As one orator proclaimed in 1783 to the Fidele Maçonne lodge in Cherbourg, names such as candor, concord, and friendship represented "the essence of Masonry" (*la Maçonnerie en elle-même*).[29]

Brethren began to realize that the title could be put to good pedagogical use, functioning as a powerful sign that conveyed an idea of the expected outward behavior and inward thoughts of the *parfait maçon*. During the 1787 inauguration ceremony of the Parisian lodge Modération, one orator drew on Lockean sensationalist psychology made popular by Condillac when he stated that "if man receives his ideas only from those objects which he sees, he nearly always needs a sensory link which feeds back to his mind." From

---

27. Dossier of Apôtres d'Heredom (Montargis), BN FM²301. A decade earlier, the Thalie lodge in Paris also wrangled with the Grand Orient over its title for similar reasons. Dossier of Thalie (Paris), BN FM²117, fols. 7r–17v. On Enlightenment secularization, see François Furet, "La 'librairie' du royaume de France au 18ᵉ siècle," in *Livre et société dans la France du XVIIIᵉᵐᵉ siècle* (Paris: Mouton & Co. and École Pratique des Hautes Etudes, 1965), 1:3–32.

28. John Stuart Mill, *A System of Logic, Ratiocinative and Inductive: Being a Connected View of the Principles of Evidence and the Methods of Scientific Investigation* (London, 1843), 1:43–44.

29. Dossier of Fidèle Maçonne (Cherbourg), BN FM²213, fol. 6v.

this principle, he went on to praise the masonic use of the title since it served as a concrete signifier which reminded members of their sworn duties to one another: "This is why we must applaud masonic lodges for their common practice of distinguishing themselves by a name or a virtue or a quality of character that suffices to remind those united under its auspices what they owe to their brethren and to themselves." Other prerevolutionary lodges shared this view, imbuing the title not only with designative but also with real ontological force. They believed that names were far more than words unrelated to lodge life, but indeed exercised a kind of referential function on members. In other words, a title not only simply reflected a membership's values—"the dominant sentiments of those who constitute the lodge" as one orator put it—but it also encouraged certain types of thought and action. During a gathering of the celebrated Candeur lodge in early 1779, an unidentified speaker related the unfortunate financial crises that had befallen one of their brethren during his travels. He indicated that the lodge's title would shape his manner of presentation: "Appointed to describe the misfortunes that have plagued one of our brethren, I will not have recourse to the ornaments of language; the facts alone will speak to your sensitive souls. . . . Candor is the emblem and the link of our society, [and] it reigns in our hearts and must so be on our lips."[30]

Masonic conviviality and friendship bonds could also be measured against values identified with titles. Addressing the Heureuse Réunion lodge in 1779, parlementaire Charles Millon proclaimed that "this distinctive title, found amongst your hearts, is the richest and purest expression of the pure, lively and endless pleasures that you experience with each other." A few years later, a speaker at the Réunion des Amis Intimes in Paris lauded friendship as "this precious gift from Heaven, reserved for sensitive souls" and everywhere present among Masons. He then went on to remark that friendship "will undoubtedly establish itself forever amongst us and particularly amongst the members of Amis Intimes who have paid homage to it in adopting it as their patron name." In a much more gushing tone, an orator of the Saint-Étienne de la Parfaite Amitié lodge reiterated this theme. He endowed friendship with animate qualities, personifying it as the life-giving source of the sociability of those lodges that chose it as a name: "O saintly and tender friendship, penetrate my entire soul! Inspire me yourself in order

---

30. Dossier of Modération (Paris), BN FM²89, "archives internes," fol. 4r; Dossier of Zèle (Paris), BN FM²128, fol. 18r; Dossier of Candeur (Paris), BN FM²58ᵇⁱˢ, fol. 60v.

to better express those constantly renewed charms that you reserve for decent and virtuous hearts! Be the guiding light of this temple which is particularly devoted to your worship!" It is also significant that brethren invoked titles during times of internal crisis. When antagonistic groups formed in early 1778 within the Frères Amis lodge in Paris, one camp announced its departure and plan to erect a new lodge. They justified this decision in declaring that the social environment no longer met the expectations implicitly set by the lodge title: "The distinctive title that this respectable lodge had chosen seemed to announce the reign of peace and friendship; on the contrary, cabals and intrigue foments in its heart."[31]

In sum, the predominance of friendship and sociability within the lexicon of lodge titles from midcentury onward reflected an ever-increasing focus among Masons on their particular brand of socializing. Lodges hoped that titles could be effectively mobilized as an ideal reference point against which actual interaction could be measured. The title was undoubtedly envisioned in such a manner in part to mitigate the reoccurring tensions between factions, to be explored later in this chapter, that could lead to the demise or severe disruption of lodges.

In order to better situate masonic associative life within the larger frame of reference of the Enlightenment, it would be helpful to compare this emergence of friendship in *titres distinctifs* during the second half of the eighteenth century with a larger, non-masonic data set: the ARTFL database.[32] This online corpus of searchable texts contains hundreds of documents spanning the gamut of eighteenth-century cultural production: journalism, correspondence, and scientific treatises, as well as classic literary and philosophical works.[33] Although this database is by no means exhaustive or even statistically representative, performing keyword searches on such a significant quantity of texts nevertheless does enable the historian to derive a general picture of what Daniel Gordon describes as "lexical trends" of the era. An analysis reveals a gradual increase in the importance of friendship within

---

31. Dossier of Heureuse Réunion (Paris), BN FM²83, fol. 15r; dossier of Réunion des Amis Intimes (Paris), BN FM²97, fol. 11r; dossier of Saint-Etienne de la Parfaite Amitié (Paris), BN FM²103, fols. 18r–18v; dossier of Frères Amis (Paris), BN FM²77bis, fol. 37v.

32. A similar approach can be found in Daniel Gordon, *Citizens without Sovereignty: Equality and Sociability in French Thought, 1670–1789* (Princeton, NJ: Princeton University Press, 1994), 48–54; and Timothy Tackett, "Conspiracy Obsession in a Time of Revolution: French Elites and the Origins of the Terror, 1789–1792," *American Historical Review* 105 (2000): 691–713.

33. The database contained 473 texts for the 1700–1799 period as of 25 April 2006.

the ARTFL corpus of Enlightenment texts over the course of the century.[34] The rate of occurrence of friendship terms per ten thousand words rose considerably from the first half to the second half of the century: whereas in the 1730s the rate stood at 6.87, forty years later it had nearly doubled to 12.63. This general lexical picture thus suggests that the emphasis on friendship within lodge titles paralleled to a large degree the wider cultural trend in which *amitié* and its derivatives were a topic of ever-increasing discussion.

✒ The Masonic Oration

To show what friendship really meant to Freemasons some two hundred fifty years ago, it is not enough to simply show that the terms *ami* and *amitié* frequently adorned lodge titles. It is necessary to probe deeper into the available documentation and try to uncover how brethren envisioned their bond with one another and set it apart from other social relations in eighteenth-century France. The speeches that punctuated significant occasions in lodge life can help reconstruct a fuller picture of masonic visions of friendship because they offer a rare first-hand account of what men in lodges believed Freemasonry was all about. Often quite vivid and elaborate in detail, these speeches were found in every region of the kingdom and in lodges that welcomed men from all walks of life, from skilled artisans to the highest echelons of the nobility. A crucial fact to keep in mind when examining the importance of these discourses is that the Freemasons who delivered and listened to them inhabited a world in which the spoken word carried considerable weight. Many speeches from the eighteenth century, including those examined in this chapter, undoubtedly strike the modern ear as repetitive and stilted in their exaggerated rhetoric. But anthologies of speeches, notably compiled from Greco-Roman texts, were quite popular in the early modern literary market as a source for both information and entertainment. Police in Enlightenment Paris also clearly understood the ability of oral communication to shape thought and action and sought to track down and muzzle *mauvais propos* against the monarch. Events unfolding at the time suggest that such draconian measures against seditious talk were hardly overblown, as the powerful oratory delivered in the halls of Versailles was one of the major factors that transformed the Third Estate of

---

34. Terms included in this keyword search were *amitié, amistié, ami, amy, amiot, amie, amiette, amis, amys, amies, amical, amicale, amicaux,* and *amicales*. The polysemes *amiable* and its derivatives as well as *amitiés* were not included.

1789 into a revolutionary body prepared to decisively break with the Old Regime.[35]

A systematic examination of the surviving archives of all Parisian lodges and a sampling of provincial cities to account for regional variation has unearthed one hundred sixty speeches delivered between 1766 and 1789.[36] This figure is obviously a low estimate of how many talks actually occurred during this period. Besides those irretrievably lost in the chaotic archival history of French Freemasonry, many discourses were probably never written down in the first place, whereas others were undoubtedly discarded shortly after their pronouncement; one Parisian Mason considered most speeches simply "routine tasks . . . destined to be forgotten."[37] Albeit partial and incomplete, the extant corpus of lodge speeches does make it possible to recover a coherent masonic perspective toward friendship.

Over 60 percent of these discourses were delivered during the opening of a lodge, and the remaining number were pronounced in adoption lodges, banquets (especially the feasts of the two saints John in June and December), initiations, and other celebratory moments.[38] Membership tables make it possible to reconstruct a collective biography of the men who addressed lodges and reveal that over half of the identifiable speakers were either men of the law (lawyers, judges, prosecutors, etc.) or military officers. Whereas the former category constituted a heterogeneous body of noble and non-noble office holders, the latter was exclusively of the second estate and comprised over 30 percent of the eight thousand or so Freemasons in eighteenth-century Paris. Officers found Freemasonry particularly attractive because, as noted earlier in this study, the initiation process supposedly guaranteed an absolute uniformity in morals and the lodge thus provided a ready-made friendship network for them during their military movements.[39] Men of the law, on the other hand, were prominent speakers in lodges not due to their overall numbers in the organization (they

---

35. Peter Burke, "Translating Histories," in *Cultural Translation in Early Modern Europe*, ed. Peter Burke and R. Po-Chia Hsia (New York: Cambridge University Press, 2007), 133–34; Arlette Farge, *Subversive Words: Public Opinion in Eighteenth-Century France*, trans. Rosemary Morris (Cambridge, UK: Polity Press, 1994); Timothy Tackett, *Becoming a Revolutionary: The Deputies of the French National Assembly and the Emergence of a Revolutionary Culture (1789–1790)* (University Park: Pennsylvania State University Press, [1996] 2006), 138–48.

36. Ninety-six of these *discours* were emitted in Parisian lodges.

37. "Mémoire pour la loge des Neuf Soeurs," Baylot BN FM²148, fol. 47r.

38. On adoption lodges, see chapter 3.

39. For views of the lodge as such a network, see Baylot BN FM²177, fol. 58r and Dossier of Celeste Amitié (Paris), BN FM²59, fol. 23v.

comprised, roughly, only 8 percent of all members in Paris), but undoubt-edly because their profession, which demanded well-honed writing and oratory skill, made them ideal candidates to compose and deliver lengthy addresses.[40] Other notable professional groups among speech authors were doctors and professors, who, combined, pronounced 18 percent of all dis-courses. Remaining speakers included clergy, government bureaucrats, mer-chants, and skilled artisans; each of these groups comprised between 4 and 7 percent of the total. Thus, although the responsibility of giving speeches tended to fall on the legal and military professions, even the most humble Frenchmen could explain, in their own words, what it meant to be part of a lodge. And what is particularly striking is that these men, despite their different socioeconomic backgrounds, expressed remarkably similar views on friendship and the overall masonic experience.[41]

Although, as we will see below, masonic visions of the individual and society changed in important ways over the course of the century, three major themes from earlier in the century still palpably shaped lodge life. First, ecumenical Christianity remained an essential ethical pillar both in Paris and the provinces. Not only did religious sensibilities continue to be taken into account when selecting a lodge title as examined above, but the Gospels also figured prominently in the initiation ritual well into the Revo-lution. Atheists, Jews, and Muslims continued to be *personae non gratae*, for brethren stressed in speech after speech that Freemasonry was where secular and Christian ethics reinforced each other, where "the moral man has become a Christian."[42] Jesus was invoked as a model of moral conduct because of his "charity, individual piety, and solidarity" and His friendship with John the Evangelist was lauded as a model of this relationship. Masons flatteringly compared themselves to the medieval Christian Knights Hospital-ler of Jerusalem, promising to defend Christianity from unspecified "infidels"

---

40. Lawyers were also predisposed to delivering speeches in the provincial context. See the figures in Beaurepaire, *Les Francs-maçons à l'orient de Clermont-Ferrand*, 181.

41. For a breakdown of membership in Parisian lodges, see Daniel Roche, *Le siècle des Lumières en province*, 2: 451. On the place of the officer corps in Enlightenment Freemasonry, see Pierre-Yves Beaurepaire, "Officiers 'moyens,' sociabilité et Franc-maçonnerie: Un chantier prometteur," *His-toire, économie et société* (2004), 541–50. On the importance of oratory in the legal profession in the Old Regime, see David Bell, *Lawyers and Citizens: The Making of a Political Elite in Old Regime France* (New York: Oxford University Press, 1994), esp. chaps. 5 and 6.

42. Dossier of Chapitre de la Constance (Paris), BN FM²65, fols. 18v–19r. On the exclusion of non-Christians, see chapter 2. See also the remarks on the necessity of belief in the Trinity and Jesus Christ as Savior in Frère Enoch, *Le vrai Franc-maçon, qui donne l'origine et le but de la Franc-maçonnerie* (Liège, 1773), 23.

with the "last drop of our blood." They also saw clear parallels between their experience and that of the early Christians under the Roman Empire who had spread the Gospel message despite persecution; like them, the masonic fraternity aimed toward "Evangelical perfection" and toward making society "purer" and "more Christian."[43]

When brethren causally related the improvement of society to the propagation of the fraternity in this way, they were illustrating the important point that Freemasonry envisioned itself throughout the century as a "utopia of reconstruction" that sought not to seal itself off from the outside world but rather attempted to ameliorate the moral character and material existence of non-Masons.[44] Lodges emphasized that they had an active role to play in improving society at large, mainly through charitable works that often were coordinated with local priests. This charitable imperative concretely demonstrated that brethren held a shared moral framework at the center of which lay alms giving. And since men continued to hold to a Ciceronian brand of friendship that stressed that friends must possess a similar worldview, this charity work solidified their bond with one another: charity and other "practices of virtue," explained one orator, "reaffirmed the knots of friendship."[45]

Second, brethren continued to stress that masonic friendship was instrumental and thus required the mutual rendering of services. One of the clearest examples of this came in a lengthy speech pronounced in an unknown lodge in Besançon in 1784. A garrison town that was a lucrative market for later editions of Diderot and d'Alembert's *Encyclopédie*, Besançon saw half a dozen lodges established during the second half of the century, made up of approximately four hundred fifty members. When compared to the overall urban population, this meant that by percentage there were about twice as many Freemasons in Besançon as in Paris. Despite this robust masonic presence, the anonymous author of this speech complained that brethren were not fulfilling the duties of mutual assistance. As soon as men are initiated, he began, they immediately contract a bond of friendship with all lodge members that is characterized by a strong emotional attachment.

---

43. Saunier, *Révolution et sociabilité*, 280; Dossier of Contrat Social (Paris), BN FM²68, fol. 29v; *La société des Francs-maçons soutenue contre les faux préjugés par le seul aspect de la vérité . . .* (Amsterdam (likely Paris), 1772), 48.

44. On Masonry as a "utopia of reconstruction," see chapter 1.

45. Dossier of Saint-Étienne de la Parfaite Amitié (Paris), BN FM²103, fol. 15r. For examples of Masons emphasizing their shared moral framework, see dossier of Amitié et Hospitalité (Sète), BN FM²205^II, fol. 35v; Dossier of Triple Lumière (Paris), BN FM²123, fol. 17r.

A fellow Mason must always be considered a close friend because he is "the person for whom we care the most and in whom we place the most trust." But feeling is not enough; brethren must also continually offer services both large and small to one another so that their friendship remains, in his words, an "active union." Otherwise, he warns, Freemasonry would lose its purpose and disappear: "Indeed," he warns, "no voluntary organization [*nulle société libre*] . . . can be useful if there is not a reciprocal effusiveness to render mutual services . . . without which the organization is without purpose and does not merit to continue." He emphasized that Masons ideally should do business exclusively with masonic merchants, seek out masonic doctors, and give preferential treatment to masonic craftsmen and artists. What the outsider might condemn as unabashed favoritism, this orator thus considered a natural expression of friendship. This orator's concern notwithstanding, masonic solidarity was alive and well in the final decades of the Old Regime, as brethren readily offered one other concrete help such as offers of money, food, and clothing, as well as assistance in finding employment for their fellows.[46]

And finally, Masons in France during the prerevolutionary era continued to evoke references to antiquity when talking about friendship. Although speakers usually were not very dutiful in recording which books may have helped shape their ideas and never explained precisely how they read or reacted to texts, a sufficient number of brethren did cite specific authors to confirm the centrality of classical works. Seventy-nine writers or their texts have been identified in the discourses, and nearly 70 percent hailed from the Greco-Roman past: Cicero (six references), Plato (six references), and Socrates (nine references, which could have been drawn from the work of Aristophanes, Xenophon, or Plato) were the most often cited. Freemasons invoked Greek figures far more frequently than Roman (thirty-nine compared with fifteen), exhibiting a wide familiarity with Hellenistic literature, including playwrights (Aristophanes and Euripides), philosophers (Aristotle, Democritus, Diogenes, and Plato), and poets (Hesiod and Pindar). Greek instruction was limited in Old Regime higher education, and most of these men would have undoubtedly encountered these authors in Latin; this does not mean, however, that late-eighteenth-century French were unfamiliar

---

46. "Discours en loge de frimaçon sur l'amitié réciproque, les services mutuels, la signification du nom de frère et la subordination," BMB MS 1782, fols. 453r–59r. For population levels, see Lepetit, *The Pre-Industrial Urban System*, 449–52. For examples of masonic solidarity, see Émile Lesueur, *La Franc-maçonnerie artésienne au XVIIIᵉ siècle* (Paris: Ernest Leroux, 1914), 219–20; Beaurepaire, *L'autre et le frère*, 136–52.

with Greek literature, as Harold Parker has suggested.[47] As we noted earlier, this affinity for the classics was reflective of the total immersion in Latin most clergy, liberal professionals, and military officers received in the eighteenth century. Whether it was in a Jesuit seminary or an *école militaire*, pupils were subjected to years of a rigorous, immersive environment in which they spent hours daily studying the language and literature of ancient Rome. The study of contemporary authors was gradually introduced into the humanities after 1760, but it may have come too late for most of the Freemasons currently under investigation, who would have been at least adolescents by the time of this reform.[48] What is particularly noteworthy is that Greco-Roman authors even found their way into speeches pronounced by craftsmen who would have had little to no formal exposure to such literature. Whether these men were examples of enthusiastic autodidacts who had acquired real familiarity with the classics in the affordable *cabinets de lecture* that dotted the capital in the final decades of the Old Regime or merely reproduced a common trope found in Freemasonry is impossible to say. But what is clear is that within lodges some knowledge of the ancients was present at all socioeconomic levels.

Although most educated Frenchmen were "children of Rome" as Laurence Brockliss has pointed out, Freemasons saw their engagement with the classics as quite different. They held that they were not merely studying ancient texts from a detached, scholarly perspective, like some "cold admirers" as they put it, but were rather actively engaged in appropriating the maxims of Cicero and others into their everyday lives. Like Rousseau, who once proclaimed that during his youth he was "ceaselessly occupied with Rome and Athens; living, so to speak, with their great men . . . I believed myself to be Greek or Roman; I became the character whose life I read," men in lodges saw themselves not simply as knowing about Greco-Roman antiquity, but actually *living* it. Nowhere was this tendency more apparent than in their speeches about friendship. At times, speakers praised Freemasonry for realizing ancient thinkers' hopes and utopian dreams of perfect friendship. The figure of Socrates, for example, was invoked for his skepticism

---

47. Harold T. Parker, *The Cult of Antiquity and the French Revolutionaries* (New York: Octagon Books, [1937] 1965), 17–20. On the limited Greek content in French higher education in the Old Regime, see Laurence Brockliss, *French Higher Education in the Seventeenth and Eighteenth Centuries: A Cultural History* (New York: Oxford University Press, 1987), 134. The masonic case also does not bear out Parker's contention that interest in antiquity waned by the 1780s. Parker, *Cult of Antiquity*, chap. 5.

48. Brockliss, *French Higher Education*, 178–81.

toward finding perfect friends in the world. Undoubtedly drawing from one of Phaedrus's *Fables*—a Latin collection based on the works of Aesop that enjoyed multiple French and Latin editions throughout the eighteenth century—brethren recounted the answer Socrates offered when asked why someone of his respected stature had built for himself such a small house: "As small as it is, if only I could fill it with true friends." Freemasonry inserted itself into this centuries-old conversation about friendship, and offered reassurance to the philosopher: "Oh! Wise Socrates, you who feared that it would not be possible to gather enough friends to fill up your small country house, if only you could still be alive, I would tell you: 'Come into our meetings, come into the home of the Freemasons and erect great edifices. The world only knows *liaisons* because friendship is restricted to Masons.' "[49]

It was also stressed that Masons must strive to model their relationships after famous examples drawn from mythology, such as the dyad of Damon and Pythias recounted in Cicero's *De Officiis*. Pythias is sentenced to death for sedition in Syracuse, but is allowed to return home to see his family one final time on the condition that Damon serves as his proxy; if Pythias does not return, it is Damon who will be put to death. Brethren cited this story as an ideal of masonic conduct for three reasons. First, it clearly embodied some of the essential virtues of friendship, as Damon trusts that Pythias will return, and Pythias remains loyal to his friend by keeping his word. Second, this friendship, at least according to how orators recounted it, displayed a formal quality that was quite similar to the sworn bond contracted through the initiation ritual as explored in chapter 2: Damon and Pythias, one Mason explained, "swore to each other a fraternal love." And finally, it was believed that Freemasonry should seek to emulate this friendship because it not only benefited the two men in question, but also improved the moral character of outsiders. After having recounted Pythias's return, one Parisian orator stressed that this action so moved the ruthless tyrant Dionysius, who had originally passed sentence against Pythias, that he not only pardoned him, but went further: "The tyrant himself could not resist praising such a friendship and . . . requested to be admitted into it." Such friends, intensely committed to each other while also making a visible impact on the world

---

49. Dossier of Réunion des Amis Intimes (Paris), BN FM²97, fols. 10v–11r. See also Baylot BN FM²176, fol. 30r. Phaedrus's fable on Socrates (Fable VIII, Book III) has been taken from *Les Fables de Phèdre* (Poitiers, 1738), 110. Rousseau's reflections on his engagement with the classics can be found in *The Confessions and Correspondence, including the Letters to Malesherbes*, trans. Christopher Kelly (Hanover, NH: University Press of New England, 1998), 8.

around them, functioned in a way quite similar to the masonic lodge, which ideally had a double role of cultivating strong bonds between members and performing acts of charity. In fitting these examples from antiquity within a masonic framework in such a way, these speeches reflected a recurrent trend in the history of friendship that stretched back to the Middle Ages, wherein Greco-Roman texts were selectively culled, and at times distorted or completely reconstructed, to render them more meaningful to later historical epochs.[50]

✎ From the *Honnête Homme* to the Man of Feeling

The men who spoke about masonic friendship during the prerevolutionary era thus echoed some main themes from earlier in the century. And yet a closer comparison of pre- and post-1760 visions of friendship reveals that brethren at the end of the Old Regime struck out in a number of new directions that were at times markedly different from some of the previous ways Masons ascribed meaning to their institution. The most important shift was in their increasing emphasis on the spontaneous and uncontrollable expression of emotions. As outlined in chapters 2 and 4, earlier Masons vaunted their friendships as grounded in a restrained sentimentalism: men were to be constantly on guard against expressing themselves through effusive language or gestures, even within the lodge. This self-conscious policing of speech and action reflected the seventeenth-century paradigm of the *honnête homme*, which still remained predominant—though it was not without its critics—at least until midcentury. The Grand Orient and individual lodges also continued to issue rules and regulations that laid out in painstaking detail the guidelines for conducting meetings. And, as examined earlier in this book, lodge officers continually pleaded with new recruits during their initiation to be fastidiously watchful to expunge pleasure-seeking self-interest from masonic life.

And yet these speeches make abundantly clear that individuals in prerevolutionary lodges were not merely more comfortable in praising friendly

---

50. Dossier of Constance Éprouvée (Paris), BN FM²65, fol. 26r; Dossier of Trinité (Paris), BN FM²119bis, fols. 21v–22v. The friendship of Pylades and Orestes was also praised. See, for example, the published speeches in Jérôme Lalande, *Abrégé de l'histoire de la Franche-maçonnerie* (Paris, 1779), 144. On the appropriation of the Greco-Roman heritage in the Middle Ages, see James McEvoy, "The Theory of Friendship in the Latin Middle Ages: Hermeneutics, Contextualization and the Transmission and Reception of Ancient Texts and Ideas, from c. 350 to c. 1500," in *Friendship in Medieval Europe*, ed. Julian Haseldine (Stroud, UK: Sutton Publishing, 1999), 4–15.

feeling, but that the open expression of inner sentiments had become by the early 1770s a *sine qua non* for being a good friend and upright moral citizen. Emblematic of this important shift was the emergence of the key term *sensibilité*. Friendship and sensibility were repeatedly associated in the masonic mental world, "inseparable companions" of one another as one orator put it. Although the word *sensibilité* had existed at least since the reign of Louis XIV to denote sensitivity to temperature, figures in the Enlightenment invested this word with new meanings. Beginning with the writings of Herman Boerhaave and Albert von Haller in early and midcentury, and continuing with the researches of the Montpellier medical school into the 1780s, the body was increasingly recognized not in a dualistic fashion, as Descartes had postulated, but rather as an amalgam of muscle fibers and organs whose reaction or "sensitivity" to external stimuli was autonomous, involuntary (in that it was beyond rational control), and self-regulating. Henri Fouquet, a Montpellier physician, summarized this "vitalist" position when he wrote the medical *sensibilité* article for the fifteenth volume of the *Encyclopédie* in 1765. Here he argued that sensibility was "apportioned to each organic part of the body" and that "each organ feels and lives in its own manner, and the combination and sum of these particular lives makes up the general life [of an organism]."[51]

The next entry in the same volume of Diderot's reference work, penned by chevalier Louis de Jaucourt, made clear that *sensibilité* was also associated with moral and emotional qualities: it was an individual's "tender and delicate disposition of the soul, which makes it easily moved and touched." Although this moral understanding of *sensibilité* was not materialistic in that it depended on the interplay between external objects and the noncorporeal soul, it did echo sensibility's physiological definition since it denoted an individual's innate susceptibility to be involuntarily moved—often to the point of displaying physical changes such as trembling, tears, or gasps—by witnessing examples of suffering or virtue. Art critic Charles Mathon de La Cour's reaction to Jean-Baptiste Greuze's *Girl Weeping over Her Dead Canary* (1765) was the response expected of the prototypical *homme sensible*: "Several times I have passed whole hours in attentive contemplation [of Greuze's painting] that I became drunk with a sweet and tender sadness." Although

---

51. Entry on "Sensibilité, sentiment (*Médicine*)" accessed via ARTFL at http://artfl-project.uchicago .edu. On Haller and the Montpellier school, see Anne Vila, *Enlightenment and Pathology: Sensibility in the Literature and Medicine of Eighteenth-Century France* (Baltimore: Johns Hopkins University Press, 1998), chaps. 1 and 2. For the linking up of friendship and sensibility, see, for example, Dossier of Vrais Amis Réunis (Paris), BN FM²127, fol. 10r.

Jaucourt acknowledged that such extreme sensitivity to external stimulation could lead to emotional excesses, he nevertheless believed that the positives outweighed the negatives; he concluded his short entry by stressing that "sensibility makes a virtuous man. It is the mother of humanity, of generosity."[52]

In their lodge speeches, brethren closely followed this definition Jaucourt put forth and may very well have had the chevalier's article in front of them when crafting their own texts. "What is sensibility?" asked a member of the Réunion des Amis Intimes in Paris in early March 1784. His answer closely echoed the *Encyclopédie* entry: "It is in general a particular quality of the soul, which makes it singularly susceptible to experience a more active imprint from external stimuli." However, he soon parted ways with standard presentations of *sensibilité*, because he used its ascribed moral qualities to differentiate between Masons and the wider public: "With a Freemason," he continued, "it is much more: it is . . . a motor of virtues, such as tenderness, humanity, and generosity." This Mason conveyed in this passage that, although sensibility as a physiological condition was universal, its impact on shaping moral behavior was restricted to brethren. Sensibility was devoid of any moral dimension among the French public, he continued, because it was too often misunderstood to endorse a materialistic worldview. Enlightenment thinkers, notably Diderot, Helvétius, and especially La Mettrie in his inflammatory *L'Homme-Machine* (1748)—La Mettrie, like Haller, had studied with the aforementioned Boerhaave in Leyden—saw sensibility and the idea of autonomous operations of the body as the intellectual foundation for a materialist cosmology. Whereas Descartes and even Haller himself saw the immaterial soul as influencing the body through some mechanism housed in the brain, materialists instead reduced all human behavior to physical origins: "the only philosophy that is relevant," La Mettrie famously quipped, was "that of the human body." Haller vigorously attacked La Mettrie in the 1750s, but sensibility's materialistic import remained sufficiently potent during the following decades, likely due to the clear materialist positions staked out in popular texts such as Baron d'Holbach's *Système de la Nature* (1770). The same orator from Réunion des Amis Intimes struck out against those who argued along materialist lines by emphasizing that whereas Masons exhibited "true sensibility," which constituted an elaborate communication circuit involving the interplay of external objects, the soul,

52. Entry on "Sensibilité (*Morale*)" accessed via ARTFL at http://artfl-project.uchicago.edu. La Cour's account is in Simon Schama, *Citizens: A Chronicle of the French Revolution* (New York: Vintage Books, 1989), 151.

and the physical body, the wider public too often simplistically understood sensibility as merely a "type of corporeal emanation, produced from the physical body only." Other speakers echoed this notion that authentic sensibility, and by extension meaningful friendship, lay beyond the grasp of most people. At the opening of his lodge in 1776, doctor Joseph Morin began his lecture on friendship by clarifying that his message was intended for Freemasons only: "If I were to speak to the general public (*des profanes*), whose hearts are not made for friendship, who have never thought about how dear is friendship, and who understand only its most superficial aspects, . . . who incessantly pronounce the tender name of sensibility [but] whose avid and cold souls will never taste its sweetness, this invocation of friendship today would be inappropriate and I would not speak about it in my discourse."[53]

Brother Morin's overture points to the importance Freemasons placed in the quality of the soul when defining friendship; friendship itself was considered a "marriage of souls," and the soul was where friendly feelings "penetrated" and bound men to one another. The masonic soul was alternatively lauded as "sensitive," "warm," "virtuous," "pure," "great," or simply "beautiful." Lodge officers lectured members on how to cultivate an *âme parfaite* because possessing a beautiful soul meant that Masons not only performed consciously willed acts of virtue but they also had a moral compass that was intrinsically bound up in the very fabric of their being. Moral behavior thus was not primarily constituted by an individual's intellectual effort to rationally adhere to an external code of conduct but was above all a deeply personal, emotional experience where morality was anchored in the outpouring of emotions rather than in deliberative reflection. It was the soul that involuntarily acted upon Masons (it is significant that orators frequently employed the phrase *ivresse de l'âme*), moving them to tears when they witnessed an impoverished family or individual, and spurred brethren to virtuous action. This was especially true if the distressed party was a Freemason. It was the "sensitivity of the soul," claimed the master of the Bons Amis lodge in March 1785, that made men "share their sufferings or pleasures," and

---

53. "Discours sur la maçonnerie, prononcé le 7ème jour du 1er mois de l'an de la v[raie] l[umière] 5784 [1784], à l'installation de la r[espectable] l[oge] de St-Jean, sous le titre distinctif de la Réunion des Amis-Intimes, à l'or[ient] de Paris," Baylot BN FM²32, fols. 19r–20r. See also dossier of Vrais Amis Réunis (Paris), BN FM²127, fol. 24v. For Morin's comments, see dossier of Saint Étienne de la Parfaite Amitié (Paris), BN FM²103, fol. 27r. On Haller and La Mettrie, see Vila, *Enlightenment and Pathology*, 16–28. La Mettrie's citation is taken from his *Machine Man and Other Writings*, trans. Ann Thomson (New York: Cambridge University Press, 1996), 39.

induced "heavy and frequent palpitations of the heart" when witnessing a fellow brother in distress.[54]

The previous passage indicates that the figure of the heart was equally as important as that of the soul in prerevolutionary conceptions of friendship; brethren at times used both terms interchangeably. As explored in the previous chapter on Bertin du Rocheret's correspondence network, individual Masons already considered the heart to be the locus of friendly feeling as early as the 1730s. Within the formal setting of the lodge, however, the rhetoric of the heart was subdued before 1760, likely on account of Freemasonry's weariness over the power of the passions and self-love. The praising of the heart had hitherto only been expressed in private letters, whereas the speeches under examination here broke new ground in making the heart a key criterion of the collective, institutionalized vision of the ideal friend. Masonic hearts were always to be "warmed" (échauffé) upon entering the lodge or when meeting a fellow brother in society, and their friendship was routinely framed as a "union of hearts." After praising Masonry as a privileged space in which the "salutary balm" of friendship always finds refuge, the abbé Louis Durand of the Trinité lodge in Paris offered a working definition of friendship as he saw it: "What is friendship? Ah! It is this tender bond that unites our heart to another, which makes our existence dependent upon another. . . . It is this precious nectar that we drink on this Earth." Another orator in the capital expressed the same notion of masonic friendship as a transparent connection between hearts when he declared that "the hearts of Masons touch one another everywhere at every point. . . . The happiness of one is necessarily the happiness of all."[55]

Within the masonic mental world, the heart functioned in a way quite similar to the soul in that it induced involuntary behavior. In speech after speech, the heart provoked "fire," emotional "outpourings" (épanchements) and sudden movements (transports). This last term is especially significant as Catherine Cusset has pointed out in her study of eighteenth-century libertine works that transport often denoted "a violent feeling of passion that carried a person beyond reason."[56] Although violence would be too strong a word to characterize the masonic sense of displacement, the impact of the heart nevertheless made it clear to men that the lodge was a space radically

---

54. Dossier of Bons Amis (Paris), BN FM²57, fol. 4v.

55. Dossier of Trinité (Paris), BN FM²119ᵇⁱˢ, fol. 21v. See also BMB MS 1782, fol. 455r.

56. Catherine Cusset, No Tomorrow: The Ethics of Pleasure in the French Enlightenment (Charlottesville University of Virginia Press, 1999), 56.

different from the outside world. The lodge, according to one member of Celeste Amitié, was a place where "I learnt to love men without fear. . . . [The lodge was] where one can surrender oneself without reservation to the movements of the heart and be enveloped voluptuously by celestial friendship, whose nature is distorted in the world. . . . Here friendship shines . . . and *transports men beyond themselves*, making them Masons."[57] The masonic penchant to employ the literary device of personification when speaking about friendship underscored that, in following the commands of the heart, brethren served a friendship that they viewed to be a self-willed, autonomous entity. "O divine friendship!" exclaimed one lodge officer who apologized to friendship on behalf of his membership for having behaved too exuberantly during one particular meeting, "Pardon me, if in your Temple a vulgar outburst seduced your children. Their excuse lies in the movements (*transports*) your fire . . . has transmitted into our hearts! The heart always remains loyal to you and entirely subjugated to your laws. . . . Everything the heart dictates to us can only please you."[58] In the discourses of prerevolutionary Freemasonry, friendship routinely smiled upon brethren, bestowed lodges with tranquility, wiped away men's tears during trying times, and staved off boredom.

Masons claimed that it was primarily through deciphering bodily gestures that a good heart and a beautiful soul were made manifest. Through a simple handshake, it was possible to detect the inner disposition of an individual: "Every brother felt a soul in clasping a hand," explained one orator in recounting a social event between two Parisian lodges during the summer of 1787.[59] Such a tendency suggests that not only sensibility, but also the related resurgence in physiognomy—the pseudoscience of deriving inner character through external appearances once again made popular by Swiss pastor Lavater's *Physiognomische Fragmente* (1775)—informed masonic culture in significant ways. Lavater was quite vocal in assuring his readers that a close examination of an individual's features could indicate if a particular person were a suitable friend, and an entire chapter of his work was entitled, "Physiognomy: The Foundation for Esteem and Friendship." He opened this section with the grandiose claim that physiognomy, "unites hearts, and only it can form the most durable and the most divine of friendships; nor

---

57. Dossier of Celeste Amitié (Paris), BN FM²59, fol. 23r. My emphasis.

58. "Travaux de la r[espectable] l[oge] de l'Amitié à l'orient de Paris, du 22ème jour du 5ème mois de l'an de la vraie lumière, 5787 [1787], jour de la réunion de la r[espectable] l[oge] des Amis Intimes," Baylot BN FM²35 (3), fol. 8r.

59. Ibid., fol. 2r.

can friendship discover a more solid rock of foundation than in the out-
lines of the forehead, the profile of the nose, the shape of the mouth and
the regard of the eye!"[60] Like most of his work, this chapter remained vague
on details, aside from questionably useful tips such as not befriending people
with severely dented foreheads or markedly protruding lower lips. Scientifi-
cally tenuous and criticized almost immediately, Lavater's belief that physical
signs—noticeably the face—could be used to scrutinize an individual's inner
disposition nevertheless held an inherent appeal to a century given over to
empiricism; a veritable "cult of physiognomy," to borrow Robert Norton's
expression, took hold in Europe that began to wane only in the nineteenth
century.[61]

By the middle of the 1780s, Lavater was widely read in France, and his
emphasis on the importance of studying facial expressions found clear echoes
in masonic speeches about friendship.[62] When a man entered a lodge, explained one orator, he simply needed to look at his fellows' jovial faces and
friendly glances to know that he was among caring companions: "What
tender satisfaction for a Mason to say that he is in a temple dedicated to friendship. Here, he considers every man to be a friend, for each brother is concerned with everyone's happiness. . . . Joy reigns in his heart and is depicted
on the face and in all of his actions. One sees in everyone's eyes sparkle
the same contentment." Conversely, a Mason could identify a distraught
brother by scrutinizing his outward form. In reflecting on how he would
react to seeing a tearful Mason, aumônier du Roi Jean-Baptiste Simonin
de Vermondans conveyed the idea that crying was expected to be a reciprocal trigger response to the joy or sadness of a masonic friend. "If I no longer
see on his lips a tender smile and gaiety," he exclaimed, "if from his eyes I see
flowing tears of sadness, oh, the waves of a rough sea would not equal the
palpitations in my heart. . . . My soul would be bathed in the tears which flow
from the eyes of my friend."[63] This passage also illustrates the importance
brethren placed on tears in validating male friendship, and Freemasonry in

---

60. Johann Caspar Lavater, *Essai sur la physiognomie, destiné à faire connoître l'homme et à le faire aimer*
(Paris, 1783), 2:48.

61. Robert Norton, *The Beautiful Soul: Aesthetic Morality in the Eighteenth Century* (Ithaca, NY: Cornell University Press, 1995), chap. 5.

62. Ibid., 208.

63. Dossier of Réunion des Amis Intimes (Paris), BN FM²176, fol. 39r; Dossier of Bons Amis
(Paris), BN FM²57, fol. 20v. Other examples of physiognomy's impact may be found at dossier of
Triple Lumière (Paris), BN FM²123, fol. 14v; and dossier of unknown lodge (Metz), BN FM²433,
fol. 37r.

fact judged a person to be sociable according to their ability to cry. Employing an oxymoronic register quite common in the literature of sensibility, an orator explained that when a reader of a play or novel displays a "pleasurable, tender tear" when encountering a scene of tragedy, he gives proof that "man is born for society."[64] Anne Vincent-Buffault has shown in vivid detail how the shedding of tears weaved its way into many arenas of eighteenth-century culture, from reading and writing practices to the rearing of children.[65] Although she does not mention Freemasonry, Masons clearly patterned their friendships in a way similar to the protagonists in the contemporaneous *La Nouvelle Héloïse* (1761) or Claude Dorat's *Les Malheurs de l'Inconstance* (1772), by authenticating their friendship through tears. What is particularly striking is that Masons considered the sharing of other bodily fluids in a similar manner, as a symbol of their intimate connection. During a banquet between two Parisian lodges, one lodge master proffered a toast to the "eternal union" of those gathered, but then deeply cut his finger on his wine glass. Despite this severe injury, the lodge secretary considered this incident to be a positive harbinger of future relations between the two groups assembled since "the blood of our dear master has sealed the agreement [between us]."[66]

From palpitations of the heart, to warm embraces and tears rolling down the face, expected behavior of masonic friends outlined in these speeches thus placed considerable weight on performing and interpreting physical gestures. Accompanying this emphasis on nonlinguistic communication was a downplaying of the importance of objectifying friendly feeling through language. Literary scholars have noted that characters in sentimental works, such as Diderot's *Le Père de Famille* (1758), often resorted to nonlinguistic signs to convey inner feeling. As David Denby notes, a prevalent "distrust of linguistic expression" to express feeling could be found in the French literature of *sensibilité*, and similar misgivings could be found inside lodges.[67] Those who volunteered or who were chosen to talk about friendship openly acknowledged the limits of using words to capture the essence of this rela-

---

64. "Planche à tracer de la cérémonie de l'inauguration de la r[espectable] l[oge] de St Jean . . . sous le titre distinctif de la Réunion des Étrangers, à Philadelphie [Paris], 5785 [1785]," Baylot BN FM²177, fols. 52r–53r.

65. Anne-Vincent Buffault, *The History of Tears: Sensibility and Sentimentality in France*, trans. Teresa Bridgeman (New York: Macmillan, 1991).

66. Baylot BN FM²35 (3), fol. 9r.

67. David Denby, *Sentimental Narrative and the Social Order in France, 1760–1820* (New York: Cambridge University Press, 1994), 83.

tionship. Some men exhibited notable difficulty in fitting the highly emotional and spontaneous form of prerevolutionary friendship within the rigid confines of prose. Midway through one speech, a Mason began to lose his train of thought as he began to praise friendship. His text slowly evolved from a cool description of Masonry to emotional outbursts punctuated by exclamation points. Apologizing to his audience, he justified himself, claiming that some inner emotional power was dictating his behavior, and he wondered aloud "what emotions are attracting me, taking me beyond the confines of what this speech has prescribed to me!" Most men did not hesitate to use the *discours* to enunciate the duties, pleasures, and rules toward friends, but brethren nevertheless clarified to their listeners that the essential meaning of friendship lay not in its intellectual comprehension, but rather in its lived experience. One orator began his speech by immediately broaching the difficulty of talking about friendship: "Do I have the skill to describe to you all of the enjoyments of friendship?" But he soon admitted that this was a *question mal posée* since any oral or written account of friendship would inevitably be incomplete: "But what am I saying? You are accustomed to feel all of its charm, and [thus] will only find in my explanations a cold, incomplete tableau. Only a sensitive heart, the heart of a Mason, can appreciate all of friendship's benefits."[68] Masons not only warned that language offered an imperfect picture of friendship, but that it could also serve as an obstacle between men in communicating feeling. For this reason, men in Masonry adopted what may be termed a rhetoric of simplicity where they strove to avoid "ornaments of language," "polished, nuanced expressions of rhetoric," and "eloquence," instead promising that "in speaking about friendship, [the] mouth will say nothing that [the] soul does not feel."[69]

Masonic stylizations of friendship thus were imbued with many of the pertinent themes of the prerevolutionary discourse of *sensibilité*. Brethren stressed that men were inextricably bound through the heart and soul, and advocated for an emotional transparency between men that did not require, and indeed lay beyond, the realm of language. The presence of these particular themes inside lodges demonstrates that Freemasonry echoed some of the most celebrated literary works of the period, notably the writings of Baculard d'Arnaud, Jean-Claude Gorgy, François Vernes, and, of course,

---

68. Baylot BN FM²176, fol. 39r. See also Baylot BN FM²32, fol. 15r; and dossier of Saint-Alexandre d'Ecosse (Paris), BN FM²100bis, fol. 40v.

69. Dossier of Saint-Etienne de la Parfaite Amitié (Paris), BN FM²103, fol. 28r. See also dossier of Vrais Amis Réunis (Paris), BN FM²127, fol. 10r.

Rousseau. Nowhere does the citizen of Geneva's discussion of friendship figure more prominently than in his 1761 epistolary novel, *Julie ou la Nouvelle Héloïse*, which quickly became a prerevolutionary bestseller, enjoying over seventy editions in French and about half this figure in English before the turn of the century.[70] Similar to the masonic speeches under analysis, the protagonists in this work continuously speak of idealized friendship as a "communication of hearts" and as a "society of hearts" where such an intimate and immediate connection is established between friends that their bond no longer even requires language to sustain itself. In a revealing letter describing his life in the pastoral estate of Clarens with the Wolmars, for instance, the tutor Saint-Preux lauds friendship as "a celestial and bracing sentiment" that is best lived in a halcyon silence that should only be broken if "the heart happens to bring a word to the mouth."[71] Did Rousseau have a direct impact on masonic thinking about friendship? Along with Voltaire, he was the most frequently cited Enlightenment author in the *discours* corpus. Voltaire's popularity undoubtedly was due to the fact that he became a Freemason just before his death in 1778, as nearly all references to him occurred after this date.[72] But because Rousseau never entered a lodge, his presence in speeches was instead more likely reflective of a sustained engagement with the philosopher's views on the moral decay of eighteenth-century society, a subject explored in the next chapter. However, on the specific topic of friendship, we will never know with absolute certainty if brethren lifted ideas and language from Rousseau's books when they sat down to compose their speeches. But the strong parallels between his idealization of friendship and Masonry's own hopes and expectations of this relationship suggest, at the very least, that lodges served as what may be termed a "site of amplification" for Rousseauean themes about this bond of solidarity.[73]

---

70. Robert Darnton, "Readers Respond to Rousseau: The Fabrication of Romantic Sensitivity," in *The Great Cat Massacre and Other Episodes in French Cultural History* (New York: Basic Books, 1984), esp. 228–49.

71. Jean-Jacques Rousseau, *Julie, or The New Heloise: Letters of Two Lovers who Live in a Small Town at the Foot of the Alps*, ed. and trans. Philip Stewart and Jean Vaché (Hanover, NH: University Press of New England, 1997), 456.

72. Parisian orators explicitly mentioned Rousseau three times and Voltaire five times. Voltaire joined the celebrated Neuf-Soeurs lodge, whose members included Camille Desmoulins, Benjamin Franklin, Jean-Baptiste Greuze, and Jacques Montgolfier, among others.

73. The notion of Freemasonry as a site of amplification has been adapted from Robert Darnton's sound recommendation that, when trying to establish crucial links between Enlightenment thought and institutions, "instead of cause and effect . . . one should imagine mutual reinforcement, feed-

In assessing this new vision of masonic friendship anchored in enflamed hearts and profuse tears, a basic yet fundamental question remains: did Freemasons acknowledge any contradiction between a friendship imbued with spontaneity and transparency and the organization's emphasis to keep close watch on the passions? Like their counterparts earlier in the century, prerevolutionary brethren believed that Masons in possession of a "truly masonic heart" must "know how to overcome their passions."[74] Over the course of this chapter, we have listened in on French Masons' own words on friendship in lodges during the 1770s and 1780s, and their vocabulary indeed sounds quite passionate; brethren in fact defined their friendship at times as a "soft and tender passion." Although it is tempting to see in such incongruous statements a certain masonic schizophrenia regarding the passions, a more satisfactory explanation is that friendship was functioning within late-eighteenth-century Freemasonry as a privileged refuge in which emotional exuberance—defined alternately in speeches as the "passions" or "excesses of joy"—was both authorized and encouraged.[75] Brethren continued, however, to be very careful to preach against other passions that were thought to engender extreme emotional states wholly incompatible with friendship. In his discussion on the passion of anger, for example, the First Warden of the Modération lodge in Paris explained to his fellows that "anger is of all the passions the most dangerous. It places a man outside of himself and removes his intellectual faculties. It deadens his soul [and] banishes friendship from his heart."[76]

↙ When Things Fall Apart: Friendship and Conflict in Lodges, 1762–1789

Focusing on the speeches about friendship inside lodges, we have thus far told only part of the story of how masonic friendship developed in the twilight of the Old Regime. We need to move beyond examining the mental furniture undergirding the masonic *mentalité* on friendship and attempt to

---

back, and amplification." Robert Darnton, *The Forbidden Best-Sellers of Prerevolutionary France* (New York: W. W. Norton & Company, 1996), 190.

74. Dossier of Caroline Louise de Lorraine (Paris), BN FM²59, fol. 14r. See also Dossier of Constance Éprouvée (Paris), BN FM²65, fol. 20v.

75. Dossier of Saint Laurent (Paris), BN FM²105, fol. 5r; Dossier of Modération (Paris), BN FM²89, fol. 14r.

76. Dossier of Modération (Paris), BN FM²89, fol. 7v.

understand the social reality of friendship within the lodge. When we shift ground from the intellectual to the social history of masonic friendship in the prerevolutionary era, the picture becomes decidedly more schismatic than the ideal put forth in masonic orations, in which all brethren were to gather in uniform harmony and conviviality.

Variety, discord, and rivalry indeed characterized much of French Freemasonry in the second half of the eighteenth century. As explored earlier, the fraternity enjoyed tremendous expansion during this period, with hundreds of lodges opening up in nearly every corner of metropolitan and colonial France; masonic membership cut across an ever-widening swath of French society that reached as far down as skilled artisans and simple clerks. But this expansion was accompanied by visible growing pains as brethren became more heterogeneous in their ritual styles. The Grand Lodge and later Grand Orient found it nearly impossible to ensure ritual uniformity as creative lodges invented a dizzying array of higher degrees beyond the third rank of mastership. There were mystical variants of the Craft operating in Bordeaux, Lyon, and Strasbourg, and the Illuminé movement in Avignon, as well as more philosophically inclined lodges such as the famous Nine Sisters lodge in Paris that welcomed the likes of Benjamin Franklin and Voltaire. Sometimes lone individuals invented an entire system that proliferated widely. Through his travels around the English and French Caribbean during the 1760s, itinerant Etienne Morin propagated his twenty-five degree "Perfection Rite," just as conman Giuseppe Balsamo convinced European brethren to partake in his "Egyptian" Masonry two decades later. Some Masons had become so concerned with the growing mass of arcana that they organized a general meeting in Paris in 1785 in the hope of "ridding Masonry of everything that is childish, useless and perhaps even dangerous."[77] But much like the contemporaneous Assembly of Notables, these intermittent meetings failed to come to any workable solution, and the masonic penchant for ritual novelty continued unabated until the Revolution.[78]

Of even greater concern than this multiplication of ritual systems, however, was the admission of men of questionable moral caliber into lodges. Already during the reign of Louis XV, dissatisfaction over lax admission criteria could be found. One Mason in Paris wrote a strongly worded letter

---

77. *L'invitation à un convent fraternel des Francs-maçons de tous pays et régimes réunis à Paris, le 15 février 1785* (Paris, 1784), Baylot BN FM²33, fol. 2r.

78. Charles Porset, *Les Philalèthes et les Convents de Paris: Une politique de la folie* (Paris: Honoré Champion, 1996).

to his lodge master in late 1764 in which he fretted over the quality of recent recruits. Lamenting what he saw as the "cheapening of Masonry" (*la marchandise de la Maçonnerie*), he complained that "I believed that when we admitted a member among us . . . it was for the pleasure of his company and not in order to benefit from his entrance fee."[79] Such concerns grew more urgent in the 1770s and 1780s, as an unprecedented number of lodges opened their doors, some of which totaled well over a hundred Masons. Bringing a sobering tone to the festivities surrounding the 1785 inauguration of his lodge in Paris, the master of Bons Amis warned his fellows that admitting too many men would have disastrous consequences: "Two causes are bringing about in giant steps the destruction of Masonry. The first is that there are too many lodges. The second is that there are too many brethren inside these lodges." His principal justification for this anxiety was the incompatibility he saw between large lodges and the masonic attempt to create lasting friendship between brethren. At the end of address, he urged the men of Bons Amis to remain small in number because "friendship is the least communicative of all the virtues. It loses its force as it extends its arms. . . . We are few, but we are united. Our temple is simple and small, but it is one of friendship."[80]

These fears over friendship were symptomatic of the disputes occurring within prerevolutionary lodges. The narratives of conflict that made their way to the records of the Grand Lodge and Grand Orient surely offer a hazy, incomplete picture of what actually occurred within meetings for three reasons. First, lodges tended to inform the masonic leadership only when a Mason had committed a serious infraction and would not have shared minor disputes and disagreements with the masonic leadership. As one orator reminded his lodge, Masons were expected to voice openly their grievances with one another and resolve them through constructive dialogue, by the end of which they "leave in agreement and remain friends."[81] Thus, the conflicts that lodges brought to the attention of outsiders—and thus generated documentation—were, by their very nature, unusual. Second, lodge secretaries often sent a mere pithy summary of conflict to the masonic leadership, listing the names of expelled or penalized Masons without further

---

79. Dossier of Saint Louis Martinique des Fréres Réunis (Paris), GODF MS AR 113.1.96, fol. 8r. 13 December 1764 letter from Second Warden.

80. Dossier of Bons Amis (Paris), BN FM²57, fols. 33r–33v.

81. Dossier of Triple Lumière (Paris), BN FM²123, fol. 17v.

comment. And third, letters from Masons were usually one-sided and accusatory, thus making reconstruction of conflict difficult.

Recorded disputes typically did not escalate beyond polite disagreement
or the exchange of colorful insults like *tartuffe* (hypocrite) or *manant* (rustic),
but tension between brethren could at times boil over into violent physical
confrontation. In late September 1780, the master of the Aménité lodge in
Paris, *parlementaire* Alexis Devaux, sent a lengthy complaint not only to the
Grand Orient, but also to the *lieutenant général de police*, Jean-Charles-Pierre
Le Noir. In his letter, he described how another member, also a *parlementaire*
by the name of Marie-Florimond Le Bas, had pushed him against a wall,
punched him in the nose, and then apparently whispered into his ear:
"You will die only by my hand." The following year in Paris, Coeurs Unis
expelled one Mason who had hit several lodge members during a banquet.
At times, this violence even spilled out into the streets. In June 1764, two
factions of the Parfaite Union lodge in Reims exchanged insults, and then
beat one another with canes in front of the city's playhouse as 150 residents looked on in amazement.[82]

What factors provoked such violence? Paris perhaps offers the most
effective laboratory to assess the origins, development, and outcomes of
conflict because it had the most lodges of any city, as well as a socioeconomically diverse membership pool. Although here we will focus on masonic life
in the capital, evidence suggests that disputes played out in a similar manner
in the provincial context.[83]

From the beginning of Grand Lodge records in 1762 to the outbreak of
the Revolution in 1789, at least one hundred eighty Masons were excluded
from or voluntarily left a lodge located in the capital.[84] This is undoubtedly
a conservative figure, since it only accounts for individuals who left for
extraordinary reasons and does not include men who simply stopped attending because of waning interest. Out of the 148 cases where it is possible to identify why a Freemason left or was expelled from a lodge, five
explanatory factors emerge. First, a small group of men were thrown out

---

82. Dossier of Aménité (Paris), BN FM²31bis, fols. 12r–15r; Dossier of Coeurs Unis (Paris), BN
FM²64, unfoliated; Dossier of Parfaite Union (Reims), GODF MS AR 113.1.121, fols. 39r–40r.

83. During the second half of the century in Paris, there were over 8000 Masons and at least 130
lodges affiliated with the Grand Orient. On the figures and social background of Parisian membership, see Le Bihan, *Francs-maçons parisiens*, 7–8; and Roche, *Siècle des Lumières en province*, 2:419, 451.
On provincial disputes, see the incidents highlighted in letters between Lyonnais Jean-Baptiste
Willermoz and his correspondents in the Midi: BML, MS 5456.

84. These findings are based on an examination of all Parisian lodges in the FM² holdings at the
Bibliothèque Nationale as well as in the AR 113.1 series at the Bibliothèque du Grand Orient.

of lodges because of conduct brethren considered morally reprehensible. Such infractions included stealing assets or items from their fellows, shady business dealings, associating with professions deemed morally suspect (usually actors), and frequenting questionable arenas of sociability like gambling houses.[85] Second, a handful of departures was the result of socio-professional restrictions on membership. A hairdresser apparently had been involved in the founding of the Bonne Union lodge in 1773, but then complained to the Grand Orient the following year that he was no longer welcome at meetings. This was because other brethren no longer recognized him—perhaps they never had, as there is no record of him on the rolls—as a brother because they considered his profession as incompatible with *la bonne compagnie*.[86] A couple of years later, Réunion Sincère likewise ejected two members when it was discovered that they were not master artisans as they had first claimed, but only *garçons*, skilled workers who were assistants to masters in their workshops.[87] Such exclusions based on profession occurred overwhelmingly during the early 1770s when lodges were in flux, reorganizing themselves under the auspices of the newly established Grand Orient. Third, because so much of Freemasonry's activity was shrouded in secrecy, Masons also expelled members who had revealed the inner workings of the Craft to outsiders by selling ritual items or holding mock initiations in taverns or private homes.[88] Fourth, we also find some men voluntarily leaving Masonry if they were unhappy with the financial status of their lodge, due either to perceived mismanagement or waste. After having witnessed creditors confiscating most of his lodge's furnishings, one brother informed Innocence Reconnue that he would not be returning.[89]

But by far the most prevalent reason (86 percent of all cases) why brethren left or were expelled from Parisian lodges from the early 1760s to the Revolution stemmed from a fifth factor: the presence of friendship cliques that threatened communal solidarity. Lodges used a host of terms to identify these self-oriented groups—which ranged in size from just a few men to a dozen or more—such as "particular" or "intimate" friends, "cabals," "factions,"

---

85. The Grand Orient, for instance, referred to actors as a "vile profession" in Dossier of Thalie (Paris), BN FM²117, fol. 12v.

86. Dossier of Bonne Union (Paris), BN FM²56, fol. 26v.

87. Dossier of Réunion Sincère (Paris), BN FM²91, unfoliated.

88. Dossier of Douce Union (Paris), BN FM²72, fol. 7r.

89. Dossier of Innocence Reconnue (Paris), BN FM²84, fol. 21r.

"conspirators," and "partisans." It is impossible to determine how many of these adullamites knew one another before joining Freemasonry, or if they instead had become especially close after initiation. What is clear, however, is that they partook in two different types of activities that other members condemned as a danger to the vitality of the lodge.

First, lodges accused these friendship cliques of some form of electoral corruption that undermined the integrity of the voting process regarding new candidates, the conferral of degrees, or the nomination of officers. In 1766, the orator of Théodore de la Sincérité lodge pleaded with the Grand Lodge to allow him to start a new lodge in the capital. He had become exasperated with his current lodge master's behavior, notably his decision to elect and initiate three close friends without consulting the entire lodge.[90] A similar situation strained the brethren of Trinité earlier that decade, where both wardens accused the master of behaving in "despotic terms" because of his persistence in initiating his friends without the lodge and then immediately granting them the next two degrees of journeyman and master.[91] The problem of friendship corruption was compounded in 1773 when the Grand Orient began requiring that members elect their masters.[92] From this year forward, the masonic leadership received a steady flow of letters from disgruntled brethren who complained about sham elections in which an incompetent master had nevertheless managed to remain in his position through his close friends' support. In 1783, a newly initiated *procureur*, Germain Garnier, complained to the Grand Orient that Sainte Sophie's acting master, fellow man of law Pierre-Louis Gouillard, delayed holding annual elections in the hope of retaining power.[93] When Gouillard finally did yield to pressure, he did not hold elections in the suite of apartments the lodge used for meetings but instead organized the proceedings at his home, to which only a handful of Sainte Sophie brethren were invited; Gouillard unsurprisingly was reelected. Following Garnier's initial complaint, other members informed the Grand Orient of their departure from Sainte Sophie, lamenting the factional strife Gouillard's actions had created. One Mason regretted that he felt compelled to "exile myself" from

---

90. Dossier of Théodore de la Sincérité (Paris), GODF, MS AR.113.1.100, fol. 22r.

91. Dossier of Trinité (Paris), GODF, MS AR.113.1.104, fol. 3r. This dispute occurred in late March 1762.

92. Pierre Chevallier, *Histoire de la Franc-maçonnerie française. La Maçonnerie: École de l'égalité, 1725–1799* (Paris: Fayard, 1974), 155.

93. The dissolution of this lodge can be found in Dossier of Sainte Sophie (Paris), BN FM²112, fols. 32r–176r.

the lodge because of the *esprit de parti* (party spirit) that had replaced the "pleasures of fraternal friendship." As more members left and Gouillard's behavior remained unchanged, the Grand Orient eventually ordered Sainte Sophie dissolved in 1787.

In addition to such cases of electoral corruption, friendship cliques also threatened community solidarity within Freemasonry when these groups kept exclusive company inside or outside the lodge. There are examples of officers disrupting the harmony of meetings by forming private discussions with select brethren. In his complaint to the Grand Orient, one Mason from Bonne Foi outlined how his wardens repeatedly banged their gavels during meetings to get the master's attention, but their efforts had been of no avail. "This is not due to the master being deaf," he sardonically remarked, "but [because] his sole focus is to converse with brethren that surround him."[94] Such instances of self-oriented friendship cliques behaving antisocially during meetings were not uncommon, but it was far more likely for these groups to partake in exclusive sociability outside the lodge. On one Sunday afternoon in early March 1782, a small group from Saint Charles des Amis Réunis lodge gathered for a festive banquet at a local *marchand de vin*, a typical custom for eighteenth-century Parisians.[95] However, other brethren condemned this event in strong terms—and later left the lodge—because not all members had been invited to participate. At times, these exclusive meals also represented a financial threat to community life, as some brethren brazenly used collective funds for these private dinners.[96]

A great many complaints also were the result of friendship cliques holding adoption lodge ceremonies in private. At times, this was because a significant portion of the lodge did not approve of women participating in Masonry, but these exclusive assemblies typically had more to do with a small number of brethren preferring to withdraw from collective lodge life in the aim of nourishing more intimate friendships, or perhaps in order to have the undivided attention of their adopted sisters. For the members of Frères Amis, adoption had become a routine part of masonic life. But when news got out that a handful of men had held an adoption assembly at a private residence in late

---

94. Dossier of Bonne Foi (Paris) GODF MS AR.113.1.75, fols. 18r–29r.

95. Dossier of Saint Charles des Amis Réunis (Paris), BN FM²101bis, fol. 64r. On the centrality of the *marchand de vin* to neighborhood sociability in the city, see David Garrioch, *Neighbourhood and Community in Paris, 1740–1790* (New York: Cambridge University Press, 1986), 25–26.

96. Dossier of Saint Louis de la Martinique des Frères Réunis (Paris), GODF MS AR.113.1.96, fol. 71v.

1777, other lodge members reacted angrily.[97] In his complaint to the Grand Orient, one Mason found such "small, secretive and selective assemblies" as completely "incompatible with the attachment and respect that we mutually owe one another." In a meeting held soon afterward, the lodge's orator roundly criticized the guilty brethren's exclusionist behavior: "Did I not already instruct you in the dangers of such anarchy? Why did my soft voice not make itself heard? It was the voice of friendship!" By 1778, the friendship clique in question had left Frères Amis, and established a new lodge, La Paix.

These lodge disputes were symptomatic of a recurrent tension between two models of friendship explored throughout this book that converged within masonic sociability. On the one hand, the participation in a wide variety of shared experiences—the performance of rituals, the listening to speeches, the attendance of banquets, and so forth—sustained what we have defined in chapter 2 as a collective "ritualized" friendship that bound together all lodge members. This form of group friendship was first forged through the rites of initiation and was what kept a lodge together. Furthermore, it was wholly grounded in activities undertaken within this setting and did not require any personal relations outside of this arena. The high value Masonry placed on shared experiences as the foundation for this collective solidarity meant that absenteeism was greatly frowned upon. How can a Mason offer "the smallest mark of friendship," an orator asked, when "months or even years go by without attending our meetings?"[98] On the other hand, masonic life also facilitated the development of deep friendship ties between individual Masons. As noted within the Bertin du Rocheret network and in the material we have examined in the preceding pages, these informal or "unritualized" friendship bonds between self-selecting brethren were nourished through letter exchange, personal visits, and exclusive acts of sociability, such as unofficial lodge meetings and private meals.

To be sure, these two forms of friendship could mutually reinforce one another harmoniously. The ritualized friendship of Freemasonry, for instance, offered men hitherto unacquainted a starting point from which to initiate deeper relationships that then could develop outside the formal setting of the lodge; this was the case, for example of Bertin du Rocheret and the chevalier de Béla. And once brethren had formed such unritualized friendships with one another, these bonds could, in turn, strengthen the

---

97. Dossier of Frères Amis (Paris), BN FM²77bis, fols. 28r–44v.

98. BMB, MS 1782, fol. 456v.

communal solidarity of the lodge. However, the above analysis has shown that unritualized friendships could also prompt behavior that posed a dire threat to the harmony of masonic life. When friendship cliques selfishly put their own interests above that of the collective, their actions could jeopardize the wider solidarity of the lodge and sometimes lead to its destruction. It is significant that this tension between ritualized and unritualized forms of friendship was prevalent in all sizes of lodges and at all social levels within masonic society, from the most well-heeled to the most humble.[99]

Because friendship could be both Old Regime Freemasonry's greatest asset and its greatest liability, the fraternity exhibited what sociologist Philip Abrams has called a classic "paradox" found in many organizations that have attempted to institutionalize friendship from the medieval period to the present.[100] Masons highly valued friendship as a source of collective solidarity and expected that brethren be emotionally invested in one another; as we have shown in this chapter, masonic friendship and emotions became even more closely enmeshed in the age of *sensibilité*. But as particular friendships between individuals strengthened, the harmony of the lodge community could be endangered.

When voluntary organizations in the past have become aware of this tension in friendship between individuality and collective solidarity, they have often jettisoned friendship entirely as a group value. In the case of European monastic communities, friendship was eventually considered to be too dangerous to remain an important value undergirding institutional life. Although monastic friendship was prized in the medieval period—though it was never without its critics—it had largely disappeared as a desirable goal by the dawn of the early modern era. This change was due in part to the growing concern over homoerotic relations between men in the cloister, but it was above all reflective of the fear that intimate friendships inevitably led to conspiracies against the head abbot. Clerical figures such as the fifteenth-century bishop of Venice, Lawrence Justinian, subsequently warned monks that friendship was a "type of assiduous and private contact . . . to be forbidden."[101]

---

99. One finds, for instance, disputes within predominately noble lodges such as Noble et Parfaite Unité as well as in assemblies catering to craftsmen, such as Désir or Trinité.

100. Philip Abrams, *Communes, Sociology and Society* (New York: Cambridge University Press, 1976), 26–27. On this tension within monastic communities, see Brian McGuire, *Friendship and Community:The Monastic Experience, 350–1250* (Ithaca, NY: Cornell University Press, 2010), 77–82; 419–21.

101. McGuire, *Friendship and Community*, 420.

But prerevolutionary Freemasonry did not abandon friendship. Lodges instead sought to mitigate the possibly corrosive impact individual friendships could have on the collective harmony of meetings in three ways. First, they openly acknowledged and warned one another in speech after speech of the potential for the creation of partial associations within lodges. One member began his address to a newly constituted group of brethren by echoing the Rousseauean notion that man is naturally sociable, and it was only within the context of lodge life that men could learn how to care for others: "Man is born to communicate [and] needs tender friends. . . . We are confident that we have established this new temple on such solid foundations. . . . It is our intimate union that will lead us to perfection and make us shine." But he immediately followed this praising of friendship with a warning that there must be "no rivalry between us. . . . Let us forcefully and firmly push away jealousy and cabals." The second term, "cabal," is significant, for it was the same used to designate friendship cliques inside lodges.[102]

Second, Masons managed the destructive potential individual friendships could have on the community of the lodge by drawing up laws of conduct that sought to limit spontaneous, unconstrained sociability within meetings. These regulations could be quite elaborate in their detail; one lodge's handsomely printed and bound conduct book numbered nearly one hundred pages![103] Most rules focused on demarcating the optimal relationship between men during meetings, and the expectation was that brethren would exercise great economy of speech and gesture. The ideal opening of the meeting or banquet began in absolute silence, and during the meeting members were allowed to speak only when authorized by an officer. Interrupting speakers was also forbidden, as was whispering to a nearby brother or communicating in a language other than French. Permission was required for members who wished to leave a meeting prematurely, to switch seats, or to even retrieve a dropped object.[104] Lodge regulations also put in place electoral mechanisms that were intended to prevent personal, unritualized friendships from damaging the harmony of the lodge. For example, most assemblies voted on new members anonymously, and if a brother happened to vote

---

102. Dossier of Innocence Reconnue (Paris), BN FM^{2}84, fol. 7r.

103. Baylot BN FM^{2}220. These were the regulations for the Parisian Thalie lodge that brethren self-published in 1779.

104. For typical examples of regulations during the prerevolutionary era in Paris, see Dossier of Coeurs Simples de l'Étoile Polaire (Paris), BN FM^{2}63, fol. 30v; and Dossier of Théodore de la Sincérité (Paris), GODF MS AR.113.1.100, fol. 14r.

against a proposed candidate, he was usually not required to explain himself publically in front of others. Such anonymity aimed to minimize acrimony between a dissenting member and other brethren who might be a personal friend of the rejected candidate.

The record of lodge disputes indicates that brethren at times did not respect this rigid etiquette, but these were undoubtedly exceptional instances. These rules were accorded pride of place inside eighteenth-century French lodges, where officers routinely read them aloud in their entirety and conspicuously affixed them to the walls of their meeting rooms. The major reason French Masons were so scrupulous about their surveillance of conduct was the fear that unrestrained relations inside the lodge could lead to anarchy. Following a series of expulsions and desertions from Amis Intimes in the late 1780s, its orator, a printer by the name of Louis Desvaux, pleaded with brethren that the rules of the lodge must be closely followed "for the love of order and special friendship that unites us" and to prevent the disagreements and enmity that destroys "the harmony and concord that should be inseparable from our meetings." In closing, he reminded his listeners that the "frequent reading of the rules . . . must be an essential part of our work. . . . [It] reminds every one of us of the obligations that we have contracted towards one another."[105] Similar to the performance of the initiation rites we explored earlier, following rules of conduct thus affirmed that the masonic social order inside the lodge was anchored in the willed subordination of the individual member to the group.

The previous section has illustrated that if lodge rules were repeatedly broken, a third extreme option to limit the harmful impact of individual friendships on collective sociability would be for members to leave or be expelled. The primary purpose of this action was for brethren to re-create a social setting where personal and collective friendships were once again complementary rather than in conflict. Following their departure from Frères Amis before having founded a new lodge, nearly a dozen brethren sent a letter to their former master that informed him that "we are going to take elsewhere the sentiments that animate us . . . this friendship and intimate fraternity that is the charm and the basis of our Order."[106]

Through these various mechanisms of coercion and exclusion at their disposal, prerevolutionary Masons sought to overcome the obstacles they faced in trying to institutionalize friendship. It is entirely possible that the

---

105. Dossier of Amis Intimes (Paris), BN FM²63, fol. 193r.

106. Dossier of Frères Amis (Paris), BN FM²77ᵇⁱˢ, fol. 37v.

masonic embrace of the cult of *sensibilité* that we have analyzed in this chapter complicated this task. By placing a premium on a Mason displaying an intense emotional responsiveness to his fellow's needs, desires, or suffering, the organization now was advocating a move away from the restrained sentimentalism that had characterized masonic visions of friendly feeling earlier in the century. Lodges perhaps experienced difficulty in integrating this new and highly effusive form of brotherly love, with the expectation that men scrupulously follow the strict laws regarding behavior that anchored associational life. In this struggle to make its ideal of male friendship more than words but also an attainable set of lived relationships, prerevolutionary Freemasonry embodied a perennial challenge, and also a limitation, that arguably all utopian communities have faced: how to transform their lofty dreams of communal life into a tangible reality.[107]

---

107. Rosabeth Kanter, *Commitment and Community: Communes and Utopias in Sociological Perspective* (Cambridge, MA: Harvard University Press, 1972), chap. 9.

✦ CHAPTER 6

Friendship under Fire
Freemasonry in the French Revolution

From its earliest history in France it was said there was something insidious about Freemasonry. In masonic lodges, it was believed, anglophile freethinkers of a deist or even atheist spirit clandestinely gathered and, in spite of tight police surveillance, hatched their dark plot against church and throne. The order's triumph lay in its deceptiveness. To the king and public at large, it portrayed itself as a benign organization of sociability with a penchant toward the occult. Within the walls of the lodge, however, brethren hammered away mercilessly against the French monarchy and openly preached and practiced democratic republicanism: laws were devised, constitutions drafted, and elections held. Ignorant of Freemasonry's true purpose, the government permitted its expansion and, as the eighteenth century advanced, so too did the masonic project to topple the Old Regime. By the eve of the Revolution, the French and the masonic mentalities, at least among the elites, had become one. It thus came as no surprise that the masonic model of politics directly influenced the Third Estate to break away from its traditional role in the Estates General to establish the National Assembly. With the creation of this body, France had become a masonic government.

This, with negligible differences from writer to writer, was the distorted caricature of Freemasonry put forth in the flood of anti-masonic tracts that appeared during the final decade of the eighteenth century in France and abroad. Conservative thinkers, most notably the abbé Barruel in his *Mémoires pour servir à l'histoire du jacobinisme*, waxed nostalgic about an Old Regime they had lost and looked out with dismay and confusion upon a France whose political, social, and cultural order they no longer recognized.[1] Perhaps driven to regain some sense of clarity, observers like Barruel sought out the "principal authors" of 1789 and singled out Freemasonry as one of the organizations most responsible for the coming of the Revolution. Adversaries of the Masons established such a tight cause-and-effect sequence between Freemasonry and revolutionary politics—at both the level of agency and political credo—that one writer simply declared, "It is difficult to explain how much the National Assembly of France owes to Freemasonry."[2]

The notion of Masonry purposefully staging the Revolution had lost much of its intellectual currency by the twentieth century, but new and equally unconvincing arguments were nevertheless put forward that refused to sever completely some type of causal link between the brotherhood and political transformation.[3] It has been only in the last forty years or so that scholars have discarded this teleological vision and have struck out in new, more fruitful directions. Beginning with the work of Maurice Agulhon and Pierre Chevallier, historians have reconstructed in great detail the socio-professional composition of membership and the geographic distribution and expansion of lodges over the course of the century, as well as the complex relationship between the brotherhood and the forces of order as the Old Regime drew to a close.[4]

---

1. On anti-Masonry during the Revolution: Jacques Lemaire, *Les origines françaises de l'antimaçonnisme (1744–1797)* (Brussels: Éditions de l'Université de Bruxelles, 1985), 81–97. On conspirational thought in the Revolution more generally: Darrin McMahon, *Enemies of the Enlightenment: The French Counter-Enlightenment and the Making of Modernity* (New York: Oxford University Press, 2001), 73–83.

2. François Lefranc, *Le voile levé pour les curieux, ou le secret de la Révolution de France, révélé à l'aide de la Franc-maçonnerie* (Paris, 1792), 34.

3. The final gasp of the "conspiracy" argument may be found in the work of Bernard Faÿ, *La Franc-maçonnerie et la révolution intellectuelle du XVIIIᵉ siècle* (Paris: Éditions de Cluny, 1935). In a more nuanced yet equally problematic fashion, the early-twentieth-century historian Augustin Cochin claimed that, because of their strong solidarity and familiarity with electoral practice within lodges, Freemasons in Brittany and Burgundy successfully maneuvered through the assemblies of 1789 in order to place themselves in positions of power. A succinct discussion and rebuttal of Cochin may be found in Malcolm Crook, *Elections in the French Revolution: An Apprenticeship in Democracy, 1789–1799* (New York: Cambridge University Press, 1996), 25–28.

4. Maurice Agulhon, *Pénitents et Francs-maçons de l'ancienne Provence: Essai sur la sociabilité méridionale* (Paris: Fayard, [1968] 1984); Pierre Chevallier, *Les ducs sous l'acacia ou les premiers pas de la Franc-*

Although this impressive and ever growing body of scholarship has definitively put to rest the idea of a revolutionary conspiracy at the heart of
the masonic project, it still leaves open the extent to which Enlightenment
Freemasonry and the Revolution were interrelated. How did political transformation affect masonic bonds of solidarity inside lodges and beyond? At
first glance, it would appear that this question leads us to the straightforward
answer Robert Darnton advanced long ago: "The Revolution turned the
cultural world upside down."[5] Pillars of the Enlightenment such as the
academies, *musées*, and salons all crumbled under the weight of 1789, and
masonic life appears to have suffered a similar demise.[6] Reporting on the
situation in Narbonne early in the Revolution, the marquis de Chefdebien
remarked that political events caused "meetings to become less frequent, less
numerous; the mutual expressions of friendship are no longer made with
the same effusion."[7] In 1789, the master of the Choix des Vrais Amis Unis in
Marseille also declared that "enthusiasm is waning."[8] The capital, along with
other areas such as the Charente, Clermont-Ferrand, Corsica, Limousin,
Lyon, Normandy, Provence, and to some degree Toulouse, all registered a
marked decline in masonic activity at some point between 1789 and 1794.
After four frustrating years wracked with financial woes, the Grand Orient—
the administrative hub of French Freemasonry—also finally ceased corresponding with lodges late in 1793. In sum, it is quite possible that fewer
than 3 percent of Old Regime lodges survived the Revolution.[9]

Such a picture of Freemasonry during the Revolution undoubtedly reflects in part the historical reality, but it is equally likely to be founded on
the archival peculiarity of masonic history. Much work on revolutionary
Freemasonry has relied heavily on the *fonds maçonnique* at the Bibliothèque
Nationale; a significant drawback of this tendency is that it has relied nearly

maçonnerie française, 1725–1743 (Paris: Vrin, 1964); Ran Halévi, *Les loges maçonniques dans la France d'Ancien Régime* (Paris: Seuil, 1984).

5. Robert Darnton, "The High Enlightenment and the Low-life of Literature in Pre-Revolutionary France," *Past and Present* 51 (1971): 112.

6. Jeremy Caradonna, *The Enlightenment in Practice: Academic Prize Contests and Intellectual Culture in France, 1670–1794* (Ithaca, NY: Cornell University Press, 2012), chap. 7.

7. Benjamin Fabre, *Un initié des sociétés secrètes supérieures: "Franciscus, eques a capite galeato," 1753–1814* (Paris: La Renaissance française, 1913), 30.

8. Daniel Ligou, *Franc-maçonnerie et Révolution française, 1789–1799* (Paris: Chiron-Detrad, 1989), 156.

9. Gérard Gayot estimates that a mere eighteen lodges affiliated with the Grand Orient were still operating in 1796 as compared with 635 in 1789: *La Franc-maçonnerie française: Textes et pratiques (XVIIIᵉ–XIXᵉ siècles)* (Paris: Gallimard, 1980), 34–35.

exclusively on the Grand Orient paper trail to confirm masonic activity. Such an approach is therefore incomplete, for it cannot account for lodge records that fell beyond the purview of the Grand Orient, notably a lodge's meeting register, the *livre d'architecture*, as well as private correspondence between brethren.

Fortunately, a new archival source has come to light in recent years, one that is particularly rich for the revolutionary period: twenty-seven thousand dossiers, now housed at the Grand Orient and Grand Lodge. It is within these so-called "Russian archives"—which migrated during the postwar period to the Soviet Union via East Germany and returned to France only in 2000—that one finds a rich record of eighteenth-century masonic life in cities where Freemasonry touched all ranks of French society.[10] Documents from Bordeaux are especially abundant, enabling the historian to trace in minute detail the transformations and continuities of Freemasonry during the most turbulent period of the Revolution—from the calling of the Estates General to the Reign of Terror.[11]

Drawing on these and other sources, we explore in this chapter the fate of masonic friendship during this transformative period. Proceeding more or less chronologically, we will first evaluate the possible connections between the masonic discourse on friendship and the new political culture taking form from 1789 onward. Our story then follows the fate of Freemasons within the bustling halls of the Estates General *cum* National Assembly in its early years, investigating how the difficult political choices brethren made either strengthened or undermined earlier ties. Finally, we will move ahead to the turbulent Reign of Terror, exploring what role friendship played in closing down those lodges that had been able to weather earlier political storms. Exploring developments in Paris and the provinces with a variety of newly available or infrequently consulted sources, we thus intend to put flesh on what has been an otherwise skeletal history of Freemasonry during this time and also to reveal something about a classic yet persistent question: How were the Enlightenment and the Revolution interrelated?

---

10. Charles Porset, "Un nouveau massif de sources: Les archives du KGB," in *Franc-maçonnerie et histoire: Bilan et perspectives*, ed. Christine Gaudin and Eric Saunier (Rouen: Publications de l'Université de Rouen et du Havre, 2003), 37–43.

11. Margaret Jacob has devoted some attention to Anglaise in the Revolution in *Strangers Nowhere in the World: Cosmopolitanism in Early Modern Europe* (Philadelphia: University of Pennsylvania Press, 2006), 107–14.

✔ Revisiting the Masonic Origins of *Fraternité*

On 6 March 1848, just a short time after the July Monarchy had collapsed in the wake of massive street protests in Paris, a cortege of Freemasons from the Grand Orient arrived at the Hôtel de Ville where they welcomed the arrival of the Second Republic. This group was led by future deputy of the Yonne Laurent Bertrand, who declared to the provisional government council that "Freemasons have always displayed on their banners the words *Liberté, Egalité, Fraternité.* In finding them once again emblazoning the flag of France, they welcome the triumph of their principles and are proud to be able to say that the entire country has received from you a masonic consecration."[12]

Bertrand's grandiose claims were a part of a rich, half-century old invention of tradition that sought to link up contentious politics with what it meant to be a Mason. As early as January 1791, lodges like Contrat Social in Paris boldly claimed that "one cannot deny that we have had much influence on the great events that are immortalizing the final years of the eighteenth century." Brethren from the Amis de la Liberté lodge echoed this view during the height of the Terror when they sent a letter to other Masons in the capital, urging them to be more explicit in their embrace of the Republic. Supporting the Revolution in symbolic ways, such as by affixing the tricolor inside the lodge, was expected, they reasoned, since "Masonry developed in most of its members the enlightenment of Reason and Philosophy that have contributed to the French Revolution and . . . masonic morals have never departed from the principles of equality, fraternity, unity and indivisibility."[13]

What these revolutionary claims all shared was the repeated insistence that the values reified in the tripartite slogan of the Republic were of masonic provenance. Historians have tended to follow this line of thinking in connecting Freemasonry and key values of the Revolution. A number of scholars have focused in particular on the new political metaphor of solidarity—*fraternité*—and have suggested that this ideal was, *mutatis mutandis,* a transposition of masonic visions into a new era. Margaret Jacob has rightly pointed out that Old Regime Freemasons used the term "friendship" more frequently than "fraternity." Nevertheless, she argues that revolutionary

---

12. An account of this meeting first appeared in the 7 March 1848 edition of the *Moniteur Universel* and was reprinted in A. Sebastian Kauffmann, *Histoire philosophique de la Franc-maçonnerie: Ses principes, ses actes et ses tendances* (Lyon, 1850), 477–78.

13. Dossier of Guillaume Tell (Paris), BN FM³31, fol. 100r.

fraternity and masonic friendship were clearly connected. "While some controversy surrounds the origin of the term *fraternity* as it was found in the revolutionary slogan," she writes, "there can be little doubt that the fraternal concept was a strong element in all masonic lodges."[14] In a similar vein, Michael Kennedy has argued that the Jacobin fraternal embrace and use of the term *"frère"* was undoubtedly due to masonic influence, and Brian Martin has claimed that the Enlightenment origins of fraternity lay within "the ritual traditions of the Masons."[15]

But the link between Old Regime lodges and fraternity was far less transparent than these historians have suggested. First, it is difficult to compare in a straightforward manner any Enlightenment precedent with fraternity because this concept was by no means monolithic during the Revolution.[16] Before fraternity fell out of fashion after the fall of Robespierre due to having acquired violent undertones during the Terror, fraternity's lexical history went through three stages: before the outbreak of international war in 1792; the period after war had commenced; and during the Reign of Terror from mid-1793 to mid-1794.[17] Briefly charting fraternity's evolution during this period is therefore necessary if we are to try to connect this idea to masonic friendship in the Old Regime.

In the early stages of the Revolution, *fraternité* was nearly always qualified by the adjectives "general" or "universal," in that it signified a union that could include not merely every French citizen, but all of humanity. During his opening speech at the Estates General, the king's Garde-des-Sceaux, Charles de Barentin, invoked the term in the effort to assuage smoldering antagonism between the orders: "Representatives of the nation, swear at the foot of the throne . . . that only the love of the public weal will animate your patriotic souls. . . . Men and citizens of all ages, unite your mind and hearts and let

---

14. Margaret Jacob, *The Origins of Freemasonry: Facts & Fictions* (Philadelphia: University of Pennsylvania Press, 2007), 113–14.

15. Michael Kennedy, "The Foundation of the Jacobin Clubs and the Development of the Jacobin Club Network, 1789–1791," *Journal of Modern History* 51 (1979): 703; Brian J. Martin, *Napoleonic Friendship: Military Fraternity, Intimacy, and Sexuality in Nineteenth-Century France* (Durham, NH: University of New Hampshire Press, 2011), 20.

16. Lynn Hunt, *The Family Romance of the French Revolution* (Berkeley: University of California Press, 1992), 12–13; Marcel David, *Fraternité et Révolution française, 1789–1799* (Paris: Aubier, 1987), chaps. 1 and 2.

17. We differ here with Marcel David who sees only two distinct stages in the history of fraternity during this period: before and after the declaration of the Republic in late September 1792. David, *Fraternité et Révolution francaise*, 12–14.

this solemn engagement unite you all in the knots of fraternity."[18] As Barentin's plea to noble and non-noble suggests, equality—be it political or social—was not a necessary precondition for fraternity during this early period. Fraternity during the opening years of the Revolution thus was roughly synonymous with unity, harmony, or peace among all ranks of citizen. Such an inclusive notion of fraternity reflected the term's Catholic past in the Old Regime, where it had designated collective solidarity within religious communities and, most importantly, the common divine origin of all humankind.[19]

From 1792 onward, this more open-ended form of fraternity did not disappear, but was soon overshadowed by two more precise forms of the concept. First, as France went to war with Prussia and then Austria, *fraternité* increasingly referred to the bonds between soldiers. Fraternity already had been closely associated to military life in the Old Regime, such as in the centuries-old term *fraternité d'armes*, which referred to a ritual pact of mutual assistance between officers or rulers.[20] But during the revolutionary wars, military fraternity became much more than an abstract reciprocal agreement, designating in addition an emotional tie synonymous with friendship. Military fraternity was enhanced by the waning of the importance of social background within the national army, and it was also undoubtedly bolstered by the foreign threat facing the Republic on all borders by 1793. In such a tense setting, suggests Alan Forrest, "the Revolutionary concept of fraternity . . . assumed a rich and evocative meaning in the ranks of the army, where young men did feel like brothers, dependent on one another in the face of shared danger."[21] Fraternity also became a strong sentimental bond akin to friendship among the *sans-culottes* in 1793 and 1794 for whom, according to Albert Soboul, it "had an emotional content and took on a mystical aura."[22] *Sans-culottes* did not hesitate to visit nearby sections in the name of "fraternization," where they participated in deliberations and

18. Verbatim of speech reprinted in *Journal général de l'Europe ou Mercure national et étranger* (1789) 3:126.

19. David, *Fraternité et Révolution française*, 18–24.

20. See, for example, Chevalier de Jaucourt's "fraternité" entry in Denis Diderot and Jean Le Rond d'Alembert, ed., *Encyclopédie, ou Dictionnaire raisonné des sciences, des arts et des métiers* (Paris, 1757), 7:290.

21. Alan Forrest, *The Soldiers of the French Revolution* (Durham, NC: Duke University Press, 1990), 102; Martin, *Napoleonic Friendship*, chap. 1.

22. Albert Soboul, *The Sans-culottes: The Popular Movement and Revolutionary Government, 1793–1794*, trans. Rémy Inglis Hall (Princeton, NJ: Princeton University Press, 1980), 153.

also offered candid displays of affection, such as the fraternal kiss and embrace. They also coordinated public banquets on the streets of Paris in the effort to cultivate fraternal bonding between all citizens, and a highly emotional register marked all these "fraternal meals," whether they took place in Paris or the provinces. A second ritual sometimes preceded or followed the civic banquet, further enhancing the emotional quality of fraternity: the planting of a "fraternity tree." This practice became especially widespread during the second half of 1793, and *sans-culottes* used this occasion to share in dance, drink, and song.[23]

The overall picture of fraternity during the years between 1789 and 1794 thus was one of increasing precision: fraternity moved from an inclusive, rather vacuous bond of solidarity to one whose meaning was restricted to certain groups with a shared experience or political vision. To what degree did this fraternal concept, in all its variety, owe anything at all to the model of male friendship within prerevolutionary Freemasonry?

Despite some formal similarities between revolutionary fraternity and masonic friendship—both often relied on rituals, for instance—the two were overall quite different both in form and content. Comparing masonic friendship with the more precise form of fraternity practiced among the *sans-culottes* and the army from 1792 to 1794 we find at least three major differences. First, as explored throughout this book, ecumenical Christianity served as an ethical pillar for the masonic community, whereas adherence to any form of Christianity was either irrelevant for or incompatible with the fraternal communion in the Revolution. The antagonism between Christianity and revolutionary fraternity became most visible during the de-Christianization campaigns in late 1793 and early 1794, and it was during this period that some of the remaining lodges judiciously suspended the use of the Gospels during the initiation ceremony until after Thermidor.[24] Over the course of these tumultuous months, we find the space in front of the fraternity tree serving as the public locale of choice for priests to renounce their vocation and faith, for citizens to burn sacred objects and writings, and for municipal authorities to urge citizens to "recognize no

---

23. During a late August 1793 public festival in Cahors, for example, several hundred citizens erected a fraternity tree in one of the town's public parks to celebrate the recent arrest of two refractory priests. After the planting, they gave one another the *baiser fraternel*, and then proceeded "arm in arm" to a banquet. At the end of the meal, they returned to the tree, again kissed one another, and concluded the festivities by dancing the *farandole*, a circular folk-dance. AP, 75:44.

24. Dossier of Guillaume Tell (Paris), BN FM³31, fol. 101r.

other religion except the virtues of the fatherland." This invitation shows how the fraternity tree could serve as an important site for revolutionaries to transfer sacral authority from institutional Christianity to the Republic. We indeed find former priests using this space to perform so-called civic baptisms on newborns, giving them classical rather than Christian names.[25]

Cosmopolitanism was a second important point of difference. Revolutionaries proclaimed fraternity open to all humanity early in the Revolution, but this soon ended with the king's attempted flight in 1791 and international war the following year. As Marcel David has observed, the threats coming from abroad incited revolutionaries to generally disqualify non-French from the fraternal community.[26] Freemasonry, on the other hand, remained on the whole faithful to the Enlightenment utopia of creating a "universal republic" wherein brethren were strangers nowhere in the world and could always find refuge within any lodge. Consider, for example, the case of Anglaise in Bordeaux, an assembly that will receive extended treatment later in this chapter. It is true that the number of non-French visitors to this lodge did in fact drop over the course of the Revolution: in 1788, seven foreign Masons entered Anglaise, whereas no more than three can be found for any year during the period from 1789 to 1794. Nevertheless, such a trend mirrored other variables such as declining meeting attendance and initiations, and therefore most likely emerged because of the overall instability and difficulty of travel during the period—especially when Bordeaux was under tight surveillance during the Terror—and did not reflect a growing penchant among Anglaise to exclude visitors along nationalist lines. On the contrary, when the occasion arose, the lodge continued to welcome brethren from England and Prussia despite the outbreak of hostilities with these powers.[27] As one orator clearly put it, cosmopolitanism and patriotism could coexist neatly alongside one another within the masonic mind: "The charms of Masonry," he declared following an initiation at the height of the Terror, "are the inviolable principles of love both of one's country *and* of humanity."[28] It is also

---

25. AP, 77:3; AP, 78:45; AP, 80:326; AP, 81:314. In a similar vein, Mona Ozouf has identified revolutionary festivals as the sites of "transfer of sacrality" in *Festivals and the French Revolution*, trans. Alan Sheridan (Cambridge, MA: Harvard University Press, 1988), chap. 10.

26. David, *Fraternité et Révolution française*, 12; Hunt, *Family Romance*, 13.

27. Masons from Berlin, Winchester, and an unspecified British colony visited Anglaise between 1792 and 1794 and were admitted without opposition. The admittance of foreigners to lodges occurred elsewhere during the same period: Dossier of Parfaite Sincerité (Marseille), BN FM³388, fol. 83v.

28. Dossier of Anglaise (Bordeaux), GODF MS AR 113.2.102, fol. 176r (2 April 1794). My emphasis.

worthy of note that, until the Terror in Bordeaux, members of Anglaise made no move to change their potentially scandalous lodge title even after the declaration of war against Great Britain in early February 1793.

A final distinction drawn between masonic friendship and revolutionary fraternity was the use of *tutoiement*.[29] Although its origins remain obscure, employing the familiar *tu* form of address in the Revolution became most visible from the proclamation of the Republic to the fall of Robespierre. The law of 11 November 1793 made the familiar *tu* form of address mandatory, and it was adopted with enthusiasm within popular societies, the army, and bureaucracy throughout France; employing the *vous* when speaking to another citizen was thereafter considered "anti-fraternal."[30] Masons, too, pledged to adopt the *tu* form in the fall of 1793, but it is questionable to what extent it was actually applied. As explained earlier in this book, *tu* had been used primarily in Old Regime Freemasonry only when belittling neophytes during the initiation process, and such a practice continued well into the revolutionary period.[31] Furthermore, when lodges did officially proclaim to do away with *vous* in late 1793, this action probably was a prudent safeguard rather than genuine testimonial to the membership's support of the change. Surviving lodges such as Guillaume Tell in Paris and Anglaise in Bordeaux introduced *tutoiement*—on 17 December and 28 November 1793, respectively—during a period when voluntary associations were under intense fire.[32] For Masons in Paris and the provinces, it was a tense atmosphere in which the *comités de surveillance* declared that "indifference was a crime." In response to this charged political climate, Freemasonry judiciously incorporated into their meetings the symbolic order of the Revolution, of which *tutoiement* comprised an important part. Other similar actions in the final months of 1793 included the adoption of lodge names perceived to be more in line with the values of Jacobin-controlled municipal governments. In Bordeaux, for instance, Anglaise became Egalité, Française d'Acquitaine now called itself Française d'Unité, and Fidèle Anglaise changed its name

---

29. Unless otherwise noted, the following discussion is based on Philippe Wolff, "Le tu révolutionnaire," *AHRF* 62 (1990): 89–94. See also David, *Fraternité et Révolution française*, 161.

30. AP, 79:49.

31. See, for example, the dialogue between a candidate and a lodge officer in G.-P. Legret *Le troubadour franc-maçon, ou recueil de cantiques maçonniques* (1793), 27.

32. Dossier of Guillaume Tell (Paris), BN FM³31, fol. 100r; Dossier of Anglaise (Bordeaux), GODF MS AR.113.2.102, fol. 162r. In August 1793, the Convention had voted to eliminate all academies and literary societies, then went on to restrict sectional assemblies to two meetings per week in September and followed this by eliminating all women's political clubs and popular societies in October.

to Liberté. In addition, lodges in Paris and the provinces placed the tricolor on all their official correspondence and decorations, in hope that these measures would shield them from any unwanted attention from municipal councils.

Despite a semantic resemblance between masonic friendship and revolutionary fraternity that has led scholars astray, these two bonds of solidarity thus differed considerably. Whereas the former was an exclusive, private, and nonpolitical tie anchored in an ecumenical Christianity, the latter was acted out in the public realm and was entirely predicated on a shared political vision that, at least initially, strove to be universally inclusive. This distinction becomes clearer when we listen in closely to the words of revolutionaries themselves when they talked about how fraternity fit into the wider history of solidarity. We find them aligning themselves with the ideas of Rousseau, Greco-Roman writers, and even the Quakers, while passing over Freemasonry in silence.[33] Of course, the historian would be ill-advised to attempt to match up fraternity neatly with any one Enlightenment precedent in a linear fashion, for such an exercise obfuscates the remarkable plularlity of meaning fraternity held during the Revolution. Fraternity undoutbedly drew from a variety of conceptual frameworks and lived experiences, and evolved dynamically over the course of the revolutionary tumult in response to political developments. It was the product of a unique and ever-renewing mix of political discourses and practices to which Freemasonry seemingly contributed little.

✦ Friendship and Classical Republicanism

On the other hand, the political discourse of classical republicanism represented a much clearer connection between revolutionary political culture and Enlightenment Freemasonry. As J. G. A. Pocock has shown, classical republicanism's early modern variant first took form during the Renaissance and is today most closely associated with the writings of Machiavelli.[34] Writers in this vein drew from the likes of Cato, Cicero, Livy, and Tacitus in their study of the elitist republics from Greco-Roman antiquity—notably Rome, but also Athens and Sparta. Although classical republicanism evolved

---

33. *Discours sur l'amitié, prononcé par le C. Manet, dans le temple de la Morale de la section Guillaume Tell* (Paris, 1793).

34. J. G. A. Pocock, *The Machiavellian Moment: Florentine Political Thought and the Atlantic Republican Tradition* (Princeton, NJ: Princeton University Press, [1975] 2003).

through many iterations in the early modern era, a central notion of this political discourse was that the vitality of the state was inextricably linked to the moral uprightness of its citizens. Equally important for this mode of thought was the idea that the polis, like the men who created it, followed a predictable life course that culminated in its inevitable demise. The objective therefore was not to render a political system everlasting, but rather to retard its eventual decline and fall. Classical republicans believed that this could be accomplished by encouraging selfless and patriotic behavior where individual citizens eschewed self-regarding impulses and instead put the common good above their own particular interests. Otherwise, moral corruption would soon take hold and hasten the degeneration of the political system.

Although Pocock largely restricted his analysis to classical republicanism in the Anglophone world, recent scholarship has shed light on its pervasiveness on the other side of the Channel. The conceptual link between private virtue and the public good was quite present in the French Enlightenment, not only in the works of Montesquieu, Rousseau, and other major figures but also in lesser-known writings found in burgeoning disciplines like political economy.[35] By the prerevolutionary decades, the politicization of private virtue clearly resonated with a wide swath of the literate public, as scores of pamphlets related the present ills of the state to the moral decay of the French. This literature devoted special attention to the kingdom's political leadership, where a classical republican hue colored scandals like the mid-1780s "Diamond Necklace Affair" that closely associated the corruption of monarchy with Marie-Antoinette's assumed moral turpitude.

Sarah Maza has estimated that at least 100,000 readers avidly followed this scandal involving the queen; undoubtedly prerevolutionary Freemasons would have been a part of this audience because they too endorsed the classical republican theme that personal virtue was of utmost relevance to political stability.[36] As we explored earlier, Masonry made a conscious effort

35. On classical republicanism in eighteenth-century France, see Keith Baker, *Inventing the French Revolution: Essays on French Political Culture in the Eighteenth Century* (New York: Cambridge University Press, 1990), chap. 6; Baker, "Transformations of Classical Republicanism in Eighteenth-Century France," *Journal of Modern History* 73 (2001): 32–53; Dan Edelstein, *The Terror of Natural Right: Republicanism, the Cult of Nature, & the French Revolution* (Chicago: University of Chicago Press, 2009), chap. 1; Andrew Jainchill, *Reimagining Politics after the Terror: The Republican Origins of French Liberalism* (Ithaca, NY: Cornell University Press, 2008); Johnston Kent Wright, *A Classical Republican in Eighteenth-Century France: The Political Thought of Mably* (Stanford, CA: Stanford University Press, 1997).

36. Sarah Maza, *Private Lives and Public Affairs: The Causes Célèbres of Prerevolutionary France* (Berkeley: University of California Press, 1993), 193.

from its inception in France to distinguish its social spaces and members from the wider "profane" non-masonic world. Such a manufacturing of distinction became ever more important to brethren in the final decades of the Old Regime because lodges were now competing in a vibrant associational landscape where hundreds of voluntary organizations from theatrical groups to agricultural societies were vying for men's time and membership fees.[37] Explaining to curious outsiders or their own ranks what made the fraternity so different from other social venues, brethren taught that, outside the walls of the lodge, France was corrupted by vice and self-interest. Although historians have uncovered speeches in which masonic orators praised material progress, it was far more common within French lodges to find an indictment of society's lax morals. In making such indictments, Masons clearly aligned themselves with the classical republican tradition and Rousseau in particular. "Should we be surprised," asked one Parisian orator, "if the Rousseaus . . . often appear moved by indignation and contempt for humanity? They have seen only selfishness and ambition directing the behavior of most men."[38]

Within the social ecology of eighteenth-century France, Freemasons found selfishness most manifest within a certain segment of high society, collectively referred to as *le monde*. Brethren identified the Parisian salon as the natural habitat of *le monde*, where men and women engaged in intellectual one-upmanship, formulaic etiquette, and meaningless witty banter. Remarkably similar to Antoine Lilti's recent description of the decidedly unintellectual nature of salon interaction in late-eighteenth-century Paris, Masons derided scholarly conversation inside these venues as shallow, "always bouncing around like an inflated balloon," and devoid of any clear focus.[39] Freemasons also attacked these circles as sites of luxury. No less so than other classical republicans, Masons were engaged in a polemic against luxury, wherein it was denounced in terms remarkably similar to the contemporaneous writings of the abbé de Mably as a "dreadful poison," an excrescence

37. Approximately 400 voluntary associations appeared in France between 1700 and 1789, with a sharp increase after 1760. This figure is based on sources discussed in chapter 1.

38. Dossier of Caroline Louise de Lorraine (Paris), BN FM²59, fols. 14r–14v. On the cautious praising of progress among British Masons, see Margaret Jacob, *Living the Enlightenment: Freemasonry and Politics in Eighteenth-Century Europe* (New York: Oxford University Press, 1991), chap. 2.

39. Théodore Henri de Tschoudy, *L'étoile flamboyante ou la société des Francs-maçons, considérée sous tous les aspects* (Paris, 1766), 1:122; Antoine Lilti, *Le monde des salons: Sociabilité et mondanité à Paris au XVIIIᵉ siècle* (Paris: Fayard, 2005), chap. 8.

that subverted morals.[40] The corruptive force of luxury preoccupied brethren to the extent that a group of Lyonnais Masons organized a public essay contest in their city with the following prompt: "Demonstrate that luxury is more harmful than useful to states." Masons proposed that luxury ineluctably fed an appetite for competitive and conspicuous consumption—women's clothing was frequently mentioned—that resulted in venues like salons becoming "scenes of dispute . . . that degenerated into quarrels and division, and which has resulted in hate."[41]

It followed from this analysis that Masons deemed friendship beyond the lodge a "meaningless word": in the social world true friendship, as they understood it, was highly problematic if not impossible to achieve. If friendly association did exist, it was described as "deformed," being typically of an ethereal and unstable quality, anchored in the unbridled pleasures of drink or pursuit of sexual gratification.[42] Most often, in fact, brethren defined the relationships the profane forged not as *amitiés* but instead as *liaisons* and qualified this latter term with a host of damning adjectives: "mercenary," "political," "unpredictable," and "deceitful." Whether speaking of the elaborate patron-client system in Versailles or the literary careerists in a Parisian salon, men in lodges imbued non-masonic sociability with opacity where "the heart and mouth are divorced from one another and [are] in an eternal contradiction." Brethren derided the social worlds of the Old Regime elite as uncompromisingly utilitarian, wherein individuals "only render services in order to then receive them" and emotional investment in others was completely absent. It was thus possible for an orator to confidently claim that in "profane society," a man has "not yet met a true friend."[43]

This masonic critique of unfriendly society went beyond mere diagnosis, however. Whereas some classical republicans contemporaneous with prerevolutionary Freemasonry were depicted as "sulking in a Rousseauian cave" as Keith Baker has noted, the fraternity, as pointed out in the opening

---

40. In his *Du cours et de la marche des passions dans la société* (1775) the abbé de Mably railed against luxury and the passions in general as the "secret poison" that would ultimately bring about the demise of Europe. Wright, *A Classical Republican in Eighteenth-Century France*, chap. 7.

41. Dossier of Saint-Alexandre d'Ecosse (Paris), BN FM²100bis, fol. 39v; BML MS 5882; "Planche à tracer de la cérémonie de l'inauguration de . . . la Réunion des Étrangers (1785)," Baylot BN FM²177, fols. 49r–51r. For the contours of the luxury debate in eighteenth-century France, see John Shovlin, *The Political Economy of Virtue: Luxury, Patriotism, and the Origins of the French Revolution* (Ithaca, NY: Cornell University Press, 2006), esp. chaps. 1 and 4.

42. Dossier of Trinité (Paris), BN FM²119bis, fol. 21v.

43. Dossier of Vrais Amis Réunis (Paris), BN FM² 27, fol. 10v; Dossier of Triple Lumière (Paris), BN FM²123, fols. 15v–16r.

chapter to this book, was a utopia of reconstruction, fully engaged in the rehabilitation of the moral fiber of society.[44] It was hoped that this process of moral regeneration could occur if the warm relationships cultivated between men inside lodges could serve as a model for other social venues. An orator of the Salomon lodge praised Masonry as a space where men "love each other here only for the pleasure of loving." At the end of a meeting, a Mason returns to his home, with "his heart still full of a noble enthusiasm. As a tender father, he will convey this sentiment of his heart to his children. As a loyal spouse, he will transmit the tenderness that he has just experienced to the [matrimonial] knot that binds him."[45]

It was above all in the Mason's interaction with his friends that he would be able to succeed in regenerating French society, one man at a time. When a musician declared to his fellows that "the need for love brings men together" in a modest Parisian lodge in 1778, he was in line with most Enlightenment thought that man was naturally sociable. Just as Rousseau's Émile was to understand that "man is naturally good . . . but let him [also] see that society depraves and perverts men," so too did Freemasons believe that friendship and morals could only be regenerated if the selfishness that corrupted human relations in society was expunged.[46] By identifying men who already stood out for their virtue and upright morals, brethren could bring them into their fold, which they believed to be the best possible environment where Christian ethics and friendly feeling were enmeshed and beneficial to both brethren and society at large. The connection between private virtue and friendship and the health of the body politic was made explicit when one lodge officer explained that friendship had a direct bearing on "public felicity." "We cultivate virtue. Offering the sovereign of the fatherland (la patrie) loyal subjects; circulating within the State the treasures of charity; adding to all the links that connect one man to another the most precious of all ties, that of a true and disinterested friendship. These are not futile tasks, but useful and precious ones, and it is Masonry that imposes them upon us."[47]

According to the masonic reading of the past, the absence of friendship was typically a harbinger of impending political doom. This was the

44. Baker, *Inventing the French Revolution*, 132.

45. Dossier of Salomon (Paris), BN FM²113, fol. 9v.

46. Jean-Jacques Rousseau, *Émile, or On Education*, intro. and trans. Allan Bloom (New York: Basic Books, 1979), 237.

47. Dossier of Salomon (Paris), BN FM²113, fol. 9r.

conclusion of one Mason from the Mediterranean port town of Sète, who claimed that the recurrent "intestinal divisions" found from the fall of the Roman Empire to the contemporaneous revolts in Geneva could all be causally linked to the lack of any meaningful connection between individuals. He therefore explained to his fellows that "the goal of this institution [Freemasonry] is to establish a tighter union between individuals than the political order has formed by bringing souls closer together through the links of tender friendship."[48] We find a similar view expressed in the capital, where a speaker brought up a question of recurrent interest among classical republicans: Why did the Roman Empire fall?[49] "Where is Rome?" he asked. "Where is the monument of so much labor and perseverance?" He granted that although sound laws, rational administration, and a robust police force could strengthen the structural integrity of a state, they alone could not prevent it from eventual moral ruin from within. This is because these were all coercive mechanisms external to individuals that did not address how subjects within a body politic related to one another on their own initiative. He then went on to enumerate other fallen states after Rome and then proudly proclaimed that "in the middle of so many revolutions and universal shaking," Freemasonry was the only establishment that has endured through the ages. He considered that the "cause of such a glorious distinction" for Masonry was "this bond grounded in beneficial virtues and which keeps in check passions, rivalries, and enmity." In order to render political entities more stable, it was therefore necessary for Masons to spearhead an ambitious project involving the "regeneration of morals" and to "teach mankind that friendship is worth more than any other treasure."[50]

This concern that the absence of friendship and associated moral decay signaled the imminent collapse of the state was all the more acute for French Masons because they shared a wider anxiety of the prerevolutionary era that the Old Regime was on the brink of implosion from within. By the second half of the 1780s, political pamphlets inundated the literary sphere, tracing the kingdom's slow moral degeneration from the sycophantic court culture of Louis XIV at seventeenth-century Versailles to recent political

---

48. Dossier of Amitié et Hospitalité (Sète), BN FM²205^{II}, fols. 35v–37v. Although the speaker was not clear, his discussion of Geneva was probably a reference to unrest in the city over the course of 1781 (this speech was pronounced in 1782).

49. For a representative example of the heuristic power of Rome in the French Enlightenment, see Wright, *A Classical Republican in Eighteenth-Century France*, chap. 2.

50. Dossier of Constance Éprouvée (Paris), BN FM²65, fols. 21r–22r. See also Dossier of Saint-Étienne de la Parfaite Amitié (Paris), BN FM²103, fol. 18v.

scandals.[51] Reflecting this broader concern, speakers inside lodges described society's moral descent from a mythical "Golden Age"—a common trope in the eighteenth century—where the laws of nature had once united men "by the ties of fraternal friendship" and where they had known "no distinction from each other."[52] But as time passed and as France saw clear advances in the arts and sciences, Masons regretted that civil society was simultaneously undergoing moral decline. Drawing insight from the "author of *Émile*"—an obvious reference to Rousseau's 1762 treatise on education—an officer of the Thalie lodge in 1776 condemned "the sciences and the arts" as "destructive plagues which carried with them corruption and disorder." The result was that many Masons felt that the Enlightenment had come at a heavy price: it was an era, one orator lamented, "so justly renowned for its great and magnificent discoveries," while also being one which was "so decried for its abandon and contempt for good morals."[53] Unlike many classical republicans, however, Masons did not see this corruption as irreversible but held out hope that their organization could reinvigorate the moral health of the kingdom and of interpersonal relations by bringing men into lodges. Prerevolutionary Freemasons thus recognized that friendship had real political power and could form the bedrock of civil society. Prefiguring the utopian musings of Saint-Just's *Institutions républicaines* during the Revolution, Masons thought that friendship was so important that those who did not believe in it should be eliminated. As one man opined: "Ah! May he perish who refuses to flatter and render homage to friendship."[54]

In the 1770s and 1780s, then, Freemasons were enunciating a form, albeit epigonous, of classical republicanism in their warnings about moral degeneration and their insistence that the health of the political state was inherently linked to the moral status of its citizens. As Keith Baker has observed, the discourse of classical republicanism in Enlightenment France was quite distinct from modern republicanism. Unlike the latter, the former variant of republicanism did not lay out a coherent "prescriptive model" advocating a republican form of government free from monarchy and with a written constitution and law-making deliberative assemblies but instead

---

51. Antoine de Baecque, "L'homme nouveau est arrivé: La "régéneration" du Français en 1789," *Dix-huitième siècle* 20 (1988), 193–95.

52. Dossier of Constance Éprouvée (Paris), BN FM²65, fol. 19r. On the Golden Age in Enlightenment political thought, see Edelstein, *Terror of Natural Right*, 51–53.

53. Dossier of Thalie (Paris), BN FM²117, fol. 11r.

54. Dossier of Trinité (Paris), BN FM²119bis, fol. 22v. Saint-Just remarks about friendship are examined below.

limited itself to a "language of opposition" to voice concern over moral or social problems that they saw as connected to the health of the reigning political regime.[55] Masonic classical republicanism unequivocally followed this model, since lodges were essentially devoid of any criticism toward the monarchy or Old Regime government institutions. A clergyman within the Parisian Réunion des Étrangers lodge made this quite clear: "It is not on the ruins of the laws of civil society that Freemasons have established their own; they respect them [and] make a particular point to observe them with fidelity."[56] J. G. A. Pocock has noted that the ultimate objective of early modern classical republicans was to create a "perfect partnership of all citizens and all values" through institutions that would ultimately strengthen the state.[57] This was precisely the objective Freemasons in France undertook in their propagation of the bonds of male friendship and an ecumenical, publically useful form of Christianity. They hoped that their efforts would be able to stave off the eventual collapse of the body politic, for like classical republicans that preceded and followed them, men in lodges subscribed to a cyclical view of history in which political states rose and fell.[58] "All states have their moments of activity and of decline," lectured one officer to his lodge, "they are born, they grow and perish. . . . What happened to those Republics that were renowned for their laws, armies and political bodies? Their existence weighed on the Earth for a moment, and a moment afterwards they disappeared."[59] Brethren were convinced that if Old Regime France had a chance to escape from this natural history of decay, it would be through their acts of charity and sociability.

Classical republicanism fundamentally concerned itself with combating self-interest and individualism, whereas the modern form of republicanism, achieved to varying degrees during the American, English, and French Revolutions, set out to reorder state and society by introducing modern forms of representation and to reorganize social hierarchies according to merit.[60] To be sure, some enemies of Freemasonry late in the eighteenth century pointed a damning finger at brethren for their republican language,

---

55. Baker, "Transformations of Classical Republicanism," 35.

56. Baylot BN FM²177, fol. 41r.

57. Pocock, *Machiavellian Moment*, 75.

58. Ibid., 75–80.

59. Dossier of Constance Éprouvée (Paris), BN FM²65, fol. 21r.

60. Baker, "Transformations of Classical Republicanism," 32–33.

seeing in it irrefutable proof that lodges were out to subvert the Old Regime. But masonic devotees in France and elsewhere during the 1770s and 1780s went to great lengths to distance themselves from subversive politics.[61] One apologist used the stock character of the *procureur* to present and refute the arguments of Freemasonry's detractors. The jurist attacked lodges as a dangerous corporate body that voiced ideologies oppositional to absolutism when he opined that "never can a republic and a kingdom be in agreement. . . . You are establishing within the state of the monarch another one that is free and independent." The remaining pages centered on the monologue of a Freemason who directly refutes this criticism by explaining to the monarch that it was moral regeneration rather than political reconfiguration that lay at the heart of the masonic project. At the end of this short piece, the *procureur* begrudgingly conceded to the Mason that "the laws condemn you and the king pardons you."[62] The anonymous author undoubtedly counted on his readers to reach a similar conclusion.

Stressing Freemasonry's classical rather than modern form of republicanism is not to suggest that lodges had no tangible connection to the Revolution, however. On the contrary, from the buzzing confusion surrounding the Estates General to the reactionary politics of the Directory, classical republicanism's vision of moral renewal was far more pervasive than the modern republican program to transform France into a political state that left monarchy behind.[63] Since over a quarter of the Second Estate deputies of the 1789 Estates General and nearly a fifth of their counterparts in the Third Estate had at one time been Masons, Enlightenment Freemasonry played an important role in the political origins of the Revolution by offering future revolutionaries an opportunity to participate in an institution that championed key tenets of the classical republican tradition.[64] Classical republicanism was quite visible early on in pamphlets such as *Mémoire sur la régénération de l'ordre public* (1789) and in Marat's paper, the *Ami du peuple*, which called for its citizen-readers to remain watchful for moral corruption that ran counter to the public interest. Later in the Revolution, one detects the influence of classical republicanism in the conviction, shared by

---

61. On British accusations along similar lines, see Jacob, *Living the Enlightenment*, 62–63.

62. Jean-Henri d'Eckhoff, *Le Franc-maçon prisonnier* (The Hague, 1777), 14–27.

63. De Baecque, "L'homme nouveau est arrivé," 196–201; Baker, "Transformations of Classical Republicanism," 43–53.

64. On the masonic affiliation of deputies, see Ligou, *Franc-maçonnerie et Révolution française*, 106.

revolutionaries of diverse political stripes, that the success of the first French Republic depended on the *mores* of private citizens. Just months before his death by guillotine, for example, the conservative deputy Rabaut de Saint-Etienne cited in a 1793 newspaper column the *Entretiens de Phocion* (1763) of the abbé de Mably—possibly the best example of a classical republican in the French Enlightenment—and wrote that within its pages the reader would discover "the austere manners and morals of the Spartans" and would subsequently understand "how a republic is constituted."[65] On the other side of the political spectrum, in the most famous speech of his political career that echoed Mably's dictum that *moeurs* "should be the principle object of politics," Robespierre emphasized that the essential task at hand for the National Convention was to "adopt all that tends to excite love of the fatherland, refine morals, elevate souls, [and] direct the passions of the human heart toward the public interest," for, in his view, "all that is immoral is impolitic, [and] all that corrupts is counterrevolutionary."[66] Classical republicanism's importance was greatest after 9 Thermidor because the National Convention introduced a Constitution in 1795 that disenfranchised more than a million Frenchmen, thus most strongly paralleling the elitist republics of antiquity.[67]

✎ Friendship and Politics in the National Assembly

If we take the conservative historian Augustin Cochin as our guide, the unprecedented elections of the Third Estate deputies leading up to the Estates General offered Freemasons a unique opportunity. Because of their decades-long experience with electoral procedure and strategy honed within Old Regime lodges, brethren were able to work in concert in the months

---

65. Originally cited in Harold Parker, *The Cult of Antiquity and the French Revolutionaries: A Study in the Development of the Revolutionary Spirit* (New York: Octagon Books, [1937] 1967), 121.

66. Auguste Vermorel, *Oeuvres de Robespierre* (Paris, 1866), 298. Other members of the Committee of Public Safety shared similar views, notably Bertrand Barère and Saint-Just. See Parker, *Cult of Antiquity*, 63, 166–70. On Mably's view that mores and politics were coextensive, see Wright, *A Classical Republican in Eighteenth-Century France*, 106. By defining Robespierre and his fellow Jacobins as classical republicans, we are parting ways with Dan Edelstein who has contended that from the trial of Louis XVI onward classical republicanism mutated into a "natural republican" program where the law of nature took precedence over positive law. On the contrary—as Edelstein himself shows (*Terror of Natural Right*, 150–51, 181, 257)—the Montagnards remained committed to a set of laws and the Constitution throughout the Terror. See also Marisa Linton, review of *The Terror of Natural Right*, by Dan Edelstein, *American Historical Review* 116 (2011): 403–6.

67. Jainchill, *Reimagining Politics after the Terror*, 31.

before this meeting to ensure a disproportionate number of their own would be seated at Versailles. Although Cochin never clearly explained the tangible political objectives of these Masons—they shared a nebulous "philosophical perspective" or "philosophism"—he nevertheless saw them embodying an efficient "machine" that closely coordinated electoral policy and excluded non-Masons from power.[68]

Historians have critiqued Cochin both for having confused lodges with other types of voluntary associations and for having glossed over the drawn out, multitiered electoral process that would have made sustained masonic influence unlikely.[69] However, few scholars have explored how his argument holds up when looking at the political sociability of brethren once they were seated at the Estates General. Do we find any degree of cooperation between Masons during the early stages of the Revolution, or was masonic solidarity and identity instead limited to the lodge and ordinary life? Since an important number of deputies had once been members of a lodge, the answer to this question can shed light on both the changing nature of masonic friendship and the personal dynamics undergirding revolutionary political culture.

The voluminous correspondence between Third Estate deputy Jean-André Périsse Duluc and his fellow Mason Jean-Baptiste Willermoz reveals that although some masonic ties were maintained, the ritual friendship between Masons often became strained or broke apart in the presence of political strife.[70] For nearly two decades, Périsse Duluc had been an active Mason who had enthusiastically embraced the Rectified Scottish Rite, a theosophically informed brand of Masonry that had adherents throughout Europe, notably in the Germanic states and Scandinavia. Since his entry into masonic life, Périsse had frequented the same lodges as Willermoz, a silk merchant and prominent Freemason in the city. The two men remained quite close until the former's untimely death in 1800 following a violent seizure; the Périsse family considered Willermoz such a close friend that they not only invited him to the funeral but also asked him to recommend a priest of whom the deceased would have approved to officiate. Years later,

---

68. Augustin Cochin, *Les sociétés de pensée et la démocratie: Études d'histoire révolutionnaire* (Paris: Librairie Plon, 1921), 221–28.

69. Crook, *Elections in the French Revolution*, 28; Ligou, *Franc-maçonnerie et Révolution française,* 95–96.

70. I thank Timothy Tackett for having brought the Périsse-Willermoz correspondence to my attention. This letter exchange has received attention in his magisterial *Becoming a Revolutionary: The Deputies of the French National Assembly and the Emergence of a Revolutionary Culture (1789–1790)* (University Park: Pennsylvania State University Press, [1996] 2006).

Périsse's wife returned some masonic documents to Willermoz and praised him as having been a "true model of friendship" toward her late husband.[71]

During his stay in Versailles and Paris from the spring of 1789 until late 1791, Périsse Duluc wrote nearly fifty letters to Willermoz; the latter's side of the correspondence is regrettably lost. Although months could transpire without a letter exchanged between them, both men made a concerted effort to maintain contact despite the unprecedented developments within the National Assembly and the fractious politics and popular violence shaking Lyon.[72] One reason they maintained this epistolary exchange was that it served the practical function of communicating vital political news. Although the French press had become more robust in the final decades of the Old Regime—a tendency that accelerated rapidly in the early years of the Revolution—private correspondence continued to serve as a trusted, albeit informal, network of information sharing.[73] The Périsse-Willermoz exchange functioned in this traditional manner, conveying facts surrounding key national and local issues such as the Réveillon riot in Paris, the opening of the Estates General, and the king's reactions to the formation of the National Assembly, as well as the opening up of political clubs in Lyon.

In this sense, this correspondence was no different from the many other missives received and sent between deputies and their constituents in the provinces.[74] But the Périsse-Willermoz letters were distinct from those read aloud throughout the kingdom to eagerly expectant townspeople in that they were intended for a very limited audience. Much of the information shared was intended for Willermoz's eyes only, and Périsse reminded his friend time and again that his writings were quite candid, written "with an open heart." As longtime members of the same lodge, these men constituted a robust example of what Charles Tilly has dubbed a "trust network," in which individuals form strong, lasting bonds of solidarity undergirded by

71. BML MS 5885 (14 April 1806). On the Rectified Scottish Rite in Lyon, see the helpful summary in John M. Roberts, *The Mythology of the Secret Societies* (New York: Charles Scribner's Sons, 1972), 109–15.

72. In the case of Willermoz, arthritis and poor eyesight also had to be overcome; Périsse praised his friend for writing despite his "difficulties with his hands and sight." BML MS 5430 (2 September 1789).

73. For an overview of the rise of domestic periodicals in post-1750 France, see Jeremy Popkin, *Revolutionary News: The Press in France, 1789–1799* (Durham, NC: Duke University Press, 1990), chap. 1.

74. For a typical example, see Lynn Hunt, *Revolution and Urban Politics in Provincial France: Troyes and Reims, 1786–1790* (Stanford, CA: Stanford University Press, 1978), 69–70.

a shared moral framework.[75] The moral quality of trust in their masonic friendship enabled Périsse to unburden himself of sensitive political issues that caused him great anxiety with the assurance that these personal thoughts would not be shared with others. He clearly sided with the patriot left on a number of issues and was concerned that the king may try to quash the National Assembly from finally getting down to its legislative business. Périsse was especially worried that the king's late June 1789 decision to significantly increase the number of troops in Paris and Versailles not only signaled the monarch's rapidly evaporating authority—later that month he confided to Willermoz that "today Louis XVI is no more king than you"—but that it was also a dangerous build up of force.[76] "You judge, my dear friend, if you think that I believe the country to be saved," he rhetorically asked Willermoz in early July, since "every moment has been used to surround us with a camp of foreign troops." In closing this gloomy report, he asked his friend to "keep this for yourself so that this story does not alarm citizens who already have enough problems, and you should work to restrain their great hopes."[77]

In some cases, Périsse informed Willermoz that information revealed had not been shared even with his immediate family. When deriding the Lyonnais municipality as trenchantly "aristocratic" and unlikely to implement administrative reforms that would be put forth in a future Constitution, the caveat of "as a patriotic citizen and as my friend, I am going to confide an observation to you only" prefaced his remarks. In the same letter, Willermoz was also instructed with whom specifically he could share other items of information. After discussing likely candidates for the position of *commissaire du Roi* in Lyon, Périsse instructed him that "you can speak about this only to my eldest brother. . . . I beg you to warn him to absolutely keep this between you and him." Périsse's circle of trust thus was quite restricted to just a handful of individuals, and his masonic friend lay at its center.[78]

---

75. Although Tilly does not discuss Freemasonry, lodges closely fit his definition of a trust network in *Trust and Rule* (New York: Cambridge University Press, 2005), 43–45. Tilly's concept has been usefully employed to describe friendship in the Revolution in Helen M. Davies, "Friendship in the Revolution: A Sephardic Correspondence (1794–1799)" in *French History and Civilization: Papers from the George Rudé Seminar* 4 (2011): 79–80.

76. BML MS 5430 (24 July 1789).

77. BML MS 5430 (9 July 1789). His reference to "foreign" troops was probably a reflection of the fact that the newly arrived regiments were composed of soldiers recruited from outside France, especially from Switzerland and the Germanic states.

78. BML MS 5430 (27 December 1789).

Their strong dimension of trust also enabled Périsse to use his friend to gather critical political information and to reveal his true views on some local and national figures of authority. Returning to the issue of selecting the *commissaire du Roi* for Lyon, Périsse not only furnished Willermoz with details about the possible men for the job but actively sought out his friend's input from a local perspective. After sharing his list of candidates, he asked his friend for a frank opinion on the matter since Périsse's own views were necessarily incomplete, as they were formed "extra muros" in Paris. Willermoz also afforded him a critical avenue from which to express his true political self. As he himself readily admitted, Périsse quite consciously crafted his public role as a moderate patriot and strove to avoid any appearance of overt factionalism, which he feared was tearing apart the Assembly; he relayed to Willermoz how he carried himself "like marble" during sessions.[79] However, his private letters served as a type of "backstage" to his public life, wherein he allowed himself to express rather strong feelings toward individuals without fear of disclosure. In discussing possible candidates for mayor of Lyon, Périsse begged his friend to "please cite nothing of me," and then launched into a tirade against a certain nobleman, Palerne de Savy, who was seriously being considered for the position. "Palerne de Savy, Mayor!!!! . . . He is a man of a violent imagination, hardened by self-love, audacious . . . [and] a friend of despotism." If elected, he feared, the aristocratic Palerne de Savy would squarely place Lyon "in opposition to the public weal."[80]

It was undoubtedly good fortune for Périsse that such personal thoughts never circulated publically, as Savy would in fact briefly serve as mayor in early 1790. It is worth noting that Périsse did not limit his scorn to local men of politics but also lashed out on more than one occasion against prominent members of the Jacobin club, which he abandoned once it began calling for a republic following the flight of the king in June 1791. In one letter, he dismissed Robespierre, Pétion de Villeneuve (future mayor of Paris), and abbé Grégoire as the "ridiculous trio" of the Jacobin leadership. He worried that they, along with the increasingly rowdy crowds that congregated at the Jacobin club, would "do us a great deal of harm because they will move away from public peace."[81]

---

79. BML MS 5430 (27 April 1790).

80. BML MS 5430 (1 January 1790).

81. BML MS 5430 (30 October 1791). It appears that the king's flight was significant in splitting Périsse and Robespierre, as the two had agreed on issues earlier in the year, such as the establishment of a national savings account for philanthropy (BML MS 5430 (4 March 1791)). Périsse's name appears on a December 1790 membership list of the Jacobins in François-Alphonse Aulard,

Périsse's masonic friendship with Willermoz thus created a space of intellectual freedom due to its ethos of trust and exclusivity. It also provided him with emotional support during these trying times, and it is quite possible that this affective component was most important to Périsse because he often felt so lonely. When he first arrived at Versailles in April 1789, he welcomed the chance to be alone in order to collect his thoughts ahead of the opening session: "I am in a complete solitude, but you know how much I prize this," he wrote.[82] Over the next two months, however, the grueling schedule of working from morning until late at night began to take its psychological toll, and he now described his conditions in much starker terms. "I am absolutely alone here," he confided to Willermoz in early July, "without a living soul who cares about me, . . . unknown, ignored outside of the meeting halls, without a friend."[83] As conservative and progressive factions began to harden in late 1789, the working environment in the Assembly subsequently became increasingly polarized. In this setting, Périsse felt that he was leading an atomized existence, completely divorced from any supportive or intimate relationships. This feeling of estrangement brought on by rancorous affairs of state soon extended even to his own sense of self, for he lamented to Willermoz the following spring that "the distractions, intrigues, cabals and plotting have so torn me from myself."[84]

In this context, Willermoz offered Périsse a vital "emotional refuge," to borrow William Reddy's term, that mitigated the tense atmosphere in Versailles and Paris.[85] The emotional strain from being separated from his friends and family was increasingly apparent as Périsse's time dragged on within the Assembly. In early 1790 he confided that "I would have never imagined that such circumstances would have taken me away from you and she [his wife] for so long. I note with chagrin that within this immense storm, unprecedented in history . . . my internal sensibility is wilting away."[86] Their

---

ed., *La société des Jacobins: Recueil de documents pour l'histoire du club des Jacobins de Paris* (Paris, 1889), 1:lxvii. On his later adhesion to the Feuillants, see Alice Joly, *Un mystique lyonnais et les secrets de la Franc-maçonnerie, 1730–1824* (Macon: Protat Frères, 1938), 289–90.

82. BML MS 5430 (27 April 1789).

83. BML MS 5430 (28 July 1789).

84. BML MS 5430 (23 March 1790).

85. Reddy cites Freemasonry and friendship as among the few emotional refuges in eighteenth-century France. By "emotional refuge," he means "a relationship, ritual, or organization . . . that provides safe release from prevailing emotional norms," in *The Navigation of Feeling: A Framework for the History of Emotions* (New York: Cambridge University Press, 2001), 129.

86. BML MS 5430 (27 April 1790).

bond stood in stark contrast to relations among deputies in many ways, but most importantly by the fact that it was not overtly utilitarian. As explained earlier, these two Masons did render minor services to one another, but this instrumental component was not as significant as the emotional investment the two men displayed toward each other. They inquired into each other's mental and physical well-being, and, as both men were devout Catholics, Périsse reached out to Willermoz to pray for him on more than one occasion to help him through what he deemed his "tough role" during sessions.[87] He also considered Willermoz a veritable second self, as he professed that there was a "union of my will to yours and of my desire to yours." Such a declaration not only shows how Ciceronian ideals continued to imbue masonic friendship late in the century, but it also suggests a likely additional benefit of this epistolary contact, for Willermoz offered Périsse a chance to reconnect to the personal traits he felt were lacking in fellow deputies, and even within himself at the time. So vital was his connection to Willermoz that Périsse often chose to write to him rather than to family during the few precious moments late at night or in between meetings. But it is important to note that friendship did not always compete with family with these men, as Périsse could ask him to transmit feelings of love to his spouse or children. "I beg you," he requested in mid-May 1790, "to bring me back in favor with my dear wife, because I am an indignant husband in not writing to her at all . . . but she knows how much I love her."[88]

The Périsse-Willermoz friendship thus was quite multistranded, displaying affective, instrumental, and moral dimensions. It was an enduring, powerful bond that withstood the rapid transformation of 1789, and its vitality is all the more apparent when thrown into relief with other, more fragile, masonic connections within the Assembly. There were some examples of Masons attempting to secure for one another positions of power—a brother

---

87. See, for example, BML MS 5430 (letters of 8 April 1789, 21 May 1789, and 23 March 1790). Willermoz's Roman Catholicism was so strong that some Protestant brethren were concerned that the primary objective of his Scottish Rectified Rite was conversion. See, for example, his tendentious letter exchange in 1785 with Lutheran Freemason of Strasbourg, Bernard-Frédéric de Türckheim in BML MS 5868, examined at length in Pierre-Yves Beaurepaire, "Lumières maçonniques et christianisme," *Dix-huitième siècle* 34 (2002): 27–40. As head of the *chambre syndicale* of printers and booksellers in Lyon, Périsse Duluc also remained lukewarm toward allowing non-Catholic texts to circulate within the city. See his November 1775 instructions to the Société Typographique de Neuchâtel, cited in Robert Darnton, *Édition et sédition: L'univers de la littérature clandestine au XVIIIe siècle* (Paris: Gallimard, 1991), 264n91.

88. BML MS 5430 (12 May 1790).

from Grenoble tried but failed to get Willermoz a post at the Paris Mint—but most inter-masonic relations soon fizzled out in this tense environment.[89] But this was not due to lack of enthusiasm, at least on the part of Périsse Duluc. When he first arrived at the Estates General, he clearly hoped that masonic affiliation would provide him with some type of ready-made friendship network, eagerly telling Willermoz with which brethren he hoped to write, speak, or visit. However, a tone of disappointment soon overtook his letters because of the frosty reception he received from Masons who either simply waved to him in passing or ignored him completely; he recounted sardonically how one brother from Strasbourg at an early session "said that he wanted to see me very much, but did not ask for my address nor gave me his."[90]

What is particularly striking was that even those men who had been actively involved in the same lodge as Périsse were unsociable toward him. Consider, for example, the case of Joseph-Jacques Millanois, a fellow Lyonnais deputy who had been a member of the Bienfaisance lodge with Périsse since at least 1781. Since both men had been committed to masonic life, serving as lodge officers for several years, Périsse expected there to be a certain degree of familiarity between them in Versailles.[91] However, his disappointment was apparent in his first less-than-cheerful report back to Lyon in late April 1789. Informing Willermoz of the postponement in the opening of the Estates General, he explained that the icy reserve of his fellow Mason compounded his frustration with the delay in setting down to work: "I am very much bothered by all of this, even more so because I do not find with our friend Millanois the friendliness that I was expecting." Although he shared an apartment in Versailles with Millanois and another non-masonic Lyonnais deputy, he noted acerbically that "they only say hello to me before leaving and when returning."[92] The situation between the two did not improve—they eventually moved into separate quarters—and Périsse was never able to understand why Millanois had adopted this "reserved air and enigmatic silence" toward him. Périsse's own psychological speculation intimated that the unprecedented chaos of the Assembly made the already

---

89. BML MS 5430 (24 May 1791). In a private meeting with newly elected constitutional bishop of Lyon, Antoine-Adrien Lamourette, Périsse Duluc also successfully petitioned for abbé Renaud—member of Périsse's Bienfaisance lodge since 1781—to be appointed a member of the constitutional clergy of the city. See BML MS 5430 (5 April 1791).

90. BML MS 5430 (3 May 1789).

91. The lodge tables of Bienfaisance during the 1780s can be found at BML MS 5479.

92. BML MS 5430 (27 April 1789).

prickly Millanois all the more irritable, but we will never know.[93] What is clear, however, is that divergent political views played little role. Throughout his correspondence, Périsse—who very quickly began referring to Millanois as a "colleague" or "co-deputy" rather than as a "friend"—praised his fellow Mason for his ardent defense of Lyon's interests and *patriote* stance. Writing midway through 1790, he informed Willermoz that "in political matters . . . he is a zealous and resourceful patriot, as well as vigilant for the interests of our city," and reiterated this view a year later when he explained that "all things considered, I admire Millanois for his zeal, his patience to carry out the most unpleasant work, and his steadfastness to complete it."[94]

In other instances, however, the new political choices facing brethren proved to be corrosive to masonic friendship. Like most of his fellow deputies of the Third Estate, Périsse Duluc harbored anti-noble sentiments, but nevertheless attempted to maintain cordial relations with aristocratic brethren early on. Over the course of May 1789, for example, he dined or spoke on more than one occasion with the duke d'Havré de Croÿ and the marquis d'Esmonin de Dampierre, both Second Estate deputies and members of the same lodge as Périsse.[95] Everything changed, however, with the political upheaval the following month, and it was now clear that political identity mattered more to these Masons than their earlier ties. In discussing the duke de Croÿ with Willermoz in early July, Périsse explained that the former's spirited defense of noble privilege was "without reason or spirit of fairness," and had definitely put the duke in the "camp of the court." Subsequently, he wrote, "neither have I sought to see him again, nor has he thought about me."[96] Although Périsse did maintain good relations with some noble brethren over the following years, it appears that the flight of the king in June 1791 definitively broke these apart. When Willermoz asked about the whereabouts of two members of Bienfaisance a few months after Varennes, Périsse reported back that "regarding [the count François-Henri de] Virieu, he flees me from afar since the events of the month of June, and I do not

---

93. "Our friend Millanois," he wrote to Willermoz in a 21 May 1789 letter, "is still the same: the slightest thing either depresses or elevates him. . . . At one moment he is up and the next moment, down."

94. BML MS 5430 (letters of 12 May 1790 and 30 March 1791). Périsse's final reference to Millanois as a "friend" or "brother" occurs on 21 May 1789.

95. BML MS 5430 (21 May 1789).

96. BML MS 5430 (8 July 1789). During the debates surrounding the suppression of hereditary nobility in June 1790, Croÿ again took a conservative stance, arguing to the Assembly that his noble status was immune to legal decrees, for it stood "outside the sphere that is touched by human law." Cited in Tackett, *Becoming a Revolutionary*, 294.

seek him out. [Jean-Antoine de] Castellas does not say hello. The friends of the national interest are hated thusly by those who are concerned only with their corporate or personal interest."[97]

The unraveling of these ties between noble and non-noble also reveals quite a lot about the ethos of egalitarianism that lay at the heart of masonic friendship in the Old Regime. Over the course of our exploration, we have seen how two forms of equal status or likeness were preconditions for entry into a lodge, since brethren endorsed a similar ethical system through the initiation ritual, and they also tended to share a similar socioeconomic background, as membership was generally drawn from professional networks. However, Périsse Duluc's Bienfaisance lodge was a less common example, wherein mixing between commoner and aristocrat within Freemasonry could be found. Did the masonic emphasis on equality have any political implications in such a context? Since the fraternity's inception, the masonic ethos of equality was tempered by the concern that outsiders might perceive in it radical politics.[98] As the stress zones of the Old Regime became increasingly apparent during the final quarter of the century—such as the growing political tension between the *parlements* and the monarchy—Masons continued to argue for the sharp distinction between masonic and political equality, and their tone had grown quite anxious by the 1780s. Perhaps due to the backdrop of the American Revolution, Masons throughout the kingdom spoke at length against an equality that was of a "legal or abstract status." In 1785, one lodge master dismissed such a principle as abhorrent because it "confuses all ranks and all conditions" and would "topple the universe if it were admitted."[99] In 1789, the Grand Orient also rejected the name Les Trois Ordres Réunis (The Three Orders Reunited), because it was "too relevant to affairs of the state."[100] Onetime Freemason and future counterrevolutionary Joseph de Maistre likewise downplayed any political connotation of masonic equality when he explained to a diplomatic correspondent in 1793 that within Old Regime lodges, it "signified absolutely nothing. It was nothing more than words." He explained that it was only

---

97. BML MS 5430 (2 September 1791).

98. See, for example, the 1742 *Apologie pour l'ordre des Francs-maçons*, reprinted in Johel Coutura, ed., *Le parfait maçon: Les débuts de la Maçonnerie française (1736–1748)* (Saint-Étienne: Publications de l'Université de Saint-Étienne, 1994), esp. 124–25.

99. *Discours prononcé le jour de S. Joseph devant une assemblée de Maçons civils et militaires* (Liège, 1785), 6. Similar views were expressed from Corsica to Paris. See, for example, Dossier of Amis Constants (Bastia), BN FM²157bis, fol. 23v and that of Coeurs Unis (Paris), BN FM²65, fol. 19v.

100. Dossier of Saint-Pierre de la Persévérance (Paris), BN FM²109, unfoliated.

once equality had become politically charged in the Age of Revolutions, where it "had become the rallying point . . . of the seditious in delirium," that the public then began to see lodges and contentious politics in a direct cause-and-effect sequence.[101]

Despite Maistre's claims and the repeated warnings from lodge officers that men should not conflate the ethos of egalitarianism within lodges with any political reconfiguration, the revolutionary context opened up the masonic ideal of equality to an unprecedented plurality of meaning. Not only did the brotherhood's attackers decry the heterogeneous social mixing within lodges as a dangerous precursor to the egalitarian principles outlined in the Declaration of Rights of Man and Citizen, but some brethren also affixed political meaning to masonic equality. Consider, for instance, an argument between Périsse and the chevalier de Rachais, another longtime member of Bienfaisance.[102] A couple of hours before a lodge meeting in Lyon in late 1788 or early 1789, Rachais confronted Périsse in his bookshop storeroom over Périsse's opinion, expressed in a recent electoral assembly, that he preferred voting by head rather than by order. Although voting by head in assemblies had already been implemented in Dauphiné and elsewhere, Rachais saw this as an unacceptable innovation that ran contrary to the "political, but also natural preeminence of the nobility."[103] Périsse was taken aback by this outburst given "the principles that he professed among us" and that Périsse considered himself to be "noble like him" while also seeing the chevalier as a "commoner like me." At this point, Rachais became visibly agitated and interrupted Périsse, exclaiming, "Sir! Sir! As a brother in the Order of the Grands Profès [a higher degree within the Rectified Rite system], I grant you this" but then stated that this did not translate into legal equality outside of the lodge. Rachais soon stormed out of the bookshop and continued to display a "feudalistic rancor" toward Périsse until the former's death by guillotine in 1793.[104]

The friction between Périsse and his aristocratic brethren show not only how political antagonism could undo masonic friendships but also that the

---

101. Jean Rebotton, ed., *Écrits maçonniques de Joseph de Maistre et de quelques-uns de ses amis francs-maçons* (Geneva: Slatkine, 1983), 132.

102. This meeting was recounted to Willermoz in BML MS 5430 (12 September 1790).

103. In 1788, voting by head had been instituted in assemblies in Dauphiné, Romans, and Vizille. Bailey Stone, *Reinterpreting the French Revolution: A Global-Historical Perspective* (New York: Cambridge University Press, 2002), 91.

104. Albert Ladret, *Le grand siècle de la Franc-maçonnerie: La Franc-maçonnerie lyonnaise au XVIIIᵉ siècle* (Paris: Dervy, 1976), 289.

line connecting the institutions of the Enlightenment to the principles of 1789 was anything but predetermined. Freemasons could exercise a great deal of intellectual creativity when (and if) they decided to extend their masonic experience into the political realm. Some brethren reinterpreted their language of egalitarianism so that it took on revolutionary significance and redefined the very nature of the body politic, whereas others adopted a more limited, apolitical view in which masonic equality simply meant an abeyance of social distinction within the restricted setting of the lodge. Undoubtedly, how men reshaped the malleable ideas encountered within Freemasonry depended largely on what they had to gain or lose by doing so. Eager to display his break from the Old Regime, for example, former Grand Master of France and cousin of Louis XVI, the duke of Orléans, claimed in an open letter published in a Parisian newspaper in early 1793 that Enlightenment Freemasonry had offered him a "sort of image of equality," but that he had now resigned from his post at the Grand Orient and devoted himself to the Jacobin cause in order to abandon "the phantom for the reality." Regrettably for him, the duke's attempts at reinventing himself came to little, and he was guillotined the following November.[105]

In sum, relations between the members of Périsse Duluc's Bienfaisance lodge in the National Assembly illustrate the great diversity of friendship found within Freemasonry. In the case of the Périsse-Willermoz dyad, we see clearly two men who offered each other a wide variety of support, from the emotional to the instrumental. Their longstanding participation in Freemasonry confirmed their similar outlook on spiritual and moral matters, and the Revolution added a political dimension to this likeness since both men quickly committed to the *patriote* camp.[106] In other instances, however, friendship between brethren was clearly circumscribed and dependent on sociability within the masonic context. Like Périsse's relationship with Willermoz, these friendships were anchored in the ritual life of the brotherhood, but they were also predicated on the lodge being free of any discussion that touched upon the rethinking of politics and social hierarchy. Once such issues forcefully came into play during the Revolution, Masons' friendships with one another rapidly dissolved. It is also likely that for many deputy Freemasons, the very experience of the Estates General, National Assembly, and National Constituent Assembly—with their rancorous crowds,

---

105. *Journal de Paris* 55 (24 February 1793), 220.

106. Willermoz helped found, for example, the *Société des Amis de la Constitution* in December 1789. On this club, see William Edmonds, *Jacobinism and the Revolt of Lyon, 1789–1793* (New York: Oxford University Press, 1990), 48–49.

moving speeches, and unprecedented legislation and political conflict—
served as a lengthy initiation process into a new friendship community
anchored in a particular set of political beliefs. Many of the brethren who
participated in this transformative moment undoubtedly shared the view
of Potevin physician and committed Jacobin, Jean-Gabriel Gallot. Writing from Paris as factions had begun hardening in the Assembly in early
1790, Gallot described how he and his like-minded deputies were now
"bound together forever. Without even knowing one another's names, we
are such good friends and so strongly liked, that hereafter, it will be impossible to travel in the kingdom, without encountering colleagues and
friends."[107]

↜ Lodges Confront the Terror

The new political culture therefore bolstered some yet strained many masonic friendships. Masonic friendship also intersected with politics during
the Revolution because such friendship could be considered dangerous in a
new order nominally grounded in an absolute transparency among citizens
and between citizens and the state. It was believed that true republicans—
men of honor and virtue—should have nothing to hide from the public,
and that, by extension, secrecy implied hypocrisy and conspiracy. The idea
was that individuals should act the same in the public realm as they do in
the private sphere of friends and family. The brotherhood's premium on
secrecy meant that, far from serving as a model for revolutionary fraternity,
masonic friendship actually earned the ire of the Revolution in 1793 and
1794.

Thanks to newly available archives at the Grand Orient, it is possible to
follow in extraordinary detail the fate of Freemasonry in Bordeaux, especially
the Anglaise lodge, which has left behind a particularly rich archive. Not
only is this city an especially useful case study because of its size, commercial
power, and large masonic presence but also because it was one of the few
sites of internal rebellion against the Convention in mid-1793, a movement
collectively known as Federalism.[108] By looking at Freemasonry before,

107. Cited in Tackett, *Becoming a Revolutionary*, 256.

108. Paul Hanson, *The Jacobin Republic under Fire: The Federalist Revolt in the French Revolution* (University Park: Pennsylvania State University Press, 2003).

during, and after the Committee of Public Safety initiated its repression of Bordeaux from mid-1793 to the summer of 1794, we will see clearly how masonic friendship became the primary justification for Jacobins to shut down all lodges.

Anglaise held its first meeting in late April 1732, less than a decade after the implantation of the brotherhood in Paris and elsewhere.[109] Despite its name, it comprised primarily Irish *négociants*; one finds such names as Boyd, Bradshaw, Knox, Madden, and Quinn on the rolls during the first decade of the lodge's existence. Such a national profile is unsurprising as Cork and Dublin were important maritime contact points with Bordeaux from the 1720s onward and a number of Irish merchants settled in the city.[110] Anglaise became decidedly Bordelais from the 1740s onward, as members were increasingly drawn from the affluent mercantile classes originating either in the city or the surrounding region. This shift can be seen as early as 1743, when the lodge decided to adopt French as the official working language. Along with Anglaise, other lodges opened their doors during the reign of Louis XV, but it was not until the final decades of the century that Freemasonry truly blossomed in Bordeaux. Almost every year from 1770 to 1789 saw the opening of a new lodge—fifteen in all—whereas a mere seven lodges had appeared during the previous fifty years.[111] The city's middling sort and its elites were attracted to Masonry because fashionable cultural currents such as mesmerism and occultism, as well as the pseudo-scientific teachings of count Cagliostro, all found their place within Bordelais lodges at some point during the prerevolutionary period.[112] For members of Anglaise, however, charity work and conviviality remained their chief preoccupations, and, as members of the oldest masonic establishment in the city, they also oversaw the founding of local lodges and

109. This account of the early history of Anglaise has been based on Pierre-Yves Beaurepaire, *L'autre et le frère: L'étranger et la Franc-maçonnerie en France au XVIIIe siècle* (Paris: Honoré Champion, 1998), 233–36; and Alain Bernheim, "Notes on Early Freemasonry in Bordeaux (1732–1769)," *Ars Quatuor Coronatorum* 101 (1988): 33–131.

110. Louis Cullen, "The Irish Merchant Communities of Bordeaux, La Rochelle and Cognac in the Eighteenth Century," in *Négoce et industrie en France et en Irlande aux XVIIIe et XIXe siècles*, ed. Paul Butel and Louis Cullen (Paris: CNRS, 1980), 51–63.

111. Alain Le Bihan, *Loges et chapitres de la Grande Loge et du Grand Orient de France (2e moitié du XVIIIe siècle)* (Paris: Bibliothèque Nationale, 1967); and Françoise Weil, "La Franc-maçonnerie en France jusqu'en 1755," *Studies on Voltaire and the Eighteenth Century* 27 (1963): 1787–1815.

112. Johel Coutura, *Les Francs-maçons de Bordeaux au 18e siècle* (Bordeaux: Glorit, 1988), 35–46.

even those as far flung as Edenton, North Carolina.[113] Brethren envisioned the lodge as a sanctum from the outside world, one in which men could devote themselves to forming lasting friendships. The importance of friendship was emphasized during a Saint John's Day banquet in the 1770s. To conclude the festivities, attendees exercised a degree of literary imagination, personifying the strong bonds of solidarity forged between them. "Tender friendship," they sang in unison, "come and kindle your flames, embrace us with your celestial flames, [and] let every day strengthen your tender bonds. . . . You flee far from the tumult and fracas of cities [and] the eyes of profane mortals. It is among us in these happy refuges that you forever make your altars."[114] By the eve of the Revolution, Anglaise largely comprised the prosperous commercial classes, a group Alan Forrest aptly crowned the "new urban aristocracy" of the period. A membership list from 1787 bears out this trend: Of the fifty-eight registered members, nearly 80 percent listed their profession as pertaining to commerce, as either *négociant* or *capitaine de navire*. Such a profile reflected the unambiguously strong presence of the mercantile classes in Bordelais Freemasonry during the closing decades of the Old Regime.[115]

With the announcement of the Estates General in early July 1788, Bordeaux resembled much of the kingdom in that it was soon awash with political talk, print, and action. Later that year, all three estates began meeting to decide on their choice of deputies and draw up respective *cahiers de doléances*. The new printing houses emerging during the period also generated a vast quantity of pamphlets, which provided the city's literate public with a running commentary on local and national events.[116] Beyond the clubs emerg-

---

113. ADG, Série 6^E 9 unfoliated, for the 1779 correspondence between the francophone Amitié lodge in Edenton with Anglaise.

114. ADG, Série 6^E 9, unfoliated, "Cantique de l'Amitié."

115. Dossier of Anglaise (Bordeaux), GODF MS AR 113.2.516, fol. 51r. Over the course of the entire century, nearly 75 percent of Anglaise members (sixty-two out of the eighty-five brethren whose profession can be identified) were engaged in trade. See the membership list in Coutura, *Les Francs-maçons de Bordeaux*, 58–205. This profile remained unchanged during the Revolution. From the summer of 1789 to the summer of 1794, absolutely no social levelling had occurred; of the twenty-eight candidates proposed for membership in this period, nearly 80 percent were drawn from the mercantile profession, exactly the same proportion as the late 1780s. Anglaise appears to have welcomed more merchants than most lodges in the city, as slightly more than half of all brethren (556 out of 1094) have been classified by Daniel Roche as involved in *négoce*: Daniel Roche, *Le siècle des Lumières en province: Académies et académiciens provinciaux, 1680–1689* (Paris: Mouton, 1978), 2: 419, 423.

116. During the 1788–1794 period, the number of *imprimeur-libraires* tripled in the city. See Ernest Labadie, *Notice biographique sur les imprimeurs et libraires bordelais des XVIe, XVIIe et XVIIIe siècles* (Bordeaux: M. Mounastre-Picamilh, 1900), 131–32. Unsurprisingly, titles of periodicals emerging in the

ing from 1790 onward, political meetings in the city could take a variety of forms, from large open-air assemblies at the Jardin Public to informal gatherings in a neighborhood café. And while Bordelais impatiently awaited correspondence from Paris, it is important to note that excitement surrounding events held grassroots appeal, especially during the years from 1789 to 1793 when the mercantile and propertied elite controlled municipal politics; they viewed the Revolution as providing the political conditions that could make possible real economic reform. As one local chronicler pithily summarized: "Effervescence is great."[117]

To live in Bordeaux in 1788 or 1789, then, would have been a gripping adventure in political apprenticeship, and the Anglaise lodge would have been in the thick of it: meetings were held in a set of rooms just off the Jardin Public.[118] In a city that expected its citizens to show enthusiasm for the Revolution, it would have been difficult indeed for these Masons to remain ambivalent or apathetic. Already by mid-1789 the cockade was a mandatory accessory; prominently displaying it was required to enter public spaces such as the theater.[119] And yet despite the profound transformations in the political climate of Bordeaux and some members' absences due to these "civic affairs of the greatest consequence," no explicit mention of the Revolution was noted in the lodge register until the middle of 1790.[120] This was not due to lack of meetings, however. As table 6.1 illustrates, Anglaise did measure a slow and steady decline in masonic life, but members still managed to gather 216 times until July 1794 and held nearly fifty meetings in 1789 alone. Why then did this lodge remain a *loge immobile* during the initial politicization of the city? At first glance, it is possible to dismiss this lacuna as a reflection of the assumed masonic prohibition against discussing matters of state in meetings. However, Anglaise brethren had in fact transgressed this supposed cardinal

---

first year of the Revolution in Bordeaux specifically referred to developments in Paris or at home, such as *Journal de l'Assemblée Nationale* (May 1789) and *Le Courrier de Paris à Bordeaux* (January 1790).

117. Michel Lhéritier, *Les débuts de la Révolution à Bordeaux d'après les tablettes manuscrites de Pierre Bernadau* (Paris: F. Rieder, 1919), 74. Entry for 20 July 1789. On Bordeaux's rapid politicization, see Alan Forrest, *Society and Politics in Revolutionary Bordeaux* (New York: Oxford University Press, 1975), 62–87.

118. Dossier of Anglaise (Bordeaux), GODF MS AR 113.2.101, fol. 96v. The lodge moved to new quarters "near the Jardin Public" in July 1787.

119. Forrest, *Society and Politics*, 62; Lhéritier, *Les débuts de la Révolution*, 74 (entry for 18 July 1789).

120. Members sent letters apologizing for their lack of attendance as early as April 1789. See, for example, GLDF MS AR 112, Opis 4, Box 9, fol. 292r. Although equally rich, the Grand Lodge's "Russian Archive" differs from that of the Grand Orient in that it is chiefly devoted to the nineteenth and twentieth centuries.

Table 6.1   Anglaise Meetings, January 1788–July 1794[1]

YEAR	MEETINGS	AVERAGE ATTENDANCE	INITIATIONS
1788	86	23	31
1789	49	19	4
1790	44	15	5
1791	32	14	6
1792	32	12	5
1793	29	10	7
1794	30	11	4

[1]More restricted gatherings such as master's lodges (*loge des maîtres*) have not been counted, as they normally occurred on the same day as general meetings. Banquets have been included.

rule on more than one occasion in the recent past. Not only had they followed the masonic consensus throughout the kingdom in celebrating the birth of the dauphin in late 1781, but local events later that decade had also prompted a banquet. In September 1788, when Louis XVI allowed Bordeaux's *parlement* to return from its year-long exile in Libourne, for having stubbornly refused to register royal edicts pertaining to creating provincial assemblies, Anglaise decided to "hold a banquet . . . to celebrate the happy return of our respectable magistrates who have returned to the seat of justice."[121] The men of the lodge undoubtedly were well aware that this episode was a part of a proud history of standoffs with the monarchy that stretched back to the medieval period. At the banquet itself, the presiding lodge master, merchant Paul Ore, began the festivities by raising his glass to the *parlementaires*, "reminding all brethren that this respectable lodge is assembled today . . . to celebrate the happy return of our virtuous magistrates and of the reestablishment of justice in the kingdom."[122]

Eighteenth-century Freemasonry thus did not merely represent a space where a distinct form of political culture, anchored in elections and following written laws, could take hold—actual talking about actual politics could and did occur within the lodge. Why then did the lodge register of Anglaise brethren remain silent on the Revolution for over a year? The most likely

---

121. Dossier of Anglaise (Bordeaux), GODF MS AR 113.2.102, fol. 16v. The banquet was held on 9 November 1788.

122. GODF MS AR 113.2.97 (Anglaise banquet register, 1781–1796), fol. 29r.

explanation was that these Masons sought out new venues specifically intended for the communication of political issues emerging throughout Bordeaux in response to the tumultuous summer of 1789. Already in late June, the Club du Café National began meeting as a group to read and discuss news from Paris and the region, and other clubs took form by early 1790; the well-off members of Anglaise were, in all likelihood, particularly attracted to the moderate Amis de la Constitution.[123] It thus appears that although overt political matters could be expressed within the masonic context during the Old Regime, brethren quickly recognized that the lodge was not the most appropriate or effective means to do so. This trend was particularly acute in the aftermath of major events over the course of the Revolution, when meeting frequency registered a noticeable decline. Consider the case of the flight of the king in late June 1791. After news of the royal family's failed attempt to flee to Montmédy had reached Bordeaux on 24 June, concern over the future of the Revolution immediately gripped the city. Bordeaux closed its port, members of the National Guard renewed their vows to the fledgling nation, the phrase "The Constitution or Death" was to be prominently displayed outside of residences, and political clubs met continuously.[124] Anglaise averaged nearly four meetings per month from January to June, but brethren were only able to organize one meeting per month on average for the remainder of the year. New political clubs, on the other hand, displayed precisely the opposite trend. Compared with monthly figures preceding the king's flight, the Société Patriotique des Surveillants Zélés de la Constitution met 30 percent more frequently from July until December of that year and nearly 80 percent more often in the summer months immediately following this event.[125]

Beyond the establishment of competing venues such as clubs and later sectional assemblies, other factors surely drained Anglaise attendance. From 1792 to 1794, we find mention in the lodge register of members who were part of the local National Guard or regular army. This is hardly surprising,

---

123. Due to the general absence of membership lists of Bordeaux's clubs and sections, it has not been possible to trace the political involvement of Anglaise brethren.

124. Richard Brace, *Bordeaux and the Gironde, 1789–1794* (Ithaca, NY: Cornell University Press, 1947), 85–98; Timothy Tackett, *When the King Took Flight* (Cambridge, MA: Harvard University Press, 2003), 159, 164; Aurélien Vivie, *Histoire de la Terreur à Bordeaux* (Bordeaux, 1877), 1: 35–37.

125. AMB, MS I 72, "Délibérations de la Société Patriotique des Surveillants Zélés de la Constitution." The averages of monthly meetings for this club were nine (before the flight), sixteen (from July to September) and twelve (from July until December).

as armed forces in the city drew heavily from the same middling sort that populated the ranks of the lodge.[126] On numerous occasions, the lodge secretary regretted the absence of brethren but found solace in the fact that they have left to be "virtuous defenders of the Republic" and to "combat the enemies of freedom."[127] In 1793, following the declaration of war with Spain and the decree on the *levée en masse*, we find no meetings held in April and only two in May; at least two thousand troops from the Gironde had been dispatched to Bayonne alone to hold the Spanish at bay.[128] A final source of depletion in the rank and file was that an undetermined number of Masons left Bordeaux, either temporarily or never to return. From late 1790 onward, one finds brethren excusing themselves for their "prompt departure" often for "the colonies," "the islands," or "America," references to the French possessions in the Caribbean.

Despite these issues, the lodge continued to meet throughout the Revolution, with the exception of a brief period after July 1794. Indeed, tracking who was visiting and corresponding with Anglaise, it also becomes apparent that at least seven other lodges in the city remained active until early or mid-1794.[129] Stubborn persistence thus emerges as the most useful way of describing Bordelais Freemasonry during the Revolution, and sweeping generalizations often advanced that French lodges emptied in 1789 may be safely discarded. In fact, compared with other regions, masonic life in Bordeaux may have been among the most vibrant in France. In his excellent monograph on Freemasonry in Toulouse, Michel Taillefer distinguished the brotherhood in Toulouse from other areas for its persistence into the Terror. Yet, whereas over a half a dozen lodges may be found in Bordeaux, Taillefer identifies only four still functioning in Toulouse beyond 1793. Furthermore, besides the exceptionally resistant lodge Saint-Joseph des Arts, Anglaise out-

---

126. Forrest, *Society and Politics*, 42. It should be noted that no mention is made of members' participation in Bordeaux's brief federalist uprising in the summer of 1793.

127. GODF MS AR 113.2.97, fols. 35r–36v. Special gatherings could be held to praise members for their military service. On 9 October 1792, a banquet was held in honor of a certain brother Estabé du Vigneau who had returned from an unknown field of conflict, probably in the northeast. The lodge master specified that he "merits our admiration and our friendship in devoting himself to go to our frontiers to finish hunting the tyrants and their puppets."

128. Forrest, *Society and Politics*, 114.

129. Dossier of Anglaise (Bordeaux), GODF MS AR 113.2.102, fol. 161r. Local lodges still corresponding with and sending delegations to Anglaise were Amitié (until January 1794), Essence de la Paix (until July 1794), Étoile Flamboyante (until March 1794), Fidèle Anglaise (until July 1794), and Française d'Acquitaine (until July 1794). One lodge remained unidentified, as Anglaise referred to seven groups operating in the city in late November 1793.

paced other lodges in Toulouse in terms of the annual number of meetings.[130] We should also bear in mind that before Anglaise's involuntary closure in mid-1794, brethren had already met on thirty separate occasions; it is thus quite likely that this year would have represented a return to, or surpassing of, prerevolutionary levels. In short, Freemasonry in Toulouse was by no means alone in continuing to operate during the most turbulent of times in the Revolution.

How can we explain Freemasonry's persistence throughout most of the Terror, and why did authorities eventually close down all Bordelais lodges at such a late date, just weeks before the fall of Robespierre? The answers to these questions have much to do with the personalities of Claude-Alexandre Ysabeau and Jacques Garnier de Saintes, two of the most important *représentants-en-mission* sent from Paris. A former priest, Ysabeau arrived in Bordeaux in October 1793 with his young colleague, Marc-Antoine Baudot, in order to realign Bordeaux with the rule of the Convention.[131] However, Robespierre and his allies eventually deemed Ysabeau insufficiently unforgiving in his application of the Terror, leading to his recall to Paris where he had to answer to the charge of *modérantisme*. Lodges enjoyed relative freedom and toleration under Ysabeau, and the fact that he was also a Freemason may have been an additional reason why the brotherhood continued unabated.[132] On the other hand, his replacement, Garnier de Saintes, the following July, expressed suspicion if not outright hostility toward all who did not unequivocally endorse the revolutionary vision of Robespierre.[133] Upon his arrival in the city on 10 July, he informed the Committee of Public Safety back in Paris that there remained much work to do: "I have arrived in Bordeaux. . . . The ground of this department needs to be sounded out. . . . There is less action at the moment but a mercantile spirit still reigns

---

130. Michel Taillefer, *La Franc-maçonnerie toulousaine sous l'Ancien Régime et la Révolution, 1741–1799* (Paris: E.N.S.B-C.T.H.S, 1984), 240–41, n12; 255. Saint-Joseph des Arts held 36 percent more meetings (294) than Anglaise. It is also possible that Coeurs Réunis surpassed Anglaise in 1794, but Taillefer only provides a table for this lodge from 1789–1793 during which time Anglaise gathered 13 percent more frequently.

131. Forrest, *Society and Politics*, 236–37.

132. On 13 January 1794, Ysabeau presided over a meeting of the Fidélité lodge in nearby Libourne. Anglaise personally invited Ysabeau to visit their lodge in late 1793, though it is not known if such a visit ever occurred. He also authorized the reopening of lodges when he returned to the city in 1795.

133. Garnier welcomed, for instance, the downfall of Danton the previous April. See his biographical sketch in Joseph Décembre, *Dictionnaire de la Révolution française, 1789–1799* (Nendeln, LI: Kraus Reprint, 1975), 2: 22–23.

and selfishness is inseparable from the speculation of business."[134] As Gar-nier's letter makes clear, *négociantisme* became a label on par with *aristocratie* in Bordeaux in late 1793, a position unlikely to have inspired much hope among Anglaise's men of commerce. The following day, he issued a public decree informing the citizens of Bordeaux that all masonic lodges had been closed. He softened the message by initially praising Freemasonry for its ethos of social egalitarianism: "In our Republic, a number of societies, known as masonic societies, have greatly advanced liberty by their hatred of tyranny. . . . Today, without a doubt, they continue to advance their love of equality which is the foundation of our Revolution."[135]

It is worth pausing here to ask how Garnier could have possibly arrived at such an image of the brotherhood as a vehicle of the key principles of the Revolution—notably social levelling—when in fact the present chapter suggests very little of the sort? It is possible that his own experience as a Freemason provided him with this interpretation, though no records have been found to confirm his membership in any lodge. Besides the cautionary measures taken by Anglaise the previous year—changing their name to Egalité, placing the tricolor on their documentation, and so forth—another explanation also emerges, one that brings us back full circle to where this chapter began: that is, with the outpouring of anti-masonic literature being generated from 1789 onward.[136] Without hesitation, scores of reactionary pamphlets pointed a damning finger at the Masons, identifying them, along with Enlightenment *philosophie*, as the corrupting historical agents that had sapped the vitality of the Old Regime. And because of the limited activity of lodges in many regions during the Revolution, these texts were the only sustainable point of contact with Masonry for the wider public, of which Garnier was a part. Though not reflective of the reality within the lodges that persisted into the final decade of the eighteenth century, Garnier's politicized perspective of masonic life was nevertheless commonplace by the time he arrived in Bordeaux. It is therefore quite ironic that enemies of Freemasonry such as the abbé Barruel sought to combat and undermine the

134. François-Alphonse Aulard, ed., *Recueil des actes du Comité de salut public: Avec la correspondance officielle des représentants en mission et le registre du Conseil exécutif provisoire* (Paris, 1903), 15:66.

135. Garnier's text has been reproduced in its entirety in Vivie, *Histoire de la Terreur*, 2:495–96.

136. The notion that Masonry lay behind much of the Revolution had become common intellectual currency very early on in the decade. In the summer of 1790, Marie-Antoinette advised her brother, Leopold II, to "watch out for any association of Freemasons. You must already have been warned that it is through these means that all the monsters here hope to achieve the same goal in all lands." Cited in the original French in Roberts, *The Mythology of the Secret Societies,* 168.

order through their attacks, and yet in the case of lodges like Anglaise, their writings had precisely the opposite effect. Because the anti-masonic literature of the 1790s had been successful in shaping the public's vision of Freemasonry as an institution entirely compatible with the Revolution, the distinctly Old Regime aspects of meetings—their politically lukewarm nature, elitism, and continued use of Christian objects and symbolism—remained concealed.

If Garnier believed that Freemasonry played an important role in the promotion of *égalité*, why then did he outlaw their assemblies? Here, we must turn our attention away from his understanding of the content of masonic sociability to his views on its form. In this second case, Garnier's perspective was more accurate than his viewpoint about masonic political orientation, for in his decree he identified the importance of friendship among brethren. Throughout this book we have argued that the rationale of Freemasonry was to create and nurture male friendship both within and beyond the lodge, and it was these strong bonds of solidarity that proved to be Garnier's overriding concern and reason to close lodges. As Marisa Linton has demonstrated, friendship—an exclusive, private, particularlistic relationship shared by a restricted group of individuals—and fraternity as the revolutionaries defined it—a vague, inclusive, collective, public sentiment to bind together the entire nation—did not necessarily line up neatly alongside one another.[137] Friendship could be seen as dangerous to the nascent political order, for the Jacobins saw in it a rival set of allegiances that conjured up images of the powerful aristocratic networks found in the Old Regime. In many ways mirroring the monarchy's paranoia over Freemasonry in the 1730s, Garnier warned that masonic friendship and the private sphere of which Freemasonry was a part had no place in the Revolution. "It is in these societies," he claimed, "where *modérantisme* can establish itself as a system; it is here that the rigidity of surveillance crumbles, where one prizes a far too intimate friendship over the austere rigidity that anchors the inflexibility of republicanism. . . . Covered by the cloak of friendship, conspirators can take up arms against liberty." For this reason, he argued, "There can exist only one lodge: that of the people."[138]

---

137. Marisa Linton, "Fatal Friendships: The Politics of Jacobin Friendship," *French Historical Studies* 31 (2008): 56–60.

138. Vivie, *Histoire de la Terreur*, 2:495–96. Less than a fortnight later in a letter to the Committee of Public Safety, Garnier reiterated the belief that closing the lodges had stifled counterrevolutionary activity: "The Revolution . . . is starting to take place in Bordeaux. . . . The measure that I took

From the streets of Bordeaux to the halls of the National Assembly, Freemasons thus experienced unprecedented challenges in the Revolution, which strengthened some friendships while dissolving many others. Exploring these viscissitudes of masonic friendship has deepened our understanding of how the Revolution affected the private sphere. On the whole, the history of private life in the Revolution has been characterized as a period in which the private sphere was subsumed into the demands of public life and scrutiny of legislation. Revolutionary assemblies paid particular attention to reconfiguring family life, generating copious legal and administrative records that historians continue to mine effectively.[139] The study of Freemasonry reminds us that the private sphere included other bonds of solidarity, namely friendship. For Garnier de Saintes in Bordeaux and others like him (records suggest that the experience of Anglaise in Bordeaux likely repeated itself in other cities during the Terror), masonic friendship, imbued with secrecy and exclusivity, was seen not only as incompatible with but as outright dangerous to a new order that remained quite wary and vigilant of private societies.[140] Of course friendship remained important to the Jacobins, but they viewed friendships as potentially corrosive to the body politic when these relations were formed in settings like Freemasonry that lay beyond their purview.[141] Revolutionaries thus recognized that friendship had real power: it could form the bedrock of a new state, but it could just as easily give birth to contrary political allegiances or trump patriotic sentiment. It was for this very reason that Saint-Just took so much care in his utopian *Institutions républicaines* to stress that although friendship was to be prized because it could serve as the sound basis of civil society, it was also to be subject to periodic rigorous scrutiny by the public. He

---

against the masonic societies has produced the most fortunate results. There existed many irregular lodges (*loges bâtardes*) comprised of all the rubbish of the Revolution. I was even aware that all those unhappy souls who were purged from the sectional assemblies considered these private societies to be rallying points where they could transplant the seeds of their plots." Letter to the Committee, 19 July 1794, in Aulard, ed., *Recueil des actes du Comité de salut public*, 15:300.

139. Margaret Darrow, *Revolution in the House: Family, Class, and Inheritance in Southern France, 1775–1825* (Princeton, NJ: Princeton University Press, 1989); and Suzanne Desan, *The Family on Trial in Revolutionary France* (Berkeley: University of California Press, 2004).

140. On other lodges that were closed down during the Terror, see, for example, Parfaite Sincerité (Marseille), FM³388, fols. 69r–83v. Like Anglaise in Bordeaux, this lodge was dissolved in the summer of 1794 (on 9 June), and attracted the unwanted attention of *représentants-en-mission* like Christophe Saliceti.

141. Beyond the work of Linton, the importance of friendship amongst Jacobins is also touched on briefly in Patrice Higonnet, *Goodness beyond Virtue: Jacobins during the French Revolution* (Cambridge, MA: Harvard University Press, 1998), 187–88.

remarked that friendship could be a panacea to hold together armies, reduce litigation, and curb crime. Friendship was important enough in the *Institutions* for Saint-Just to proclaim it as a chief criterion of citizenship: "He who will have said that he does not believe in friendship will be banished. . . . If a man has no friends, he is banished." He also declared that all friendships between adult men (including those that had been dissolved) were to be publically declared every year during the month of Ventôse.[142] It is therefore clear that friendship and private life, which at first glance may appear to be quite unrelated to the political history of the Revolution, lay in fact at the heart of one of the most fundamental challenges facing France in these most turbulent of times: how to preserve the freedom of individual action while assuring the structural vitality of the burgeoning state.[143]

---

142. Louis-Antoine de Saint-Just, *Oeuvres complètes*, ed. Michèle Duval (Paris: Ivréa, 1984), 983–84. On friendship in the thought of Saint-Just: Patrick Rolland, "La signification politique de l'amitié chez Saint Just," *AHRF* 56 (1984): 324–38.

143. On this issue, see the illuminating Howard Brown, *Ending the French Revolution: Violence, Justice and Repression from the Terror to Napoleon* (Charlottesville: University of Virginia Press, 2006).

Conclusion

By focusing on the institution of Freemasonry, we have sought to contribute to the social history of male friendship in Enlightenment France. Scholars have long recognized the prominence friendship held in the social and moral thought of the period, but rarely have they considered how men who were not writers thought about and experienced this relationship. I have argued here that two forms of friendship converged within masonic sociability. The first was what anthropologists have called "ritualized friendship." Contracted through the initiation ritual, this sworn bond of solidarity resonated with more formal forms of friendship that historians have found in earlier periods, from Greco-Roman antiquity to the dawn of the early modern era. Similar to the form of classical friendship found in the writings of Aristotle and Cicero, masonic ritualized friendship was above all anchored not in an inexplicable personal attraction between two unique selves but rather in a shared moral vision of the world.[1] The Greco-Romans remained the standard model for friendship from the Renaissance to the Revolution, but their reception varied considerably over time. Sixteenth-century humanists remained rather optimistic

---

1. This book is clearly part of what Dan Edelstein has called the "classical turn" in Enlightenment studies. Dan Edelstein, "The Classical Turn in Enlightenment Studies," *Modern Intellectual History* 9 (2012): 61–71.

toward the potential for classically inspired friendship, but a much more pessimistic view emerged in the seventeenth century. Eighteenth-century
Freemasonry thus represented a cautious reengagement with Ciceronian
friendship, in that brethren were confident that virtuous friendship between men was possible but only in a tightly controlled setting in which the
ritual process functioned as an effective filter between the lodge and the
outside world. Freemasonry thus served as a response to what historians
have called a "crisis" in Renaissance friendship brought on by the reluctant
concession that the teachings of antiquity were designed for relatively com-
pact city-states, and simply could not be adapted to life in the burgeoning
cities of early modern Europe.[2] The associational world of early modern
Europe undoubtedly grew in popularity from the seventeenth century
onward because it offered smaller social arenas like lodges that were better
suited to such classical models.

We must be cautious, however, in claiming that the ritualized friendship found in Freemasonry simply represented an updated version of the
classical civic friendship. Although I have drawn attention to the strong
parallels between the masonic and classical experiences of friendship by
defining them both as founded on a type of *Gemeinshaft*, in which shared
morals defined as "virtue" served as the bedrock of communal living, there
was an important difference. Whereas the ritualized friendship of the ancients was obviously pre-Christian, Freemasonry predicated its solidarity
on Christian values. In this sense, Masonry "Christianized" the classical
model of friendship through its rituals just as the eighteenth-century com-
mentators of Cicero went to great lengths to show how the Roman's moral
lessons fit perfectly with a Christian way of life.[3] Whereas many *philosophes*
drew from pre-Christian antiquity to attack Christianity, Freemasonry
blended Europe's Christian and Greco-Roman pasts in its own novel and
constructive way.

The Christian foundation of the masonic bond that we have uncovered
also reveals that David Garrioch's argument that eighteenth-century

2. Carolyn James and Bill Kent, "Renaissance Friendships: Traditional Truths, New and Dissenting Voices," in *Friendship: A History*, ed. Barbara Caine (Oakville, CT: Equinox, 2009), 153–54.

3. In his preface to the early-eighteenth-century French edition of Cicero's treatises on old age and
friendship, academician Philippe Dubois-Goibaud writes that because of its "pagan spirit," Cicero's
thought "must not be presented to the Christian without some type of corrective" and therefore
advises his audience to attentively read his editorial footnotes whose intention was to bring the Roman's moral precepts into conformity with "the truth that Christianity has made known to us."
Philippe Dubois-Goibaud, *Les livres de Cicéron de la vieillesse et de l'amitié, avec les paradoxes du même
autheur* (Paris, 1708), "Avertissement."

friendship was moving toward a "secular sentimentality" may be only part of the story. In his admirable synthesis, Garrioch furnishes much evidence to suggest that in the writings of some thinkers, and within certain circles in Britain and France, friendship was no longer grounded in shared religious values, as had been the case with earlier organizations such as Catholic confraternities.[4] To be sure, a confraternity demanded much more religious uniformity than a masonic lodge, but this does not mean the former held a monopoly on spirituality. Freemasonry, too, required candidates to affirm their Christian beliefs during the initiation, and although masonic Christianity was explicitly more ecumenical and tolerant than Catholic orthodoxy, Mason and confraternal associate alike would agree with father Malebranche's statement on friendship in his *Traité de morale* (1684): "If we are true Christians on Earth, we will be loyal friends and we will never find loyal friends except in those who possess a solid piety."[5]

Excavating the Christian values at the center of the masonic experience forces us to reject the notion that eighteenth-century Freemasonry was an unrelentingly secular institution. This view, first made popular by masonic apologists and detractors alike in the nineteenth century, continues to influence historical writing, such as Edward Muir's recent statement that Old Regime lodges "practiced explicitly non-Christian collective rituals."[6] If Freemasonry resembled other private venues of sociability in the French Enlightenment in its pursuit of a "heavenly city" where the subjects of absolutism were free to develop a wide range of social relations, the masonic heavenly city was unequivocally Christian.[7] Margaret Jacob is therefore correct when she notes that the fraternity in eighteenth-century France was far less radical than in other national contexts, notably the Low Countries where masonic coteries displayed a penchant toward pantheism and materialism. If Dutch Freemasonry was a part of the Radical Enlightenment, French Freemasonry can surely be framed as part of the Christian *Aufklärung*.[8] The masonic embrace of Christianity also reminds us that the French

---

4. David Garrioch, "From Christian Friendship to Secular Sentimentality: Enlightenment Re-evaluations," in *Friendship: A History*, esp. 204–6.

5. Nicolas Malebranche, *Oeuvres*, ed. Geneviève Rodis-Lewis (Paris: Gallimard, 1979), 2:642.

6. Edward Muir, *Ritual in Early Modern Europe* (New York: Cambridge University Press, [1997] 2005), 296.

7. Daniel Gordon, *Citizens without Sovereignty: Equality and Sociability in French Thought, 1670–1789* (Princeton, NJ: Princeton University Press, 1994), 5–6.

8. Margaret Jacob, *The Radical Enlightenment: Pantheists, Freemasons and Republicans* (Burlington, NC: Temple Publishers, [1981] 2003), 280.

Enlightenment, despite all its anticlerical *philosophie*, was not inevitably an enemy of traditional religious faith but indeed could be quite accommodating to it. Of course, Freemasonry in France today largely sees itself as the descendant of the Third Republic and has gone on to become a champion of republican *laïcité*, and the Catholic Church remains officially hostile to the order. But the historian must move beyond these perceptions and resist teleologically pigeonholing Old Regime Freemasonry into the wider history of secularization, a developmental process that is today increasingly contested.[9]

In its emphasis on ritualized friendship as a relationship grounded in restrained sentimentalism rather than emotional freedom, Freemasonry also complicates the emotional history of eighteenth-century France laid out in the work of William Reddy. Implicitly building on the work of Philippe Ariès and others who have argued that Old Regime elites increasingly sought out private venues like Freemasonry to escape the tightly policed atmosphere of the court and the rigid expectations of family life, Reddy identifies the masonic lodge as one of a handful of "emotional refuges" emerging in the period. By this term Reddy means that lodges, like salons, did not adhere to "the requirements of self-control expected in other venues where power, influence and rank were expressed." Within the masonic context, Reddy contends, there was a general "letting down of vigilance" where brethren were bound in a kind of "natural, gentle harmony."[10] Although the masonic lodge obviously had a different set of objectives and requirements for membership from the court, we have shown that it too was a part of Norbert Elias's "civilizing process," in that it expended much energy on policing the actions, gestures, and speech of its members not only during the initiation but at all moments. We have seen, for example, how officers read out loud lengthy codes of conduct to brethren that forbade a host of actions, from whispering into the ear of another man to excusing oneself without permission. Reddy's strict demarcation between the court and masonic lodges dissolves further if we bear in mind that whereas Versailles under Louis XIV could be quite cold and impersonal, the atmosphere during the eighteenth century was completely different. The king and queen as well as nobility in residence routinely organized intimate, informal dinners and social gatherings—*sociétés particulières* as they were

---

9. Hugh McLeod, "Introduction," in *The Decline of Christendom in Western Europe, 1750–2000*, ed. Hugh McLeod and Werner Ustorf (New York: Cambridge University Press, 2003), 1–26.

10. William Reddy, *The Navigation of Feeling: A Framework for the History of Emotions* (New York: Cambridge University Press, 2001), 152–53.

known—where attendees ate, drank, sang, and talked at length into the wee hours of the morning.[11] Whether they were at the court or in a masonic lodge, the elites of the French Enlightenment participated in social forums that comprised a constant interplay between prescribed formal structure and unpredictable individual action.

Reddy's definition of friendship as an "emotional refuge" does, however, more accurately describe the second form of friendship we have uncovered in Freemasonry: "unritualized friendship." Exploring the Bertin du Rocheret network, the conflicts plaguing prerevolutionary gatherings, and masonic ties during the Revolution, we have traced how some brethren could cultivate more informal, casual ties through letter writing, personal visits, and private gatherings outside the lodge. Those Freemasons who became exceptionally close relied on each other as a potential outlet through which they could voice varying levels of dissatisfaction regarding their personal or professional circumstances. The study of these unritualized friendships between Freemasons also forces us to rethink our current assumptions about private life in this period, in that it cautions us against regarding emotionally close friendships as ineluctably gendered female. When historians have looked at friendship between men in the Old Regime, it has often been to study something other than friendship *per se*, such as heavily instrumental patron-client ties or erotic homosexuality. This scholarly trend is perhaps due to the fact that male friendship today adheres to what one scholar has called the ideal of "heterosexual masculinity," where men generally define themselves against any form of behavior that can be construed as homoerotic, such as the sharing of emotions.[12] But the ideals and practices of male friendship that we have examined here indicate that eighteenth-century men could express their affection for one another in explicitly romantic terms that closely mirrored the female vocabulary of the period.[13] In their letters, speeches, and apologias, brethren left accounts of sharing thoughts, hearts, embraces, and tears. Masons saw no contradiction between this behavior and masculine norms, despite the fact that we have also seen that their behavior could attract suspicion from

---

11. Antoine Lilti, *Le monde des salons: Sociabilité et mondanité à Paris au XVIIIe siècle* (Paris: Fayard, 2005), 73–76.

12. Gregory Herek, "On Heterosexual Masculinity: Some Psychical Consequences of The Social Construction of Gender and Sexuality," in *Changing Men: New Directions in Research on Men and Masculinity,* ed. Michael Kimmel (Newbury Park, CA: Sage Publications, 1987), 68–82.

13. Dena Goodman, *Becoming a Woman in the Age of Letters* (Ithaca, NY: Cornell University Press, 2009), chap. 1.

outsiders that they were not "just friends." Although some historians have argued that such romantic friendship between men was generally limited to early adulthood before marriage, it is significant that Freemasons from all ages and social groups prized friendship as the underlying rationale of their organization.[14]

Through the analysis of the many speeches men pronounced in their lodges during the 1770s and the 1780s, we have traced how a particularly emotionally effusive form of male friendship became embedded in Freemasonry, a phenomenon reflective of the values championed in the new literature of *sensibilité*. Brethren in the prerevolutionary era could still on occasion refer to one another as *honnêtes hommes*, but this seventeenth-century model of masculinity had largely given way to the personae of the man of feeling. Although some historians have seen the emotional control so emblematic of the *honnête homme* as dictating masculine norms throughout the century, we have seen that this older ideal gave way to a celebration of spontaneous and transparent affection."[15] Despite the efforts of some literary scholars and intellectual historians to push the rise of sentimentalism back to the early eighteenth century, the masonic case clearly supports the view that distinguishes the post-1760 period as one in which a marked sentimentalism pervaded all aspects of intellectual production, from the theater to moral philosophy.[16] This development was due not only to the emergence of the *homme sensible* in the writings of Rousseau and other authors but also was a result of the recurrent concern that *honnêteté* constituted little more than a system of empty signs frequently employed for deceptive ends. Pierre de Laclos's (also a Freemason, it is worth noting) *Les Liaisons dangereuses* (1782) was but one case in which libertines exploited the language of *honnêteté* with

---

14. E. Anthony Rotundo considers romantic friendship at the turn of the nineteenth century between young men as dying off once marriage and adult life began. See his *American Manhood: Transformations in Masculinity from the Revolution to the Modern Era* (New York: Basic Books, 1994), 87–91.

15. Robert Nye sees the paradigm of the *honnête homme* as predominant throughout the Old Regime in *Masculinity and Male Codes of Honor in Modern France* (Berkeley: University of California Press, 1998), chap. 2. In a similar vein, David Garrioch speculates that the paucity of fictionalized male friendships relative to female ones during the era of *sensibilité* suggests that highly sentimental friendship was considered "essentially female." "From Christian Friendship to Secular Sentimentality," 182.

16. See Daniel Mornet's general remarks in *La pensée française au XVIIIe siècle* (Paris: Armand Colin, [1926] 1969), 137–39. In a contrary vein, Mark Hulliung has argued that "some of the ways in which scholars have structured the eighteenth century are defective—for instance, the claim that the age began with reason but ended with tears of sentimentality. On closer examination, tears were plentiful throughout the century, early and late." Mark Hulliung, *The Autocritique of the Enlightenment: Rousseau and the Philosophes* (Cambridge, MA: Harvard University Press, 1994), 4.

destructive consequences.[17] Unlike British and German critics of sensibility of the 1780s who strongly associated sensibility with women and chastised the "effeminate tenderness" of sensibility as incompatible with manly ideals, the masonic case suggests that sensibility remained decidedly less gender-bound in the French context.[18]

We have also seen that friendship in eighteenth-century daily life comprised a delicate combination of both affectivity and instrumentality. Although prominent social theorists of the Enlightenment such as David Hume and Adam Smith downplayed the importance of rendering services in friendship relations, and indeed expressed, according to sociologist Allan Silver, an "abhorrence of instrumentality in personal relations," masonic ties functioned concomitantly as an intellectual exchange, an emotional refuge, and a bond with tangible material benefits. It was this versatility that undoubtedly made masonic relationships so different from other forms of male friendship historians have studied in Old Regime France. Political friendship at court, for example, was often quite unstable and prone to betrayal because of the constant jockeying for coveted appointments, power, and status. Historians like Sharon Kettering have shown that the bedrock of state-building in Ludovician France was patronage and that this relationship mobilized a language of friendship. However, behind this vocabulary lay a form of solidarity analytically quite distinct from friendship since the relationship between a patron and his client was a purely utilitarian, emotionally muted, vertical relationship between unequals. As we have seen in previous chapters, this relationship was quite different from the masonic tie anchored in an ethos of horizontal egalitarianism and wherein emotional investment mattered and where utility was not the ultimate rationale for friendship. And although more lasting friendships took form in the early modern Republic of Letters, these relationships largely restricted themselves to the reciprocal circulation of ideas and texts.[19] Masonic friendship moved well

---

17. On the linguistic overlapping between *libertinage* and *honnêteté*, see Elena Russo, "Sociability, Cartesianism, and Nostalgia in Libertine Discourse," *Eighteenth-Century Studies* 30 (1997): 383–400.

18. Janet Todd, *Sensibility: An Introduction* (New York: Methuen, 1986), 141.

19. On political friendship and patronage, see Sharon Kettering, "Friendship and Clientage in Early Modern France," *French History* 6 (1992): 139–58; Christian Kühner, "'Quand je retournai, je trouvai toutes les cabales de la cour changées': Friendship under the Conditions of Seventeenth-Century Court Society," in *Varieties of Friendship: Interdisciplinary Perspectives on Social Relationships*, ed. Bernadette Descharmes, Eric Anton Heuser, Caroline Krüger, and Thomas Loy (Göttingen: V&R unipress, 2011), 59–75. On intellectual friendships, see April Shelford, *Transforming the Republic of Letters: Pierre-Daniel Huet and European Intellectual Life, 1650–1720* (Rochester, NY: University of Rochester Press, 2007), 39–44.

beyond the life of the mind and spread far outside the walls of the lodge. Although the masonic bond could be more multistranded than other forms of friendship that hitherto have attracted scholarly attention, it is unlikely that Freemasonry was unique within the associational landscape of eighteenth-century France. Other voluntary associations—the Ordre de la Félicité, for example—resembled Freemasonry and also no doubt provided a space to develop robust friendships that drew on similar moral themes and shared values.[20] In this way, the story of Freemasonry sheds light on a key element of the wider social history of the period, in which friendship and its pleasures lay at the heart of living the Enlightenment.

In sum, the friendly feeling traced in this book was the result of a dialectical movement of continuity and transformation. Freemasonry in Enlightenment France blended an older, more formalized brand of ritualized friendship with a new culture of sentimentalism or *sensibilité* that became ever more pronounced as the Old Regime drew to a close. As the cases of lodge disputes in prerevolutionary Paris suggest, these two forms of friendship did not always coexist harmoniously. The deep, unritualized ties that some men forged through more exclusive acts of sociability—such as private dinners or parties that did not include all lodge members—could create friendship cliques and subsequently erode the collective, ritualized friendship of the group.

Exploring male friendship through Freemasonry also helps us answer a long-standing question central to the intellectual and political history of the period: What did the political culture of the Revolution owe to Enlightenment modes of sociability like Freemasonry? Historians have attempted to connect the associational culture of lodges with Jacobin totalitarianism, constitutionalism, the ideology of *fraternité*, or a "bourgeois" public sphere, but the evidence presented here suggests that a more tangible connection lay in the discourse of classical republicanism. Classical republicans were chiefly concerned with assuring political stability; they looked upon selfishness, avarice and luxury as morally corrupting and celebrated patriotic and civically minded male citizens who were bound in a friendship anchored in shared virtue. By the 1730s these themes were already central to French Freemasonry, in writings such as those of Andrew-Michael Ramsay, one of the founding fathers of the movement. Men like Ramsay embodied the spirit of the Enlightenment, which sought to contribute to the public good

---

20. On the similarities between lodges and other organizations, see David Garrioch, *Neighbourhood and Community in Paris, 1740–1790* (New York: Cambridge University Press, 1986), 176–77.

and saw the lodge functioning as a utopian platform that offered the kingdom a model of how the ideal political community could be constructed:
citizens bound in fraternal friendship and linked to the outside world through
philanthropy. Ramsay was so convinced of Freemasonry's public utility that
he reached out to Versailles to obtain royal approval early on in the reign of
Louis XV. In the spirit of Aristotle and Cicero, who stated that friendship
between men of excellent character served as the social glue that held together the wider political community, Ramsay and other French brethren
hoped that lodges could serve as an institutional prop to the Crown by instill-
ing civic virtue and initiating a vast project of moral regeneration.[21] Although
recognition from the government never came, down to 1789 men continued to hold that their activities could have real import to the moral and
political health of the kingdom. By the prerevolutionary decades some fifty
years later, the masonic message about the moral corruption of the kingdom
had become quite anxious in tone and their depictions of the sordidness of
the "profane" world quite vivid. Would France, brethren wondered aloud
to one another, soon suffer the collapse that befell the Roman Empire?

From this analysis, it becomes clear that it is inaccurate to see the fraternity as an "intellectual weapon" against absolutism, as Reinhard Koselleck
once argued, or even to include the lodges among Jürgen Habermas's institutions of eighteenth-century civil society that generated rational criticism
of the state. This is because masonic criticism always remained focused on
improving the *mores* of society and was essentially devoid of any disapproval
of the monarchy or Old Regime government institutions. Margaret Jacob
has glossed over the importance of classical republicanism, instead arguing
that Masonry was connected to the more modern form of republicanism
that emerged in mid-seventeenth-century England, which aspired to reorganize social hierarchies according to merit and to create a *novus ordo* by introducing modern forms of representation. Thus she writes that lodges "became
one link in the chain that connects English political culture, and in particular its revolutions, to the late eighteenth-century democratic revolutions on
the Continent."[22] The affinity between the masonic emphasis on constitu-

---

21. On the political importance of friendship for the classical world, see Paul Rahe, *Republics Ancient
and Modern: Classical Republicanism and the American Revolution* (Chapel Hill: University of North
Carolina Press, 1992), 24–25, 30–31, 56–57, 106, 122.

22. Margaret Jacob, *Living the Enlightenment: Freemasonry and Politics in Eighteenth-Century Europe*
(New York: Oxford University Press, 1991), 219. See also pp. 9, 17, and 51. Classical republicanism
is mentioned in passing on p. 209.

tions, laws, and elections and revolutionary politics is indeed suggestive but ultimately inconclusive, as her analysis does not extend into the Revolution itself. We should not lose sight, however, of a more important point Jacob makes time and again: Freemasonry belonged squarely to the cultural universe of the Old Regime. It is this second observation that leads one to conclude that masonic political culture was imbued with an older form of republicanism that conceived of private virtue and public life as inextricably linked. Freemasonry thus was a powerful apprenticeship in classical republicanism for the men who later made the Revolution, because whereas the political writings of the French Enlightenment offered readers utopian or historical examples of societies that shunned libertinage and luxury and celebrated brotherly love and virtue, lodges provided tens of thousands of men a social microcosm of classical republicanism in practice. The masonic politicization of the private prefigured the revolutionary concern from 1789 onward to create a morally regenerated citizenry that would anchor the new nation and leave behind the decadence of the Old Regime.

Studying the Revolution enables us not only to trace some of the ways lodges helped shape the political culture of modern France but also to see how the revolutionary tumult itself profoundly transformed Freemasonry. The Revolution clearly marked the beginning of the "politicization" of Masonry, meaning the gradual process by which values not inherent to Old Regime Freemasonry began to infiltrate masonic life to the extent that admission into the brotherhood meant subscribing to them. In hope of avoiding harassment from authorities, lodges in the Revolution demanded that candidates affirm their absolute fidelity to the First Republic and their status as full-fledged French citizens, and this association with modern republicanism became a critical component of masonic identity into the nineteenth century and beyond. Unlike British Masonry, which styled itself as a loyalist institution firmly committed to constitutional monarchy, or German lodges, which sought to avoid politics altogether, French brethren embarked on a path unique in the history of the brotherhood.[23] Rather than shun party politics or uphold the political establishment, masonic identity in modern France developed around a political position that may be loosely defined as "oppositional republicanism." Louis-Napoleon Bonaparte's

---

23. Jessica Harland-Jacobs, *Builders of Empire: Freemasonry and British Imperialism, 1717–1927* (Chapel Hill: University of North Carolina Press, 2007), chap. 3; Stefan-Ludwig Hoffmann, *The Politics of Sociability: Freemasonry and German Civil Society, 1840–1918*, trans. Tom Lampert (Ann Arbor: University of Michigan Press, 2009).

repression of the left after the Revolution of 1848 constituted the crystalliza-
tion of this identity, as political minorities of all stripes—from utopian so-
cialists to liberals—sought refuge within lodges.[24]

Most important, the Revolution inaugurated a pattern of governmental
repression against Freemasonry that continued to haunt brethren well into
the twentieth century. Although its politics were obviously on the left rather
than the extreme right, the Reign of Terror dealt with Freemasonry in a
manner chillingly similar to the collaborationist regime of Pétain. After
World War I, conservative voices denounced Freemasonry as the source of
France's economic woes and as a refuge for political undesirables such as
Jews and Communists. With the arrival of a conservative authoritarian rule
in 1940, these anti-masonic delusions were given full rein. The newly established Service of Secret Societies (SSS) organized museum expositions,
produced films, and held public conferences revealing the evils of the
brotherhood. At the head of the SSS was the historian Bernard Faÿ, editor
of the monthly *Les Documents maçonniques*, the main anti-masonic propa-
ganda mouthpiece of Vichy. In one of its first installments (1941), Faÿ
wrote a lengthy editorial in which he explained why the regime had out-
lawed Freemasonry the previous year and then proceeded to publish lists of
tens of thousands of Freemasons. Just as the *représentants en mission* of the
First Republic saw in masonic friendship a potentially dangerous network of
political subversives, so too did Faÿ explain to his readers that the secretive
ties between Masons had sapped the vitality of the French state, making it
easy prey for the German military. He opened his piece by praising friendship in abstract terms—"friendship is one of the firmest foundations of
social life"—because it could engender a convivial atmosphere within the
army, university, and government. However, he distinguished these friendships from the masonic variety, which he considered inherently dangerous
to the state. Echoing the concern found in Saint-Just's *Institutions républicaines* (1794) that friendships formed in secret were dangerous for the body
politic, Faÿ condemned "masonic complicity" because it was not subject to
periodic "evaluation of public opinion." Looking back over recent French
history, he lamented that masonic favoritism had proceeded unchecked, for
it resulted in a "profound corruption of French administrative life, which
instead of working in favor of general and national interests, served above

---

24. Philip Nord, *The Republican Moment: Struggles for Democracy in Nineteenth-Century France* (Cambridge, MA: Harvard University Press, 1995), chap. 1.

all the special interests of Masons."[25] Because Faÿ and others like him considered masonic friendship antithetical to the public good, they applauded closing down lodges, banning brethren from public office, publishing names of individual Masons, and hunting down obstinate brethren as all necessary steps in the Marshal's "National Revolution." For the thousands of brethren arrested or imprisoned, and especially for the hundreds of Masons who lost their lives during these dark years, friendship came at a heavy price.

---

25. Bernard Faÿ, "La camaraderie maçonnique," *Les documents maçonniques* 3 (November 1941): 3–7.

❧ INDEX

Abrams, Philip, 197
absolutism. *See* monarchy
actors, excluded from lodges, 193
adoption lodges: growth of, 83–88; and
    male Masonry, 100–109; opposition to,
    85–86, 195–96; use of the term "soeur"
    in, 103–04. *See also* sodomy
Anglaise lodge (Bordeaux), 70–71, 167,
    209–10, 233–39
Anglomania, 18, 22
anti-masonic literature, 6, 8–9, 30–31, 51–52,
    84, 89–93, 98, 201–2, 240–41, 254–55
antiquity, Greco-Roman. *See* Enlighten-
    ment; male friendship
apologias, of Freemasonry, 8–9, 26, 40–42,
    67–70, 81–83, 89–90, 94, 96–97,
    137–38, 218–19
Apologie pour l'ordre des Francs-Maçons
    (apologia), 69–71
archives, masonic, 16, 20, 104, 154–55, 203–4
Ariès, Philippe, 4–5, 247
aristocracy. *See* nobility
Aristotle, 32, 34–36, 176
atheism, masonic refutation of, 69–70, 174,
    181–82
Les aventures de Télémaque (Fénelon), 37, 39

Baker, Keith, 214–15, 217–18
banquets, in lodges, 22, 24, 83–84, 87, 89,
    100, 105–6, 110, 113, 138, 165n20, 186,
    192, 195, 198, 234, 236, 238n127
Barruel, Augustin, 91, 98, 202, 240–41
Beaurepaire, Pierre-Yves, 8, 67, 70, 114
Béla, Jean-Philippe chevalier de, 115,
    144–47, 153–54
Besançon, 175–76
Bible, use of in lodges, 63–66, 174, 208
Bienfaisance lodge (Lyon), 227, 229
Bodin, Jean, 15, 31
Bordeaux, 23, 70–71, 167, 209–11, 232–41
Buffier, Claude, 34n63, 44–45

Burke, Janet, 87, 108
Bray, Alan, 78–79
British Freemasonry, compared to French,
    28, 71, 213n38, 253–54
Bussi-Aumont, lodge of, 23–24, 104n82,
    110–16

Calvières, Charles-François marquis de,
    114–15, 136–37, 150
Castagnet, Charles Tanchon de, 114, 117,
    119, 125–26, 152–53
catechisms, in initiation ritual, 66–67
Catholic Church, views on Freemasonry,
    20, 61, 93
charitable works, by lodges, 37, 87, 175
Chevallier, Pierre, 8, 88, 90, 202
Chevaliers du jeu de l'arc (organization), 114
Christianity: Enlightenment, attacks on,
    48–49; importance to French Freema-
    sonry, 60–71, 138–40, 168–69, 174–75,
    208–9, 226, 245–46
Cicero, 34–36, 76, 129, 175–77, 226, 245
civil society, defined, 25n27
classical republicanism: defined, 14–15,
    211–12, 217–19; in French Revolution,
    219–20; masonic friendship and, 214–17,
    251–52
clientage, compared with friendship, 73–74,
    152, 214, 250
clubs: Freemasonry compared to, 102, 114,
    212–14, 236–37; growth in France, 5,
    24–27, 213, 236–37
Cochin, Augustin, 202n3, 220–21
confraternities, 114, 246
Constitutions of the Freemasons, The (Ander-
    son), 28, 71
correspondence: as conduit for news, 144,
    222; and friendship, 120–28; models of,
    120, 131; and postal service, 127;
    reciprocity in, 124–27; vocabulary of
    orality in, 122–23